PRESERVATION *and*
CONSERVATION
for Libraries *and* Archives

PRESERVATION and CONSERVATION
for Libraries and Archives

Nelly Balloffet
and
Jenny Hille

Judith Reed, *Technical Editor*
Jenny Hille, *Illustrator*

AMERICAN LIBRARY ASSOCIATION
Chicago   2005

Photographs by Nelly Balloffet, Gwen Denny, and/or Jenny Hille, with technical help from Cristina B. Carr, Harald Hille, and Liza Wallis (unless otherwise noted)

Composition, cover, and text design by ALA Editions

Printed on 50-pound natural offset, a pH-neutral stock, and bound in Arrestox B cloth by McNaughton-Gunn

The paper used in this publication meets the minimum requirements of American National Standard for Information Sciences—Permanence of Paper for Printed Library Materials, ANSI Z39.48-1992. ∞

Library of Congress Cataloging-in-Publication Data

Balloffet, Nelly.
    Preservation and conservation for libraries and archives / Nelly Balloffet and Jenny Hille ; Judith Reed, technical editor ; Jenny Hille, illustrator.
        p.   cm.
    Includes bibliographical references and index.
    ISBN 0-8389-0879-9 (alk. paper)
    1. Library materials—Conservation and restoration—Handbooks, manuals, etc. 2. Archival materials—Conservation and restoration—Handbooks, manuals, etc. 3. Library materials—Storage—Handbooks, manuals, etc. 4. Archival materials—Storage—Handbooks, manuals, etc. 5. Paper—Preservation—Handbooks, manuals, etc. 6. Books—Conservation and restoration—Handbooks, manuals, etc. 7. Library exhibits—Handbooks, manuals, etc. 8. Archives—Exhibitions—Handbooks, manuals, etc.   I. Hille, Jenny. II. Reed, Judith A.   III. Title.
    Z701.B234 2004
    025.8'4—dc22   2003062371

Printed in the United States of America

09 08 07 06 05   5 4 3 2 1

Dedicated to
Judy Reed,
dear friend
and gentle
gadfly

Contents

A library has always been considered a special place for reading, study, or reference, and librarians have always been charged with the care and management of their books.

The word "library" has expanded to include computer disks, films, documents, works of art, artifacts, and more. The duties of librarians have also expanded. They now need to include a knowledge of preservation practices, and that is what this book is about.

Libraries have always been treasured and cared for to a greater or lesser degree. Their first need, of course, was a plan of organization for access. Four millennia ago, in Mesopotamia, librarians stored their clay tablets so that they would be available for reference. (Clay tablets are virtually indestructible, so their chief preservation dangers were only conquest or pillage.) Over the centuries tablets changed to rolls and finally rolls changed to codexes, that is, the book format we know today.

In the Middle Ages preservation mostly consisted of chains attached to some books, chiefly in monastic libraries for security; metal bosses to prevent abrasion of leather covers; and before the general use of paper, fastenings to preserve the parchment contents of books from climate changes.

In the fifteenth century King Matthias Corvinus of Hungary had a bookbindery attached to his palace and, much before his time, had bookshelves built in his palace with curtains to keep out the dust. Books that needed it were sometimes rebound.

In *The Enemies of Books*, the printer and bibliophile William Blades (1829–1890) wrote: "The surest way to preserve your books in health is to treat them as you would your own children, who are sure to sicken if confined in an atmosphere which is impure, too hot, too cold, too damp, or too dry."

Today's librarians, curators, and bibliophiles have become more and more aware of the need for the proper treatment and handling of the varied objects in their care, in other words, preservation.

The authors of this book, Nelly Balloffet and Jenny Hille, have both studied bookbinding. Nelly studied with Laura Young in New York, and in an internship with Carolyn Horton, author of *Cleaning and Preserving Bindings and Related Materials,* a landmark of the present-day interest in preservation. Jenny studied in New Haven with me in the Conservation Studio of the Yale University Library. They both know about the materials books are made of, how they are put together, and how they are affected by their environment and handling.

Both have earned M.L.S. degrees, Nelly at the Columbia University School of Library Science and Jenny at Southern Connecticut State University. For some years they have given preservation workshops funded by the New York State Library's Discretionary Grant Program. Both maintain studios in which they conserve books, documents, and prints.

Nelly is the author of *Emergency Planning and Recovery Techniques: A Handbook for Libraries, Historical Societies and Archives in the Hudson Valley* (1999) and coauthor (with Jenny Hille) of *Materials and Techniques for Book and Paper Repair* (2001). She collaborated with Hedi Kyle and others on a *Library Materials Preservation Manual.*

In addition to training in this country, Jenny studied and taught bookbinding and conservation practices in Switzerland for three years. She has also done private conservation work and worked in the Yale Library Conservation Studio and is the coauthor with me of *Headbands: How to Work Them.*

Preservation and Conservation for Libraries and Archives is a comprehensive manual covering the preservation requirements of library and archive materials. It treats such subjects as the making of book supports and simple repairs; the materials, tools, and equipment needed to perform conservation work; the environmental needs of paper and books in storage and out, and on exhibition; the education of patrons and staff in conservation awareness and safe practices; disaster prevention and recovery planning; the treatment of materials on loan and in transit; and a great deal more. It is well illustrated with drawings by Jenny Hille.

This book also takes into account the following fact, which the authors themselves set forth: "Compromise and accommodation are always necessary in the real world."

Jane Greenfield

Preservation and Conservation for Libraries and Archives was written in response to the interest expressed in such a work by preservation librarians. Research and archival collections need special care, and librarians need a manual that covers all the aspects of preserving working collections. The authors are well qualified for the task.

Nelly Balloffet, the principal author, has worked in libraries and privately in her own conservation studio for thirty years. She studied with Laura S. Young in the 1970s and worked for Carolyn Horton in the 1980s. Nelly initiated and ran the workshop program for the Guild of Book Workers in the early 1980s. This program ended with the growth of regional chapters, and workshops remain the major tool for education in specific techniques for practicing bookbinders and conservators. Nelly has taught various aspects of library preservation throughout her career, and has always been generous in sharing her knowledge and exchanging ideas with colleagues.

Jenny Hille trained and worked with Jane Greenfield at the Conservation Studio of the Yale University Library and at the Centro del Bel Libro in Ascona, Switzerland. She served as New York chapter chairman of the Guild of Book Workers, a position she held until 1994. In addition to twenty-five years' experience as a private conservator, Jenny also brings her designer knowledge to the book and her illustration skills to the clear line drawings which illustrate the procedures.

While conducting library surveys over several years, the authors became increasingly aware of the need for preservation training in smaller institutions. Together they developed and presented several short courses sponsored by the Lower Hudson Conference and the Southeastern New York Library Resources Council. The short manuals created from these courses have now been expanded into this comprehensive volume.

Institutions with limited staff, equipment, and training will find answers to their preservation questions in this book. The first section covers the basics of preservation—environment, education, disaster planning and response, and storage methods. The book then moves on to simple preservation techniques, paper conservation techniques, book conservation techniques, and setting up small exhibitions. Five appendixes and an index round out the book.

All of the techniques described and illustrated here have had extensive testing at the workbench, with continuing revision of the procedures taught to students. Throughout this book the authors emphasize that while all the techniques described are accepted book and paper conservation methods, they are a guide for preserving working collections and are not intended as instruction for the treatment of rare or unique materials.

After many years as Laura Young's assistant, I took over the operation of her New York City studio where I continued to teach and accepted commissions. Since 1998 I have been employed as conservator at the Frick Art Reference Library in New York. My thirty-year involvement with teaching bookbinding and conservation makes me aware of the need for publications like this one, which presents sound, well-illustrated techniques in an easy-to-follow format. It is especially helpful that all of the information on both preservation and conservation is available in one volume. As our colleague Judith Reed has said, this book is truly "a teaching tool for people who teach."

We are fortunate to have this unique manual which reflects so many years of accumulated knowledge, experience, and sensitivity in the fields of preservation and conservation.

Jerilyn Glenn Davis

Acknowledgments

The following people helped us in many different ways. They are listed alphabetically; the order in which they appear has no relation to the value we place on their contribution. We are very grateful to each person; we could not have done it without them.

Myriam de Arteni	Maria Holden
Joe Bamberger	Sidney F. Huttner
Amy Braitsch	Marsha Lieberman
Ines B. Brown	Barbara Lilley
Cristina B. Carr	Olga Souza Marder
Simon Carr	Susan B. Martin
Ann Chernow	Ellen McCrady
Marie Culver	NEDCC Field Services Staff
Mary Davis	Xuan-Thao Nguyen
Paula De Stefano	Ralph Ocker
Gwen F. Denny	Sherelyn Ogden
Mindell Dubansky	Patsy Orlofsky
Margaret H. Ellis	Kelsey Osborn
Beverly P. Feder	Ronald D. Patkus
Jesse Feder	Roberta Pilette
Elaine Feiden	John F. Reed
Susan Fraser	Maija Reed
Julie T. Graessle	Marc Reeves
Jane Greenfield	Elaine Schlefer
Tema Harnik	Jean-Paul Sémeillon
Pamela Hatchfield	William Streeter
Harald Hille	Liza Wallis

Thank you also to many other colleagues, friends, and relatives who helped and encouraged us during this project.

Ana B. Hofmann is the author of appendix A, "Care of Photographs."

Photographs that appear without credit were taken by Nelly Balloffet, Gwen F. Denny, and/or Jenny Hille, with technical help from Cristina B. Carr, Harald Hille, and Liza Wallis. Nelly Balloffet's photograph is by Liza Wallis Photography.

We owe a great debt of gratitude to the LuEsther T. Mertz Library of the New York Botanical Garden, both to the present staff as well as to dear friends and colleagues who have retired.

Both of us have worked at the botanical garden (Nelly as part of the Book Preservation Center staff from 1979 to 1981 and Jenny as a conservator in the late 1980s). In addition, we are involved in a long-standing program to conserve books in the special collections, serving as contract conservators. Through the years we have benefited from generous sharing of information and technical advice, but it was during the preparation of this manual that our connection with the Mertz Library became invaluable.

Jerilyn Glenn Davis, friend and mentor, read the manuscript; we thank her for many helpful suggestions.

PRESERVATION AND CONSERVATION: WHAT'S THE DIFFERENCE?

There is some confusion about the meanings of the words "conservation" and "preservation." According to *Webster's Unabridged Dictionary* (2nd ed., 1960), the primary meaning of "conservation" is "the act of preserving, guarding, or protecting; preservation from loss, decay, injury or violation." "Preservation" is defined as "the act of preserving, or keeping in safety or security from harm, injury, decay, or destruction." These two definitions seem very similar.

In *Bookbinding and the Conservation of Books: A Dictionary of Descriptive Terminology* by Roberts and Etherington, "conservation" is defined as

1. The conscious, deliberate and planned supervision, care and preservation of the total resources of a library, archives, or similar institution, from the injurious effect of age, use (or misuse), as well as external or internal influences of all types, but especially, light, heat, humidity and atmospheric influences.

2. A field of knowledge concerned with practical application of the techniques of binding, restoration, paper chemistry, and other material technology, as well as other knowledge pertinent to the preservation of archival resources.

There is no separate entry for "preservation."

In the twenty years since *Bookbinding and the Conservation of Books* was published, the word "preservation" has more or less assumed meaning no. 1. It encompasses all the steps and activities needed to ensure that the holdings of a library or archive remain in the best possible condition for as long as possible. This includes concerns about storage methods, the building's envelope and environment, security, and other aspects that broadly affect every item in the collection.

"Preservation" includes safeguarding not only physical materials but also information. To this end, reformatting, replacement, and the use of protective containers are employed to extend access to information that might be lost once paper or electronic books or documents deteriorate.

"Conservation" has retained the second meaning, with emphasis on the physical treatment of specific items or collections. It includes simple preventive steps as well as major procedures that may require many weeks of work.

The words are still often used interchangeably, so we will have to be patient and see how the usage evolves. In this book, "preservation" refers to steps that address the overall safekeeping of all the holdings. "Conservation" is used to mean hands-on treatment.

Preservation and Conservation for Libraries and Archives came about as a result of our experience working with small and medium-sized libraries, archives, historical societies, and private collections. In particular, it was inspired by the handouts that Jenny and I created for the series of workshops we developed and taught over the last twelve years. The courses covered a number of preservation subjects, as well as hands-on instruction in simple but sound conservation techniques. These programs were sponsored by the Lower Hudson Conference and the Southeastern New York Library Resources Council, with funding from the New York State Library's Program for the Conservation and Preservation of Library Research Materials, as well as from the Institute of Museum and Library Services.

The workshops attracted a varied group: archives, libraries, and historical societies were represented by professional staff as well as by technicians, volunteers, student workers, and occasional board members. There were also some students from library and history programs and occasionally a private collector. In general, people came looking for ways to handle various specific situations, for instance, how to preserve oversize materials or how to exhibit books and documents without damaging them. They brought many sample problems and we gave many impromptu demonstrations in addition to the scheduled material. As the seminars progressed, we noticed that our students became much more capable of working out good solutions on their own. And this was, of course, our goal.

We wrote this book as a resource for the entire library or archive: for staff in charge of the general preservation of holdings, as well as for those who are involved in the actual repair or presentation of specific items.

In this book we cover many aspects of caring for a reference collection or archive. While the latter portion of the book is devoted to hands-on treatment, that is only one aspect of a total preservation plan. As part of our consulting practices, we conduct general preservation surveys in libraries and archives. After site visits to many institutions, we are convinced that providing a good environment for collections, with proper storage conditions, is the step that provides the most benefit to the greatest quantity of materials of permanent value.

The first section of the book touches on the subjects of environment, disaster planning, storage furniture, storage containers, and other matters that directly affect the well-being of the whole collection.

The second section has information on setting up a work area and includes descriptions of useful equipment, as well as working tips. Section 3 deals with rehousing and gives directions for making simple enclosures. We give directions for making simple paper repairs in section 4, and book repairs are covered in section 5, the largest in the manual. (Books are complicated structures.)

We've also noticed that most libraries and many archives produce exhibitions from time to time, often with limited resources. The task of preparing materials and setting up the exhibits frequently falls to preservation/conservation staff, and sometimes volunteers or staff members from other departments are involved as well. Since we could not find very much literature on the subject of exhibitions outside the museum setting, we decided to devote the last section of this book to the topic of small exhibitions. The guidelines include steps to help produce an attractive show without causing harm to the materials on exhibit.

Finally, there are five appendixes containing additional information. Appendix A, on the care of photographs, was written by Ana B. Hofmann, a conservator of photographs. It is included because photographs comprise a large part of many collections, and it gives a great deal of basic information in one convenient location. Two appendixes list suppliers and sources of help, and the last two appendixes are a glossary and a bibliography.

This is not a book to read cover to cover but rather a place to find information on a variety of subjects. The first section, on the basics of conservation, will be more useful to administrative staff. The second section, on setting up a work area, can help when planning a new lab or remodeling an established one. The other sections are designed for use by preservation department staff. We suggest that you first read through a procedure to make sure it is suitable for your needs and then go back and begin carrying out the instructions. As with anything, it makes sense to start with the simpler steps and to practice on discards or on items that can be replaced.

Many of the procedures are not new; we have simply endeavored to present techniques in a clear way after field-testing them in our seminars. Over time, we have gained a good idea of what technicians at small institutions can be expected to accomplish, given limited time, equipment, and training opportunities. While some staff members may stay at their positions for many years, it is more likely that there will be frequent changes. So we have concentrated on methods that can be learned fairly quickly and that produce reliable results.

We base our teaching on professionally accepted paper and book conservation methods. Some of the techniques are traditional bookbinding steps, modified for use in a mending facility with limited equipment. But we do not teach bookbinding as such in our workshops or in this volume because learning to bind books takes many months or years. Furthermore, libraries routinely send books that need new hard covers to library binders.

In like manner, the section on flat paper repair is limited to the simpler mending steps that are most frequently needed in an archive or library. Lining, deacidification, fills, in-painting, etc., are better left to skilled professionals with adequately equipped studios.

The techniques provided in this book are suitable for research and archival materials without great artifactual value. The goal is to get books or documents back on the shelf so their information can be accessed, and to do so in a reasonably cost-efficient way, with no damage to the materials.

When there is any doubt about the artistic, historical, or monetary value of an item, it is preferable to box or folder it and restrict its use until a librarian or archivist can be consulted. In the section on rehousing, we give information about different types of preservation containers, as well as instructions for making book enclosures in two styles. If treatment for rare materials is indicated, a conservator can help determine a course of action. Although the instructions in this manual are sound, they are no substitute for the experience and skill required to treat a rare item.

In the workshops we have taught, as in the preparation of this book, it has been our aim to disseminate sound information to technicians who have little access to professional training. We realize that instructions can be misinterpreted. A key element to developing a successful in-house conservation program is to have a knowledgeable subject specialist review all materials to be treated. In this way, rare and historic items can be set aside for further evaluation.

Nelly Balloffet

Section 1

The Basics of Preservation

IN THE LAST THIRTY YEARS, AWARENESS OF WHAT needs to be done in order to preserve research materials over the long term has increased tremendously. Librarians and archivists understand that mending, rebinding, and microfilming are not the sum total of preservation and that other issues, sometimes hard to notice at first, come into play. Administrators who are in charge of the overall running of a library or archive will find useful information in section 1.

In the following pages, we'll take a look at some of the factors that contribute to the survival of paper-based collections. It is not an exhaustive study of the topic because there are other works devoted exclusively to the subject. But we start this way because these are the preliminaries that must be in place in order to have a successful conservation program.

This section is divided into four main parts:

1. "Environment." A key contributor to long life for library and archive materials is storage in safe environmental conditions.
2. "Education." Staff and patrons must learn how to handle research materials.
3. "Disaster Planning and Response." There must be a plan in place to safeguard patrons and staff, as well as preparations to lessen damage to the collections.
4. "Storage Methods." We describe various types of storage furniture and locations. Storage materials, such as folders and boxes, are discussed in section 3.

The section concludes with a summary of basic preservation measures, advice on procedures to avoid, and two work flow charts.

ENVIRONMENT

One of the most effective steps any library or archive can take to preserve its holdings is to maintain safe humidity and temperature levels, good air quality, and controlled light. This move benefits every single item in the collection. Without a good environment, books, documents, photographs, and all other materials will become dirty, faded, moldy, brittle, or pest-infested, and generally deteriorate or even be destroyed. (At the beginning of section 6, there is a discussion of environmental conditions suitable for exhibitions of books, documents, and art on paper.)

Temperature and Humidity

Guidelines for archival and library storage spaces emphasize controlled relative humidity (RH) and moderate temperatures. Since the late 1960s, many preservation specialists have recommended an RH of 50% and a temperature around 60°F (16°C) for storage areas, 24 hours a day, 365 days a year. Frequent fluctuations are harmful to many materials; the key is to *maintain* the desired temperature and RH around the clock, with no major changes.

However, in an ordinary building designed for public use, the heat and air conditioning are programmed to maintain a comfortable temperature for patrons and staff while the building is open. It is fairly easy to have constant temperatures with a heating and air conditioning system that is in good operating condition. Regulating the RH is much tougher, and it is difficult to provide adequate conditions for archival and library materials housed in older buildings.

An understanding of the climate in the region is helpful. Does your area have a mild or severe climate? Is it humid or dry? In the northeastern United States, conditions can range from more than 100°F (40°C) and humid to well below 0°F (−20°C) and dry. Other geographical areas are dry year-round or are humid all the time. Some regions have a much narrower temperature range over the course of the year, and some have even greater changes from summer to winter. These variations make a difference in the way indoor air reacts to heating and cooling.

In cold winter areas, heating makes the air much drier than is safe for the long-term storage of archival materials. If the heat is turned down when the building is not occupied, the relative humidity goes up. When the heat cycles on again, the RH goes down again.

During hot weather, air conditioning will lower the RH as long as it is running. But for reasons of economy, central air conditioning is often turned down or off when a building is closed. For safety, window units are not generally left running unattended. As soon as the air conditioning is turned off, the relative humidity begins to climb. A storage space that had 50% RH during the day may well have 75% RH at night.

Auxiliary dehumidifiers are sometimes used in storage spaces. They must be monitored, emptied, and adjusted as needed. An unattended dehumidifier can overflow from a poorly adjusted collection container or pose a fire hazard from overheating if the coils freeze up.

Unless the central heating, ventilation, and air conditioning (HVAC) system is designed to dehumidify during humid times and add moisture during the heating season, chances are that RH will fluctuate widely despite the best efforts.

Some Facts about Relative Humidity

Air includes a variable amount of water vapor; the warmer the air is, the more water vapor it can hold. The word "relative" in the term "relative humidity" refers to the amount of moisture actually in the air compared to the amount of moisture that it *could* hold at that temperature. (Air pressure, altitude, and some other factors enter into the equation as well, but it is temperature that most dramatically influences the air's capacity to hold moisture.)

Temperature and relative humidity (RH) are closely linked. When we hear that the temperature is 70°F and the RH is 100%, it means that the air is holding all the water vapor it can, at 70° (21°C). If the temperature drops, the air's capacity for moisture will drop and the RH will rise. At 100%, the air is saturated ("full") and cannot hold additional moisture as vapor. The additional water vapor becomes rain, condensation, dew, snow, etc.

Conversely, as the air gets warmer, its RH goes down. If the RH is 50%, it means that the air has half the amount of water vapor it is capable of holding at that particular temperature. The air is no longer "full," but it would like to be, and so it begins taking up moisture from any material that will release it.

PRACTICAL CONSEQUENCES
OF CHANGES IN RELATIVE HUMIDITY

When the temperature in an enclosed space, like a room, goes up and down, the RH changes in inverse relation to the temperature: when the temperature goes up, the RH goes down because the warmed air is able to hold more moisture than it did when it was cooler. So it is "relatively" drier than it was before. Conversely, when the air cools and the temperature goes down, the air can hold less moisture and the RH goes up.

LOW RH

In winter, heating the air causes its RH to go down. Because it then has less moisture than it is capable of holding, the air begins to take up moisture from materials such as paper, leather, wood, photographs, and textiles, which are hygroscopic (i.e., they readily absorb, retain, and give up moisture). Items made from parchment and most photographs are especially likely to shrink and be damaged in dry conditions, but all library materials become desiccated and suffer mechanical stress. The emulsion on slides and negatives often starts to separate from the film carrier. Brittleness, delamination, warping, and other damage, often irreversible, follow.

HIGH RH

During periods of high humidity, hygroscopic materials absorb water and swell. This causes strain to bindings and may make it difficult to remove books from tightly packed shelves or folders from very full file cabinets. Another major danger is the onset of a mold outbreak. (See more on mold below, p. 17.)

When the heat is raised and lowered daily, or air conditioning is turned up and down, the change in temperature causes the relative humidity of the air in the building to change every time. As the temperature goes down, the relative humidity goes up, and vice versa. The materials shrink and swell repeatedly, increasing the damage. Furthermore, there is the likelihood of condensation during periods of higher RH. Condensation can cause water damage as surely as can a flood.

This is only a very simplified introduction to the link between temperature and relative humidity. For more information on the subject, consult Appelbaum, *Guide to Environmental Protection of Collections; The Story of Humidity;* and the publications of the Library of Congress Preservation Directorate (see appendix C).

Naturally, a building must be in good repair before the indoor environment can be regulated. It is a good idea to have a schedule of inspection and maintenance that addresses every area of the building from roof to basement. In this way, small problems can be taken care of before they become emergencies.

When a building has multiple problems that cannot effectively be solved, it may be time to start preparing for renovations or a new location for the collections. This is usually a complex, expensive, and very time-consuming project, one that will be several years in the planning.

During this period, staff can do research to determine what changes are most needed. It is always more efficient to incorporate desired features during the renovation or building stages. It will be very helpful to consult with an engineer who specializes in library and museum buildings. *Conservation Environment Guidelines for Libraries and Archives* by William L. Lull is a helpful publication with clear explanations of many technical aspects of environmental regulation.

Heating, Ventilation, and Air Conditioning (HVAC)

When a library or archive is planning a new or renovated building, every effort should be made to include a modern HVAC system designed for the needs of libraries and museums. It should have the capacity to provide constant relative humidity and moderate temperature in storage spaces, 24 hours a day, 365 days a year. Within a 24-hour period, the RH should not change by more than 12%. (This means 2% above or 2% below the specified level, not "approximately 2%.")

Air Pollution Filters

In addition to regulating relative humidity and temperature, the HVAC system should include filters capable of removing various particulate and gaseous pollutants. (The exact combination of filters will be determined by the air quality at the site, which will depend on whether it is located in an industrial area, a high-density urban location, a rural setting, etc.) It is important to note that much more stringent exposure limits are set for collections than for people. As Lull says in *Conservation Environment Guidelines for Libraries and Archives:* "Part of the reason the collection has a lower tolerance than human occupants of the same space is that the human body is living and can effect repairs to itself—the collection has no such self-renewing mechanism. The collection is also expected to have a longer life and exposure period, hopefully several hundred or thousand years, which means that even a low level of gaseous pollution will have a significant cumulative effect."

A good HVAC system, properly maintained and operated, will help preserve all the materials in the library or archive by reducing the stresses caused by constant changes in relative humidity. Moderate or cool temperatures help retard many kinds of deterioration.

Coping with Old HVAC Systems

Humidifying Air in Winter

In the past, preservation specialists emphasized that a constant 50% RH was a desirable goal year-round, and so it is, *if* the building and HVAC are designed for it. Institutions in cold winter areas experimented with retrofitting old systems to humidify air in winter. There are difficulties with this approach. The main problem is damage to buildings without proper moisture barriers. Water vapor penetrates into walls where it condenses on cooler materials closer to the outside. Moisture also condenses on window glass and metal window frames and runs down to puddle on window sills or floors. This causes rot, rust, and mold and encourages insects and vermin.

Another common result of haphazard humidification is mold inside the building, on collections, and also in air ducts. Constant monitoring of many different locations within the building is necessary to verify that the RH is not going above 50%. Attention to weather conditions is very important, so that water is not added to the system during humid periods. It has to be a very hands-on process, not one run by the calendar.

Once mold gets into the air ducts, it can spread to other areas served by the same air handler. The institution may then be saddled with a persistent problem because mold is hard to eradicate. (See "Mold," p. 17.)

Even if your HVAC system is able to add moisture to the air in winter, *don't* do it if any of these conditions exist:

- The building is an older one, not designed to be humidified.
- The HVAC system does not have the capability to *maintain* RH at the required level, without allowing it to go higher than indicated. (This is normally the case in most older systems.)
- Facilities personnel are not thoroughly trained in the operation of the system.

In Winter: Lower the Heat for Higher RH

A much safer way to raise relative humidity in winter is to lower the heat in storage areas to around 60°F (16°C), or even lower. At these levels, the RH stays at a higher level, perhaps approaching 35–38%. These cooler conditions are much healthier for hygroscopic materials like paper, leather, parchment, and so on. Patron and staff areas can be maintained at a comfortable temperature; storage areas should be much cooler in winter.

In Summer: Use Air Conditioning to Keep RH at 50% or Below

During warm weather, the interior temperature can be a little warmer, as long as the air conditioning is able to dehumidify to 50% or below, 24 hours a day, every day.

In Spring and Fall: Adjust HVAC for Dehumidification

In much of North America, spring and fall are seasons when the weather can be cool *and* very humid. It is often quite changeable. The weather may be pleasant enough for people, but danger lurks behind the moderating temperatures. At these times, neither heat nor air conditioning may go on and humidity can become trapped in the building, or in certain areas. Mold is always a threat if the relative humidity stays high for several days.

The HVAC system should be able to dehumidify storage areas over a broad range of temperatures. Some systems are not able to dehumidify when the outside air is humid but is below a certain temperature, when the AC would not normally go on. The facilities engineer or an outside contractor should determine whether the building's HVAC system has this capability. If not, perhaps modifications can be made, with added reheaters, chillers, or other changes to ensure that RH at or below 50% can be maintained during all seasons.

Keep in mind that relative humidity which goes up and down repeatedly causes more stress to hygroscopic materials than a steady level that is not quite ideal. Barbara Appelbaum in her *Guide to Environmental Protection of Collections* makes this point very clearly (pp. 34ff.). She suggests that a "*steady* RH every day and night of the year at any feasible level between about 40 and 60% would be virtually ideal for most collections." Because it is very difficult to maintain one level year-round (in a building without a specially designed HVAC system), a more attainable solution might be to maintain the lower level in the winter and very gradually go up to the higher RH in summer. Fluctuations within a 24-hour period should be very small and the change from one month to the next no more than 5%.

We would add to this, from experience working in libraries and archives, that 60% RH in summer may permit mold growth in materials that have dormant spores. This is fairly common in archival and special collections that include donations. The closer to 50% in summer, the better.

Cold Storage

Certain materials are more sensitive to high temperatures and will benefit from cooler storage conditions. If your institution has important collections of color photographs, film and glass negatives, slides, motion pictures, microfilm, and magnetic tapes (audio or video), consider including a cool room (40–60°F, 5–16°C) when planning renovations. An engineer with experience designing libraries should be consulted.

Until suitable storage can be provided on-site, it may be advisable to store irreplaceable originals in a remote archival storage facility, at 25–40°F, –4 to –5°C (cold storage). It might be possible to make user copies of certain items to keep in the library for the convenience of researchers.

These recommendations are based on information available from the Library of Congress Preservation Directorate. It would be advisable to consult with a person experienced in the preservation of nonprint media before deciding on any particular type of storage.

Monitoring Environmental Conditions

Even if the building and HVAC system are state of the art, do not simply rely on the fact that the system is run by a computer. (Almost everything is these days.) Conditions in many areas of the stacks or storage spaces must still be monitored to make sure that what the computer says is in fact what is happening. Complicated systems must be scrupulously maintained by specialized technicians.

Watch Temperature and Humidity for a Year

To determine what conditions prevail in different areas of the building, place monitoring devices in several storage or stack areas. Select a variety of locations, e.g., high shelves, low shelves, near outside walls, in the middle of the room, and especially places where there does not seem to be very good air circulation, like L-shaped corners.

Conditions at off-site storage areas can be monitored using data loggers with remote sensors. Study the space to determine how many sensors should be used and likely locations where they should be placed. Many types of sensors are available; some have alarm or warning mechanisms to alert staff at the main location when conditions depart from safe limits.

Keep a log of conditions at various times of the day and night for a full year to see what patterns emerge. Having detailed information will help make your case when interacting with facilities personnel about the need for more controlled conditions. Incidentally, a brand new HVAC system, no matter how advanced, will generally require at least a year before it is properly calibrated. It is up to you to keep records to determine if the promised conditions are in fact being provided.

Monitoring Equipment

There are various methods to read and record temperature and relative humidity. A combination of instruments often works well. The first two instruments described below provide a running record or printout, while the others give readings that must be read and noted manually.

Recording *hygrothermographs* were the museum standard for many decades and are still preferred by many. They need regular calibration. The paper charts must be changed and the information gathered manually. Hygrothermographs provide both a running record and current readings (fig. 1-1). They run on batteries and do not need electricity. The instruments are available from conservation and museum suppliers; they range in price from about $800 to $2,000.

Fig. 1-1

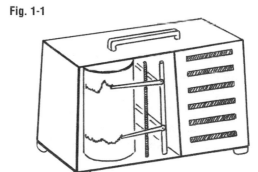

Data loggers are small battery-powered digital instruments that record environmental information. Loggers can be set to take readings at specified intervals; some instruments have a window that gives current readings as well. Software is included so that they can be connected to a personal computer that is periodically downloaded. Some loggers can be permanently connected to staff computers so that information from a remote location can be had at any time. Charts can be generated showing the temperature and humidity during a particular time. Various models cost from about $100 up to $1,000 or more; their price continues to drop as time goes by. They are available from conservation suppliers (see appendix B) and other suppliers of industrial instruments.

Digital psychrometers are battery operated (fig. 1-2). They show current relative humidity ranging from 0% to 100% and temperature from –4°F (–20°C) to 120°F (49°C). The memory feature displays maximum and minimum readings. The humidity sensors of these instruments can be recalibrated. The cost is between $80 and $140; two models are available from conservation suppliers.

Fig. 1-2

Digital hygrothermometers, also battery operated, show current temperature and humidity (fig. 1-3). They have a memory function; push-buttons reveal the highest and lowest temperature and humidity since the last time the memory was cleared. They cost between $25 and $40 and are available from conservation and household catalogs, electronics stores, and other suppliers. They cannot be calibrated and are not as accurate as psychrometers, but they can be used to observe patterns: compare read-

Fig. 1-3

ings on the same instrument over a period of time and trends will become apparent.

Hygrometers measure humidity. Very small instruments are available, for example, the one made by Arten, which is only 2" (5 cm) long. It has a dial for temperature and one for RH and also a row of squares along the bottom that show RH by color change from pink to blue (fig. 1-4). Since the color change strip remains accurate indefinitely, a marked difference between the RH dial and the strip means that the instrument needs calibration. A kit is sold for this purpose.

Fig. 1-4

Dial hygrometers are available at various prices. Don't buy one unless there is a way to recalibrate it periodically.

There are various other small humidity meters on the market. All hygrometers tend to overestimate humidity over time, sometimes by more than 10%. When selecting one, ascertain whether and how it can be recalibrated. (Thermometers do not need to be recalibrated.)

Temperature/humidity cards provide a very inexpensive way to monitor many spaces, and even different areas of the same room (fig. 1-5). There are several kinds; we like model 6203 LCC made by Süd Chemic (formerly Humidial Corp.) because they are easy to read (see appendix B). The cards last at least a year, but if they get wet they will not read true and should be discarded. They are available from conservation suppliers as well as from Poly Lam Products Corp. in quantities of 100 or more.

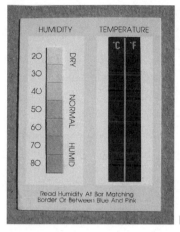

Fig. 1-5

Light

In areas occupied by patrons and staff, lighting should be adequate for comfortable reading and work. The light can come from fixtures of various kinds or from windows and skylights, or from a combination of sources.

However, prolonged exposure to light levels that are suitable for reading and working can cause damage to books, documents, and art on paper. The most obvious effect is fading. But light also helps break down the internal structure of many materials, including paper, leather, and textiles. They become brittle and eventually fall apart.

Damage from light is irreversible, and it is cumulative. This means that the longer the material is exposed to light, even at low levels, the more serious the effect will be. The quantity and quality of light that falls on materials must be controlled.

Rooms or areas that are used exclusively for storage should be dark when no one is in the room. Most archival materials are kept in boxes or cabinets of various kinds, so very little light reaches them.

Most likely to suffer light damage are those items that are stored in areas used by patrons and staff. Prints, documents, maps on permanent display, and book bindings, especially the spines, are typical casualties. In addi-

tion, carpeting, furniture, and curtains deteriorate more quickly from excessive light exposure, causing added expense.

Some Facts about Light

NATURAL LIGHT

We are mainly concerned with three types of rays found in natural light: ultraviolet (UV), visible, and infrared (IR).

Ultraviolet Light

Sunlight is rich in ultraviolet rays, which are not visible to the human eye. However, this is the part of the light spectrum that is most damaging to paper, textiles, and leather (including book bindings), many plastics, and all kinds of photographic processes. Fading, color changes, brittleness, cracking, and delaminating are all results of the accelerated aging that is caused by UV light.

Direct sunlight has the greatest amount of UV radiation, but even the indirect light from a north-facing window has a great deal. UV-filtering coatings and shades are available for windows and skylights. The filters remove a good portion of UV light and are an excellent investment.

Another good option is to use paint or ceiling tiles that contain the white pigment titanium dioxide. This substance has the capacity to absorb UV radiation while reflecting visible light.

Visible Light

This is the part of the light spectrum that we actually perceive as light. Although not in the UV range, high levels of visible light still cause deterioration, but at a much slower rate than UV light.

Infrared Light

Infrared light is not visible to us but is felt as radiant heat. Sunlight coming through skylights and windows generates significant amounts of heat; this often affects the temperature and relative humidity in that part of the building.

ARTIFICIAL LIGHT

Even though artificial light is much less bright than sunlight, it can still cause fading and deterioration. There are a few types in common use for indoor lighting. Each has different properties. (See also "Lighting" in section 6, p. 151.)

Fluorescent Lamps

After natural light, the most common source of UV radiation is fluorescent lighting. This is the kind commonly used in institutional buildings. Some method, or combination of methods, must be used to reduce UV radiation in areas where collections are kept. Plastic sleeve filters are available from conservation suppliers. (See appendix B.) Make sure that the sleeves are long enough to cover the ends of the tubes where much of the radiation is produced. The sleeves last at least ten years as long as they are not damaged. Throw out any sleeves that are cracked or torn.

Fluorescent tubes with built-in coatings that significantly reduce UV output were available in the past from conservation suppliers, but they have largely been discontinued by the manufacturers. However, tubes with shatterproof plastic coatings are still made, for use in the food industry. The coatings contain an ultraviolet stabilizer that reduces the amount of UV light transmitted.

In the case of recessed lighting, UV-filtering sheet acrylic shields can be used. This eliminates the step of removing and reinstalling the sleeves when tubes have to be replaced.

Paint pigmented with titanium dioxide or ceiling tiles coated with the paint will also help reduce UV radiation from fluorescent tubes, sometimes by as much as 90%, depending on the design of the lighting.

Incandescent (Tungsten) Lamps

The normal light bulbs found in homes are tungsten lamps, also called incandescent lamps. They give off very little UV, and their warm-colored light is much safer for paper-based materials. They do produce heat, but HVAC systems are generally able to compensate for this. The lamps should be at least four feet away from any object likely to be damaged by heat.

Tungsten-Halogen (Quartz-Halogen) Lamps

These small, powerful lamps are efficient light sources. Depending on the model, they give off significant levels of UV radiation. Filters are available for them. They also produce a lot of heat, sometimes more heat than light. Some fixtures have the transformer separate from the lamp; this helps to reduce heat in the room.

Halogen lamps should not be installed inside enclosed spaces, and they should be shielded to prevent any contact with flammable objects. Observe the manufacturer's or designer's guidelines to avoid the risk of fire.

High Intensity Discharge (HID) Lamps

There are several different kinds of HID lamps. They are somewhat similar to fluorescent lamps and require some time to light up completely after they are turned on. High-pressure sodium lamps give off very little UV and are sometimes used in large storage spaces. Mercury and metal halide HID lamps have very high UV output and are not suitable for indoor lighting.

Protect Sensitive Materials from Excessive Light Exposure

A combination of methods is often necessary to achieve the degree of protection needed by various materials. See "Measuring Light Levels" in section 6, p. 152, for information about measuring visible and ultraviolet light.

USE APPROPRIATE FILTERS

Make sure that there are UV filters on all fluorescent fixtures and that windows and skylights have filtering coatings or shades. This will cut down on the amount of ultraviolet radiation reaching exposed materials. In some cases, consider using opaque shades on certain windows or skylights during the brightest part of the day, especially in summer. (The window coverings will also keep a lot of heat out.)

USE UV-ABSORBING PAINTS AND CEILING TILES

Products containing titanium dioxide absorb a great deal of UV radiation. After the paint or tiles are in place, no further action is needed except a periodic vacuuming of the tiles to remove dust. Paint should be reapplied or cleaned when it is no longer bright.

ROTATE EXHIBITS OR MAKE FACSIMILES

Many libraries have framed maps, portraits, charters, and other pertinent documents that are on permanent display. Because light damage happens so gradually, years may pass before the staff notices that the color of a map, for example, has faded or even disappeared. Signatures on letters or charters likewise become very faint. This is a continuing process; in addition, the paper or parchment of the document deteriorates and loses its strength. The longer the item is exposed to light, the worse the damage will be.

A good strategy for avoiding further damage is to make a facsimile for framing. Afterwards, place the original in a folder and store it in a flat file drawer or box with similar items. A professional photographer can make a full-size print of the document; this can provide a remarkably close reproduction as well as a copy negative for other uses in the future. Color photocopies are a less costly alternative and may well be suitable for many situations. Digital and other reproduction techniques can be employed to deal with large sizes, faint originals, and other problems.

If a library or archive prefers to show original material, follow the guidelines in section 6 regarding temperature and humidity, light levels, and framing and mounting methods. Light that reaches the object on exhibit should be limited to 5–15 foot-candles as measured with a light meter; this may require relocating some exhibits away from very bright areas. Even with low light levels, limit the time that any item is on view to no more than three months. Substitute a similar document or print after that, or alternate originals and reproductions.

USE OPAQUE PROTECTIVE CONTAINERS

The surest way to protect light-sensitive materials is to enclose them in suitable archival containers. This will be discussed in "Storage Containers (Preservation Enclosures)" in section 3, p. 57.

For a more detailed explanation of light and its effects, as well as types of lighting fixtures, see NEDCC Technical Leaflet 13, "Protection from Light Damage," by Beth Lindblom Patkus.

Maintenance and Housekeeping

Regular Maintenance

To avoid problems with insects and other pests, and to reduce the chances of mold developing, the whole building and all its systems must be kept in good operating condition. Meticulous roof and gutter maintenance is essential. Inspections of the ventilation and heating system that are performed on a regular schedule may identify potential problems before they happen.

No Smoking

Smoking is not normally allowed in libraries and archives for reasons of health and also for the safety of the materials. If smoking in out-of-the-way areas is a problem, try to find who is doing it. Explain that smoke is disseminated throughout the building by the HVAC system and that this violation is putting the institution at some risk. Furthermore, clandestine smoking is more likely to lead to fires. It may be possible to compromise by providing a lounge area, perhaps in a nearby building, with proper ventilation and fire-suppression systems.

Restrict Food to Specific Areas

Food should be restricted to specific rooms; these areas should be inspected regularly by pest control personnel. Public and staff areas should be cleaned daily, or as needed. Frequent cleaning ensures the removal of trash and other possible sources of food for insects or rodents; in addition, an orderly appearance lets patrons know that the staff cares about the materials under its care. Maintenance is not an exciting subject, but it is one of the cornerstones of preservation.

Maintain Grounds

The grounds around the building must likewise be kept in good condition. Shrubs and foundation plantings should be thinned or pruned as needed to make sure that they do not provide shelter for rodents and pests. Plant bushes a few feet away from walls; air circulation will help reduce humidity buildup near the building. Check also that lawns or open areas are graded away from the building. Install curtain drains or other means of keeping water away from the foundation. Common sense and low-tech steps very often are the best ways to prevent or even reverse troublesome conditions.

Housekeeping and maintenance are frequently performed by personnel from departments that are not under the control of the library or archive. It is possible that the maintenance staff have been in the institution for a long time and have been in the habit of doing things a certain way. If these methods are not producing the best results as far as preservation needs are concerned, it sometimes requires great diplomacy to bring about changes. The maintenance staff must see themselves as a respected part of the team whose mission is to safeguard the collections. A good working relationship between the head of the library and the head of the maintenance department will facilitate day-to-day operations and will pay off handsomely in emergencies.

EDUCATION

Basic Rules for Using Research Materials

When most researchers come into a library or archive, their primary goal is to obtain information. They see the materials as providers of that information and that's about it. People who are looking for specific facts or figures are often only dimly aware of the physical characteristics of the books, documents, or other media that they use. An important task for administrative or preservation staff is to raise patrons' awareness of proper handling techniques.

Prepare a preservation booklet, flyer, bookmark, or other handout with some basic rules. Illustrations are very helpful and help maintain a light, friendly tone.

Here's an example of what to include in the brochure.

- Leave food and drink outside the library.

- No smoking in the library or archive.

Fig. 1-6A

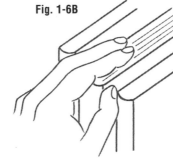

- What happens to a book when it is removed from the shelf by pulling the top of the spine (fig. 1-6A).

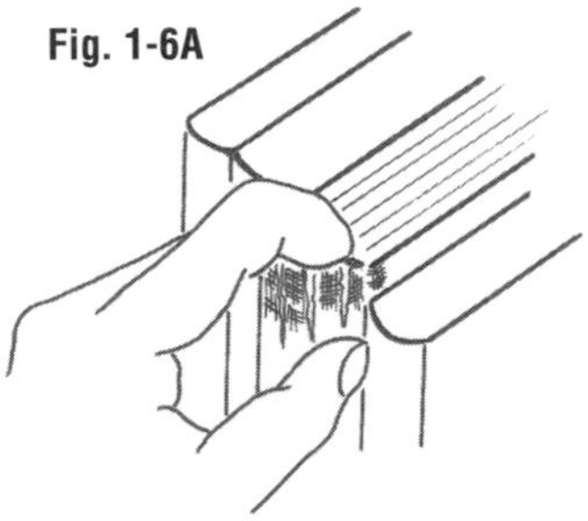

- Proper way to remove a book from the shelf.

  Move the book toward the front of the shelf by placing your fingers on top of the pages (fig. 1-6B)

  Fig. 1-6B

  Push adjacent books in, leaving the book you need at the front of the shelf (fig. 1-7A)

Fig. 1-7A

If there is no bookend available to support books, prevent them from sagging by placing a few books on their sides next to the last book (fig. 1-7B)

Fig. 1-7B

- Always handle materials with clean hands (or wearing cotton gloves, depending on the situation).

  - To mark your place in a book, use pieces of acid-free paper only.

    Don't fold down and crease the corners of pages

    Don't leave objects in books as bookmarks. This includes pencils, paper clips, pieces of paper, notebooks, etc.

    Don't put repositionable adhesive notes (e.g., Post-its) on book pages while doing research. The adhesive leaves a residue which can cause pages to stick together. It also attracts dirt, which sticks to it.

  - *Don't* use highlighters or write in books.

  - Show damaged materials to a staff member; never make any repairs yourself.

- Use care when photocopying; *do not* press down hard on a book that has a stiff binding (fig. 1-8). If having trouble, ask if there is a better copier for that type of book.

Fig. 1-8

Don't crush books on the copier

Staff Training

All new employees should get a copy of the flyer or booklet, with an explanation of why the procedures are important.

In addition, develop a set of instructions for staff members who actively handle books or other materials. These include all of the topics covered in the handout as well as:

- Shelving:

  Books should stand up straight on the shelf, the spines even with the front edge of the shelf. (See fig. 1-7B.) Use appropriate bookends; to prevent distortion, don't allow books to sag.

  Don't place books on top of a row of other books (fig. 1-9). If the shelf is full, shift books. If the book is too tall for the shelf, take it to a supervisor and explain.

  Don't shelve books on their fore edges (i.e., the edge opposite the spine). If too tall, see above.

  Reshelve books found out of call number order

- Damaged materials:

  Bring to supervisor

- Be observant and report irregular conditions:

  Problems with the heat or air conditioning

  Leaks or flooding

  Unusual dirt accumulations

  Mold

  Insects or rodents

  Doors or windows left open

  Unauthorized persons in areas not open to the public

Fig. 1-9 This is an example of poor shelving

One of the main goals of the administration should be to create a feeling among all of the staff that they are guardians of something important and that each person's job is crucial to the smooth functioning of the institution.

Patron Education

Distribute the preservation flyer or bookmark to all users of the library or archive. Enlist the aid of the staff to keep a discreet eye on patrons and be ready to help with problems. Most academic libraries present orientation programs for new users; include preservation tips in these sessions.

To encourage the use of safe bookmarks, many libraries provide small pieces of acid-free paper on reading tables and other areas used by patrons. These slips of paper don't cause distortion to the text block and, if accidentally left in the book for a long period, will not cause staining to the pages. If the library has bookmarks printed with information about hours, regulations, collections, and so on, make sure that they are printed on acid-free card stock. (State this fact on the bookmark.)

Occasionally, the director will give a tour of the library to groups such as Friends of the Library, local political figures, visiting faculty members, and so on. This is another opportunity to mention the ways that the institution is working to preserve the collections.

Library or archive staff should emphasize that collections in good condition can be used but materials that are allowed to deteriorate will eventually be lost. The importance of proper care for rare or valuable items is usually easy to demonstrate, but it is not always easy to prove that materials valuable primarily for their information also need favorable conditions to continue to be useful.

In dealing with the public, the staff of the library or archive should demonstrate that preservation of the collections is a very high priority and one that can only be accomplished with the collaboration of people who use the materials.

DISASTER PLANNING AND RESPONSE

Making plans for responding to emergencies is preservation at the most basic level, yet it is often overlooked in favor of the day-to-day activities of a library or archive. While this book is not primarily concerned with disaster planning, a few aspects of the topic will be discussed briefly. (For more information, see the bibliography.)

There are three main parts to planning for emergencies.

- The *first* is to make provisions for the safety of patrons and staff.
- The *second* has to do with maintaining the institution's ability to continue functioning during and after a major emergency.
- The *third* is making provisions to reduce damage to the collections. This includes developing priorities for salvaging materials.

Fires, hurricanes, tornadoes, acts of terrorism, etc., can cause great devastation. Often the damage is not limited to the institution but affects a whole region. When a major disaster occurs, the *number one priority* is to get everyone out of the building and to account for every person.

Evacuation of Patrons and Staff

Most public institutions have evacuation plans. These include the appointment of fire marshals among the staff, directions for evacuating the building, floor plans posted in various locations on each floor, phone lists indicating the appropriate person(s) to be notified in case of emergency, fire drills, and other procedures. If there is no evacuation plan, this is the first place to start, and without any delay.

Contingency Arrangements during an Emergency

After instructions for the evacuation of patrons and staff are in place, the institution should make contingency plans for continuing to function during the restoration of the building(s). This involves arranging for temporary office space, computers, storage areas, and sometimes additional staff. The head of the library must understand what insurance will cover. This is also a good time to make sure that there is a clear chain of command in the institution so that, in the event of a major salvage operation, needless time will not be wasted in obtaining approvals.

Collection Priorities

Assess the collections and develop priorities for salvage so that emergency workers can be directed effectively. The importance of the materials to the collection affects this decision. The nature of the materials must also be considered. For instance: can the items survive prolonged immersion or wetting? When books printed on coated paper get wet, they cannot be allowed to dry closed because the pages may fuse together. This is called "blocking" and is *not* reversible. If a library has a collection of such books and this collection is one of its important holdings, those books should be among the first to be salvaged. The same applies to collections of photographs since most types of photographic materials cannot survive prolonged soaking.

The cost and availability of replacements enter into the equation. Is it possible to replace a certain book, and at what cost, or is it a unique artifact, valuable in its original form? An accurate inventory makes it easier to determine priorities for salvage.

Mercifully, most crises are not in the major disaster category, and much of the effort can be directed at preserving the collections affected. The most common emergencies are related to water coming into the building, either as flooding from ground level or as roof or pipe leaks. In addition, small fires, quickly put out, often involve a fair amount of water damage. These events usually come without warning. But some emergencies can be predicted and prevented or made less severe by a study of the building and its surroundings.

General Assessment or Survey

A general preservation survey has several goals. One of them is to assess factors that pose a risk to the preservation of the collections.

The survey can be conducted by one or more staff members who should take some time to explore the building. It is easy to take many things for granted when a person has worked in a building for a long time. During the assessment, however, the surveyor should look at it with a fresh eye in order to assess risks.

Consult the building engineer or head of maintenance for information on building details. Note environmental conditions in all areas. Observe what type of storage furniture is used for various materials. Determine the locations of key collections. (Templates are available to help institutions compile surveys.)

Sometimes an outside contractor is hired to compile the general assessment or survey. A permanent staff member, who is part of the disaster planning team, should meet and work regularly with this consultant. The more involved the regular staff can be in the survey, the more they will learn from the consultant and the more pertinent the report will be.

The survey may uncover risks that can be corrected, thus preventing some emergencies. And it will be a logical first step toward emergency planning: forewarned is forearmed.

Compile a Disaster Plan

Compiling a disaster response plan is a lengthy process and requires a person (or team) who is persistent, detail-oriented, and patient enough to keep working on a project that does not seem to have much immediate relevance to the functioning of the library.

In some cases, an outside consultant is brought in to compile the disaster plan. This is helpful in cases where there are severe staff limitations; in addition, a person familiar with the process can bring in good ideas gleaned from previous experience. However, the consultant should work closely with one or more permanent staff members who will continue to be involved with the plan by updating it periodically and explaining it to other staff members. Otherwise, it is possible to end up with an excellent plan that nobody in the institution understands very well (or has actually read).

Calling Chains

Among the things that need to be established by the disaster plan is who must be called in various types of emergencies. This should include 911, the head of the department, security, maintenance staff, the head of the response team, and so on. The creation of a calling chain or telephone tree should be the first task of the disaster planning team.

Response Team

A response (or disaster action) team typically includes the chief administrator or director, the head of security, the building engineer or equivalent, the research librarian, archivist, or other person in charge of collection development, and the head of technical services or registrar. The list will vary depending on the institution, but the object is to have people who can fulfill a variety of duties. Remember to include additional staff who could substitute for response team members away on vacation or who work only part-time. The person (or persons) who compiled the plan may be part of the response team, but this is not always the case.

Some larger libraries have a preservation librarian. This person's job often includes performing or supervising surveys and creating a disaster plan; the preservation librarian would logically be on the disaster response team and is sometimes the head of the team.

The chief administrator or director can play a variety of roles during a disaster but is not generally the head of the team. The director should be somewhat detached from the actual mud and debris so that he or she can continue to function as the chief administrator. The director will authorize procedures and expenditures and provide cash or a credit card for necessary purchases. The director (or his administrative staff) will contact insurance companies to find out exactly how the library is covered in this case; contact salvage companies; and provide news releases to the media.

Keep in mind that the head of the response team should be a person with stamina and good people skills who can function well under stress. It does not need to be a high-ranking officer. The director and the head of the response team should be able to communicate comfortably with each other.

The other members of the disaster action team will be in charge of actually implementing the actions needed to respond to the emergency.

These suggestions apply to larger institutions. A smaller library or historical society might not have people in all these positions, nor would it need a large disaster response team. One or two dedicated persons are sufficient; it is simply necessary to have the cooperation of the head of the institution and of the chief financial officer (the person who authorizes expenditures).

Members of the response team should each be assigned specific roles to avoid duplication of some steps and neglect of others. All team members should be very familiar with the disaster plan and with the response techniques outlined in it. They can, in turn, train other staff members or volunteers as the need arises.

If the library or archive shares a building with other tenants, or other branches of a larger institution, the person writing the disaster plan should cooperate as much as possible with the other tenants or departments for the greatest common benefit. Conversely, the plan must include any off-site locations used for collections storage.

Emergency Instructions

Early in the planning stages, develop a set of very simple directions that can fit on one page. This form can be included in the written plan; multiple copies can be printed and posted near the evacuation instructions and at the entrance to all collection areas. A sample of instructions used at the LuEsther T. Mertz Library of the New York Botanical Garden is shown, with permission, on p. 15. This form gives directions for taking care of relatively minor emergencies. It assumes that certain supplies are on hand.

Emergency Supplies

Having some essential supplies ready can mean the difference between a minor emergency and extensive damage. The salvage kit should contain a copy of the disaster manual. The supplies can be kept in one or more convenient locations. Some items (e.g., flashlights, scissors, tapes) are extremely tempting to borrowers, so there should be an inventory from time to time to make sure everything is available and in working order. Many institutions keep the supplies lashed to hand trucks: this makes it easy to transport them to the scene, and it also provides hand trucks to assist in removing materials from the disaster area. Book trucks are another good option.

The kit should contain plastic sheeting. Order enough to cover priority collections. Precut to suitable sizes, refold, and label the bundles so they can be taken immediately to the appropriate areas.

Other useful items to have on hand include plastic or rubber gloves and boots, cartons, plastic crates, newsprint, paper towels, mops, buckets, and plastic garbage bags (fig. 1-10). Wet/dry vacuums are very useful for removing small amounts of standing water.

More complete lists can be found in various works cited in the bibliography. Many items can be purchased by the institution's central purchasing department, at great savings.

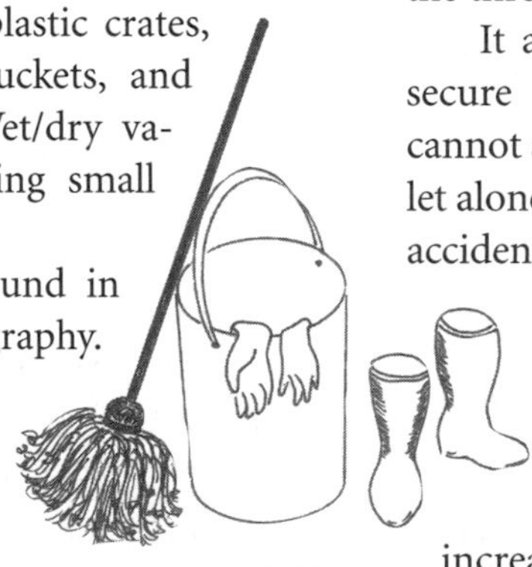

Fig. 1-10

Recovery Plans

Arrange for off-site locations where materials can be taken while the building is being restored. The disaster plan should also have information about local resources needed to cope with various types of emergencies. Include cleaning services as well as more specialized vendors, such as dehumidification companies.

Compile a list of volunteers or other possible helpers from the community or other departments. Trusted former employees and current volunteers are also good sources of temporary assistance. Make contacts among sister institutions to secure mutual aid agreements.

Distribute the Disaster Plan

The disaster plan should be distributed to all departments in the institution, to fire and police personnel, and to others who have agreed to help in emergencies, such as volunteers and staff of nearby institutions. Alarm codes, the location of certain valuable collections, and other sensitive information should be blanked out from versions that go outside the institution. Key staff and disaster response team members must have copies of the plan at home in the event that no one can enter the building to get an on-site copy.

Construction and Renovations

A significant number of disasters happen during construction and renovation projects. Fires can start from electrical and mechanical equipment brought in by the contractor, or from a cigarette. The roof or walls might be open for a time, and windows and doors may not close well, allowing water and air pollution to enter the building. If the construction takes place in the summer, there is an increased risk of mold outbreaks. With winter projects, the threat of pipes freezing and bursting is a real concern.

It also becomes more difficult to keep the building secure when outside contractors come and go. Staff cannot always do their own work efficiently at these times, let alone be on the lookout for doors or windows left open accidentally. And a stranger in the building during the renovation project might not arouse much concern.

Collections and storage spaces should get more frequent security inspections, and there should be a heightened awareness throughout the building. Security staff may need to be increased temporarily. During construction, the collaboration of security staff and building maintenance workers is essential for keeping the collections safe. Perhaps the building engineer can serve as liaison between the construction crew and the institution's staff.

Sample EMERGENCY INSTRUCTIONS *Form*

adapted from the

Disaster Preparedness and Recovery Plan,

the LuEsther T. Mertz Library of

the New York Botanical Garden

DO NOT PANIC

FIRE

1. Pull fire alarm
2. Evacuate the Building
3. Call 911 (dial 9 for an outside line)
4. Call NYBG Security 000 000-0000; after 4 P.M., call 000 000-0000

WATER

1. Call NYBG Security 000 000-0000; after 4 P.M., call 000 000-0000
2. Call Physical Plant (Name of contact person) 000 000-0000
3. Call Maintenance (Plumber) 000 000-0000
4. If problem persists, call Dept. of Water 000 000-0000 (dial 9 for an outside line)
5. Protect the area getting wet

A. Water from above

1. Remove library materials from shelves and move to dry area. Use book trucks if possible; otherwise hand carry materials to dry location.

   AND/OR

2. Cover immediate and adjacent areas with plastic sheeting (use plastic sheeting located in box at the _____ Bldg. side of each collection floor)

B. Water from below

1. Remove library materials from lower shelves first; use book trucks if possible; otherwise, hand carry materials to dry location. When this is complete and if problem persists, remove all materials from shelves.

CALL THE DISASTER ACTION TEAM

Before beginning the project, isolate nearby collections. It may be sufficient to simply cover a section of stacks with plastic sheeting, tightly taped in place. But a more extensive project might require more elaborate steps. A temporary wall, preferably made of fireproof materials, can be erected to separate the construction site from the rest of the building. HVAC ducts should be sealed or reconfigured so that construction dust does not permeate the rest of the building. In this way, disruption can be reduced and security will be less compromised.

If it is not practical to isolate the construction site, then the collections should be moved to a secure storage location. This could be in another part of the building, in space at a sister institution, or in off-site commercial storage. When selecting a storage location, consider the physical condition of the collection and the type of environmental conditions it will have. If space must be rented, this cost will have to be added to the project. Determine if access is needed to the material during the construction. All these options have to be evaluated and decided before construction starts.

Temperature and humidity will be much harder to control with part of the building open. Discuss this problem with the building engineer and emphasize the importance of stable conditions to the continued survival of the collection. HVAC filters will need changing more often during and after the project, and the ducts may need to be cleaned to remove all traces of debris. Before cleaning air ducts, cover any materials under the ductwork. Even if the cleaning is done carefully, stirred-up dust sometimes falls on areas below.

Construction can put a great deal of dust into the air, no matter how well isolated the renovation site might be. Accumulated dust can damage computers and peripherals as well as diskettes and magnetic tapes. Use a vacuum with a HEPA filter or equivalent to remove dust from surfaces frequently and be especially attentive to backing-up routines during this time.

Keep in mind also that new portions of the HVAC system may need very close monitoring for at least a year before they are fully calibrated.

Water Emergencies: The Importance of Quick Action

Fires, earthquakes, bomb blasts, and other disasters are certainly extremely destructive. But after the initial damage is over, there is usually no further immediate danger to the collection (except in cases where materials are left exposed to the elements or vulnerable to theft). Salvage can proceed at a reasonable pace, as circumstances permit.

When water is involved, however, the situation is completely different. Unfortunately, the most common emergency in research collections is flooding of some sort: streams overflow, water mains break, heating or water supply pipes in the building break, roofs and windows leak, etc. And there is almost always water damage after a fire.

In the case of a minor leak, much damage can be averted by simply covering materials with plastic or moving them to another location, as directed in the "Emergency Instructions Form" from the New York Botanical Garden discussed previously.

Major floods usually require quick help from a professional salvage company in order to minimize the damage. Books and other materials can suffer damage from being submerged for long periods; paper-based, photographic, and other materials that are wet but not submerged will begin to mold within a short time. Generally, mold develops sooner during warm weather, but other factors, such as a history of prior mold infestation, also determine how long it takes for mold to start.

To prevent wet materials from becoming moldy or otherwise deteriorating, they must either be air dried immediately or frozen until they can be dealt with. Air drying a large number of items is not always possible, and it is not the best way to dry bound books (cockling almost always results). Disaster recovery companies can pick up materials to freeze-dry in their plants or in special trucks brought to the site. The disaster plan should make provisions for transporting materials to local freezers as quickly as possible if they cannot go directly to freeze-drying facilities.

The building and storage furniture will also need to be dried and cleaned. When compiling the disaster plan, contact one or more disaster recovery (or salvage) companies. Most vendors will send helpful literature and some may send a representative to meet with staff during the planning stages in order to answer questions about costs, response times, and services offered. (Several companies are listed in appendix B.)

Failure of HVAC System

Although not usually as dramatic as a flood, failure of the HVAC system during a humid stretch of weather is quite serious. Mold (also called mildew) can develop surprisingly quickly, particularly in buildings where the HVAC malfunctions more or less regularly. Sometimes it will affect a large portion of the library; other times it will occur in pockets.

It is very important that all staff members know what mold looks like and that they be alert to its development. If a book or an area smells like mildew, the problem must be investigated. It is much easier to head off a small mold outbreak than to have to treat all the materials and shelving in a library. Since failure of the HVAC system is another situation that calls for a quick response, we are treating it as a disaster.

Mold

When mold is found growing on books and other materials that were not affected by flooding, it means that environmental conditions are favorable for its growth. These conditions include high humidity, high temperatures (as would occur during an HVAC failure in summer), darkness, still air, and undisturbed dirt.

If the mold is still confined to the covers of books or outer containers of archival materials, the outbreak may well be curtailed by cleaning the visible mold from the book covers, or rehousing the archival materials, and then carefully disinfecting the shelving and the air ducts serving that area of the building.

Cleaning a Small Mold Outbreak

Dormant mold and mold that is just beginning to form can be cleaned in-house if there is a well-ventilated area that can be separated from the HVAC system serving the rest of the building.

Workers should protect themselves against exposure to the mold by wearing goggles and a snug-fitting respirator with the appropriate cartridges. Face masks should be fitted to each person. Hair and clothing should be covered with smocks, aprons, and hats or caps that can be disposed or washed with bleach at the end of each session. Work clothing should be changed after each session, placed in plastic bags or other tight containers, and washed or discarded. Workers can wear well-fitting cotton or plastic gloves. Avoid touching the face, eating, drinking, or smoking with dirty hands or gloves. Shower and wash hair after each session or, at least, before going to bed. Mold does cause a variety of allergic reactions in different people. *Persons with respiratory problems should consult their physicians before doing this work.* Staff should take frequent breaks in separate, well-ventilated areas or

outdoors, and wash their hands before eating, drinking, or smoking. Provide snacks, happy music, and any other cheerful amenities that will keep morale up.

CLEANUP PROCEDURE

Thoroughly examine nearby shelves to make sure that the mold has not spread there. Staff should learn the difference between mold and dust: mold tends to grow in uneven patterns or in little dots. It is just as likely to appear on horizontal surfaces as on vertical areas. Dust is even, and always thicker on horizontal surfaces. If uncertain, use a magnifying glass (5× power or higher) to look at some genuine dust. Then look at the suspected mold. A web of little hairs or plantlike growth with spores indicates mold. A mycologist should be consulted to identify the particular strain and determine whether unusual health risks are involved. You can get the name of a mycologist from a local college or hospital.

Cover unaffected ranges of shelves with plastic sheeting. Tape the film to the edges of the bookshelves. Close or block HVAC vents in the affected area to cut down on the spread of airborne spores to other areas of the building. Lower the humidity by using dehumidifiers, and increase local air circulation with fans or air movers. Or open windows, if feasible, when the humidity is lower outside than inside, and use exhaust fans. You may need to rent commercial equipment.

Pack the moldy books into disposable cartons, or transport them out of the library on book trucks that can be disinfected later. Metal or fiberglass book trucks are easier to disinfect. (See "Packing and Moving Books" in section 5, p. 102, for tips on packing books into boxes.)

If possible, the books should first be cleaned using a vacuum cleaner with a HEPA filter. Use the brush attachment and, if the books are fragile, place a piece of cheesecloth between the brush and the wand to catch any loose pieces (figs. 1-11 and 1-12).

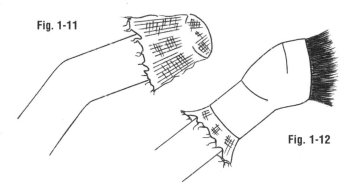

Fig. 1-11

Fig. 1-12

The vacuuming can be done as the books are removed from the shelf or in the area where the major cleanup will be done, depending on conditions.

Make sure to discard the bag immediately after a mold cleanup and to disinfect the brush attachment by washing it in hot, sudsy water.

The next step is to remove surface mold from bindings and edges of books or from document boxes, folders, or other containers. Use a soft brush or cloth, such as flannel, or a One-Wipe cloth (available from supermarkets), or a "magnetic" cloth such as a Dust Bunny (available from conservation suppliers). *Don't open books or folders* at this stage, to avoid getting mold spores inside. When cleaning the tops of books, work from the spine out to the fore edge (figs. 1-13–1-15).

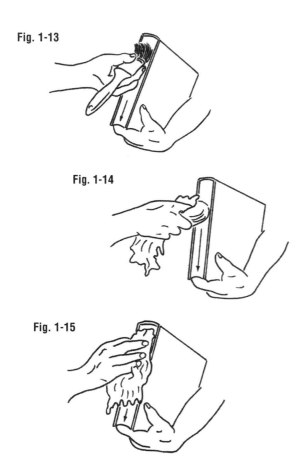

Fig. 1-13

Fig. 1-14

Fig. 1-15

Natural rubber sponges, such as Gonzo sponges, are always used dry and are excellent for removing mold. Slice some sponges into sections about 2" (5 cm) thick to make it easier to work on curved areas of books. As the surface of the sponge gets dirty, cut it away with scissors. Be sure to discard the sponges after using them to clean mold.

Note: The directions above can be modified to clean books and shelving that are merely dusty. It is not necessary to use a disinfectant on the shelving and floors. The books need not be removed to another room; they can be cleaned on book trucks brought into the stacks.

Take the cleaned books to a well-ventilated, clean, dry (below 50% RH) area. Stand them fanned open (fig. 1-16). Softcover books may need to be supported with bookends in order to stay upright; the same is true of very thin or very tall books. With clean hands, spot check for signs of mold inside. Let the books stand open for several days (fig. 1-17). This will reduce humidity in the pages to safe levels.

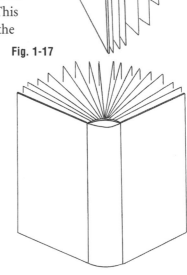

Fig. 1-16

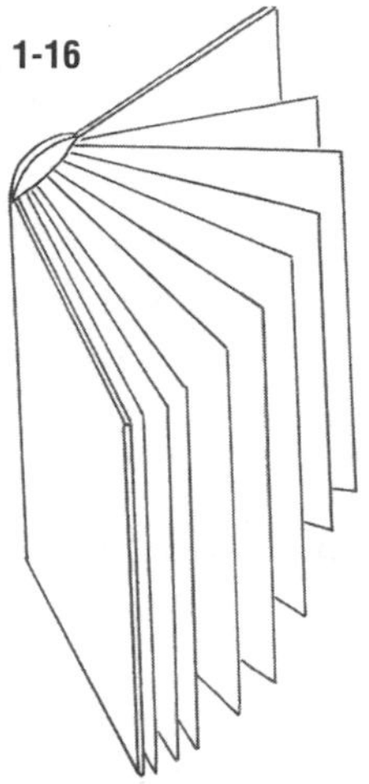

Fig. 1-17

In the meantime, the shelving, walls, floor, etc., should be disinfected with a fungicide such as Lysol liquid or bleach (five parts water to one part bleach). Do not use great quantities of aerosols such as Lysol spray without protecting the worker with a properly fitted organic vapor (cartridge) respirator. Liquids are more economical and effective than sprays as a rule. Good air exchange and circulation should be maintained during the cleanup. Make sure to use appropriate plastic or rubber gloves and protective clothing.

Note: In the United States there are numerous regulations regarding what products can be used in different circumstances. This varies according to each state, the type of institution, union representation, and other factors. In some situations, the regulations may make it impossible for staff to clean mold. The work will have to be done by an outside contractor.

Carpeting should be cleaned with a fungicide added to the water. It may be necessary to remove the bottom shelves in order to gain access to the space below each range. In cases of recurring infestation, it is usually necessary to remove carpeting and install flooring that can be mopped clean. Carpets are excellent breeding places for mold because they hold much moisture, even when they don't appear damp.

Examine the cleaned books. If there are still traces of mold on the covers but not on the pages, the best solution is to send the books to the bindery for recasing. In the case of rare or historical books that must be retained in their bindings, consult a conservator. Do not use any chemicals to clean book covers.

As soon as the shelving and books are clean, carefully remove the plastic from nearby ranges and inspect the books again to make sure they did not develop mold during the cleanup. The cleaned books can be reshelved.

Don't leave the plastic covering on the shelving any longer than necessary since it prevents air circulation. It also makes it difficult to notice if mold begins to develop later.

Prevent Future Mold Outbreaks

The conditions that caused the mold outbreak must be corrected. If the HVAC system is not able to maintain relative humidity at around 50% during humid weather, it may be a good investment to hire an HVAC engineer for a consultation. Referrals can be obtained from the American Society of Heating, Refrigerating and Air-Conditioning Engineers (see appendix C).

Problems with roof leaks or groundwater need to be investigated and corrected. Good cleaning practices and adequate air circulation are also key factors in preventing a future occurrence of mold.

A collection that has never had a mold outbreak can usually ride out a period of humid weather without problems, but once there is a history of mold it really is critical to watch the relative humidity. There are always many kinds of mold spores in the air waiting for favorable conditions to bloom, and materials that have previously been moldy are more likely to become moldy again than items that have never been infected. The humidity must be controlled not only in the summer but also during the cool, damp months in spring and fall. At these times, it may be necessary to run heat and air conditioning at the same time in order to achieve a safe level of humidity.

Major Mold Outbreaks

More extensive mold outbreaks are beyond the capacity of staff to handle in-house and will require quick action by a disaster response company. They may bring in dehumidification equipment so that whole rooms and the materials in them can be dried enough to retard mold growth. Their staff or a cleaning company will need to clean the mold off books, walls, floors, shelves, and other surfaces. The HVAC ducts should be cleaned and filters changed. (See appendix B for companies that can provide these services.)

Another method is to freeze books to stop the mold damage and postpone the cleanup until a more convenient time. A few books can be wrapped in plastic bags and frozen on-site; larger numbers will need to be sent to a commercial salvage company. Freezing does not kill mold spores, but it does make them inactive.

Good results have been obtained by the use of a fairly new technique. It involves enclosing the affected materials in a container with a very low oxygen atmosphere. This can be done by some specialized companies, on-site or at their plants.

For further information, contact the Library of Congress Preservation Directorate or a regional conservation center such as the Conservation Center for Art and Historic Artifacts, the Canadian Conservation Institute, or the Northeast Document Conservation Center (NEDCC). They can provide literature, technical advice, and referrals to conservators. Some of this information is available at their websites. (See appendix C.)

Disaster Recovery

Disaster recovery involves various steps. Restoring the building to a functioning state, or finding a new location for the library or archive, is obviously of great importance but is outside the scope of this book. When it comes to dealing with damaged collections, options vary according to the kinds of materials affected. A library may be able to replace or simply discard certain books. Other items may need to be reformatted. It may be possible to rebind some materials or to repair them in an economical way. The instructions given in sections 4 and 5 can help staff make a variety of sound repairs. Rare or valuable items, once stabilized, should be placed in containers until a subject specialist and a conservator can evaluate them. See "Storage Containers (Preservation Enclosures)" in section 3.

STORAGE METHODS

Providing a safe environment is one of the chief ways of preserving collections. Another is good storage. While safe environmental conditions protect against chemical deterioration, good storage practices protect against light and dust, keep fragile materials intact, and keep materials from becoming distorted. Proper storage containers can reduce damage from rough handling and act as a buffer between the materials and a less than perfect environment.

Storage Furniture

Storage furniture tends to last for many years, so it is worth investing in shelving and cabinets that will not hasten the deterioration of materials placed in them. When planning renovations or additions, look for furniture that does not give off formaldehyde or other harmful volatile components.

Powder-Coated Steel

Powder-coated steel is currently believed to be a safer material, in contrast to baked enamel steel, which was favored in the past. Baked enamel coatings may off-gas (emit noxious gases as they cure) if not properly applied and sealed. This would be a particular problem for materials that are enclosed in cabinets with doors or drawers.

Other safe materials include anodized aluminum, which is strong and lightweight although expensive, and chrome-plated steel, which is often used to make wire shelving for box storage.

Wood Shelving

Avoid purchasing wood shelving or other furniture in which to store collections of lasting value. Wood gives off acid gases that are damaging to paper, leather, textiles, and other library and archival materials. Although more gases are emitted when the wood is new, some woods continue to off-gas indefinitely. Oak is among the more harmful woods. Composites such as plywood, chipboard, or Masonite are very damaging because the adhesives and sealants used in their manufacture also off-gas. In addition, the manufacturer may change the makeup of a product at any time, further confusing the issue.

Existing Storage Furniture

In a less than perfect world, furniture that is not optimal must sometimes continue in use. Some steps can be taken to make it better.

A cabinet or bookcase with shelves made of chipboard or compressed wood can be modified by replacing the shelves, preferably with powder-coated steel or chrome-plated steel wire shelves. If this is not possible, solid wood shelves can be made using one of the woods that gives off the least acid gases. These include mahogany, poplar, spruce, and walnut. All surfaces of the wood should be sealed. Water-based polyurethane is easily available and is a safe coating (as of this writing). After sealing, the shelves should be allowed to dry for three or four weeks before being installed.

In addition to coatings, barrier products of various kinds can be used. For instance, the shelves can be covered with polyester film (e.g., Mylar). Drawers in flat files can be lined with Mylar, acid-free mat board (museum board), archival foam board, or combinations of materials to provide a safe surface. The concept of barrier products is addressed further in section 3, where we discuss barrier sheets for acidic pages in books; and in section 6, which includes information on lining exhibit cases to prevent acid migration.

Enclosed Cabinets and Bookcases

Bookcases and cabinets with doors provide security as well as protection from dust and light. The same applies to file cabinets, flat files, and other furniture where the materials are enclosed. But if the collections are not used frequently, dangerous conditions can develop undetected. This is a particular problem in storage spaces where the temperature and relative humidity are not well regulated.

The most common problem with metal furniture is condensation. Humid air can be trapped in the cabinet or bookcase. Moisture condenses on metal surfaces when the temperature in the room goes down. The extra trapped moisture can cause the furniture to rust, as well as encourage mold growth on the materials stored inside. This problem is made worse if the cabinet is against an outside wall, which becomes cooler than the rest of the room.

Pull cabinets and bookcases a few inches away from outside walls if this can be done safely. Another option is to install sheet insulation, such as polystyrene, behind the cabinets.

Place a small hygrometer or humidity card in suspected cabinets. Cases with glass doors can be checked without having to open the doors. Monitor conditions for several months. If the relative humidity exceeds 50%, move the collections to a different type of cabinet or otherwise change conditions so that the RH does not go above 50%. Occasionally, a change as simple as opening the doors from time to time can improve matters greatly. Sometimes the doors can be completely removed without damaging the cabinet.

Encourage air circulation by other means. If the shelves can be shifted forward, pull them out so that there is space behind them for air to move from top to bottom of the cabinet. To ventilate fixed wooden shelves, large holes can be drilled near the back edge.

There can be condensation inside wooden cabinets as well, but it is less noticeable than on metal furniture because the wood holds some of the moisture. The trapped humid air encourages mold growth just the same.

Whatever type of furniture is selected, there should always be an open space about six inches high below the bottom shelf or drawer, to encourage air circulation. This is most important when materials are stored at or below ground level.

Compact Shelving

These high-density storage systems feature bookcases or cabinets of various configurations which move along tracks. When closed, the shelving is very close together and a great deal of space is saved. In each section of shelving, only one aisle is open between ranges at any one time. Most of the materials will be shielded from light most of the time. The mechanism that moves the shelving can be powered by electricity or cranked by hand.

Compact shelving has been in use for several decades, and the design has been refined to eliminate some problems of the past. The hand-cranked mechanisms are much smoother than in earlier models and the ranges move quite easily. On electric-powered models, sensors stop the shelves from moving when they detect an obstacle. But there are still some drawbacks.

As the ranges move, the vibration can shift books or objects on the shelves and possibly cause them to fall off.

The more efficient systems move fast enough that the top shelves actually tilt slightly as they move, again posing the chance of having books fall off. If this effect is noticed, adjustments can be made to counteract it.

High-density shelving is by its nature very heavy: many more ranges will fit in the same space as conventional stationary ranges, and the shelving itself is sturdier and heavier. It may not be suitable for all locations. Consult a structural engineer or an architect who specializes in storage units for libraries and archives to determine which types would be most appropriate for your needs, particularly if the shelving is being installed in an existing building. Floors need to be strong enough to support the additional weight of the heavy-duty shelving plus the books, especially since the load must move frequently.

Lack of air circulation in the closed ranges can lead to mold forming on books. This is a difficult problem in spaces without good environmental controls. If the location has a history of dampness, even if only occasionally, it is better to sacrifice the extra storage space. In any case, check humidity levels at regular intervals, or use data loggers that can transmit an alarm if the humidity rises above 50%. Place the monitoring equipment on lower shelves, corner locations, and other suspect areas.

One additional consideration is that, in case of fire or flood, the salvage of materials stored in movable shelving might be more difficult. This should not preclude the use of this type of shelving, but it should be taken into account when composing a disaster plan.

Book Storage in Libraries

In libraries, most books are stored upright on shelves. This time-tested system makes books easily accessible and is a very safe method as long as the spacing of the shelves leaves ample room to insert and remove books. Shelves should be deep enough so that books do not protrude out into the aisles.

Books must be adequately supported so they are perpendicular to the shelf. If they are allowed to sag, they will become distorted and may start to break out of their bindings. Tall, thin books are particularly likely to become distorted from sagging; thick, heavy books are most prone to start ripping at the hinges. Books of roughly similar sizes support each other well, but a large book next to a tiny book will sag over it. Insert a support between them to keep the large one upright and to prevent the tiny one from getting lost. Another option is to separate books according to size. (See "Oversize Designation" below.)

Book Supports (Bookends)

When buying bookends, consider the size and shape of the books they will support. There is no set formula for how big a book support should be in relation to the size of the book. Books should not sag over the support, and the design of the bookend should prevent it from sliding and letting books lean or collapse. When in doubt, err on the side of too large.

Book supports are made of steel or plastic. The steel ones are usually more rigid and sturdier. Some designs do have quite sharp edges that can "knife" the pages of books accidentally pushed into them. They might not be suitable for collections on open stacks that are used heavily by patrons. Other designs have flanges that make them less likely to get pushed into books.

Adjustable wire book supports slide on a track on the shelf above. They are convenient for collections that get heavy use because they don't get lost as easily as free-standing bookends. Books can be jammed into them, however, and they sometimes come off the track accidentally. Depending on the height between the shelves, these bookends often support only the top of the book next to them, and occasionally a book is too short to be caught by the bookend.

Other adjustable book supports clip onto the front of the shelf on which the books are resting. These come in metal or plastic and tend to be rather small. They often have a space where a label can be inserted.

Request samples from suppliers before making a large purchase of bookends. More than one size will be needed and probably more than one type as well.

Avoid Crowding

Don't allow shelves to get so full that it becomes difficult to get a book in or out. Crowding inevitably leads to damage; sometimes books get pushed behind or into each other, or into bookends that are no longer visible in the jumble. When a book doesn't fit, patrons or shelvers sometimes lay it on top of books on the shelf. The extra book can fall to the back of the shelf, where it can remain lost indefinitely. It can also become distorted. Shift books periodically to make sure there is always some growing room. Some libraries leave a quarter of each shelf empty; less might be sufficient in a collection not expected to grow very much.

Oversize Designation

The height at which a book becomes "oversize" can vary according to the nature of the collection and the shelving available. There can be more than one "oversize" dimension (e.g., small folio, folio, large folio) in order to best accommodate the books. Libraries with closed stacks often shelve books according to many height categories, to conserve space. A side benefit of this system is that each book gets full support from its neighbors.

Height alone does not necessarily mean that a book should be stored flat. Some libraries have large numbers of tall books. If they are in good condition, always kept well supported, and not allowed to sag, tall books up to 18 inches or more can be shelved together in the upright position, provided the shelving can bear their weight without buckling. Patrons or pages should be instructed in proper methods of removing books from shelves (see "Basic Rules for Using Research Materials" above, and also "Removing a Book from the Shelf" in section 5, p. 100).

In situations where a book is a little too tall for the shelf, some libraries choose to place the book on the shelf on its fore edge (the edge opposite the spine). This allows the call number to be read easily. Unfortunately, when a hardcover book is placed on its fore edge, the weight of the pages pulls them down and eventually they start to break away from the binding at the inner hinges.

If there are a number of these largish books, there are two good solutions. One is to increase the space between the shelves; the other is to designate the books "oversize" and shelve them elsewhere. The latter requires modifying the catalog record; the former does not.

A tall book can be placed on its spine safely if it is securely supported on both sides. The weight of the pages pulls the book *into* the binding, which is fine. Since the title and call number are not visible, this method is less convenient for the user. The book can be placed in a wrapper or phase box with the call number in a visible area, if this is suitable for the collection.

Storing Books Flat

Some books are best stored flat, in stacks of from one to a few books. These include tall, thin books; very thick volumes; and very fragile books as well. The exact number in a stack depends on the thickness, weight, and condition of the volumes and also on whether there is a safe place nearby to rest the top books while getting out the bottom ones.

For the largest books, metal cabinets with sliding shelves are available. One book is placed on each shelf. Once the shelf is pulled out, the book can be removed by lifting it straight up rather than sliding it off, as is the case with stationary shelves.

Very large, thin books can also be kept in flat files. This is often convenient in archives. They should be large enough to fill most of the drawer to prevent excessive movement. (See "Storage of Larger Items" below for more information on flat file cabinets.)

For safety, it is best not to store heavy or large books more than five feet or so off the floor. Regardless of whether large books are stored upright or flat, provide a surface nearby where the book can be taken and examined. If there are no tables or shelves for this purpose, take a flat-shelf book truck to the stacks and use it to rest the book or books as they come off the shelf.

In the case of quite large books, always move them with the help of another person. Before removing them from the shelf, be sure there is a clear surface to take them to and there are no obstacles on the floor on the way to that surface.

Book Storage in Archives

The arrangement of archives is quite different from the way library materials are organized. Books are not generally stored together on shelves according to subject matter. Instead, they may be kept with other materials that pertain to particular collections, in record storage cartons or document cases. Ledgers and other large books are sometimes stored flat on shelves, or they may be in the drawers of file cabinets.

Most books in archives have value as individual artifacts; for instance, they may have belonged to the person who created the collection. Or they may be unique items, such as municipal or corporate ledgers. Generally, ready access is not as important as long-term preservation. (Some archives microfilm or otherwise reformat some of their materials to facilitate access to the information.)

It may require some ingenuity to store books in archive boxes or document cases, together with other items in a collection, without damaging the books or the other materials in the box. There are three ways that offer good support for books: lying flat on the bottom of the box; standing upright as they would on a shelf; or placed on their spines, perpendicular to the bottom of the box, with their fore edges up. Don't let books lean at an angle

or try to stuff them into a space that is not big enough. It's often helpful to wrap a book in acid-free paper or put it into a phase box or wrapper before placing it into the archive box. Put the title or accession number on the part of the wrapper that should face upward, to reduce rummaging while searching for a book and to make it easier to put it back in the box properly.

When books are placed in boxes that are not very full, support them with spacers made of acid-free corrugated or archival foam board, or even wads of acid-free paper, so they stay put and do not shift or sag when the box is handled. Try to distribute the weight so that the box is balanced when it is picked up. This will help reduce damage to the books as well as to documents or other materials in the box.

It is good practice to separate fragile objects from documents or books. For example, a silk bonnet from the mid-nineteenth century should be stored in a separate box, with appropriate notations made on the finding aid to indicate its location.

Be especially careful to isolate leather-covered books that have red rot, an advanced, irreversible type of leather deterioration. Books with red rot leave rust-colored stains on paper or other materials they touch. Wrap such books in acid-free wrapping paper or make book jackets. (See "Polyester Dust Jackets" in section 3, p. 72, for instructions on making book jackets.)

Smaller, lightweight books can be kept in file cabinet drawers, if desired. They should be wrapped in acid-free paper or enclosed in an acid-free envelope and placed spine down in a folder. Books that are too big to be stored this way should be stored separately in boxes or on shelves.

As a rule, it is not a good idea to store large books lying flat in file cabinet drawers because they can be damaged as they slide around when the drawer is opened and closed. As time goes by, other items are often put on top of the books, making it more difficult to find and remove the books. Drawers without backs are especially unsuitable because books can fall out the back.

Document Storage

Documents, pamphlets, photographs, and other unbound materials need mechanical protection to prevent crushing and tearing, and to keep related materials together. This protection can be provided by acid-free file folders, envelopes, polyester sleeves, or other enclosures made of inert or acid-free materials. These can then be placed in document storage cases, record storage cartons, file cabinet drawers, and so on. (There is more information on this subject in section 3.)

Storage of Larger Items

Materials that are too large for file cabinets or document storage cases can be stored flat in larger boxes or in flat file drawers, or they can be kept rolled in various types of tubes and long boxes.

Flat File Cabinets

Flat file drawers are designed to store unbound maps, prints, posters, and other large, flat items with convenient access and good protection. Regardless of the size of the materials, place them all in folders that closely fit the interior dimensions of the drawers. Don't place several different sizes of folders in the same drawer, because when artwork is stored in folders that correspond to the size of each piece and all the folders are put in the same drawer, the smaller folders shift to the back or sides of the drawer as it is opened and closed.

Blueprints and other large-format architectural plans are often light-sensitive and should be stored in lightproof containers. These can be roll storage boxes or tubes as described below, or they can be placed in acid-free folders of appropriate sizes for storage in flat file drawers. If flat files are not available, the folders can be put into large, tightly covered boxes. They should be placed on oversize shelving that is deep enough so the boxes don't stick out, to avoid sagging and the possibility of getting bumped off the shelf.

Different types of blueprints and other duplicated plans should be separated because some duplicating processes react chemically against one another. Place them in separate folders or interleave them with polyester film. For more information on this subject, consult the Library of Congress Preservation Directorate web page (see appendix C) and Kissel and Vigneau, *Architectural Photo Reproductions*.

Flat file drawers are also a good way to keep repair papers in good condition. When setting up a conservation work area, make sure to include space for a flat file cabinet. Select cabinets with drawers no more than 2" (5 cm) deep, to reduce the likelihood of stacking too many items in them.

Atlases in Flat File Drawers

Flat file drawers offer good protection to large, thin atlases or books of plans that don't have hard covers. They should be wrapped or enclosed in folders, according to condition and frequency of use. If the drawer is much larger than a book, install dividers or make partitions of acid-free corrugated board to keep the book from shifting very much. Shallow storage boxes, or their lids, can sometimes be used to subdivide drawers. They also function as trays to facilitate removing large, fragile atlases or similar materials.

In the case of books with covers, double deep shelving generally provides better storage than drawers. Metal cabinets with sliding shelves are available for oversize, heavy books.

Very thin, tall books that are in good condition can also be kept in flat files if this is convenient. However, it is quite easy for smaller books to shift around and damage other materials in the drawer. Small books should not be stored in flat files because they will eventually migrate to the back of the drawer where they will be lost until the next time the drawer is rearranged.

Art Storage in Flat File Drawers

Matted art or documents can be safely kept in drawers, but framed art should not be stored this way. The glass can break, causing harm to the artwork, and the eye hooks and other hanging hardware can abrade or make holes in nearby materials. In addition, the frame itself can be damaged from shifting in the drawer or from other things landing on top. Framed materials should be stored upright; this is the correct way to store sheets of glass as well. Provide proper storage for these items elsewhere. (See "Framed Art Storage" below.)

Roll Storage

There are several options when it comes to storing rolled materials. If the rolls are thin enough, they can be stored loosely in one layer in flat file drawers. Do not crowd them, and don't force thick rolls into a drawer that is too shallow. Make sure the rolls don't get caught in the back of the drawers. Ideally, each map or plan should be wrapped in acid-free paper (don't use rubber bands or adhesive tape to keep the maps rolled; flat cotton twill tapes or strips of polyester film with Velcro dots are okay). The wrapping should extend a few inches beyond the edges of the rolls for extra protection. Identifying information about the maps should be written in pencil on the outside. Computer-generated labels can be used as well; select a good-quality label stock that will not fall off, from a supplier of conservation materials.

Another solution is to use roll storage containers. These are available in various configurations from many suppliers. For additional support, large documents can be rolled around a rigid core first and then placed in a storage tube (fig. 1-18). If the document is fragile, wrap

Fig. 1-18

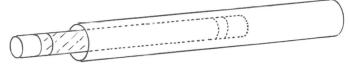

it in acid-free tissue or bond paper, or in Mylar, before placing it in the tube. Very brittle maps or plans can be interleaved with acid-free tissue or bond paper. The interleaving material should be larger than the item it is protecting. Blueprints and other large-format architectural plans can be kept in roll storage boxes or tubes, with opaque endcaps to keep out light.

The tubes or boxes can be stored flat on deep shelving, as in figure 1-19, or in upright or horizontal bins or boxes, as shown in figure 1-20.

A cubby-hole-style bin which can be placed on oversize shelving or on top of flat files will keep the tubes from rolling off the shelf (fig. 1-20).

Fig. 1-19

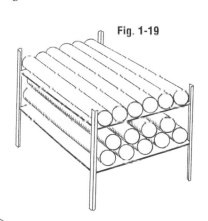

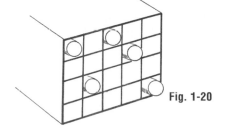

Fig. 1-20

Some roll storage bins have casters and can be moved around easily (fig. 1-21).

Framed Art Storage

All framed items should be stored vertically, either hanging on sliding storage systems or in padded frame racks.

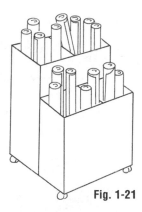

Fig. 1-21

Padded Frame Rack

A ready-made bin can be used, such as the kind used by framers to store mat boards upright (fig. 1-22), or one can be made with lumber that has been sealed with polyurethane or acrylic paint (fig. 1-23). The sealant should be allowed to cure for at least two weeks, to prevent off-gassing once the bin is in use. The bottom of the bin should

Fig. 1-22

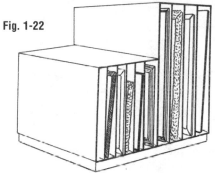

be several inches off the floor, for air circulation and for protection against moisture. The bottom of each compartment should be padded with

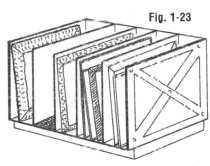

Fig. 1-23

foam board or other cushioning material to protect the frames. A piece of cardboard or foam board should be placed between adjacent frames; it should be bigger than the frames.

Store one to four pictures in each section, depending on size. Label each compartment of the bin, indicating what art is in each section. This simple method provides safe, upright storage as well as easy access to particular items.

Institutions with large collections of framed items may prefer to install sliding storage systems (fig. 1-24). Metal grill panels are suspended from parallel tracks on the ceiling, and frames of any size can be hung on hooks. To inspect a particular piece, the panel holding it can be pulled out. This is easier than moving frames around in a frame rack, particularly in the case of large pieces.

Courtesy of Archival Matters, Inc.

Fig. 1-24

Manufacturers can use various components to configure units to fit the needs of each client. As with other storage furniture, be careful of installations on outside walls. Add insulating panels behind the racks as needed. The frames on the racks can be covered with large sheets of wrapping paper or with cotton cloth to keep out dust and light. (Some manufacturers of these systems are listed in appendix B.)

Off-Site Storage Spaces

Many institutions rely on off-site storage, either as a temporary measure during construction or moving, or as a permanent means of housing materials that are used less frequently.

In addition to questions of cost, security, and convenience, the environment at the remote location should be investigated. It is better to send a staff member to check rather than to rely entirely on descriptions and assurances from the storage company. Storage spaces that are below grade should be avoided in most circumstances; attics and barns should never be used.

Temperature and humidity should be regulated 24 hours a day, 365 days a year. In summer, the relative humidity must be kept at about 50% and the temperature at 70°F (21°C) or below. There should be no daily (or hourly) fluctuations in relative humidity. A *gradual* rise of 10–15% in RH between winter and summer is acceptable. There should be low to moderate heat in winter and the capability to dehumidify in spring and fall. The HVAC system should have appropriate pollution control filters. Look for a building that is maintained well and shows no signs of past leaks, mold, insects, rodents, or other dangers to collections. In fact, the same guidelines apply here as in the main location.

After a collection is sent to the storage space, a staff member should visit and check conditions periodically.

Storage below Grade

When rivers flood or water mains burst, basements fill with water. Before making a decision about what materials to put in storage spaces that are below grade, make a thorough study of the area around the building and the flooding history of any nearby rivers. The location of nearby water mains should be researched as well, because when they break the results are often disastrous. On a smaller scale, lawn watering systems may malfunction, causing excess water to accumulate near the foundation. During a heavy rainstorm, badly graded lawns or inadequate drains can direct several inches of water into basements.

The safest policy is simply not to store any materials of lasting value, such as archives, rare books, or art, in basements. (See "Disaster Planning and Response" earlier in this section.)

If necessary, a sound, *dry* basement can be used to store materials that are easily replaceable. Basement floors are usually cool and this can lead to condensation. To avoid the possibility of mold, storage furniture should be raised several inches off the floor. This will also provide some protection from flooding if an overhead pipe bursts or water enters the basement from outside.

Water Alarms

Water alarms should be placed at locations where water could come, either from outside or from pipes. There are different types of alarms; select a model that can be wired to a central station, the same as the fire alarm. Some alarms can be attached to the water supply itself and can stop the flow of water when they detect a leak.

No Storage on the Floor

It is always a good rule *never* to store anything directly on the floor, not even temporarily, at any level of a building. Even if a deep flood is unlikely, a small leak is always a possibility, and water tends to run along the floor until it finds a drain or is stopped by some absorbent material such as a box of books.

Attics, Barns, and Other Unheated Spaces

These spaces are never suitable for the storage of paper-based materials. Temperatures may vary by more than 100°F, and the relative humidity can range from very low to 100%, depending on the season. Very high temperatures in summer make paper and leather brittle and destroy photographic materials. As the weather cools in the fall, air in a closed building also cools gradually, but it often retains the higher moisture content of the warm weather for weeks or even months. This causes condensation on storage furniture and on the materials. It is usually a matter of a couple of years before mold begins to form on clean materials. In the case of archives or books with dormant mold spores, a full-blown infestation can develop in a few days.

There is much more to be learned about proper storage methods than we have covered here. See the Library of Congress Preservation Directorate leaflets (in appendix C); NEDCC Technical Leaflets 28 through 38 on "Preservation of Library and Archival Materials" (appendix C and bibliography); and the Gaylord Bros. Pathfinder pamphlets 2, 3, and 5 (appendix B).

SUMMARY OF BASIC PRESERVATION MEASURES

- Provide a good environment and good storage conditions.
- Educate staff and patrons on proper handling techniques.
- Create a disaster plan.
- Catalog or process materials; sort, weed, replace, and reformat as appropriate.
- Evaluate donations:

    Not only should the materials be pertinent to the collection, but they should be free of mold and insects. Beware of any materials that smell musty or like mildew.

    Consider requesting donors to fund treatment of materials in poor condition.

- Evaluate materials that need repair to determine what type of action is most suitable.
- Provide containers for materials that cannot, or should not, be repaired.
- Perform sound conservation treatments that are economical and within the capability of the staff.
- Keep good records indicating types of preservation steps, numbers of items treated, and time spent on various operations.

- Create work flow charts. Charts serve as visual aids, letting staff know at a glance how labor and responsibilities are divided. The samples at the end of this section can be modified to suit your needs.

Procedures to Avoid

In addition to the basic preservation steps outlined in this section, there are many other procedures that can be carried out safely in-house. However, in order to have a successful preservation program, it is just as important to exercise judgment when selecting materials for treatment as it is in deciding which measures are appropriate.

Always take all factors into account when deciding whether and how to treat a particular book or document. The following are situations where in-house treatment should be avoided.

Repairs to Items That Have Historical, Artistic, or Monetary Value

While the conservation techniques we discuss in the next sections are sound and will not cause damage when done correctly, it is not possible to learn from reading this book the many nuances of what is proper treatment for a book or document that has value beyond the information it holds. Such unique and special items, sometimes said to have "artifactual" value, should *never* be repaired in-house. To do so will very likely diminish that value.

When a rare book, valuable print, or historical document needs help, it should be placed in an appropriate container and restricted from use. (Section 3 discusses many types of containers, or "preservation enclosures.") The librarian or curator should evaluate the importance of the item to the collection and consult a conservator to determine what extent of conservation is needed. As funds become available, it can be scheduled for professional treatment by a competent conservator. In some cases, it may be possible to make a duplicate copy for the use of researchers.

Repairs That Are Very Time-Consuming

The techniques in this book are primarily intended to keep a research collection in good condition and extend its life as long as possible. Most of these materials could be replaced in some way or another, at varying costs. There is no point in spending a week repairing a book that could be replaced for fifty dollars, including processing. On the other hand, a loose hinge can be repaired in just a few minutes when it is first noticed, but if left untreated it can lead to a broken binding and a major repair.

The goal is to treat quickly as many items as can be done well. Even in the case of a document or book that is hard to replace, there could be other options for preserving the information. These include reformatting: preservation photocopying, microfilming, or digitization. Once a copy is made, the original may be put into a preservation enclosure and withdrawn from use.

Rebinding

In the past, major libraries did their own binding of serials and monographs. However, making a new hard-cover binding for a book requires considerable skill. In addition, in order to bind great numbers of books economically, a lot of large and expensive machinery is needed. Binding is now done by library binderies or outside contractors, and we do not address it in this book.

In some cases, one or more staff members may learn how to bind a book by hand. This might be appropriate treatment for occasional books. A board shears (cutter) and iron presses are needed for hand binding. See section 5 for descriptions of the equipment and supplies needed for book repairs.

Work on Very Fragile Materials

Do not make repairs on books or documents that are extensively damaged. There is no point in repairing the covers of books that have brittle pages because the pages will break apart and fall out of the binding, whether it is repaired or not. Explore other preservation options, such as replacing the book. If that is not possible, then some type of reformatting will preserve the information. After reformatting, the original may be placed in an enclosure and withdrawn from use.

Many leather-bound books in research collections are affected by "red rot." This is a nasty, irreversible form of deterioration that leaves red stains on shelving, other books, and users' hands and clothing. Adhesives do not stick well to rotten leather, and it is useless to try to repair these bindings. See "Consolidating Leather Rot (Red Rot)" in section 5, p. 119, for ways to deal with red rot.

Many old and rare materials are fragile or have delicate components. These should not be treated in-house in any case. Place the item in a preservation container and consult a conservator.

Projects That Are too Large for the Work Space

Large books or maps take up enormous amounts of work surface. In addition to the space needed to work on them, there will need to be clear countertops to leave things drying, prepare the repair materials, and perform other operations. A large project can take over so completely that there is no space left for routine operations. So unless the repair is a quick one, oversize and large-format materials might best be sent to an outside contractor.

Another point seems obvious but is worth repeating here. The work surface must be a good bit larger than the object to be repaired. (See "Setting Up a Work Area for Preservation Activities" in section 2.) If the object cannot fit and be shifted to different angles on the counter, it should not be treated in-house.

Operations That Require Sprays and Chemicals

We recommend that you stay away from chemical treatments. This includes the use of solvents and deacidification solutions. Chemicals require proper ventilation and a fume hood or appropriate respirator, as well as gloves and eye protection.

Furthermore, paper, inks, and colors can react in unexpected ways to solvents and deacidification solutions. It is better to leave treatment with chemicals to conservators who have the training, equipment, and experience to use them safely. Use buffered barrier sheets or enclosures instead.

Work Flow Charts

Creating a chart often helps clarify how duties are distributed among the staff and serves as an organizing tool. Since the preservation process involves different groups of people, we have made a sample chart showing steps carried out by library or curatorial staff, followed by one that outlines the procedures carried out by preservation department staff. The charts are models and should be modified to suit the needs of each institution.

Decisions Made by Administrative Staff

The first chart (fig. 1-25) shows steps in the preservation process that are carried out under the direction of administrative staff, i.e., a librarian or curator.

Survey and Sort. A librarian, curator, or subject specialist is able to gauge the importance of particular items to the collection and can therefore decide the best way to handle materials that are not in good physical condition.

Withdraw. It may be that a book or document is no longer relevant and can simply be withdrawn from the collection.

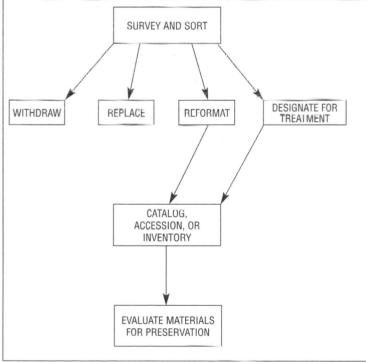

Fig. 1-25

If the item is to remain part of the collection, it is necessary to determine whether it is important mainly for the information it contains. If that is the case, practical decisions have to be made regarding whether to replace it, reformat it, or keep it in its original form and repair it by various treatment options.

Replace. Replacing a book is sometimes the best solution. There are at least two situations where replacement is a better choice than repair: one is when it is possible to purchase a new copy of a current book for less than it would cost to repair it, taking staff time and materials into account. Another is when a publication, such as a directory, is out of date and will shortly be replaced by a new edition.

Reformat. "Reformatting" is a term that includes microfilming, making paper facsimiles by photocopying or other means (and then binding, in the case of books), making photographic reproductions, and reproducing by digital means. At present, photographic reproductions, microfilming, and paper facsimiles made on acid-free paper are considered long-term preservation options.

Digitization is an exciting and promising development which extends access to knowledge in wonderful ways. It helps remove fragile items from use while making the information easily available. However, until we are assured that the data will be readable indefinitely, caution indicates that digitization cannot be considered a substitute for more traditional methods of preservation.

With all types of reformatting, the institution needs to decide whether to retain the original. There are arguments for and against retaining copied or microfilmed originals. However, when materials are digitized, every effort should be made to retain the originals.

Designate for Treatment. If the librarian or archivist determines that a damaged work should be kept in its original form, there are several treatment options. These are determined by the nature of the materials, the severity of the damage, and the capabilities of the preservation staff.

Catalog, Accession, or Inventory. Once it has been decided that a work should be preserved, it should be cataloged or inventoried if not already done. This makes it possible to keep track of materials while they are undergoing preservation steps, and needs to be done eventually in any case.

Procedures Carried Out by Preservation Staff

The second chart (fig. 1-26) shows steps in the preservation process that are carried out by or under the direction of the preservation staff.

Evaluate Materials for Preservation. The preservation staff, preferably in conjunction with the person who made the earlier choices, should evaluate all the materials that were designated for treatment to determine whether each item can be treated in-house or not.

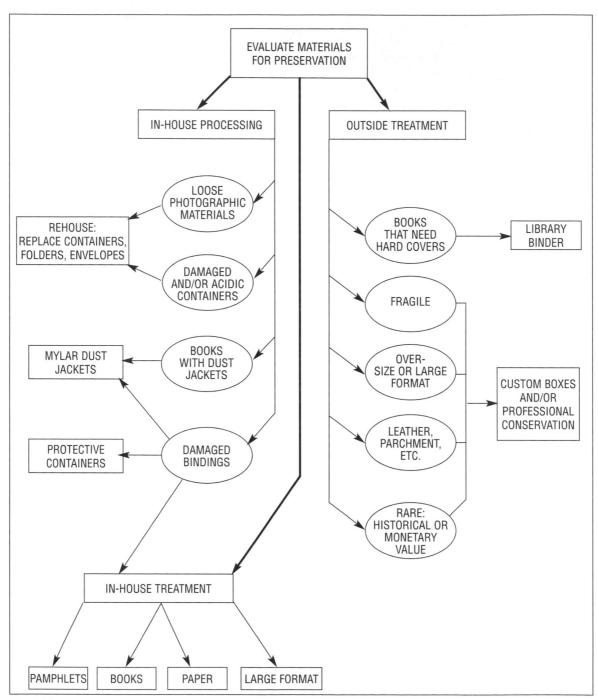

Fig. 1-26

Outside Treatment (right side of chart). Certain operations are usually better left to outside contractors. These include:

Library Binder. Books that need new hardcover bindings should be sent to a library binder. Most libraries have guidelines indicating publication date cutoffs and other factors that help determine whether a book should be sent to such a bindery. Books that fall *outside* these guidelines must be evaluated to decide whether they should be reformatted, replaced, or treated by a hand bookbinder or conservator.

Custom Boxes. Outside vendors are a good choice when clamshell boxes and other custom-made containers are needed, as in the case of special collections materials that must be presented in a sturdy yet elegant way. Such boxes require a great deal of skill as well as access to good quality, well-maintained bookbinding equipment. Many library binders and certain suppliers make clamshell and other special boxes. Some hand bookbinders also provide this service. (See appendix B for the names of a few commercial box makers.)

Professional Conservation. This category will vary according to the capabilities of the staff and equipment and space available in the lab of the library or archive.

Books or flat paper items that are very fragile or larger than can be handled in the work area, items made of parchment or leather, and works that have artistic, historical, or monetary value *should not be repaired in-house.*

Photographs should likewise not be treated in-house because they have very different characteristics from other works on paper and there are many types of photographs, each needing a distinct type of treatment. If a photograph needs treatment, consult a conservator who specializes in photographic materials.

When materials that need outside treatment are identified in the collection, they should be placed in appropriate preservation containers to prevent further damage. Administrative staff or subject specialists can establish priorities for treatment, since the costs are typically much higher than for other forms of preservation. As funds become available, these materials should be sent to conservators who specialize in treating works of their type.

In-House Processing (top left side of chart). This is a broad category, encompassing both old and new materials, bound and unbound, print and nonprint. The group includes items waiting for treatment as well as other materials that will be kept in their present form but need rehousing or other protection, such as archival materials. (Rehousing is addressed in section 3.)

Unbound materials, such as photographs or documents, may be put into sleeves or folders and then into storage boxes or other containers.

Nonprint media such as magnetic tapes and film should be stored in adequate enclosures.

Materials in damaged or acidic storage containers should be placed in new, conservation-quality enclosures.

Polyester dust jackets should be placed over publishers' paper dust jackets. This simple process preserves the paper jacket and provides added protection for the binding.

Books with damaged bindings which are not candidates for the library binder can be covered with polyester dust jackets, placed in preservation enclosures, or sent on for in-house treatment. Occasionally a combination of these is best.

In-House Treatment (bottom left side of chart). Materials designated for in-house treatment can consist of books, flat paper items, pamphlets, and some large-format materials. This is the subject of sections 3, 4, and 5 of this book.

Section 2

Getting Started

Work Space, Equipment, Tools, and Techniques

ONCE THE LIBRARIAN OR ARCHIVIST HAS DETER-mined what materials should be treated in-house, some preparations will be necessary. These will depend on the types of work to be carried out and the space available.

In libraries and archives where rehousing is the primary preservation activity, the main requirements are adequate work surfaces and one or more good cutters. In institutions where mending and other forms of conservation work are carried out, more equipment, access to water, and individual workstations are needed.

Storage space for supplies and for work in progress is needed in both cases.

In this section, we will look at various elements to consider when setting up a room or area for preservation activities. There is no one perfect solution. A large institution that carries out extensive conservation activities needs one or more rooms where several people can work and where repair and rehousing materials can be stored. Workstations and equipment should be arranged to facilitate efficient production. A small library or archive may have just a portion of one room, and that room may be used for a variety of other activities not related to preservation. In these situations, it is essential to have a dedicated storage area where work in progress and supplies can be stored between work sessions.

This section is divided into three parts.

1. "Setting Up a Work Area for Preservation Activities" has information about the essential features of a work space, as well as other desirable factors.

2. "Equipment" contains descriptions of several types of equipment, with details on their uses.

3. "Working Tips" explains how to carry out key steps that are used in procedures throughout the book.

SETTING UP A WORK AREA FOR PRESERVATION ACTIVITIES

Before setting up your work area, try to visit the preservation departments or conservation labs of institutions similar to yours and talk with the staff. Find out what type of work they do and what features and equipment are useful to them. Don't be discouraged if their facilities are dazzling and state of the art. Even the fanciest labs have aspects that didn't work out as expected, especially if the staff was not able to make the final design decisions. And many, many institutions produce excellent work in labs that are not ideal.

The following are some factors to consider when setting up your work area.

Dedicated Space

In order to put books or documents into preservation enclosures or do in-house repairs, there must be a space with suitable work surfaces that can be dedicated to these activities. This area should be used for preservation only and it must be secure, i.e., it must be possible to lock it so that work can be left safely from one work session to the next. These are really the main requirements. Many steps need a drying or pressing period during which the materials must remain undisturbed, and this is not feasible if the work surface has to be cleared at the end of each session. Having a dedicated space is particularly important in situations where preservation activities are carried out on a part-time basis. The technician should be able to leave work half-finished and expect to find everything in the same place upon return.

Many institutions have processing or technical services rooms or areas. These spaces often have many features that are desirable in a work area, including countertops, a sink, storage space, and so on. It is also logical to be close to where other shelf preparation activities are taking place. Even a small corner of such a room is a good place to start.

It is possible to carry out small projects in shared spaces that do not have sinks, storage space, or other desirable features, as long as there are tables or other work surfaces. Is there a closet or cabinet somewhere where work in progress and supplies can be stored between sessions? A good solution in these situations is to keep hand tools and small supplies in toolboxes or other containers with lids. A book truck with flat shelves is very useful for transporting the tools and supplies, as well as materials that need work, between the storage area and the work area.

Access to Water

When planning for a new space, include a sink. It's much easier to keep hands, work surfaces, and brushes clean, get water to make paste, and perform many other operations with a source of water nearby. Shallow sinks are most suitable; get one that is as large as possible. It's very important that a large sink be installed correctly so that it will empty completely. Make sure that you can reach the faucets easily before the contractor leaves. A hose or spray attachment is useful.

It is uncomfortable to work with a deep, restaurant-type sink, and it is very difficult to keep it clean. Chances are that the sink will not be replaced for many years, so it's worth getting a good one at the beginning. The sink should be near at least one workbench or countertop.

Some operations, such as the rehousing activities described in section 3 and many of the steps described in section 4, can be carried out without the need for a dedicated sink. It is enough to have a nearby restroom or other place where workers can wash their hands as needed. But for paper and book repairs, a sink is really very desirable and every effort should be made to have one included at the planning stages.

Floor Coverings

Preservation work produces a lot of scraps and debris. A floor that can be vacuumed and mopped easily is best. Carpeting is the worst choice. Very hard floors can be made more comfortable by using anti-fatigue mats at workstations. The mats are available from industrial and safety supply catalogs.

Workbenches

It is most helpful to have several work surfaces at different heights. Not only are people of various sizes, but also some activities are more comfortably carried out at different heights. Kitchen counters are 36" high and many people are used to working at that height. Sturdy reading room or refectory tables make good work surfaces for activities that can be done sitting down.

A table or workbench can be raised to suit a tall person. One way is to set it on wood blocks (such as sections of railroad ties), or to place lengths of 2" lumber under each set of legs. Check in a building supply store to see what sizes are available. After attaching the supports, make sure that the table is very stable before starting to use it.

Another method of raising a work surface is to have a new countertop built on top of it, covered with plastic laminate. If desired, the countertop can be made a few inches wider than the table, in order to provide knee space for sitting. Make supports for it out of 1" × 6" or 2" × 6" lumber, sealed with water-based polyurethane, to form compartments under the countertop. This method also provides storage space for large papers, boards, and other repair materials. Even though these storage compartments are not enclosed, as exhibit cases are, if they are made from materials that emit noxious fumes, they can cause the papers and boards to deteriorate faster.

Board and paper are heavy, and so is a laminate-covered top. Examine the construction of the table and if necessary, put some 2" × 4" supports under it to prop up the middle. Do this *before* the table starts to sag (fig. 2-1).

Fig. 2-1

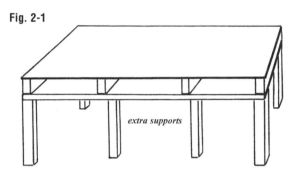

extra supports

Laminate countertops are waterproof and easy to keep clean. But other smooth, sturdy tops can be used, especially if they are already in place. They can be covered with newsprint, wrapping paper, sheets of binder's board cut to size, or other materials at hand. These coverings have to be changed from time to time in order to provide a clean surface.

Keep work surfaces uncluttered and don't use them for storage.

Chairs

An adjustable task chair with good back support makes a big difference. Many kinds are made, and the best thing is to have the person who will be using the chair test-sit it. If this is not possible, at least try to match the size of

the person to the size of the chair. Preservation work often calls for getting up and down frequently. It is easier to get in and out of chairs without armrests.

For counter-height work surfaces, various drafting chairs and stools are available. Make sure there is an adjustable footrest or ring.

Chairs or stools on casters can be moved around easily and are convenient for the user. Chairs on casters can roll away unexpectedly, so always look to be sure the chair is where you think it is before sitting down. This will avoid injury to the worker and possible damage to objects being carried to the workbench.

Carts or Stands on Casters

Smaller equipment can be kept on carts or stands with casters (fig. 2-2). This leaves more counter space available for working and also makes it easy to store the equipment in corners of the room or even under workbenches when not in use.

Printer carts, projector stands, and similar wheeled furniture are often discarded when an institution changes to a different type of equipment; check to see if something suitable for your needs is available among the old equipment.

Fig. 2-2
A small encapsulator is shown. It is bolted to the cart for safety.

Lighting and Environment

Light

Bright light without glare is essential. Full-spectrum bulbs or tubes make color matching easier. In addition to ceiling fixtures, each work area should have a task light that can be directed as needed. Since there will always be library and archival materials or artwork in the preservation area, filters should be used on any fixtures that emit ultraviolet light.

Natural light has a great color and is wonderful for the spirits. If you are lucky enough to have windows, make sure that there are shades or blinds on them. Depending on the orientation of the room, the shades will be needed to cut down on sun glare. They are the best protection against ultraviolet light. Remember that even north-facing windows admit a lot of UV light. Never leave library or archival materials uncovered on workstations within about 15' (4 or 5 m) of a window, even if the sun doesn't directly hit there. Consider installing tinted film shades or coatings that admit visible light while filtering out much of the ultraviolet.

At the end of the day, pull down shades or blinds to keep light out. As the days get longer, the sun comes out hours earlier than the beginning of the workday and likewise sets later. (See "Light" in section 1, p. 7, and "Lighting" in section 6, p. 151, for more information on light.)

Environment

Materials may be in the preservation area for several months while treatment is completed. The same environmental conditions adequate for spaces where books, documents, and works on paper are stored are also recommended for the preservation department. (See "Environment" in section 1, p. 2.)

Floors should be cleaned frequently and trash should be removed every day. Don't have lunch or coffee breaks in the work area. Besides the danger of damaging materials, there is also the likelihood of attracting pests to discarded wrappings and drink containers. Taking a break in another area is safer and more restful as well.

Many people like to have a sip of water now and then during the workday. If your institution allows this, use common sense to avoid spilling the water. Never place the water bottle on the same surface where the work is; put it on a book truck or on another countertop that is *lower* than the work surface.

Another good way to prevent damage from spills is to place water bottles in a plastic or metal container, like a cake pan or shallow storage tub. The side of the container often prevents a bottle from tipping all the way and if it does, the water will be contained.

The same precautions apply when you need to have a container of water at hand to carry out a treatment step.

Storage

The preservation area must have shelving, flat files, and cabinets of various types in order to store materials waiting to be processed. The same guidelines that apply to furniture used for the permanent storage of collections also apply to furniture used to store materials while in the preservation department. (See "Storage Furniture" in section 1, p. 20.) Some of this storage furniture can be built under and around workstations.

Tools and repair supplies need adequate storage to stay in good condition. Cabinets with drawers and shelves with doors are good for tool storage. Some frequently used items can be placed in boxes or other containers kept at each workstation, or they can be kept on pegboards hung on a nearby wall.

Metal flat file cabinets are extremely useful for storing large documents and art on paper and also for keeping repair papers neat and clean. Papers and boards can last for years, but if they are not kept in an orderly fashion, after a while it's hard to know what is in stock. Japanese paper is particularly likely to be damaged and should be kept in folders within drawers.

Wooden flat files are not suitable for the long-term storage of acid-free paper supplies because the wood gives off gases that hasten the deterioration of paper. If you have paper or board that has been stored in wooden furniture, be sure to test it with a pH pen before using it. Sometimes the outer edges of the sheets, as well as sheets at the top and bottom, turn acidic while the paper inside remains acid-free.

Some supplies come in the form of long rolls. Make a space for roll storage, using any of the methods described in "Roll Storage" in section 1, p. 24. Cutting dispensers are a good choice for large, heavy rolls that are used frequently, such as acid-free wrapping paper. They can usually be mounted on a wall; some are designed to be used standing vertically and can be moved to the workstation as needed.

Established institutions frequently have unused desks, chairs, tables, storage furniture, and sometimes equipment that are no longer used by any department. If your budget is slim, be sure to see if items that you need are available, but don't accept anything that is clearly unsuitable. Once a poor-quality workbench, for example, is in place, it will be much harder to get funds for a better one.

A small historical society or library might not be able to set a room aside for preservation work. An option is to keep tools and materials in one or more toolboxes, milk crates, or other sturdy containers. A closet or cabinet can be used to store the equipment and supplies between uses, as well as the books or other materials that need work or are in progress. When a staff member is ready to work, all the necessary tools and materials will be ready and can be brought to the work area.

Office Area

In a somewhat larger preservation department, a small "office" area is useful for research, record keeping, ordering of materials, and other administrative tasks. The phone and computer can be used quietly and without interfering with hands-on activities. Shelving or temporary partitions can be arranged to define the area. This is a good place for file cabinets, which can be used as partitions around the office while providing handy access to administrative records.

EQUIPMENT

Most techniques we will discuss in this book can be carried out using only hand tools (which we'll discuss later), but the process will be slow and probably not cost-effective. A few pieces of equipment are worth investing in. Chief among these is a good cutter. The specific type can vary according to the sort of work that will be done, as well as other considerations, such as space available and budget. If you will be doing extensive book repairs, some presses will make the work much more efficient. Read the following descriptions to see what is most appropriate for your situation.

Cutters

In order to cut large sheets of paper, board, Mylar, and other materials quickly and accurately, it is necessary to have some type of cutter. The following are the types of cutters that are most useful in preservation activities.

Board Shears

The traditional machine used by bookbinders and box-makers is called a board shears. It has a curved steel blade bolted into a cast-iron arm, which is hinged to the bed of the cutter at the far end, just like the familiar office paper cutters. A long, sharpened piece of steel called a "knife" is bolted to the cutting edge of the bed, and the blade cuts against that edge when the arm is lowered. The action is similar to a scissors, hence the name "board shears" (fig. 2-3).

A metal guide, sometimes stationary and sometimes adjustable, is located on the near side of the bed, at a 90°

angle from the cutting edge. The paper or board is jogged against this guide and positioned for cutting.

The main thing that sets a board shears apart from an inexpensive paper cutter is the long clamp, or pressure bar, that runs along the cutting edge. After the paper is positioned, the clamp is lowered by stepping on a pedal. This prevents the material from shifting as the blade comes down and ensures a square cut.

Fig. 2-3

There are usually two means of setting measurements for repeat cuts. The "inside gauge" or "back stop" is a bar that slides on a guide or track on the bed of the cutter and can be set and locked at various distances from the cutting edge. The "outside" or "rollout gauge" is sometimes called the "front stop." It is to the right of the blade and cranks in and out. Each is useful for various types of cuts.

Board shears are made of hardwood and cast iron and are *very* heavy. This is what makes them so solid and stable when in use. The legs are normally bolted to lengths of 2" × 4" lumber to spread the load. The weight has to be taken into account when deciding where to place one. Cutting thick materials is sometimes rather strenuous and would certainly be heard and possibly felt by occupants of the floor below in certain types of buildings.

The blade assembly of a board shears is quite heavy. If it were released in mid-cut and came down by itself, it would fall with great force and could cause serious injury. To prevent this, a round counterweight made of cast iron is attached to a bar that extends from the blade assembly and fits through a slot in the counterweight (fig. 2-4). The position of the counterweight is adjusted on the bar so that when the blade is released it returns gently to the upright position. To prevent the counterweight from accidentally coming off, a small bolt and nut can be installed through a hole found at the end of the bar.

When well maintained, a board shears is capable of making accurate cuts on all weights of paper, mat board,

Fig. 2-4

and binder's board. New ones cost several thousand dollars; used ones cost much less, depending on location and condition. A used one may need to be repaired and adjusted; sometimes a shop that does metalwork and sharpening has someone with the skill to do this. Otherwise, it is better to get one in working order. A board shears is a very desirable piece of equipment, which will last indefinitely. Many institutions have board shears that are over a hundred years old and show no signs of wearing out.

Other Good Cutters

If space or budget does not allow a board shears, there are several alternatives. Select a cutter with a good clamping mechanism, to keep the paper or board in place as the blade comes down. This is essential for making accurate, square cuts, so don't invest even a small amount of money in a cutter without a clamping system. Cutters differ in the length of cut as well as in the thickness of the material they can cut. In general, the machines with shorter blades can cut thicker boards with less effort. Consider what type and size materials you will normally be cutting and select a machine that meets your needs.

We have personal experience with the following cutters; there are many other options and we by no means imply that these are the only good ones. Consult with colleagues in similar institutions to see what works well for them. Used cutters can be found occasionally; if in good condition when offered for sale, they should give good service for many years.

KUTRIMMER

This cutter comes in two versions: four tabletop models with different cutting lengths and two freestanding models with longer cuts. They have very good-quality blades that can be removed for sharpening and make excellent cuts. Kutrimmers offer most of the features needed in a preservation workshop.

The tabletop models have hand-operated clamps, and the two larger models, no. 1058, which cuts 22.5" (57 cm), and no. 1071, which cuts 28.5" (72.5 cm), have both inside and outside gauges. The freestanding models have foot-operated clamps as well as both gauges. Model no. 1080 can cut 31" (79 cm), and no. 1110 can cut almost 44" (111 cm). Models from different years have varying details, clamp assemblies, and other features.

The larger tabletop models (fig. 2-5) can be used to cut all materials from paper to medium-weight binder's board. They are a good choice for smaller workshops and excellent second cutters for bigger operations.

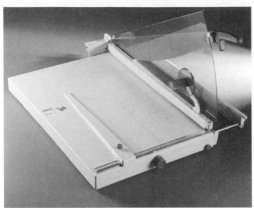

Fig. 2-5

Courtesy MBM Corporation

Although the freestanding models (fig. 2-6) can accommodate full sheets of board, they are really only adequate for lighter boards such as museum board. These models would be suitable for a workshop that produced preservation enclosures or prepared materials for exhibitions. The machine is not sturdy enough for the vigorous action of cutting binder's board, and the clamp cannot restrain the board firmly enough to get an accurate cut.

If you foresee needing to cut full sheets of binder's board, consider a used board shears in good condition. The cost difference may not be that great.

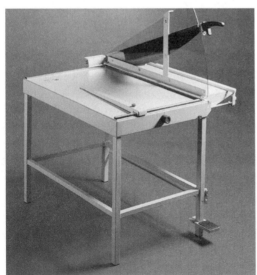

Fig. 2-6

Courtesy MBM Corporation

The clamp on older Kutrimmer models is hinged at the far end and secured with a latch at the near end. When the latch is released, the clamp can be swung out of the way. A sheet of board that is too wide to fit under the clamp can be cut this way, to divide it into smaller pieces. (See "Cutting and Trimming," p. 49, for instructions.)

DAHLE

This company makes several types of quality cutting machines designed for use from hobby to professional levels. All have clamping mechanisms, but not all models have stops or gauges to facilitate making repeat cuts. They are accurate and suitable for thinner boards, paper, Mylar, and foam board but are not designed for binder's board.

There are quite a number of choices. Two tabletop cutters with clamps, two gauges, and safety features are Model 567 with a 21.5" (54.5 cm) cut and Model 569 with a 27.5" (70 cm) cut. The hand-operated clamp cannot be moved aside (fig. 2-7).

Fig. 2-7

Courtesy Dahle North America, Inc.

There are also two freestanding models, no. 580 with a 32" (81 cm) cut and no. 585 with a 43" (109 cm) cut (fig. 2-8). They both have two gauges and a foot-operated clamp. The same comments apply to these as to the freestanding Kutrimmers.

Dahle and some other manufacturers refer to these cutters as "guillotines," but they are not what bookbinders know as guillotines. (See the glossary for a definition.)

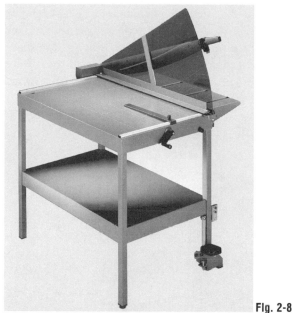

Courtesy Dahle North America, Inc.

Fig. 2-8

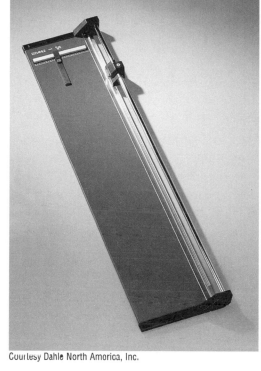

Courtesy Dahle North America, Inc.

Fig. 2-9

The blade assemblies of both Kutrimmer and Dahle cutters have an adjustment that keeps the blade from falling down when it is released. The action of the blade should be checked periodically and the adjustment screw tightened as necessary. For safety, form the habit of always raising the blade at least 90° to lessen the chance that it will fall toward you. Never attempt to disable the safety shields on these machines.

In addition to cutters, Dahle and many other companies also make rolling trimmers. These machines cut on a different principle. A self-sharpening cutting wheel enclosed in a housing runs along a track, as in a mat cutter. There is a clamp to hold paper or thin board firmly, and some models have gauges or stops on the bed. Rolling trimmers are very good for cutting Mylar. They are much less expensive than cutters with blades and the larger Dahle models, nos. 556 and 558, can make excellent cuts up to 37.5" (95 cm) and 51" (129.5 cm), respectively.

Some trimmers can be wall mounted. As a group, they are much lighter and more compact than cutters, so it is easy to move them around or store them when not in use. The trimmer shown in figure 2-9 has a 51" (129.5 cm) cut and weighs 16 lbs (7 kg).

MAT CUTTERS

There are a great number of mat cutters available. This type of cutter also has a cutting head that runs along a track (fig. 2-10). The cutting head holds a replaceable blade and can usually be set to cut at a 45° angle or at a 90° angle. It is important to use blades that are designed for the particular brand and model of mat cutter. Generally, the clamp is integrated into the track assembly: the track is lifted, mat board is inserted, and then the track (and clamp) are lowered onto the mat board.

Mat cutters come in lengths up to 60" (152.5 cm). Like trimmers, they are compact and lighter than cutters, and much less expensive. Larger models can be wall mounted.

Courtesy Logan Graphic Products, Inc.

Fig. 2-10

The following are some rules of thumb for selecting cutters:

- If the only large materials you cut are lightweight, such as paper, thin board, and polyester film, a large mat cutter or a rolling trimmer provide the longest cuts at the most modest cost. They are compact and safe to use.
- To cut smaller materials of most weights, cutters like the Kutrimmer are fine.
- In order to cut thick, large boards, especially binder's board, a board shears is preferable and a Kutrimmer is a good second choice.

One more detail about cutters: they are designed for right-handed people. We have never seen one built for "lefties," although they may exist. However, the fact is that people who work with their hands after a time become somewhat ambidextrous. Most of us sew or use a knife with either hand rather than turn the work around. So don't let the fact that you are left-handed dissuade you from getting a cutter.

Presses

Presses come in various sizes and shapes and are used for many different purposes. Some types are especially useful for book repairs; others are more suitable for pressing flat paper items. It's not essential to have one to set up a workshop, but presses help make so many operations quicker and more efficient that it is worth obtaining a few over a period of time. As you work through some of the procedures in sections 3, 4, and 5 you will see what kinds of presses will work best for you.

Nipping Presses (Copy Presses)

These cast-iron presses were originally used for copying letters and documents onto the pages of thin, blank books where office records were kept. (For a history of copy presses, see Rhodes and Streeter, *Before Photocopying: The Art and History of Mechanical Copying.*) They were used throughout the nineteenth century and the first few decades of the twentieth century. Because they were used in most offices and are fairly indestructible, a lot of them survive. They are often found in antique shops, but there are more economical sources.

Bookbinders use these presses to press or "nip" books, and they can be used to press any bound or loose

pages that fit between the platen and the base. The presses came in many sizes and styles. When looking for one, check the amount of "daylight," which is the space between the platen and the base. Since they were intended to press just one rather thin book at a time, many copy presses have only a couple of inches of daylight. Look for at least 3" (7–8 cm), but more is better. (See fig. 2-11.)

Fig. 2-11

Standing Presses

The term "standing press" is used for presses made of iron, or wood and iron, with a relatively large platen size, e.g., 14" × 18" (35 × 46 cm) or more. They may stand on the floor or on a stand. They were designed for bookbinding and have at least 15" (38 cm) of daylight between the platen and base. Many nineteenth-century standing presses are still in use. The most decorative are the French presses; these are much sought after by collectors, and one in good condition commands a premium price.

Figure 2-12 shows a French press. It stands about 5.5' (168 cm). The ingenious mechanism provides much more torque than a nipping press, so it is possible to press things tighter. A large stack of books or a number of flat paper objects between boards can be pressed at the same time.

Many types of large presses were made in the past; most were made of hardwood and iron, some entirely of iron or hardwood. There are a few models still made today. Old presses in good condition are often better than new ones. If you are considering purchasing a press, try to see it first and observe how it operates to see if it is suitable for your needs.

Fig. 2-12

The presses described above hold books or other items horizontally. The following types are meant for holding books perpendicular to the work surface, so that the spine can be worked on.

Finishing Presses

This type of press consists of two planks of hardwood, about 7 or 8" (18 or 20 cm) wide by about 20" (51 cm) long and about 1½" (4 cm) thick. Two wooden screws, at the ends, hold them together (fig. 2-13). These small, light presses are extremely convenient to use and can be stored standing on end if necessary. When purchasing a wooden press, make sure that the screws work smoothly. Keep the screws parallel by tightening or loosening them simultaneously. This will prevent the screws from getting stuck and possibly damaged. Occasionally, the holes on the two boards are not aligned perfectly and the screws won't turn easily no matter how you turn them. If a press with this problem was purchased new, it should be exchanged. An old press with this problem can some-

times be helped by waxing the threads of the screws with beeswax or paraffin. Older finishing presses have gently rounded or beveled edges along the top; many new ones do not.

Fig. 2-13

Lying Presses

A lying press consists of two thick, heavy pieces of hardwood held together with wooden screws. Older ones can be quite large and can be unwieldy; the press in figure 2-14 is 30" (76 cm) long and weighs over 20 lbs (9 kg).

Originally, these presses were placed in stands called "tubs" and were used for many operations, including edge gilding. Most of the old presses found today have lost their tubs and must be propped up on some type of sturdy supports in order to use them. This can be a risky operation in a busy lab. They are not usually a top priority for a preservation department.

Fig. 2-14

Smaller versions, with 12"–18" (30–45 cm) capacity between the screws, are sometimes called finishing presses and can certainly be used in the same way, although they do not support the whole book as well as a regular finishing press does. To improve this, small pressing boards can be used with the press.

Handle presses with wooden screws with care; do not drop or bump them when using or moving them to avoid breaking or damaging the screws.

Job Backers or Backing Presses

A backer is a cast-iron press with two jaws that are opened and closed by a screw wheel. It works somewhat like a vise. This is a heavy piece of equipment that is not at all portable, and it takes up a fair amount of floor space. But if your institution does a lot of book repairs and there is room for it, it is a wonderful machine to have. When a book is in a backer, it is held perfectly steady, leaving both hands free to work. Used ones can be found from time to time.

The backer shown in figure 2-15 has 20" (51 cm) jaws and can accommodate books over 6" (15 cm) thick; there are bigger as well as smaller versions, including some models that are mounted on wooden bases or legs. The legs of this backer are bolted to lengths of 2" × 4" lumber to spread the weight.

Combination Presses

This press design has been in use for at least fifty years and can be made from materials available at lumberyards or hardware stores by people who are handy. (See fig. 2-16.)

Fig. 2-16

The combination press consists of two pieces of plywood at least ¾" (2 cm) thick held together by four carriage bolts. Brass strips line two edges and protrude about ¹⁄₁₆" (2 mm). They help set the grooves on the joints of book bindings, as shown in figure 2-17A.

Fig. 2-17A

On older models, such as the one shown in figure 2-17B, the edges on the opposite side of the press are beveled and there are brass strips on the bevels. This makes it possible to do some of the operations performed on a book in a backer. Current versions available from catalogs do not have this feature.

Fig. 2-15

Fig. 2-17B

Gaylord Bookcraft Press

A Gaylord press is an ingenious device that can press up to five average-sized books at once. It comes with Masonite boards that are used to separate the books, but small brass-edged boards can also be used in it, with the brass edges on the side away from the book protected by Masonite boards. It is small and can be put away when not needed. (See fig. 2-18.)

These presses were found in almost every library in the past, and many old ones are still around. The company offers replacement parts.

Courtesy Gaylord Bros., Inc.

Fig. 2-18

Dry Mount Presses

A dry mount press is handy for pressing papers or thin boards and is often used without heat (figs. 2-19 and 2-20). Look for one that is at least 18" × 23" (46 × 58.5 cm). A used press is worth considering, even if it does not heat, if the hinging mechanism is in good condition (and the price is right). Used presses may have upper platens that are encrusted with adhesive. Since the press will be used with additional boards or blotting paper, this is not usually a problem.

The base of the press is too spongy for our purposes, but this is easily remedied by the use of boards of various thicknesses. Have two pieces of fairly thick binder's board, e.g., .098 (U.S.), cut a little larger than the pressing area. The article that needs pressing is placed between blotters that are inserted between the binder's boards and the whole assembly is put into the press. For more pressure, add more layers of binder's board. As with any metal press, be careful not to leave damp boards in a closed dry mount press to avoid rusting the platen.

Fig. 2-19

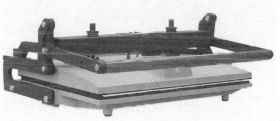

Fig. 2-20

Boards, Pressing Boards

Several types of boards are useful in the work area. But before describing them, we should clarify that the term "board" is used in three senses in conservation. The word can refer to a rigid or semi-rigid material, or a part of a book, or a piece of wood or thick plastic used for pressing work. The three meanings are as follows.

1. There are paper-based boards, such as binder's board, mat or museum board, bristol board, and corrugated cardboard. Plastic boards include, among others, plastic corrugated board and foam board (which has paper linings). These boards may be incorporated into repaired objects or they may be used for making protective containers, pamphlet binders, mats, exhibit mounts, etc. They are described in the sections dealing with their uses.

2. In the terminology of bookbinders, book historians, and booksellers, the front and back covers of books are called boards.

3. In the equipment category, "boards" are rectangular pieces of good-quality plywood or acrylic sheets at least ½" (1.3 cm) thick, which are used for pressing. Masonite or similar composition boards are sometimes used where thin, rigid boards are needed. Birch veneer plywood is very smooth; get boards that are good on *both* sides and give them an additional fine sanding, especially around the edges. It is good to have an assortment of sizes, at least two of each size.

Brass-Edged Boards

Some wooden boards have strips of brass along the edges that protrude about ¹⁄₁₆" (2 mm) above the surface of the board. The brass may overhang the bottom side of the board or both the top and the bottom (figs. 2-21A and 2-21B). They are used for some book-pressing tasks described in section 5.

Fig. 2-21A

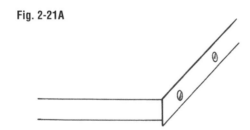

Fig. 2-21B

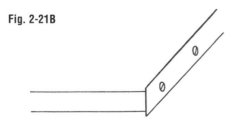

Brass is a soft metal, easily nicked and scratched. When pressing books in a press, protect edges that are not next to a book with plywood or Masonite boards so that the edges do not touch the platen or the base of the press. (See fig. 2-22.) Damaged edges can cause damage to books being pressed.

Fig. 2-22

Store brass-edged boards with Masonite or plywood boards between them, so the brass edges do not touch (fig. 2-23), or stack the brass-edged boards so that alternate edges face front and back.

Fig. 2-23

Hand Tools

Descriptions of spatulas, brushes, knives, and other small hand tools are given in sections 4 and 5, with the instructions for procedures that require them. But because bone folders are used so frequently in most aspects of preservation, we introduce them here.

Bone Folders, Teflon Folders

These handy tools are used to score and fold, rub down pasted areas, mark distances, burnish materials, and many other techniques. They come in several sizes and shapes for different purposes, and they really are made from animal bone. Bone folders can be polished and shaped to suit the user; conservators have very strong preferences about this. Occasionally, plastic folders may be found. They are more likely to scratch and cannot be shaped as well as bone.

In the mid-1990s folders made from Teflon were developed. (Two are pictured at the top of fig. 2-24.) They are chunkier than bone folders. They are very good for smoothing operations and tend to make materials less shiny than bone folders do. Adhesives do not stick to them. They become smoother with use and can be reshaped by filing or sanding, if desired.

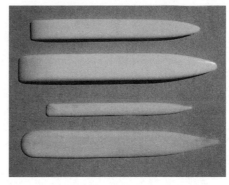

Fig. 2-24
An assortment of bone and Teflon folders

WORKING TIPS

We will provide here directions for carrying out techniques that will be used in a variety of procedures discussed in the following sections. Many of the working tips throughout this manual came from Nancy Russell, a bookbinder who worked at Columbia University and at the Metropolitan Museum of Art from the 1960s to 1981. Before that, Mrs. Russell had worked for a time in a commercial bindery, where she learned the value of using time and motion efficiently.

Some tips have their origins in traditional bookbinding customs that determine the way particular steps are carried out. In a bookbinder's shop with apprentices, it is essential that everybody does things in a uniform way, and the same applies to a conservation lab with several technicians and interns. Although it may seem arbitrary to say that a book should be put into a press with the head to the left, forming this habit will save you from inadvertently applying an old spine upside down. New workers learn faster and make fewer errors when procedures are standardized, especially in a lab where more than one person works.

Measuring

Learning to take and transfer measurements accurately is one of the cornerstones of conservation training. Conservators use several techniques to simplify this critical step.

There are many situations where rulers and measuring tapes are useful, of course, but conservators often use other means to transfer measurements. Marks can consist of small holes made with a very fine awl point, pencil dots, short slits made with a scissors or knife, or a simple crimp or indentation made with a fingernail or bone folder. Different methods work well in various situations and are a matter of personal preference. It is seldom necessary to draw long pencil lines to indicate cutting or folding lines; it is quicker and neater to make just a few small marks.

Strips of scrap paper work well, especially when measuring round or irregular surfaces such as book spines. Mark the measurement of the object on the strip and transfer it to the material to be cut (figs. 2-25 and 2-26).

Fig. 2-25

Fig. 2-26

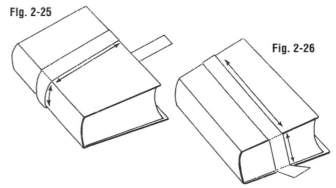

Another method is to place the object on the board or paper to be cut. Mark the measurement directly on the material (fig. 2-27).

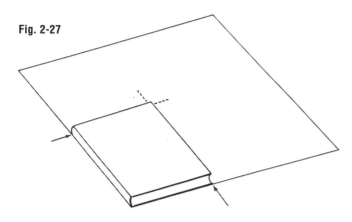

Fig. 2-27

To order custom-made boxes or other enclosures for books, they must first be measured accurately. Several of the vendors in appendix B sell devices for doing this. If you don't have a measuring device, the following method is easier than measuring a book that is just lying on the counter.

Slide the backstop (the gauge on the bed of the cutter) toward the left side of the cutter and lock it in place. This provides a firm, square corner. Place a ruler against the backstop, parallel to the bottom guide of the cutter. Put a book on top of the ruler, snug into the corner and note the width (fig. 2-28). Then turn the book to measure the height.

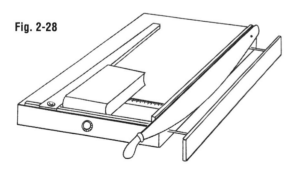

Fig. 2-28

To cut a piece of paper, Mylar, or board to the same size as another object, such as a board from a book cover, have the blade of the cutter in the lowered position and place the board against the backstop (or inside gauge) of the cutter. Move the gauge until the object touches the blade. Lower the clamp to hold it securely and lock the gauge in place (fig. 2-29). Release the clamp and raise the blade; remove the original item from the bed of the cutter. The measurement is now locked onto the cutter. This is sometimes referred to as "having a gauge." If another worker needs to use the cutter when the inside gauge is locked, it is the custom to ask if anyone still needs that measurement before changing the position of the gauge.

Fig. 2-29

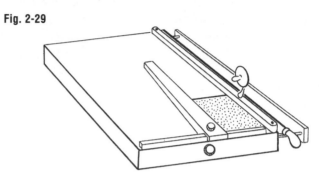

Grain Direction

Grain plays a major role in how paper handles and works. It is worth taking a little time to understand this important characteristic.

Most of the materials that come to the mending department will be made of paper or board that has a definite grain direction. Practically all papers and boards used to make repairs or protective containers also have grain, sometimes called "machine direction."

Paper and board tear and bend more easily *with* the grain than *against* it. Think about tearing a clipping out of a large newspaper. The tear from the top of the newspaper is fairly straight while the one from the side is often extremely ragged. This means that the grain of the newspaper goes from top to bottom, or is "grain long." The printing press prints on rolls of paper and the grain is always along the length of the roll, not across the width. (See also "Overview of Western and Japanese Paper" in section 4, p. 76, for more information about papermaking.)

Any procedure that calls for folding and creasing will turn out much better if the crease is along, or with, the grain. Going back to the newspaper example, the fold between two leaves is with the grain and is neater than the one that folds the newspaper in half, which is against the grain. At the second fold, the fibers of the paper may be broken and fuzzy.

This effect is greatly magnified when heavier papers or light boards are folded, with creases made across the grain significantly more ragged than those made with the grain. For neatness, and to prolong the useful life of preservation enclosures, the folds should be *with* the grain whenever possible.

Testing for Grain Direction: Paper

There are several tests for telling the grain in paper.

Manufacturers often mark the grain direction on the packaging of their papers by underlining one of the numbers indicating the size of the paper. A ream labeled 8½" × 11" is "grain long," that is, the paper will fold in half more easily the long way, resulting in a folded sheet 4.25" × 11".

Chain Lines. Many papers have lines that are visible when the sheet is held in front of a light source. The very closely spaced lines are called "laid lines." The widely spaced lines at right angles to the laid lines are called "chain lines" (fig. 2-30). In *handmade paper,* the grain is always parallel to, or "with," the chain lines.

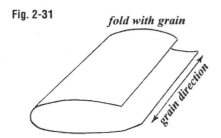
Fig. 2-31 *fold with grain*

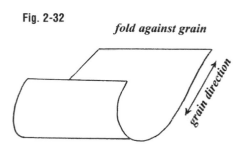
Fig. 2-32 *fold against grain*

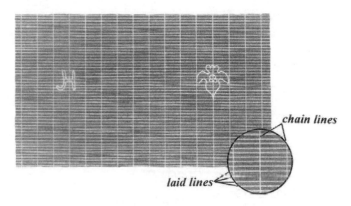

Fig. 2-30 A sheet of laid paper held against the light

The next two tests are suitable for *new materials only,* not for documents or book pages.

Moisture. Wet the corner of the sheet, just along the two edges, with a cotton swab (fig. 2-33). The grain is parallel to the edge that stays smoother. The other wet edge will curl and ripple (fig. 2-34).

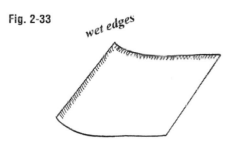
Fig. 2-33 *wet edges*

On *machine-made paper,* chain lines are made artificially and the grain could go either way. By tradition, the chain lines run in the machine direction, with the grain, but it is prudent to confirm this with one of the following tests.

Bending. Curl the sheet over in one direction and then in the other direction, pressing and bouncing gently with your hand. Note which way bends more easily. The direction with the *least* resistance is parallel to the grain (figs. 2-31 and 2-32).

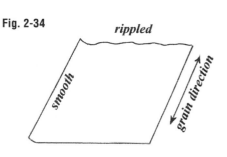
Fig. 2-34 *rippled*

Tearing. Tear a test piece. The paper rips easily with the grain. Ripping against the grain offers more resistance and produces a ragged tear. The grain is parallel to the straighter tear (fig. 2-35).

Fig. 2-35

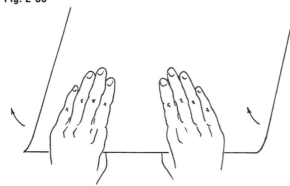

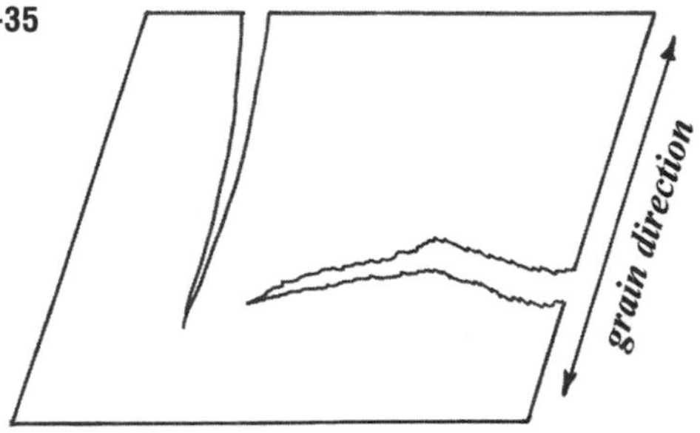

Testing for Grain Direction: Board

Place a piece of museum, bristol, or binder's board on a flat surface; place your thumbs under the board and your fingers on top and bend the edge up slightly (fig. 2-36). Turn the board 90° and try this on the edge at right angles to the first. It is better not to look at the board; instead, let your fingers tell you in which direction the board bends more easily. That is the grain direction.

Fig. 2-36

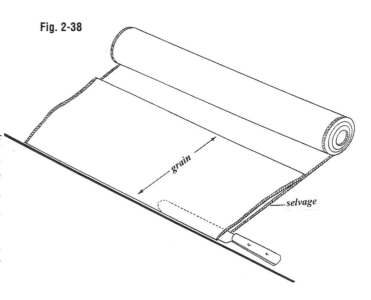

Sometimes it is difficult to determine the grain of laminated boards like museum board because the board is made up of several layers (plies). As with plywood, the grain of each ply alternates in order to make the board as stable as possible. These boards can usually be used in either direction.

For applications where grain direction is important, cut a piece of the laminated board and brush paste or PVA mix on it. Let it dry. Observe how the moisture dis-

torts the board. The grain goes in the direction that stays straight; the board is "against the grain" in the curled direction (fig. 2-37).

Fig. 2-37

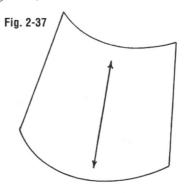

After determining the grain direction, it is helpful to draw a pencil line on the leftover board or paper, near the edge. This saves time in future when looking for a piece of the right size and grain direction.

Testing for Grain Direction: Cloth

The grain of cloth is along the length of the bolt, parallel to the selvage. It is the direction of the warp threads. However, this is not always obvious in scraps. The surest way to know the grain is to preserve the selvage on cloth that has been cut from the bolt. Form the habit of cutting cloth in pieces the whole width of the bolt (fig. 2-38). Then cut the quantity needed for the job at hand from that segment, starting at one edge and making sure to leave the selvage on the other edge of the piece until it is used up.

Fig. 2-38

If a usable scrap with no selvage is produced, make a pencil line on the back near the edge indicating the grain direction before putting it away.

Cutting and Trimming

A scissors is fine for rough cutting paper or light board, but for good, straight cuts, a cutter with a clamp is best. If an object cannot be cut in a cutter, a knife and straightedge work better than scissors.

A steel ruler works well for short cuts on lightweight materials. (Plastic, aluminum, or wooden rulers get cut by the blade and will be full of nicks and dents in a short time.) For long cuts, a heavy metal straightedge with a non-skid bottom is much less likely to slip. This is safer for the user and results in less wasted materials. It need not be marked in inches or centimeters. Thickness and rigidity are what matter; a heavy straightedge can be clamped to the work surface to leave both hands free if desired. They are available from art and drafting supply vendors.

Self-healing cutting mats are made of a relatively soft plastic. As the name indicates, cut marks tend to close over. But they are not indestructible, and a light hand will help preserve the surface. They come in many sizes and in different colors. The translucent ones can be put on a light box. They are more expensive than the opaque mats.

When cutting with a knife, put the material on a self-healing cutting mat or on a large piece of waste mat board. Crisscrossed lines from previous cuts on a mat can deflect the knife. Try always to cut in the same direction on the mat; turn the work as needed. Avoid cutting on binder's board; there may be tiny pieces of metal in this board, which dull knives quickly.

Mark the cutting line on the material, align the straightedge, and hold it very firmly. Make several light cuts (fig. 2-39). Put more pressure on the straightedge than on the knife. As you cut, pay attention to how you hold the straightedge down: the fingertips should be well out of the way of the blade.

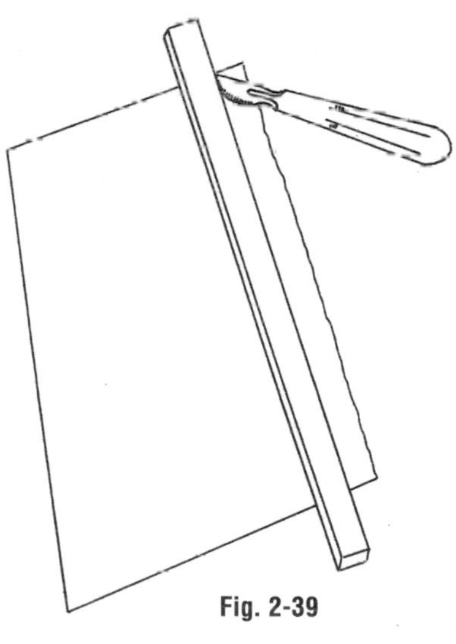

Fig. 2-39

For long cuts, cut about 7" (18 cm). Stop cutting but don't lift the knife out of the cut, then "walk" your fingers down the straightedge before you continue cutting.

If the point of the knife drags and does not produce a smooth cut, the blade may need to be replaced (or sharpened). If your blade is rounded rather than straight, try lowering the angle of the knife so that the round part of the edge does the cutting. That area of the blade remains sharp long after the point becomes dull or damaged.

Fragile paper that shreds or breaks apart when cut with the point of a blade can often be cut neatly using the round part of a sharp scalpel blade. Lower the handle until the point is off the paper entirely and be sure to hold the straightedge down very firmly.

When a thick material seems to be beyond the capacity of a board shears or other cutter, place it against the guide near the hinge of the blade. Clamp it firmly and cut slowly. There is much more power at the hinge end of the cut than at the handle end. Furthermore, the blade is likely to be sharper there, since most cutting is done at the near end of the cutter.

A board that is a few inches too wide to fit under the clamp of an old Kutrimmer can be divided into smaller pieces. Release the latch that secures the clamp at the near end of the cutter and swing the clamp out of the way of the blade. Remove the backstop (inside gauge) from the bed of the cutter.

Place the board on the bed of the cutter, against the guide at the hinge end, and hold it down firmly with your left hand. Cut about two-thirds of the blade length. *Be careful because the clamp and safety shield will not be in place to protect your left hand.* Remove the board from the cutter and turn it over, so the cut edge is toward you (fig. 2-40). Align the partial cut along the cutting edge as well as possible, hold the board down with your left hand, and complete the cut. This initial cut will be *very rough* and might not even meet in the middle, so make it a little oversize. Latch the clamp in place again, square one end of the piece, and cut off smaller pieces of board to size.

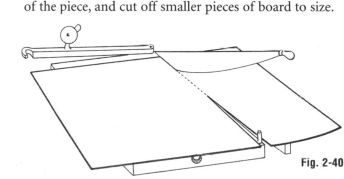

Fig. 2-40

An office-type cutter without a clamp can be used to divide board into smaller pieces as well, but it should not be used for subsequent cutting, where accuracy is important, because the cuts will not be square.

When making wrappers (protective enclosures made of lightweight board), sort the books by size in order to get the most economical cutting layout for the vertical and horizontal pieces of each wrapper.

When cutting cloth from a bolt or paper from a roll, place the roll or bolt on the counter, parallel to the front edge. Roll out the cloth or paper so a little more than you need is flat on the counter. Mark the spot to start the cut on one edge and fold the cloth or paper back so the edges are aligned. Fold and crease as in figure 2-41. Bring the creased material near the edge of the counter, to make room for your knuckles. Place a knife with a straight blade into the crease and slit with one pulling motion all the way across. Move your whole body, from the start of the cut to the end, rather than just using your wrist. To produce a neat cut, avoid a sawing motion.

Fig. 2-41

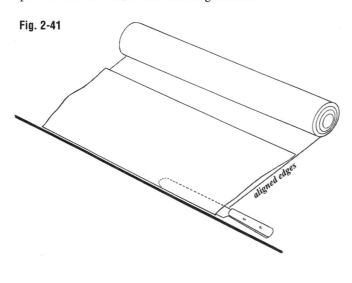

Note: Cutting the selvage first with a scissors, at the edge where the cut starts, may make it easier to slit heavier cloths.

Squaring Board or Paper

Most board and paper sold in sheets have square corners. However, to make sure that a piece you cut will be square, it is prudent to check that the sheet is square before you start cutting from it. T-squares, carpenters' squares, and triangles can be used to check a corner. Another good way to check is to place the sheet in a good cutter with an accurate bottom guide. If the corner doesn't line up well with the cutting edge of the cutter, slide the board under the clamp so that a small portion of the whole board protrudes beyond the cutting edge. Keep the board snugly against the bottom guide. Put the clamp down and cut the sliver off. Then cut off the amount needed for the job at hand.

The board left on the cutter after cutting off the first piece has a square corner, at least at the lower right side. This should be the starting point for future cuts from that sheet. Mark the corner with an "X" in pencil to indicate this (fig. 2-42).

If the edges of a sheet have become damaged during shipping or storage, trim two adjacent edges to produce a square corner and use the sheet for smaller projects.

Fig. 2-42

Scoring and Folding

Folding

A large sheet of paper or thin board, such as 10-point bristol or card stock, can usually be folded without first scoring it. The fold will be easier and neater if it is made with the grain (see "Grain Direction" above).

Mark the crease line at one edge of the sheet and position it on the work surface so that the fold will be near the edge of the counter. Fold the sheet back and align the edges. Hold the sheet down firmly with one hand and with a large bone folder start the crease near the middle of the fold (fig. 2-43).

Run the bone folder across the fold, creasing from the middle out and off the edge of the paper. Repeat the

Fig. 2-43

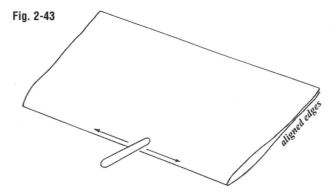

motion from the middle toward the other direction. Make sure to keep the paper firmly restrained with your other hand during the process.

Scoring and Folding: Making a Simple Folder

A simple folder can be made by folding a sheet of bristol or other lightweight board in half. But thicker boards such as map folder stock don't crease well unless the fold line is first scored. Folds made against the grain should *always* be scored first, even in lightweight materials. Scoring compresses a line into the paper or board and results in a neater crease, with fewer broken fibers.

Scoring by hand is easier if the board is placed on a somewhat padded surface, such as a large piece of waste mat board or a self-healing cutting mat.

Make marks at the edges of the board, to define the line to be scored. Line up a straightedge on the marks and hold it down securely. Run the pointed end of a bone folder firmly along the straightedge, as if drawing a line. Keep pressing the bone folder against the straightedge the whole length of the scored line (fig. 2-44).

Be careful not to press too hard when scoring thin boards to avoid cutting them. Heavier boards may need to be scored a second time to get a good indentation.

Continue to hold the straightedge in place and slide the bone folder under the board, folding it up against the straightedge. Draw the bone folder sharply against the straightedge, creasing the board at a 90° angle (fig. 2-45). Remove the straightedge and crease the paper or board completely, using the folder as necessary. Rub the crease with the bone folder, starting at the center and going out in each direction, as shown in figure 2-43.

If the countertop has sharp, square edges, you can score and fold board down over the edge (fig. 2-46). Then sharpen the crease with a bone folder.

Fig. 2-46

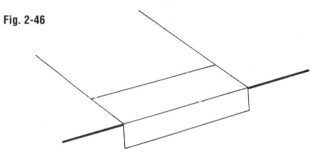

A board shears or other large scissors-type cutter with a clamp or pressure bar can be used for scoring and folding. The blade should be moved up and *back,* safely out of the way. Mark the line or lines that need to be scored on the paper or board and place it against the bottom guide of the cutter. Slide it under the clamp until the area to be scored is precisely at the cutting edge.

Press the clamp down tightly but *do not cut.* Instead, use a large bone folder to rub the board down against the cutting edge of the cutter (fig. 2-47).

Fig. 2-47

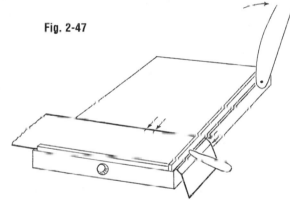

This method makes it easier to make several folds close together on the same piece of board, as when making wrappers. The guide and clamp ensure that the folds will be parallel. Push the board out, making sure it is snugly against the bottom guide, until the next line is over the cutting edge. Put the clamp down, and score with the bone folder.

After all the lines on the piece of paper or board have been scored, remove the piece and sharpen all the folds with a bone folder.

Fig. 2-44   **Fig. 2-45**

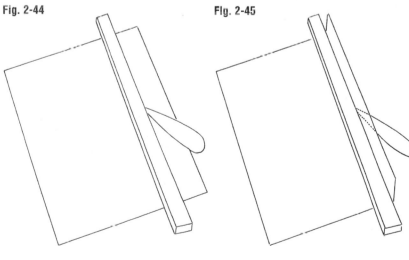

Using Adhesives

Many of the conservation techniques in this book call for the use of adhesives. The properties of starch paste, methylcellulose, and PVA are described in sections 4 and 5; here we give some tips for handling and applying adhesives. (Recipes for preparing paste and methylcellulose are in "Adhesives" in section 4, p. 79. Instructions for making a PVA-methylcellulose mix are in "Adhesives" in section 5, p. 104.)

Although cooked starch paste does not keep for very long, its useful life can be prolonged by keeping the main supply refrigerated and clean. The starch powder lasts for years if kept clean and dry.

Methylcellulose comes in powder form and must be mixed with water. The mixed adhesive lasts many months if it is not contaminated. The powder lasts for years if kept clean and dry.

PVA (polyvinyl acetate), a white plastic glue used in book repairs, is sold under various trade names. It keeps for many months if not contaminated. It is damaged by freezing or prolonged storage at low temperatures. Make sure to order enough PVA in the fall so that it won't need to be shipped during the winter. (Some suppliers charge extra for winter shipping, and a few will not ship in cold weather.)

To avoid contamination, don't dip the brush into the *main* container of any type of adhesive. Instead, decant some adhesive into a small, heavy, wide-mouth container, like a straight-sided jam or salsa jar with a lid, to use for a few days or for a particular job. Select a container that will not tip over from the weight of the brush or from wiping the brush. Put about 1"–2" (3–5 cm) of adhesive in the jar, or just enough so that the ferrule of the brush does not get covered with adhesive (fig. 2-48).

Clean the rings of adhesive containers and the inside of lids before putting the lids back on the containers, to make it easier to open the jar the next time. This works better than putting wax paper or plastic wrap under the lid.

Put jars of adhesive into a shallow plastic container on the workbench, to keep spills contained. Keep brush handles clean while working by always wiping excess adhesive on one side of the jar and then resting the brush on the clean side of the jar (fig. 2-48).

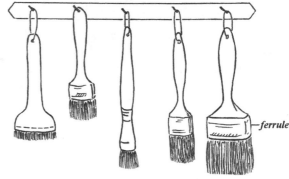

Fig. 2-48

Brushes will last a long time if they are not allowed to dry out with adhesive in them. They should be clean, or *in* the adhesive, or in water until they can be washed. Wash brushes at the end of the day to avoid rust on the ferrules. Let dry with the bristles pointing down. Once dry, store brushes hanging on a rack (fig. 2-49), or in an open container, bristles up.

Fig. 2-49

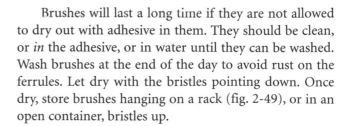

ferrule

Select brushes with short handles, like paintbrushes, to reduce the chance of accidentally knocking over the adhesive. If you have long-handled artist brushes, break off part of the handles. Smooth the ends by sanding, or put tape around the broken ends.

When getting ready to start a job that requires the use of adhesives, be sure to have a supply of clean waste paper at hand. Unprinted newsprint is absorbent and inexpensive. It is available from moving companies and shipping supply vendors.

Apply adhesive from the center out to the edges, to avoid getting adhesive on the front of the work (fig. 2-50). Make sure your fingers are clean before handling the pasted sheet.

Fig. 2-50

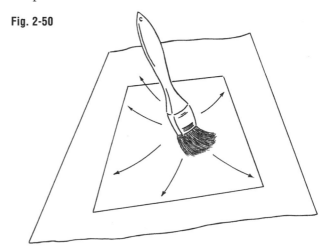

Discard waste paper immediately after applying adhesive. Or fold it in half, if it's a large sheet. This is important: many a project has been ruined by being set down on pasty paper.

General Working Tips

Keep hands clean. A slightly damp paper towel, square cotton pad, or piece of cheesecloth can be kept in a plastic container near at hand. Shop aprons are good for protecting clothing; they will stay soft much longer if you don't use them to wipe adhesive off tools or hands.

If working too far from a sink to wash hands, e.g., in the stacks shifting books, you can use waterless hand cleanser and paper towels to keep hands clean.

When using water for a task, always put it on a surface lower than the work.

Don't use repositionable adhesive notes (e.g., Post-it notes) on archival or library materials. Some adhesive remains behind when they are removed, causing pages to stick together. Dirt is also attracted to the adhesive residue even if the area doesn't feel sticky. If left in place for long periods, the adhesive becomes hard to remove.

Don't use rubber bands to keep objects together, even temporarily. They cause indentations and, if left longer than anticipated, the rubber deteriorates, sticking to objects and giving off harmful gases.

Section 3

Simple Preservation Techniques

Rehousing Library and Archive Materials

ONCE A SPACE IS SET UP, WORK CAN BEGIN. BUT IT is not usually possible to treat every item in poor condition right at the start. Conservation work requires time and trained technicians, and it may take many years to repair a collection. Generally, an assessment is carried out to determine what materials need work as well as priorities for treatment. In the meantime, many institutions protect fragile materials by putting them into containers of various types.

A box or envelope provides good protection from light and dust and also provides some buffering against fluctuations in temperature and humidity. It also protects materials from mechanical damage, such as abrasion, and keeps loose fragments from getting lost. A whole collection can be protected in this way in a much shorter time and for a fraction of the cost of making repairs. In time, particular items may be selected for conservation treatment. They will be much cleaner and more likely to be successfully repaired if they have been in boxes or other containers.

This section is divided into four parts.

1. "Rehousing Library and Archive Materials" looks at the concept of protecting a collection by putting materials into boxes, folders, or other enclosures and discusses some of the preliminary steps involved.
2. "Storage Containers (Preservation Enclosures)" discusses some aspects to consider when selecting enclosures.
3. "Handling Certain Types of Materials" gives guidelines for preparing and rehousing particular types of materials.
4. "Making Simple Enclosures" includes directions for making some simple storage containers.

REHOUSING LIBRARY AND ARCHIVE MATERIALS

The word "rehousing" is used here to mean the process of putting library and archive materials into new enclosures or storage furniture. The term does not imply that the materials are moved to a different building (although rehousing is often carried out in conjunction with moving collections). It is a somewhat confusing term, but it has been in use since the 1990s and seems to be established usage, at least in North America and Australia. We have heard the term used either when old boxes and folders are being replaced or when books and documents are being put into enclosures for the first time.

Rehousing can be a big undertaking, requiring additional supplies and labor and, often, extra shelving or storage space. The project should be included when planning upcoming budgets or grant proposals.

Determining What Materials Need Rehousing

When a general preservation assessment is carried out, an institution is often advised to rehouse a collection. The following factors, among others, should be considered when making decisions.

A. *What sort of use does the collection receive?* Materials of permanent value that get a lot of use need to be placed into sturdy, individual enclosures that are easy to open and close. The enclosure must indicate the title of the book or contents of the folder and the inventory or call number. At the other end of the spectrum are limited-retention archives that may never be looked at again. These documents are generally placed into large storage boxes that are often taped shut. Other materials fall somewhere in between, for instance, older editions of books or municipal maps. Items that may be consulted sporadically can be wrapped in acid-free paper, labeled, and tied.

Some materials may no longer be appropriate or pertinent; consider whether these should be replaced or withdrawn.

B. *What is the physical condition of the materials?* Two categories are generally put into enclosures: fragile, incomplete, or otherwise damaged materials, to prevent further losses; and valuable or rare items in good condition, to keep them that way.

When deciding whether a book should be boxed, take the following characteristics into account:

- Is it very old, fragile, misshapen, unbound, or much smaller than its neighbors on the shelf?

- Does it have leather rot, suspected dormant mold, sharp metal clasps, or any other condition that makes it dangerous to its neighbors on the shelf?

- Is the book in pristine condition, or does it have association value through inscriptions, enclosures, or other means? The value of such books is very much tied to their condition.

Similar questions can be asked when it comes to rehousing flat paper items.

If in doubt about whether to put something into an envelope or box, remember that nothing is ever harmed by being put into an acid-free enclosure of the correct size and type. It is a completely reversible step.

C. *How appropriate is the storage furniture?* If the materials are going into state-of-the-art cabinets professionally designed for the particular situation, very simple enclosures will be adequate. But if the storage furniture is marginal at best, selecting the right combination of containers may enable the institution to postpone replacement of the storage furniture.

The right enclosure can be determined by balancing the kind of use, the condition of the item, and the type of storage furniture.

Circulating materials are not usually good candidates for preservation enclosures because boxes and envelopes tend to get separated and lost. Such materials are normally replaced or sent to the library binder.

After the materials to be rehoused have been selected, some preparations are necessary before the supplies can be ordered.

Preliminary Stages

1. The first step is to examine the materials, to ascertain that everything is actually part of the collection and has been cataloged, accessioned, or inventoried. For example, a box of archives may include extraneous items that are clearly not related to the collection. These items should be brought to a librarian or archivist.

2. After this initial step, follow the guidelines above to select specific materials for rehousing. It may be that only some items will be placed in enclosures, as in a collection of books in various conditions. In other situations,

every item will go into an enclosure, as is common in archival collections.

3. The next step is to select the *type* of enclosure that is best suited to the situation. More than one kind can be ordered, to accommodate particular problems, but it will be easier for patrons and staff to use the collection if a uniform system is maintained. (See the sections below, "Storage Containers (Preservation Enclosures)" and "Selecting and Adapting Ready-Made Products," for some guidance on what sorts of containers are appropriate for various materials.)

Counting; Ordering Supplies

Count the materials to be rehoused to determine how many enclosures you need, and how many of each type if you will be using more than one. Ordering larger quantities always results in better prices; 5,000 envelopes might cost 25 cents apiece, while an additional 500 ordered later might be 45 cents each. On the other hand, you can't always return unused quantities, so it pays to have a fairly accurate count.

Check prices and availability with several suppliers. You may find that certain items are not sold by all suppliers. It may also be more economical to order different materials from different suppliers. Place the orders for boxes, envelopes, folders, and other supplies well in advance of the time you expect to begin working. Some items, such as custom-made enclosures, may take longer than others to arrive.

If your project requires many boxes, keep in mind that the boxes in their shipping containers will take up a lot of room while the project is going on. Arrange for a space to store them where they can be retrieved as needed. If this is not possible, try to have the supplier send them in two or more shipments.

Cleaning Materials

All materials to be put into enclosures (or treated) should be inspected for dust, mold, insects, and so on, and cleaned before proceeding with other steps. (In fact, cleaning is a basic form of preservation. Keep a dust cloth and soft brush handy whenever you handle research materials. If your hands get dirty from working in the stacks, take a break to wash them.) Instructions for cleaning mold from books are given in "Mold" in section 1, p. 17. Dust can be cleaned in the same way, but requires less stringent personal protection measures.

It is a good idea to confine the cleaning activities to one area and to carry the cleaned materials to another table or workbench where they can be put into the new enclosures. If you need to use the same area for both activities, divide the work into "cleaning periods" and "enclosure periods." Work on a surface that can be cleaned easily, such as plastic laminate. If this is not available, cover the surface with unprinted newsprint or wrapping paper while cleaning materials, and discard the paper before starting to put them into enclosures. Detailed information on the steps involved in cleaning and refurbishing a book collection can be found in *Cleaning and Preserving Bindings and Related Materials,* by Carolyn Horton. This book includes useful handling information and basic repair techniques. Many of the procedures it describes are intended for use on leather bindings. We suggest that you consult a conservator before using chemicals or dressings on books or paper objects, in order to select a safe course of treatment appropriate for your particular collection. Chemicals are not needed in a normal rehousing project.

If evidence of insects is discovered, the area where the materials came from must be inspected and treated as necessary by a pest control contractor. Books can be placed in a freezer (0°F, −18°C) for a few days to kill insects. Conditions in the storage space must be corrected to prevent them from coming back.

For more information on pest control, see NEDCC Technical Leaflet 26, "Integrated Pest Management," by Beth Lindblom Patkus (includes a recent bibliography); and *Approaches to Pest Management in Museums,* by Keith O. Story.

It may make sense to start cleaning the materials before the rehousing supplies arrive. A suitable place to store the cleaned items temporarily is necessary. The labels should be ready when the materials are placed into the enclosures, although it is possible to make pencil notations on the enclosures until the labeling can be completed.

STORAGE CONTAINERS (PRESERVATION ENCLOSURES)

Enclosures

In the book world, the word "enclosure" was originally used to mean an item found in a book, such as a letter, newspaper clipping, money, metal fasteners, rubber bands, etc. The enclosure might have been left there intentionally or accidentally. (See Roberts and Etherington, *Bookbinding and the Conservation of Books.*) A librarian or subject specialist should examine the enclosure to determine whether it should be retained. In the preservation department, the concern is how to treat an enclosure that is damaging a book. We will address this below.

In her *Library Materials Preservation Manual* (1983), Hedi Kyle introduced a new meaning for "enclosure," using it to mean an envelope or container for an item in need of protection. This meaning caught on and is used in professional literature and in preservation catalogs, where they are generally called "preservation enclosures."

We use the word "enclosure" primarily in the second sense, and occasionally in the traditional sense, where the meaning is clear from the context.

Research and special libraries use many of the same enclosures that are used in archives and also use several kinds of book boxes. Enclosures are used much less frequently in circulating collections because the materials tend to be withdrawn or rebound when they start to fall apart. Furthermore, patrons may not put books back into their preservation containers and the enclosures are often lost or discarded.

Many kinds of containers are available; some may need some assembly or modification to accommodate the object. Envelopes come in many sizes and shapes and even various weights (thickness of paper). There are boxes for documents, photographs, artwork, newspapers, nonprint media, and artifacts. And there are folders to fit most boxes and flat file drawers. Clear plastic sleeves may be closed on one, two, or three sides and there are various types of plastics as well as different thicknesses.

Boxes are routinely used in archives to keep collections together. Folders, envelopes, and sleeves protect individual items within the boxes. Materials that are too large for boxes may be placed in folders in flat file drawers, or they may be wrapped in acid-free paper.

The following are the principal types of enclosures used to preserve books and documents.

Envelope: usually made of buffered paper, sealed on three sides. It may have a flap closure on the fourth side or it may be open, with thumb notches to facilitate inserting and removing materials. Tyvek, a thin, strong material made from spun-bonded olefin (high-density polyethylene), is also used for envelopes. It allows vapor to escape but resists penetration by liquids, and it also resists punctures and tearing. Tyvek envelopes make a quick, inexpensive enclosure for small books.

Envelope sling: a long piece of sturdy paper. Slings are sold in various sizes, to correspond with a variety of envelopes. The sling is folded and a document or small pamphlet is placed in the fold. Slings protect fragile items as they are slid into envelopes. If you make them in-house, cut the paper short grain for neater folding.

Sleeve: generally used to mean a see-through enclosure. They may be closed on one, two, or three sides. Select sleeves made of polyester, polyethylene, or polypropylene and avoid acetate and vinyl.

Folder: open on three sides, with the fold on one long side. The basic folder is similar to an office file folder, but many sizes and shapes are available, with different features. Folders may come with flaps, sleeves, or envelopes attached inside and they may have a soft or hard cloth spine. Buffered versions of most office types of folders are available from conservation suppliers.

Wrapper: a simple enclosure generally made in-house from two pieces of lightweight board folded to fit a particular book. It is a type of "phase box" (see below).

Dust jacket: a plastic cover made to protect the paper jacket on a hardcover book as well as the covers of books without publishers' dust jackets. These enclosures are called "book jacket covers" or "jacket protectors" by some suppliers. They are available in versions with paper linings as well as without linings. Select jackets made of polyester or polypropylene and acid-free paper, if they have linings.

Pamphlet binder: a quick means of providing a hard cover to a thin booklet or pamphlet. Pamphlets are an old library standby, available in many acid-free styles.

Album: a book-shaped binder with three-ring or other mechanisms to hold plastic sleeves for document or photo storage.

Box: a large category of enclosures made from boards of various weights as well as from polypropylene and other inert plastics. Some designs can be stored flat and assembled as needed; others are reinforced with metal at the edges.

Boxes with flip-up lids are designed for upright storage of documents, photographs, and other flat paper items.

Clamshell boxes are a one-piece design consisting of two trays that close over each other. There is a great range of models. Economy designs are made of various cardboards and have paper labels; sturdier boxes are usually covered with cloth. Cloth-covered boxes for valuable or rare items are custom-made to the exact size of the book and may have gold-stamped leather labels. Clamshell boxes may be stored upright or flat and are used for books or collections of documents, prints, or photographs.

Boxes with separate lids may have drop fronts on the bottom tray, to make it easier to insert and remove prints or other large or fragile items. Boxes with lids are always stored flat.

There are also boxes of various shapes for artifact and textile storage, for the storage of rolled items, and for most other needs.

"Phase box" is a term used to describe containers made from a variety of cardboards to fit specific books. They may be considered temporary protection until the book can be conserved or a better box made. A wrapper is one kind of phase box.

In addition, suppliers offer an assortment of boards, tissues, and wrapping paper that can be used to fill out or pad the contents of boxes.

Protection for books can be provided by adjustable two-part rare book storage boxes, costing under five dollars per book, or by any of numerous stock and custom-made designs, including made-to-order, cloth-covered clamshell boxes with leather labels stamped in gold, costing $75 to several hundred dollars, depending on size and supplier.

Each enclosure has merits, and prices vary greatly. If you are contemplating a rehousing project and are overwhelmed by the breadth of choice, consider having a preservation consultant come and look at your materials and storage furniture. The consultant will likely have seen much messier collections than yours and will have suggestions that can save you time and money when ordering supplies.

Archival? Acid-Free?

"Archival" and "acid-free" are the two big catchwords in supply catalogs. "Archival" originally meant "pertaining to archives or records; or, [information] contained in records" (*Webster's New Twentieth Century Dictionary of the English Language, Unabridged,* 2nd ed., 1960). Sometime in the 1970s, the word was gradually extended to mean that a paper, board, or other item was acid-free or inert and therefore not harmful when used with archival mate-

rials, e.g., documents meant to be preserved. The further implication was that the paper or board would last "a long time," a vague period that could be anywhere from five to five hundred years. By now, when we hear the term "archival materials," we don't immediately know whether it refers to envelopes, boxes, and polyester sleeves or to documents, microfilm, photographs, etc.

A similar blurring has occurred with the term "acid-free." It can mean that a certain material has a neutral pH (7) *or* that it is alkaline (between 7 and 14). But the term is often used indiscriminately to indicate a desirable feature, even when the pH is in fact extremely high. This is the case with some glue sticks, which have a pH between 10 and 14, high enough to discolor and damage paper.

Alkaline Reserve

Paper is usually considered acid-free when it has a pH between 6 or 6.5 and 7, and "buffered" when its pH has been raised to about 8.5 or 9 by adding an alkaline substance like calcium carbonate during manufacture. Such paper is said to have an "alkaline reserve."

So the word "acid-free" does not give an exact description, nor does it mean that something is necessarily safe to use.

Some suppliers use "acid-free" and "archival" interchangeably. For instance, polyethylene sleeves may be referred to as "acid-free" when the really important factor about plastic sleeves is whether they give off noxious vapors or not. If they do not emit harmful gases, they are considered inert (safe). Polyester, polyethylene, and polypropylene are inert plastics. Avoid vinyl and acetate sleeves; they break down in time and emit harmful gases. Look for sleeves that pass the PAT test (see below).

What Does "pH" Mean?

The term "pH" is commonly used to express the acidity or alkalinity of a solution on a scale that runs from 0 to 14. A value of 7 is neutral, below 7 is acidic, and above 7 is alkaline. The symbol "pH" refers to the words "power" and "hydrogen." (For technical details, consult a work on basic chemistry, such as the Museums and Galleries Commission Conservation Unit's *Science for Conservators,* vol. 2, *Cleaning.*)

PH TESTING

Testing the pH of a solution is relatively quick and can be done with meters or indicator strips. Testing a dry material, such as paper or board, is another matter. The paper may be shredded and mixed with water (sometimes heated and sometimes cold), and then a meter can be inserted into the pulp. This is a "destructive" test that cannot be used on original documents, but it can be used to test new materials.

Fortunately, it is not necessary to test book pages or documents in the course of a normal rehousing project or when planning minor repairs. Simply stick to the rule of using appropriate conservation-quality materials for repairs or enclosures at all times.

Two methods for obtaining approximate pH readings in a small preservation department involve the use of indicator strips and felt-tip pens. Both are available from conservation suppliers.

Indicator strips can be used to test documents or book pages. The strips have little squares that are impregnated with indicator substances. If done carefully, the test should not leave a mark on the paper.

Place a scrap of Mylar under the paper to be tested. Dampen the paper by rolling a cotton swab moistened with distilled water over an area about 1" (2.5 cm) long. Place an indicator strip on the moistened area, then put a blotter and a weight over it. Leave at least five minutes, pick up the strip, and compare the color change on the indicator squares to the scale printed on the box. It may take some time to get a reading.

Caution: Tide lines (water stains) may develop on some papers if too much moisture is used. Various papers react differently to water. If testing pages in a book, test at the gutter or some other inconspicuous spot in the middle of the book, *not* on the title page. Be aware that the pH may be different in various parts of the book.

It takes too long to get a reading on the indicator strips to make them useful for routine testing of new materials. The strips are also fairly expensive.

PH pens are felt-tipped pens filled with an indicator solution. This is a quick and easy way to find out whether paper or board is acidic or not. When selecting materials to use for repairs or rehousing, make a small mark on the new material with a pH pen. If it is neutral or buffered, the mark will change from yellow to magenta (or from green to blue, depending on the indicator chemical in the pen). Instructions for use come with the pens.

If you find old repair papers or boards that have been in storage for several years, test them before use. Although the material may have been acid-free when it was bought, it might have become acidic while in storage, from exposure to environmental pollutants. It is also a good idea to spot-check new materials from time to time.

Caution: Do not use the pH pens to test documents or book pages because the mark cannot be removed. The pen's reading tells whether a material is neutral or above but gives no indication of how alkaline the tested material is.

PAT Test

The American National Standards Institute defines standards that materials must meet. Standards IT 9.2-1998 gives specifications on types of enclosures, papers, plastics, adhesives, and printing inks. Enclosures for photographic materials must pass the Photographic Activity Test (PAT) as well. The test checks for harmful chemicals that cause image fading or staining.

Enclosures that pass the PAT test are suitable for photographic as well as other types of archival materials. This is a better indication of quality than a simple statement that a sleeve is "acid-free" or "archival."

If you purchase rehousing materials from established suppliers, such as those in appendix B of this book, you have a better chance of getting good quality than if you purchase similar materials from an office products supplier, for instance.

For more information about pH and acid-free and buffered materials, consult McCrady, *North American Permanent Papers;* NEDCC Technical Leaflets 31, 38, and 57; Museums and Galleries Commission Conservation Unit, *Science for Conservators,* 3 vols.; and Roberts and Etherington, *Bookbinding and the Conservation of Books.*

Testing New and Old Folders and Boxes with a pH Pen

Materials newly purchased from reliable conservation suppliers are usually what they claim to be. If you wish, you can spot-check a shipment of acid-free envelopes, for instance, by making a small mark on one with a pH pen and observing the color change of the mark. It should change immediately to magenta or to blue, depending on the indicator solution in the pen.

Periodically test the pH of older storage containers, even if they have never been used. Do not be surprised if materials that were acid-free or buffered when bought have become acidic after a number of years. This might be due to atmospheric pollution or to inadequate outer boxes or contact with wooden furniture. Generally, the outside of the container becomes acidic first, while the inside remains buffered or neutral somewhat longer.

This does not mean that the containers have failed; instead, it indicates that the folder or box reacted to acidic pollutants in the air or storage furniture, in effect forming a barrier of protection for any materials inside. This is what they are supposed to do. However, enclosures that test acidic with a pH pen should not be used to protect documents or books, even if they *look* undamaged.

On the other hand, acidic contents, such as newsprint, leather bindings, and certain types of photographic materials, can cause acid-free or buffered enclosures to become acidic. This is normal. Regardless of what caused them to become acidic, the containers need to be replaced.

Sometimes it is difficult to know whether to select a paper or board enclosure that is neutral or one that is buffered. Both are acid-free. However, buffered enclosures will stay acid-free much longer than neutral ones and will not need to be replaced as soon.

In the past, curators were advised to use only neutral pH enclosures for certain photographic materials. It is now generally believed that this is not necessary. See NEDCC Technical Leaflet 38, "Storage Enclosures for Photographic Materials," by Gary E. Albright; and appendix A, "Care of Photographs," by Ana B. Hofmann.

Selecting and Adapting Ready-Made Products

Suppliers of conservation materials offer a tremendous assortment of enclosures for storing almost any type of object. In many cases, there are several equally valid ways of storing an item and the choice can be made on the basis of convenience or cost. For instance, documents can be stored in paper envelopes or folders, or in polyester or other see-through sleeves. They can be in file folders, which might be placed in flip-top document storage cases or put into hanging files in file cabinet drawers. A small quantity of documents might be kept in a small, flat box, or in a four-flap binder with rigid covers.

The idea is to provide protection from mechanical damage, light, dust, and air pollution. Look for an enclosure that is rigid enough to protect the item in the type of storage system you use. For instance, a six-page pamphlet can be placed in a paper envelope or Mylar sleeve if it is stored with other documents in a file folder within a box or drawer. But if it is shelved with books, it needs to

have a much more substantial binder or portfolio around it to give it enough bulk so that it will not be damaged or get lost behind larger books. The binder can be labeled with a call number or other inventory identification.

Similarly, a shallow box with lid, a little bigger than the book, will serve to protect a single book that is stored flat in a cabinet or in a drawer. If desired, rolled up or crumpled acid-free tissue or other paper can be inserted to fill up the extra space. But when hundreds of books that are shelved upright in stacks need protection, the boxes must fit accurately and enable the books to stand on their bottom edges.

Occasionally a stock product can be modified to serve a specific need. For example, an envelope sealed on three sides can be adapted to provide safe storage for a fragile document. Slit one side of the envelope to create a flap that can be peeled back. This allows the document to slide in more easily, with less chance of snagging.

Some enclosures have several scored lines so they can be folded to fit individual items. This includes several types of adjustable rare book boxes and portfolios with flaps. And some enclosures are meant to be used with other containers, for instance, envelope slings. These are folded pieces of acid-free paper that are useful when storing fragile documents or pamphlets. The delicate item is first put into the sling and then both are slid together into an envelope.

If you cannot find a container that suits your needs in the book and paper section of a catalog, look in the sections that offer supplies for artifacts, textiles, herbarium specimens, and so on. A wedding gown storage box might be the perfect way to store a few fragile, lightweight rolled maps.

When there is nothing ready-made in the size and shape you need, some suppliers will make enclosures to your design. You can make a prototype or send a detailed description and get price quotes. Of course, this is more economical when larger quantities are being ordered, but it is even possible to get a single folder made.

Many library binders and other small companies make book boxes of various types, to the exact sizes you supply.

The price of enclosures, whether stock or custom-made, goes down as the quantity ordered goes up. When ordering quantities above the largest listed, ask if there is a further discount.

HANDLING CERTAIN TYPES OF MATERIALS

Scrapbooks and Albums

These one-of-a-kind books often have irregular shapes. Older ones are frequently in poor condition; they may be stuffed with memorabilia and may not close well. They are not always able to stand properly on the shelf. Many institutions wrap such books in acid-free wrapping paper, label the package, and store them flat on shelves. Another good option is to enclose them in boxes. (In the case of damaged scrapbooks and albums, it may be wise to first wrap them in tissue or wrapping paper and then box them.) Boxing may make it possible to store fragile albums upright on shelves without subjecting them to further damage.

Custom-sized phase boxes made from acid-free board are available at reasonable prices (see appendix B for sources). The institution supplies the vendor with measurements and copy for a label.

Sturdy premade boxes are available from many conservation suppliers in dozens of stock sizes. They may not be the exact size for the book, but acid-free tissue can be rolled up or crumpled and stuffed into the extra space to prevent the book from shifting. This option is suitable for books that will be stored flat on shelves. Label the box on the side that will be visible. A *few* lightweight boxes can be stacked, but be careful because the boxes can become distorted. When that happens the lids will gap open and dust and light can get inside.

Photographic Materials

In recent years, the market value of many photographs has increased dramatically. Since it is not always possible to judge which prints are or will be collector's items, it is best to treat all photographs that are part of the collection as rare. This means no in-house treatment, good environmental conditions, and proper storage containers.

Good storage containers work together with a good environment to protect photographs from light, dust, abrasion, warping, fingerprints, and so on. A great variety of enclosures that pass the PAT test can be ordered from several conservation suppliers. Select the styles that work best in your situation.

Gloves

It is important not to touch the emulsion of photographic materials (prints and negatives of all types) because oils in the skin etch the emulsion and will become indelible fingerprints in time. This also applies to microfilm, motion picture film, and similar media. Cotton gloves are often recommended for that reason. However, gloves can make a person clumsier; it is not really possible to feel through them and the fingertips have very little traction. If you are able to hold prints and negatives by their *edges only,* you may be able to work without gloves. However, if you are more comfortable wearing gloves (or if they are required by your institution), be sure to get gloves without any sort of pattern or dots on the fingers, since these can leave marks.

Separate Prints and Negatives

Prints and negatives are sometimes found in the same envelope. While this may be convenient in a personal collection, it is not a prudent method for an institution. First, in case of a disaster, both print and negative would be affected and the image might well be lost. And second, plastic negatives and paper prints have different storage requirements.

Put the negatives and prints into individual paper or plastic sleeves that pass the PAT test and store them separately, in boxes of the right size and shape. Provide good support by inserting dividers or spacers as needed so that the materials don't sag.

Protect Prints and Slides in General Files

Photographic prints and slides are often included in files containing other documents. They may be loose or in old envelopes or sleeves. Discard any vinyl sleeves or acidic envelopes and place the prints or slides in suitable plastic sleeves or paper envelopes to protect them from damage during browsing and handling. (If there is information on old envelopes, transfer it to the new enclosures *before* putting the photographs or slides into them.)

Paper or Plastic?

There is no one perfect enclosure recommended for every photographic material. Select sleeves or envelopes that pass the PAT test and suit your particular situation.

Paper envelopes or folders are usually cheaper than plastic ones and they are opaque, so that light does not reach the object inside. Paper breathes and prevents the buildup of moisture and damaging gases. Many envelopes and folders are available in either acid-neutral or buffered versions. The fact that paper is opaque might be a disadvantage in some cases, since the print cannot be viewed until it is removed from the envelope. However, it is easy to write identifying information on paper with a pencil before inserting the print.

Plastic enclosures can be made from polyester (e.g., Mellinex) or from polypropylene or polyethylene. Polyester is the most stable and inert plastic used for enclosures. It is extremely clear, does not distort easily, and it comes in several weights or thicknesses. Polypropylene enclosures may be rigid or flexible. Polyethylene enclosures are flexible, like household plastic bags.

Avoid purchasing vinyl (polyvinyl chloride, or PVC) sleeves. As they deteriorate, they give off harmful gases and stick to the emulsions of prints or negatives. If you find prints, negatives, or slides that are stuck to old vinyl sleeves, do not attempt to separate them. Consult a conservator.

The plastic enclosures are clear and allow the image to show through. Researchers can browse through a box of prints without touching them. Plastic enclosures do allow light to reach the object, but this is not normally a primary concern in photographic collections because the sleeves are stored in opaque boxes or drawers.

Plastic provides more protection from atmospheric pollution than paper does. On the other hand, plastic enclosures trap harmful gases that are produced by some deteriorating materials and this speeds up the process. Polyester creates a static charge that can remove loose flakes of emulsion from deteriorating prints or negatives.

Polyester enclosures can be heavier than paper and are several times more expensive. Polypropylene and polyethylene are less costly and usually thinner than polyester; some enclosures made of these two plastics may cost about the same as paper.

The comments about enclosure choices for photographs also apply when deciding what types of enclosures to purchase for documents and other paper items. If a sleeve passes the PAT test, it should be safe for anything in the collection.

Glass Plate Negatives, Lantern Slides

Glass negatives and lantern slides have similar housing requirements. They need to be protected from abrasion and from breakage. Store similar sizes together.

Each negative or slide should be placed in a paper envelope that is buffered or acid-neutral. Envelopes with three sides sealed as well as four-flap folding paper enclosures are sold in various sizes. The envelopes take up less room than the four-flap enclosures, but the latter might be more suitable for fragile slides or negatives. If replacing old envelopes, be sure to transfer all information to the new enclosure before inserting the negative or slide into it.

Sleeved glass plate negatives should be stored on edge in boxes designed for their size, e.g., 8" × 10". Glass is heavy; for safety when handling the boxes, calculate the number of plates so that each box doesn't weigh more than about 8–9 lbs (3.5–4 kg). Select a box that will be nearly filled with the plates and will not allow them to sag. Insert dividers of acid-free corrugated cardboard, the same size as the plates, every few plates to pad them. If the front of the box is much lower than the glass plate, insert a cardboard divider in front of the first plate to prevent it from breaking against the edge of the box.

Lantern slides are smaller, and it's not usually necessary to insert cardboard dividers among them in the boxes; they should be kept upright in boxes designed for lantern slide storage. If they don't fill a box, put a spacer or a wad of crumpled acid-free tissue paper behind them.

Waterproof Storage

Many types of photographic materials are very likely to be damaged beyond saving if they get wet. Consider this when planning their storage location. As with *all* other library and archival materials, *never* store boxes directly on the floor, and avoid below-grade locations if at all possible. It is occasionally recommended that certain materials be stored in waterproof containers. Since a waterproof container would also be airtight, consult a conservator or preservation specialist to determine if particular materials can be safely stored that way.

More details about the care of photographs may be found in appendix A, "Care of Photographs."

Maps, Posters, Architectural Photoreproductions

Architectural plans, maps, large posters, and other large-format materials can be stored in two ways: flat or rolled. Flat files or large boxes can be used for the flat storage of items that fit in drawers or boxes, while larger materials must be kept rolled.

If you have a collection of architectural photoreproductions, e.g., blueprints, you may wish to consult a person who can identify the various reproduction processes because some interact adversely with others. If this is not possible, be sure to isolate each print with a barrier of polyester film. (See "Barrier Sheets; Interleaving," p. 70.) Prints made by a few techniques require storage in a neutral rather than a buffered environment. (See Kissel and Vigneau, *Architectural Photo Reproductions*, for more information on this subject.)

Rolled Storage

There are various ways to protect a rolled map or plan. A plan in good condition can simply be inserted into a tube or long box, available from suppliers. These should be labeled to indicate the contents. A more fragile item should be rolled around an acid-free core a little longer than the item to protect the rolled edges and then wrapped in acid-free wrapping paper or polyester film before inserting it into a tube or box.

Storage containers are available in the form of cardboard boxes or tubes of various diameters and lengths. Plastic storage tubes in various styles are also offered by some suppliers. Some of these are waterproof or water-resistant.

In cases where there are many tears and loose pieces, it might be prudent to roll the map together with a sheet of acid-free paper or polyester film for support, as shown in figure 3-1.

Fig. 3-1

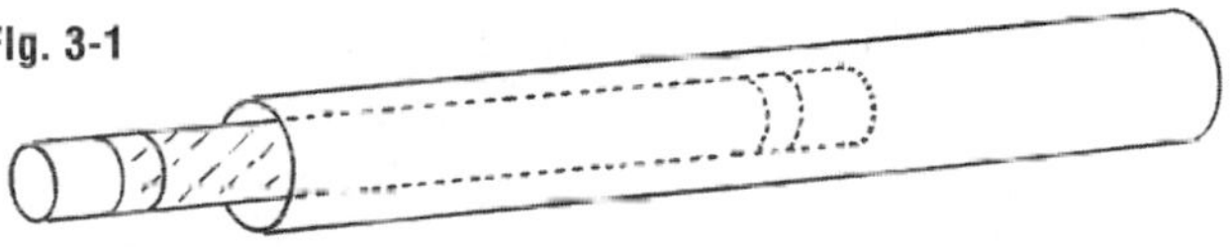

Very large, bulky groups of plans which are seldom used can be rolled around an acid-free core and then wrapped with sturdy acid-free paper. To hold the paper closed, use cotton twill tape or make reusable straps from strips of polyester film with hook and loop fasteners (figs. 3-2 and 3-3).

Fig. 3-2

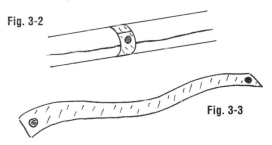

Fig. 3-3

In "Roll Storage" in section 1, p. 24, we discuss various types of shelving and furniture that can be used to store tubes and rolls.

For more information on this subject, consult NEDCC Technical Leaflet 36, "Storage Solutions for Over-sized Paper Artifacts," by Mary Todd Glaser.

Unrolling Large Maps or Drawings for Flat Storage

Rolled materials that fit in the drawers of flat files can be unrolled and stored flat. However, an item that has been rolled for several years or decades will not usually lie flat and has to be opened gradually. (See directions below.) Make sure drawers or boxes large enough for these items are available before starting an unrolling project.

Sometimes it is not possible to unroll materials for flat storage because they are just too fragile to unroll without damage. Get help from a conservator before proceeding; in the meantime, wrap and store these rolls as discussed above.

To prepare rolled items that are relatively sturdy, remove paper clips, staples, pins, and old, loose repair tapes. Don't pull off any tape that is still attached. If you find a piece of tape dangling and in danger of being pulled off, trim it neatly, close to the document.

If the piece is large, this will be a two-person job.

Open the roll gently as far as it will unroll easily (fig. 3-4).

Place a piece of blotter and a wooden or acrylic pressing board over the unrolled area and weight down with wrapped bricks or books (fig. 3-5). Do not force the

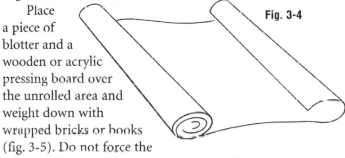

Fig. 3-4

roll open. You may have to do it in several stages, progressively opening and placing weights on the unrolled portion. Let it relax a few days, then open it a bit more, moving the weights farther out, and so on.

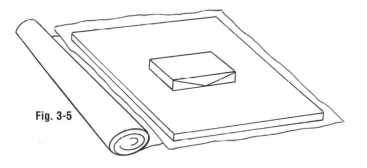

Fig. 3-5

Once the item is totally unrolled, cover it completely with acid-free blotters, and place wooden or acrylic pressing boards or weights on top.

Let the document remain under weight for several days. After this initial flattening, turn the document over and put the blotters and weights on it for another few days. It is ready for storage in oversize archival folders when it doesn't curl back spontaneously if left uncovered.

Some materials will always try to curl again and must be placed in storage folders that will keep them flat.

A light weight, such as a piece of museum board, can be placed on the folder to keep the item flat in the drawer.

The best time to unroll documents is during periods of higher humidity, when the building's heat is not on, because the extra moisture makes paper much more flexible. If the roll does not relax sufficiently by this method, you may need to place it in a humidity chamber, as described in "Relaxing and Flattening Paper" in section 4, p. 84, and then repeat the unrolling steps.

MAKING SIMPLE ENCLOSURES

Map Folders

Storage folders of many sizes and several weights are available from most conservation suppliers, and some suppliers will make folders to custom sizes. But if you need just a few, it is easy to make them from large sheets of bristol board, map folder stock, or other light- or medium-weight boards.

Lightweight Map Folders

Follow the directions for folding and scoring light boards in "Scoring and Folding" in section 2, p. 50. After the board is folded, the resulting folder can be trimmed down to size if necessary.

Hinged Folders or Portfolios

To construct portfolios or large folders for heavy materials, cut two sheets of a medium-weight board, such as pressboard or mat board. Cut them just a little smaller than the inside of the flat file drawer or storage box into which they will be placed. Don't use or make folders that are much smaller because small folders get shuffled around when the drawer is opened and shut or the box is moved, resulting in damage to the contents.

Cut a piece of 2" or 3"-wide pregummed linen tape (sold in conservation and framing supply catalogs) that is about 2.5" (6 cm) longer than the length of the board. Book cloth, which is available in rolls a few inches wide, can also be used. Crease the cloth in half, lengthwise. Cut a second piece of tape or cloth about 1" (2.5 cm) shorter than the length of the board and set it aside.

Place the objects that will be stored in the folder on one board and align the other board on top of them; measure the space between the boards. (Use a ruler, or a triangle, as shown in figure 6-36, p. 174.) This will be the distance between the boards; in this example, let's say that the distance is 1", or 2.5 cm. Remove the objects and line up the edges of the boards, overhanging the edge of the work surface by an inch or two. Put a weight on the boards to keep them from shifting.

Fit the creased tape or book cloth around the two boards, so that the fold in the tape is about ½" (1.3 cm) from the edges (one half of the measurement obtained in the previous step). Make a few light pencil marks on the board where the edge of the tape will be aligned.

It is much easier to attach the tape to one board, allow it to dry, and then attach the second board to the other half of the tape. Moisten the pregummed tape with water or apply a 50-50 mix of PVA and methylcellulose to the strip of book cloth, down the length of the piece but on one side of the crease only. Use a brush in either case. (See "Adhesives" in section 5, p. 104, for information on making a PVA-methylcellulose mix.)

Attach the gummed tape or pasted book cloth to the first board, using the pencil marks as guides. It should extend about 1½" (4 cm) at each end (fig. 3-6). Put waste paper or blotter over the tape and rub down with a bone folder. Allow to dry.

Fig. 3-6

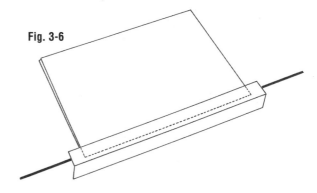

Turn the boards over and move them 2"–3" (5–7.5 cm) back from the edge of the counter. Make sure that they are well aligned, one on top of the other. Place a weight on the boards. Fold the tape or book cloth over the second board and mark where the edge of the tape should go. Place waste paper under the tape or cloth. Open out the tape and moisten it (or apply adhesive to the book cloth) from the crease to the edge. Discard the waste paper. Fold the tape up and attach it to the second board (fig. 3-7). Put clean waste paper or blotter over the tape and rub down with a bone folder. Allow to dry.

Fig. 3-7

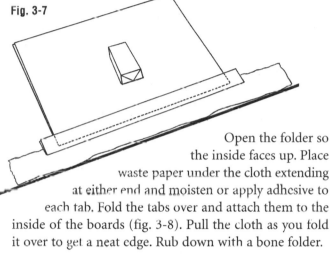

Open the folder so the inside faces up. Place waste paper under the cloth extending at either end and moisten or apply adhesive to each tab. Fold the tabs over and attach them to the inside of the boards (fig. 3-8). Pull the cloth as you fold it over to get a neat edge. Rub down with a bone folder.

Fig 3-8

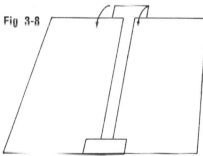

Crease the second piece of pregummed tape or book cloth to help center it. Moisten (or apply adhesive to the cloth) and position it over the joint between the two boards. Using a bone folder, work it down so it sticks to the reverse side of the first piece of cloth and rub it down to the boards (fig. 3-9).

Fig. 3-9

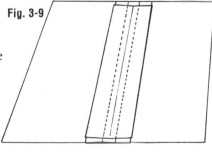

Self-Closing Wrappers: Protection for Books

In this context, the term "wrapper" refers to an enclosure made to fit a book. Wrappers are relatively quick to make and although usually considered a temporary measure, they can last quite a number of years. They provide excellent protection for fragile books. Wrappers are most suitable for smaller books: if you need both hands to pick up a book, it is probably too heavy for a wrapper. A box made from heavier board should be ordered for it from one of the suppliers listed in appendix B.

Wrappers can be made from various lightweight boards. Many boards measure 32" × 40" (81 × 101.5 cm) in size; in order to make wrappers efficiently, it is necessary to have a cutter that can cut at least 32" (81 cm). (See "Cutters" in section 2, p. 36, for descriptions of cutters.) A knife and straightedge can be used, but the process becomes much more time-consuming and generally gives less accurate results.

We give directions for making two styles of wrappers. Both can be made from boards of various thicknesses. Ten-point bristol or card stock can be used, but 20-point board will give better results in most cases. Board may be sold under the names bristol, card stock, map folder stock, folder stock, and others. Other light boards may be used if they can be folded as explained in "Scoring and Folding" in section 2, p. 50. Heavier boards generally require the use of a creasing machine, a major piece of equipment.

In both versions, the wrapper is made in two pieces, one vertical, the other horizontal. The grain direction of both pieces must be parallel to the folds to ensure sharp folds (in the short direction of each piece). Labs that produce a large number of wrappers often precut a quantity of pieces in several frequently used sizes. The board pieces can be trimmed quickly for a custom fit.

Each piece is wrapped around the book at right angles to the other and the two pieces are fastened together with double-coated tape. Wrappers of both styles stay closed without the need for fasteners.

Place a triangle against the fore edge of the book to determine its thickness (fig. 3-10).

After measuring the thickness of the book, proceed to cut board for the style of wrapper you prefer.

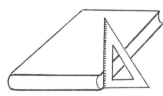

Fig. 3-10

Kyle Wrapper

This wrapper was developed at the New York Botanical Garden around 1980 during the time that Hedi Kyle was head of the preservation department.

VERTICAL PIECE

Place the book on a sheet of board, making sure the grain of the board is at *right angles* to the spine of the book (this way the folds will be *with* the grain). Align it along two edges, and mark the measurements (fig. 3-11).

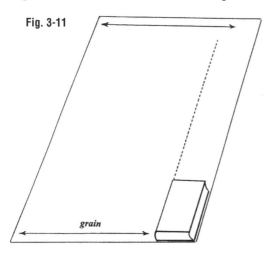

Fig. 3-11

grain

Cut a piece of board the width (W) of the book by approximately 2½ times its height (H) + twice its thickness (T), or W × 2.5H + 2T.

Center the book on the vertical piece. Mark the folds on the board with a bone folder, using the top and bottom edges of the book as guides. Remove the book, fold the board at each crease, and sharpen with a bone folder. (Or place the board in a cutter, as shown in fig. 2-47, on p. 51, and crease the folds against the cutting edge of the cutter.) Make sure the folds are parallel to each other (fig. 3-12).

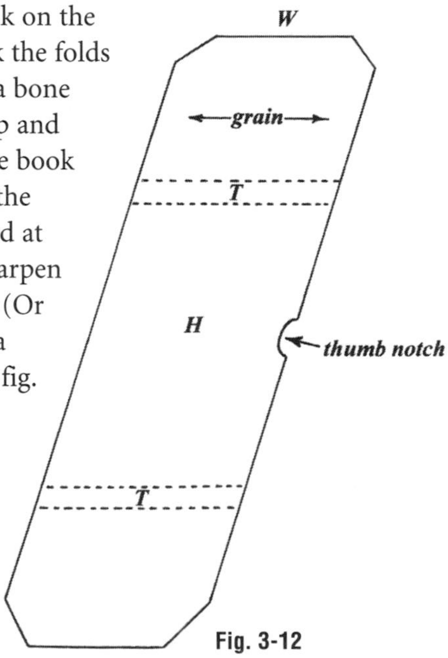

W

←grain→

T

H

←thumb notch

T

Fig. 3-12

Cut a thumb notch on one side. A ¾" gouge (a type of chisel) is useful for this step (fig. 3-13).

Fig. 3-13

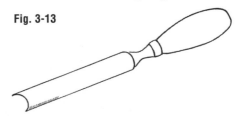

Place the vertical piece on waste mat board; put the blade of the gouge on the spot where the notch will go and use a hammer to cut the notch away.

You can also use a quarter as a template. Draw around it lightly with a pencil and then cut with small scissors.

A V-shaped notch can also be made, but it is more likely to tear than a rounded one.

Angle the corners of the flaps.

Fold the flaps around the book (fig. 3-14). It should fit snugly. Keep the book in this piece of the wrapper while measuring for the next part.

Fig. 3-14

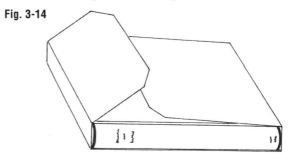

HORIZONTAL PIECE

Place the book, wrapped in the vertical piece, on the board, this time with the grain running parallel to the spine of the book (fig. 3-15).

Cut a long piece the height (H) of the book wrapped in the vertical piece by twice the width, plus 3 times the thickness, plus 2" (5 cm), or H × 2W + 3T + 2" (5 cm).

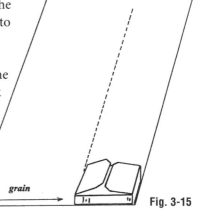

grain

Fig. 3-15

Fig. 3-16

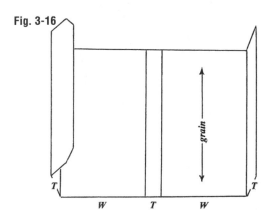

grain

W   T   W

T   T

Make the first fold a little less than one thickness (T) from the right edge and stand the flap up. (See right side of fig. 3-16.) Push the wrapped book against this flap and continue to fold and crease around the book. Sharpen folds with a bone folder. After making the last fold, trim off the excess board, leaving a flap about 2" (5 cm) wide. Angle the corners (fig. 3-16).

Apply double-coated tape to the middle section of the vertical piece, opposite the thumb notch.

Place the horizontal piece on top of the vertical piece. When they are aligned properly, take the paper strip off the double-coated tape and rub the two parts together.

Wrap the book, folding the flaps in the sequence shown in figure 3-17.

Pull flap 5 over the short flap (3) and insert it into the space behind the thumb notch.

Attach title and call number labels on the outside of the narrow panel between flap 5 and panel 4.

Fig. 3-17

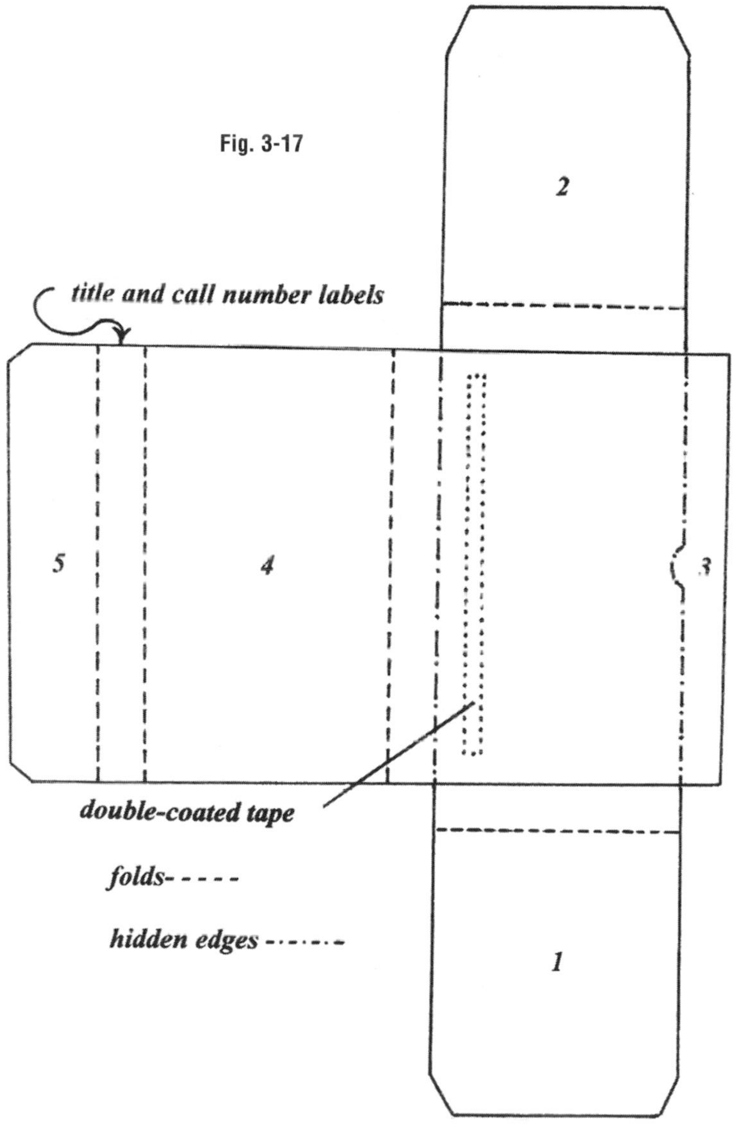

title and call number labels

2

5   4   3

double-coated tape

folds- - - - -

hidden edges - - · - · - · -

1

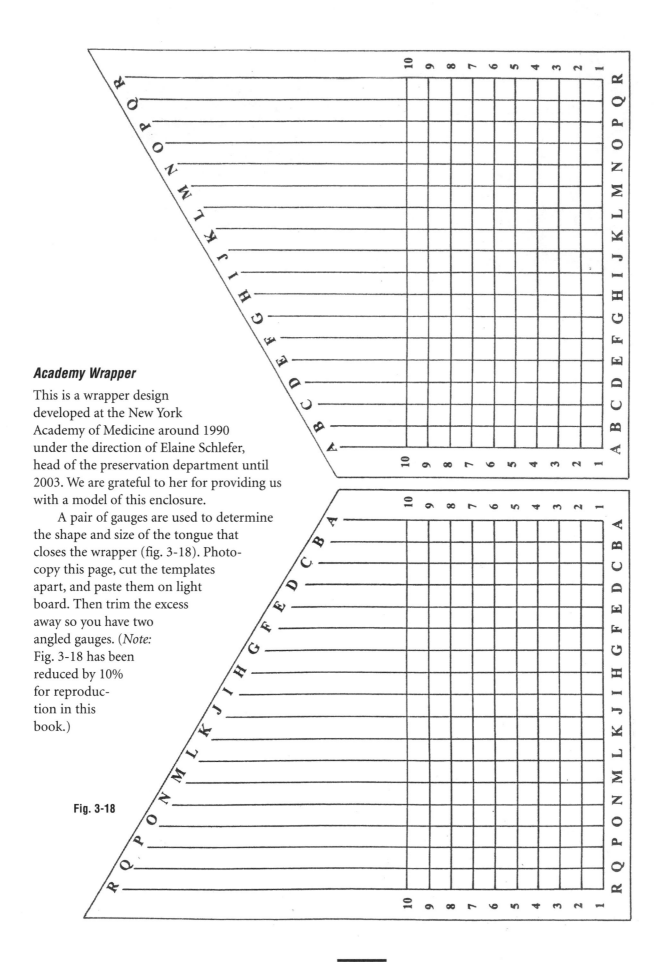

Academy Wrapper

This is a wrapper design developed at the New York Academy of Medicine around 1990 under the direction of Elaine Schlefer, head of the preservation department until 2003. We are grateful to her for providing us with a model of this enclosure.

A pair of gauges are used to determine the shape and size of the tongue that closes the wrapper (fig. 3-18). Photocopy this page, cut the templates apart, and paste them on light board. Then trim the excess away so you have two angled gauges. (*Note:* Fig. 3-18 has been reduced by 10% for reproduction in this book.)

Fig. 3-18

VERTICAL PIECE

Place the book on a sheet of board, making sure the grain of the board is at *right angles* to the spine of the book. Align it along two edges and mark the measurements. Cut a piece of board the width (W) of the book by 3 times its height (H) + twice its thickness (W × 3H + 2T).

Center the book on the vertical piece. Mark the folds on the board with a bone folder, using the top and bottom edges of the book as guides. Remove the book, fold the board at each crease, and sharpen with a bone folder. (Or place the board in a cutter, as shown in fig. 2-47, on p. 51, and crease the folds against the cutting edge of the cutter.) Make sure the folds are parallel to each other (fig. 3-19).

Fold the flaps around the book. It should fit snugly. Keep the book in this piece while measuring for the next part.

HORIZONTAL PIECE

Place the book, wrapped in the vertical piece, on the board, this time with the grain running *parallel* to the spine of the book.

Mark the height of the book, wrapped in the vertical piece, on the board and cut a long piece the height (H) of the book by 3 times the width + twice the thickness (H × 3W + 2T).

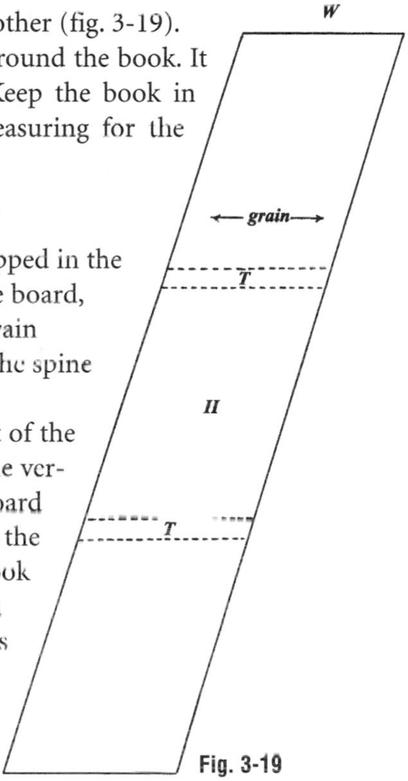

Put the book (in the vertical piece) at one end of the horizontal piece and mark the folds. Take the book out, and crease the folds sharply, making sure they are parallel to each other.

Open the horizontal piece out on the countertop to mark the flap where the tongue will be cut. The tongue should be about 2" (5 cm) wide by about 2" long, but can vary according to the size of the book.

Use the gauge to mark the board so that a tongue of the appropriate size will be left when the excess board is cut away. If the same letters and numbers show at the edges of the board, the tongue will be centered. In figure 3-20, the gauges are positioned at 4, to determine the

Fig. 3-19

length of the tongue, and at P, to determine its width. The tongue is less likely to tear if holes are punched at the corners with an awl before cutting. Cut the board away and then cut the sharp points off the tongue to make it easier to insert into the slit (fig. 3-21).

Fig. 3-20

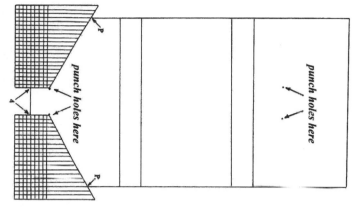

Fig. 3-21

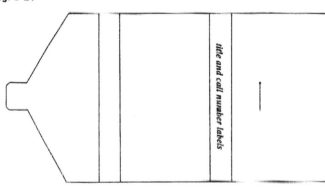

Assemble the two pieces, with the book inside, making sure that the tongue is on top. Make two pencil marks for the slit, using the corners at the base of the tongue as guides. (See right side of fig. 3-20.) Take the horizontal piece off and place it on a cutting mat. The slit should be about ¹⁄₁₆" (2 mm) wider than the tongue. Punch holes at each end, then line up a straightedge with the two holes and cut the slit with a knife. Be careful not to go past the punched holes. (See right side of fig. 3-21.)

Using double-coated tape, connect the two parts of the wrapper together, with the vertical piece *inside* the horizontal one.

Number the flaps as shown in figure 3-22. This is the order in which they should be closed. Put the book in the wrapper, close it, and insert the tongue into the slit.

Attach title and call number labels on the narrow panel next to the panel with the slit. This ensures that the wrapper won't open when it is inserted between books on the shelf.

Fig. 3-22

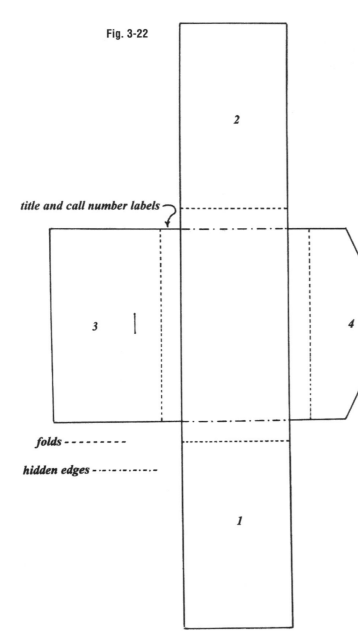

title and call number labels

folds - - - - - - - -

hidden edges - - · - - · - - · - -

Other styles of wrappers are described in NEDCC Technical Leaflet 33, "Card Stock Enclosures for Small Books," by Richard Horton.

Barrier Sheets; Interleaving

It often happens that a book has acidic covers or endpapers that cause the outer pages to become stained. This is sometimes called "acid migration" and is not just a cosmetic problem: as the pages become dark, they also become acidic and brittle.

A simple, very safe way of slowing down the damage is to insert pieces of buffered bond paper between the acidic components and the text pages. This should be done in the course of rehousing, in-house repairs, or whenever the condition is noted. A slightly heavier-weight bond, e.g., at least 24 lbs, is less likely to wrinkle. Cut the paper so it is just a little smaller than the size of the covers and tuck it into the gutter as far as it will go. It will stay in place better if it's cut long grain. Adhesives are not normally used in this step, but it is possible to tip a barrier in place if necessary. (See "Tipping" in section 5, p. 108, for directions on tipping.) Be careful not to adhere the barrier to the title page or other important pages.

Occasionally certain leaves in a book are more acidic or stained than others. Place a barrier sheet on either side. For this application, thinner paper is preferable, to avoid distorting the spine of the book.

Whenever an acidic clipping or document must be stored with other materials, enclose it in a fold of buffered paper, or in a buffered paper envelope, to prevent it from damaging the other items.

The barrier principle can be used in many situations.

Photographs are often mounted to album pages that have become very brittle. Interleaving barrier sheets may make it easier to turn the pages.

Adhesive sometimes oozes from pressure-sensitive tapes used to attach photographs or documents to scrapbooks, or old repairs made with tape may be deteriorating. The barrier sheets will prevent the adhesive from sticking to the facing pages.

When wrapping a particularly brittle map or document, roll it together with a large sheet of buffered paper. This will make it easier to handle the map when it is unrolled and it will also absorb some of the acidity from the object.

When storing brittle maps or prints flat in folders, place barrier sheets of buffered paper between them. If several maps or prints of different sizes are to be stored together in the same folder, interleave them with buffered sheets the same size as the folder.

Conservation suppliers offer buffered wrapping paper, and this is an economical choice for many interleaving operations. For smaller projects, buffered paper is available in sheets of various sizes. Replace interleaving paper or barrier sheets when they look stained or test acidic with a pH pen.

Polyester film can also be used. It does not provide the buffering effects of paper, but it is a superior moisture barrier.

Polyester Encapsulation

In book and paper conservation, the term "encapsulation" refers to the process of sealing a document or other flat object between two sheets of polyester film. The goal is to protect the object during handling and storage and to isolate it from environmental conditions that are likely to damage it.

The technique was first used at the Library of Congress over thirty years ago, when conservators were looking for ways to treat brittle paper without the use of lamination. Lamination with various sheer materials had been practiced for several decades, and it was apparent that some forms of lamination were harmful to paper and also very difficult to undo, or reverse. In contrast, because the polyester film is sealed at the edges only, it does not adhere to the document and the process can be reversed by simply cutting the sealed edges away.

The technical name for polyester film is "polyethylene terepthalate." It is one of the most transparent and colorless plastics and is considered chemically inert. This means that it does not give off noxious gases. There are several types and many thicknesses; not all are suitable for conservation uses.

Over the past three decades, Mylar type D, made by the DuPont Corporation, and Mellinex 516, formerly made by International Chemical Company (ICI) of Great Britain, have been used. DuPont acquired the Mellinex line from ICI several years ago.

The name "Mylar" has become somewhat like "Kleenex" in that it is used in a generic way, as in "Mylar balloon." The Mylar line itself, however, has been discontinued by DuPont, although the Mellinex line is still made. So when we talk about Mylar encapsulation or Mylar sleeves we are really referring to the Mellinex line of polyester film.

A flat item, such as a document or a map, is placed between two sheets of polyester film. The thickness of the film should vary according to the size and weight of the object; the most commonly used thickness is 3-mil, followed by 4-mil.

Originally, the polyester was sealed using double-coated tape. But after a few years, the tape tends to ooze adhesive, and occasionally the document slides into the sticky area and gets caught in it. Sometimes the tape gives way and the polyester comes apart.

While instructions for joining the polyester with double-coated tape are still found frequently, we do not recommend the practice, for the reasons given above. Instead, the edges of the film can be sealed together using one of several machines which weld using ultrasound or heat. The equipment varies widely in price, size, and capabilities. Tabletop models are sold by conservation suppliers, while larger machines are generally built to order.

If you do not have access to an encapsulating machine, there are other options. One is to find a regional center or library binder that offers the service. This might be a very economical choice for an institution with only a few items to encapsulate.

Polyester Sleeves:
An Alternative to Encapsulation

Another solution is to use polyester sleeves, which are available in many sizes and configurations from most conservation suppliers. The sleeves are intended for use with documents, photographic materials, oversize objects, postcards, stamps, and other flat items. Several suppliers can make sleeves to your specifications.

Sleeves with two adjoining edges sealed, often called L-seals, are particularly useful because one layer can be lifted to facilitate inserting the object. The document or print can be set close to the corner and the sealed edges; static will keep the other two edges together. (Make sure the sleeve is at least an inch or two larger than the document.) For materials that will be stored in folders, this may be sufficient protection and there is no need to seal the open edges (fig. 3-23).

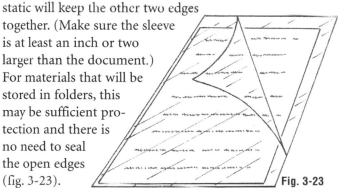 **Fig. 3-23**

It is also possible to purchase L-seals or other sleeves, insert the documents in-house, and then send them to be sealed by a library binder or at a regional center. This reduces handling of fragile originals and makes shipping safer.

Possible Dangers of Polyester Sleeves or Encapsulation

Polyester does not allow moisture to go through it and there is minimal air exchange. When acidic materials are encapsulated, the sealed enclosure may accelerate the process of deterioration. Likewise, dormant mold on encapsulated materials that are stored in sub-ideal conditions may grow more rapidly. To avoid these problems, select a different type of enclosure for questionable materials. If the benefits of polyester outweigh the disadvantages, insert a sheet of buffered paper behind the object to be encapsulated, or in the sleeve. The paper will act like a barrier sheet and will need to be replaced when it becomes acidic.

Polyester film develops static; this is what keeps documents in position in their sleeves. However, static is a hazard for objects that have powdery pigments like pastel or loose flakes such as deteriorated emulsions on photographs. The static can pull the pigment or fragments off the object. This effect becomes much more pronounced in overheated, very dry storage conditions. For such items, select paper enclosures.

The static may also be a hazard when inserting very brittle paper into a sleeve. Place the document on a sheet of buffered paper and slide it in that way. If both sides of the document must remain visible, very gently remove the paper after the document is in place. Otherwise, leave the paper in the sleeve for its buffering effect..

Sleeves can also be made from other plastics, but they cannot be sealed in the same way as polyester. (See "Paper or Plastic?" p. 61, for more information on other safe plastics.)

Polyester Dust Jackets

Polyester film is a very good material for making dust jackets for books. A jacket can be used to protect a book with a deteriorated binding or to keep an intact book in fine condition.

Libraries have used plastic covers to protect the paper dust jackets of circulating books for decades; conservation suppliers now offer a good assortment of styles that are suitable for use with books of permanent value.

They are made from polyester; some styles are made from polypropylene.

Some jacket covers have a white paper lining; a paper dust jacket is inserted between the white paper and the polyester. A torn paper dust jacket can be kept together without repairing it by putting it carefully into this type of cover. Other styles do not have a lining; the plastic is simply folded around the top and bottom edges of the paper dust jacket.

We give instructions for making two types of jackets that are primarily designed for use on books without paper dust jackets. Two-mil or 3-mil polyester film works well for small books; 4-mil or 5-mil is better for larger books.

Simple Book Jacket

A simple polyester dust jacket can be made in six steps.

1. Cut a piece of polyester the same height as the book by about four times the width.

2. Insert one end of the piece inside the front cover of the book, to measure for the first flap. It should reach to about 1" (2.5 cm) from the inner hinge.

3. With your fingers, crimp the polyester at the edge of the book cover, making a mark at the top and another one at the bottom. Remove the polyester from the book and place it on a soft surface, such as a self-healing cutting mat. Score a line connecting the marks, using the pointed end of a bone folder. Fold the polyester and sharpen the crease with the edge of a bone or Teflon folder.

Note: Polyester scratches easily. Rub through a piece of waste paper placed over the polyester to prevent marring the jacket.

4. With the bone folder, make another set of marks next to the first, the thickness of the board, which will be about ⅛" (3 mm). Score the second line and make a second fold, making sure it is parallel to the first (fig. 3-24).

Fig. 3-24

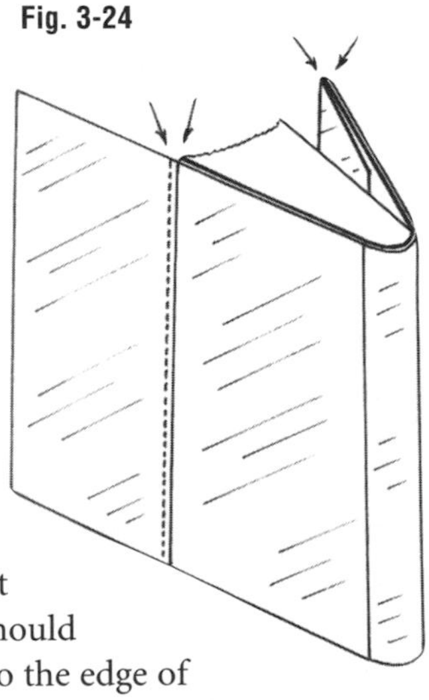

Fit the folded polyester around the front cover. The parallel folds should keep it firmly anchored to the edge of the board. Wrap the polyester around the spine snugly.

5. If the book has a rather squarish spine, the jacket will fit better if the spine is creased.

With your fingers, crimp the polyester at the top and at the bottom to mark the position of the spine (fig. 3-25). Remove the book from the jacket; crease and fold these two lines.

6. Put the jacket back on the book and close the book; make sure the jacket fits snugly. Mark the location of the edge of the back cover on the jacket. Make two folds on the polyester to accommodate the thickness of the board, the same as at the front.

Fig. 3-25

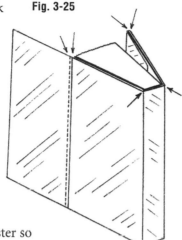

Cut the excess polyester so the back flap comes to about 1" (2.5 cm) from the inner hinge.

Tape is not needed; the creases at the edges of the boards and the wide inner flaps will keep the jacket from coming off the book.

Some older books have very rounded spines. Do not make folds for the spine on those jackets; skip step 5 and go directly to step 6. Make sure to wrap the polyester around the spine snugly and make the folds for the boards of the book accurately.

Tube Book Jacket

This jacket is made the way children used to make jackets for school books from brown paper. Two-mil or 3-mil polyester is suitable for this jacket. The style is particularly useful for books with red rot because it covers the edges of the boards. It can also be made from acid-free wrapping paper or from a decorative paper, if the book needs to be made presentable for an exhibition or other purpose. The jacket is made in ten steps.

1. Measure the book and cut a piece of polyester 2½ times its height by four times its width.

Mark the height of the book at both ends of the polyester as shown in figure 3-26. Crimp with your fingers or mark with a thin waterproof marker.

2. Place a long straightedge on one set of marks and score. Repeat with the second set. This defines the outside panel of the jacket.

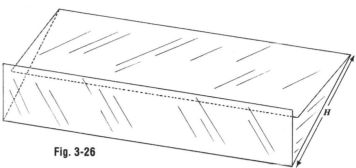

Fig. 3-26

3. Crease the flaps down over the outside panel and rub them down with a bone folder through a piece of waste paper, to avoid scratching the polyester. The flaps will overlap on the inside of the jacket (fig. 3-26).

4. Center the book on the folded polyester and wrap the jacket around it snugly.

5. Mark the location of the corners of the covers on the polyester, at the top and at the bottom. Remove the book from the jacket and place the jacket on a soft surface such as a cutting mat, with the inside facing up.

6. Align a straightedge on the marks, score the polyester with a bone folder, crease it, and then rub it down with the bone folder.

7. Make a second set of marks, ⅛" (3 mm) from the first fold. Score and crease another fold, making sure it is parallel to the first fold (fig. 3-27).

Repeat these steps on the other end of the polyester tube.

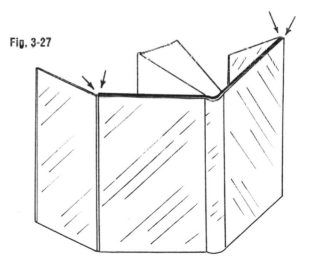

Fig. 3-27

8. Put the jacket around the book and tuck the flaps in. They should end about 1" (2.5 cm) from the inner hinge; trim if too long. If the jacket fits well, take the flaps out and open the book.

9. Open one flap a little and insert the front board of the book into it. Repeat with the back board.

10. Smooth the polyester around the boards and make sure that the edges fit well into the parallel creases.

If desired, you can put a short strip of double-coated tape on the inside of the book jacket. Open the book, to allow the jacket to move away, and insert the tape near the edge. Remove the paper lining of the tape to fasten the flaps to the inside of the book jacket (fig. 3-28).

With this method, the jacket can slide back and forth as the book is opened and closed but it does not come off. The tape is not in contact with the book cover or the endpapers and there is no danger of adhesive oozing onto the book.

Fig. 3-28

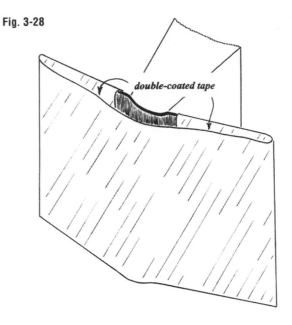

double-coated tape

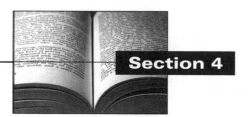

Paper Conservation Techniques

MOST MATERIALS IN A LIBRARY OR ARCHIVE ARE composed at least in part of paper. For this reason, a basic grasp of the nature of paper is helpful for understanding the steps required to preserve and repair books, documents, maps, prints, and so on. We will also give information about supplies and equipment, to assist people who are setting up a work area. The handling techniques in part 3 of this section include preliminaries that often come before repairs. This information supplements the advice found at the beginning of section 3 and should be helpful to those who are primarily involved in rehousing archives and other materials.

The repair techniques in part 4 are intended for use on research collections. This category includes materials that have permanent scholarly value but are not considered rare. These techniques are not meant to be applied to artwork, photographs, or rare books.

This section is divided into four parts.

1. "Overview of Western and Japanese Paper" gives a brief account of the history of paper and explains some of the characteristics that affect the way it works.
2. "Supplies and Equipment Needed for Paper Repairs" describes the materials and tools used to make paper repairs.
3. "Techniques for Handling Paper" covers methods for cleaning, flattening, and moving paper objects.
4. "Paper Repair Techniques" contains illustrated instructions for making simple paper repairs on loose documents as well as the paper in books.

OVERVIEW OF WESTERN AND JAPANESE PAPER

Note: The following account is but a tiny glimpse into the fascinating and extensive history of papermaking. Dard Hunter's *Papermaking: The History and Technique of an Ancient Craft* is considered by many to be the bible of papermaking history books. It is listed in the bibliography with several other works on the subject.

Although paperlike materials were developed in Egypt, Ethiopia, Mexico, and doubtless other places as well, the ancestor of paper as we know it is said to have been invented in China around AD 100. In the eighth century, Arabs learned of it from the Chinese and its use gradually spread to the West by way of the trading routes. It was introduced by the Moors into Spain in the tenth century. According to paper historian Dard Hunter, paper began to be used in Italy, France, and Germany in the twelfth and thirteenth centuries and arrived in the Netherlands and England in the early fourteenth century. The manufacture of paper is thought to have started about a hundred years after its introduction in each locale.

The word "paper" comes from "papyrus," the writing material of the ancient Egyptians and other Mediterranean peoples. Papyrus was made by slicing the pith, or inner portion, of sedge plants, soaking the strips in water and then laying them side by side in a rectangle. Another layer of wet strips was put crosswise on top of this and the two layers were pressed until they were dry and stuck together. This differs considerably from true paper, as we will see below.

European paper was originally made from linen and cotton rags that had been shredded and broken down into fibers. The shredded rags and some sizing material were added to a large quantity of water to form the "pulp" from which the sheets were made. The sheet-forming method developed then is still the basis for modern hand papermaking. A mold (i.e., a screen) is dipped at an angle into the vat of pulp, then lifted out, also at an angle. This allows most of the water to drain away, while the fibers remain on the screen. The mold is shaken back and forth and left to right to drain more water. In the process, the fibers interlock. The pulp is then left on the mold for a few minutes to let more water drain. After a while, the mold is turned over, positioning the freshly made sheet of paper on a blanket made of wool felt. This is called "couching." Another felt blanket is placed on the sheet and the next wet sheet of paper is couched on the top blanket. The process is repeated until the stack, or "post," of sheets is the proper size. Then the pile is taken to a large press, where the remaining water is pressed out. Next, the post is removed from the press and the sheets are separated from the blankets. They may be pressed again without felts or they may be hung to dry, depending on the surface finish desired. Handmade paper is still made essentially the same way, but it is an infinitesimal portion of the paper produced today.

In the nineteenth century, the demand for paper in Europe and America became so great that there were not enough rags available to make pulp in the traditional way. Papermakers started experimenting with different types of plant fibers. By midcentury, wood pulp began to be used. But wood pulp must be treated with various chemicals to make it fit for papermaking, and many of the additives that have been used for the past 150 years decrease the paper's durability.

Characteristics of Western Papers

Laid Paper

In Europe before about 1800, molds were made by attaching individual wires to a rectangular wooden frame. Wires placed close together go from left to right and are secured to each other by wires installed at right angles and about an inch apart. The wires impress the familiar "laid" pattern on the sheets of paper. The very closely spaced lines are the laid lines. The widely spaced lines at right angles to the laid lines are called chain lines (fig. 4-1).

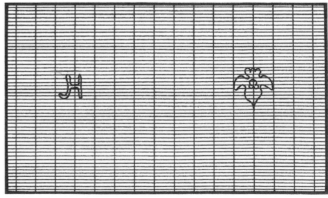

Fig. 4-1 Laid paper mold

WATERMARKS

A watermark is a design made from wire and attached to the wires of a laid mold or to a wove screen. As the sheet of paper is formed on the mold, the design is impressed into it, so that the sheet is slightly thinner over the outline of the watermark. The marks are easy to see when the sheet is held up to the light because the paper is more translucent in that area (fig. 4-2).

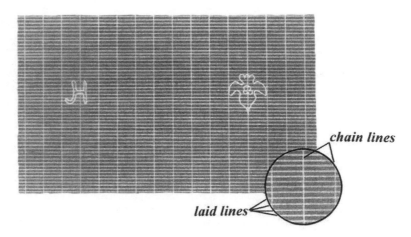

Fig. 4-2 A sheet of laid paper held against the light

Wove Paper

In the late eighteenth century, the manufacture of drawn brass wire was refined and improved; this made it possible to manufacture very tightly woven screens that could be attached to the frames of molds. The paper made on screen molds does not show any lines. It is called "wove" (not "woven"). Wove paper became more common as the nineteenth century progressed.

For several decades at the beginning of the nineteenth century, both wove and laid papers were used in Europe, often in the same book. For instance, the text pages of a book might be printed on laid paper, while the plates were engraved on the smoother wove paper.

Both laid and wove papers were watermarked to indicate the mill where they were made and other characteristics as well, such as size or date of manufacture. But paper might be stored for many years before it was used, so the watermark date might be quite a bit earlier than the imprint date of the book.

Machine-Made Paper

Papermaking machines began to be developed around the year 1800. For the next few decades, both hand and machine-made paper were produced.

The machines perform all the steps needed to turn pulp into a roll of paper. The pulp flows onto a moving belt. As it moves forward, the belt vibrates, keeping the fibers from sinking to the bottom and also causing the water to drain away. This combined motion makes the fibers interlock but it also makes them align themselves in the direction the belt is moving. The comparison is sometimes made to logs floating down a river. Most of the logs are parallel to the flow of the river, not across it.

The grain of machine-made paper is always the same as the belt direction, along the length of the belt, not across it, and it is quite pronounced. It is sometimes called the "machine direction." Paper has much more strength in the grain direction.

Machine-made paper may show laid and chain lines as well as watermarks; they are made by a series of rollers that pass over the belt as the paper is being made. So the presence of these patterns on Western paper is not necessarily an indication that the paper is handmade.

Characteristics of Japanese Papers

Japanese and other East Asian papers have always been made directly from plants rather than from rags. The plant material is treated in various ways to break it down into fibers and then added to a vat of water. Most Japanese papers have much longer fibers than Western papers; this characteristic makes them very strong and good choices for repairs. The surface of the paper is usually quite soft and the sheets are very flexible.

The manufacturing method has remained fairly constant for centuries. The paper is made on matlike molds which have thin bamboo strips (producing the "laid" lines) laced together with horsehair or vegetable fiber (which produce the "chain" lines). The sheets are formed by dipping the molds into a vat of pulp. The molds leave chain line and laid line marks on the paper. Some of the steps are done with the assistance of machinery, but most Japanese paper is basically handmade.

The grain of handmade Japanese papers runs with the chain lines. It is not as pronounced as it is in Western paper, but it is easier to tear Japanese paper in the grain direction. (In conservation work, the paper used for repairs is almost always torn, as we will see.)

Machine-Made Japanese Paper

In the late twentieth century, rolls of machine-made Japanese papers became available. They are wove papers; i.e., they do not show chain and laid lines. The grain of these roll papers is in the machine direction, the same as in Western papers. It is somewhat more marked than the grain of handmade Japanese papers.

Testing Paper for Grain Direction

The grain affects how paper behaves when it is folded, moistened, and torn. Determining grain direction is a basic skill that must be mastered when learning how to repair books and papers. The following are some tips to help you find the grain direction of paper. (See "Grain Direction" in section 2, p. 46, for information on determining grain in other materials.)

Chain Lines. Many papers have lines that are visible when the sheet is held in front of a light source. In handmade paper, the grain is always parallel to ("with") the chain lines. Since chain and laid lines are artificially imposed on machine-made paper, the grain could in theory be either way. But by tradition, the chain lines run in the machine direction, with the grain.

The following are several tests for determining the grain of paper.

Folding. Curl the sheet over in one direction and then in the other. It will fold more easily one way. The direction with the *least resistance* is parallel to the grain (figs. 4-3 and 4-4).

Fig. 4-3   *fold with grain*

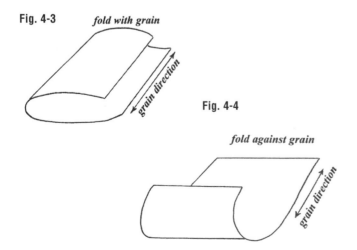

Fig. 4-4

fold against grain

The next two tests are suitable only for *new materials* used for repair or rehousing, not for documents or book pages.

Wetting. Wet the sheet along just two edges with a cotton swab (fig. 4-5). The grain is parallel to the edge that stays smoother. The other wet edge will be much more rippled (fig. 4-6).

Fig. 4-5

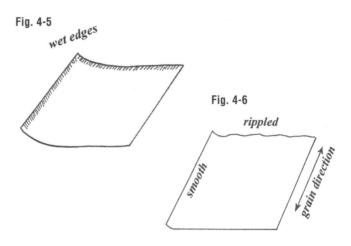

wet edges

Fig. 4-6

rippled

smooth

grain direction

Tearing. Tear a test piece. The paper rips easily with the grain. Ripping against the grain offers more resistance and produces a clearly ragged tear. The grain is parallel to the straighter tear (fig. 4-7).

Fig. 4-7

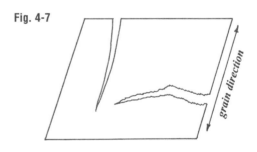

grain direction

Testing pH

It is important to select acid-free paper or boards to use for repairs. Acidic materials can stain and damage documents or book pages; furthermore, repairs made with acidic paper or board will not last as long.

The simplest way to determine whether a particular paper or board is acid-free is by using a pH pen, available from conservation suppliers. A small mark is made on the material being tested; if the material is neutral or buffered, the mark changes from yellow to magenta (or from green to blue, depending on the indicator chemical in the pen). Instructions for use come with the pens.

Do not use a pH pen to test documents or book pages. The mark cannot be removed.

If you find old repair papers or boards that have been in storage for several years, test them before use. Although the material may have been acid-free when it was bought, it might have become acidic while in storage, from exposure to environmental pollutants.

Photographs

This book does not cover any type of treatment for photographs because it is a separate field of paper conservation that requires special training and equipment. There are many types of photographs, each needing distinct types of treatment. Good environmental conditions and proper sleeves, envelopes, and other storage containers will keep photographic materials in stable condition. (See appendix A, "Care of Photographs.") For the treatment or repair of photographs, consult a conservator who specializes in this field.

SUPPLIES AND EQUIPMENT NEEDED FOR PAPER REPAIRS

Repair Papers

Papers of various types (mostly Japanese) and adhesives are the two main materials used to mend papers. A few hand tools are necessary, and it is helpful but not essential to have some pieces of equipment.

When to Use Japanese or Western Paper

Japanese paper is preferred for almost all mending steps. It comes in many thicknesses and different shades of white as well as many colors. Sekishu and Kizukishi are two papers of a natural white color that are carried by most conservation suppliers and can fill a wide variety of needs. But many other papers are available from more specialized distributors (see appendix B). It is a good idea to purchase a swatch book, to get an idea of the differences in color and weight. Some Japanese papers are costly, but there are also many good, economical choices. Repairs generally require quite small pieces, so the sheets can last a long time.

The surface of Japanese paper is usually soft, and repairs blend in. The long fibers make even very thin papers quite strong. One of its most useful properties is that it can be torn into strips or pieces with feathered edges. Torn edges are softer than cut edges and are not so likely to cut or damage the paper being mended, especially if it is fragile. In time, an assortment of scraps of various weights, sizes, and tones will accumulate. Keep them in a box or envelope and you will frequently find the perfect piece for a repair right at your fingertips.

Western papers are most appropriate for endpaper replacements and for making storage containers, barrier sheets, and book covers. In general, Western papers are stiffer and have a harder surface than Japanese papers.

Be sure to have a good way to store your repair papers so they are not damaged (see "Storage" in section 2, p. 35).

Adhesives

For repairing book pages and other paper objects, select an adhesive with the right properties.

A. It should have the right amount of strength to hold the object indefinitely, but the hold should not be stronger than the paper itself. Ideally, the adhesive should release before the object tears.

B. It should not leave a residue, and it should be easy to reverse without causing damage to the object. The adhesive itself should not discolor and it should not stain the paper over time.

Few commonly available adhesives meet all these criteria. Furthermore, the formulation of commercial products can change without notice, so it is better to rely on products made specifically for the conservation field.

Problems with Some Adhesives

COMMERCIAL TAPES

Pressure-sensitive (self-adhering) tapes should be avoided. These tapes have two layers: the film "carrier" and the adhesive. Most of the adhesives cause staining over time or else ooze out from under the carrier. They require solvents and technical skill for removal.

In the late twentieth century, pressure-sensitive tapes advertised as "archival" were introduced. Many are more stable than regular tapes; they do not yellow and adhesive does not ooze out from the edges even after aging. But they are hard to remove and their aging properties are not really known yet. Do not use them for anything of lasting value. The tapes are quick and convenient fixes for circulating and other materials that are not meant to be kept, e.g., an annual directory that is discarded when the new one comes in. They are often used for repairing newspapers before microfilming.

WHITE GLUES

White glues are not normally used in paper repair because their hold is too strong. They are very difficult to remove once dry, and even more so when they have aged. Mends made with white glue are stiff and translucent; the edge of the mend is usually shiny and the whole repair has a sloppy look. The glues are appropriate for use in book repairs and are described in "Adhesives" in section 5, p. 103.

GLUE STICKS

There are several brands of these on the market, and many are advertised as being "acid-free." And so they are, but unfortunately, they err on the side of being too alkaline. Some glue sticks range between pH 10 and 14. For comparison, paper is considered neutral or acid-free if it is between 6 and 7 pH. Buffered materials usually have a pH of 8.5. The highly alkaline glue sticks cause color changes in paper after several months or a few years. The adhesive sometimes dries up and the mend comes apart. Glue sticks are good for temporary uses such as general office work, but they are not suitable for materials of lasting value.

RUBBER CEMENT

Never use rubber cement! It gives off toxic gases that are harmful to the worker. As it ages, it dries up, releasing its hold and staining paper. It damages paper irreversibly.

Good Adhesives for Paper Repair

STARCH PASTE

Starch pastes, made from wheat, rice, and other plants, have been used to repair paper for many centuries. Paste is a reliable adhesive with a known track record, both in Asia and in the West.

Paste is prepared by mixing a powdered starch with water and cooking it while stirring. It can be made thick, with less moisture content, or thin, for easier spreading. It is slow drying and gives plenty of time for positioning

fragments of paper as desired. Any excess that might ooze out from a repair can be removed and will not usually leave a stain. Repairs made with paste can be reversed easily with moisture.

Cooked paste does not have a long shelf life. It will grow mold after a time and may also separate and become "weepy." When either of these conditions are noticed, the paste must be thrown out.

Recipe for Making Paste

Make a slurry of two tablespoons of starch paste powder added to a few teaspoons of *cold* water in a large heat-proof cup or bowl. Pour approximately one cup of boiling water into the slurry while stirring briskly. It should thicken and become translucent. Put the mixture in a microwave oven, cook one or two minutes, take out, whisk, cook another couple of minutes, etc., until the paste is smooth and tacky. Transfer to a very clean, smaller container and cover the surface of the hot paste with boiled water or with a piece of plastic wrap. Let cool. Keep the container in the refrigerator.

When a task calls for paste, do not take the main supply to the workbench. Instead, take out the amount needed and sieve it into a heavy glass or ceramic bowl (or strain through a double layer of damp cheesecloth). If the paste is too thick, add water a few drops at a time to achieve the desired consistency.

The paste may keep for a week or two, depending on the weather and on how clean the storage container was when the paste was put in it. Sometimes older paste can be reconstituted by giving it a brief boil on the stove or in the microwave oven. (Never try this if the paste looks or smells bad or moldy.) Stir it with a whisk while reheating and after sieving. Try using the reconstituted paste on a test piece and see if it is still sticky. If not, discard.

Stickiness Test

Pick up a little dab of paste and roll it between your index finger and thumb. It should feel tacky and not just wet. Next, separate your fingers and see if the paste stretches a bit as they open (fig. 4-8). If the paste breaks apart immediately, it will be not be sufficiently sticky to make paper repairs. It may need to be cooked and stirred more, or in the case of older paste, it may have started to turn bad. Discard and make fresh paste.

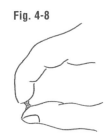

Fig. 4-8

Making Paste on a Stove

Starch paste can also be made on a hot plate or stove. A double boiler is ideal; otherwise, you can use a Teflon-coated pot. Make a slurry of two tablespoons of starch paste powder added to a few teaspoons of *cold* water. Pour approximately one cup of boiling water into the slurry while stirring briskly. Mix constantly during cooking, to prevent the formation of lumps and to keep it from sticking or burning. The technique is similar to making gravy.

Do not add any preservatives to paste. If you need a slow-drying, easily reversible adhesive only occasionally, it will probably be more efficient to keep a supply of methylcellulose on hand. It will last for several months if it doesn't become contaminated.

METHYLCELLULOSE

This adhesive is made from cotton fibers treated with an alkali; it is sold as a white powder to be mixed with water by the user. It is not as strong as starch paste but is a perfectly suitable and safe adhesive for the type of paper mending carried out in most libraries and archives.

Recipe for Mixing Methylcellulose

Stir five tablespoons of methylcellulose powder *briskly* into one cup of *very hot* water; this step is key to making the powder disperse rather than clump. When the powder is thoroughly mixed, add enough *cold* water to make one quart. It should start to thicken immediately. Cover and let sit for several hours; preferably overnight. To thin, add a few drops of water, mix, let stand. When ready to use, decant a small amount into a heavy, wide-mouth jar. Never dip the brush into the main supply; this will contaminate the adhesive and it will spoil more quickly. Thick methylcellulose can be used for mending paper with Japanese tissue and to clean off the spines of books. The mixed adhesive needs no refrigeration and will last for months if kept clean.

Hand Tools

A few small tools are needed for paper repair. Keep them in good condition and don't use them for other tasks. Some items can be purchased from the suppliers listed in appendix B; others come from art supply, building supply, or hardware stores.

- Bone and Teflon folders, of different sizes. They are described in "Hand Tools" in section 2, p. 45.

- Microspatulas. Stainless steel ones are inexpensive and useful for many operations; it's good to have several on hand.
- Paste brushes. An assortment of sizes, e.g., ¼", ½", 1", is helpful. Nylon or polyester paintbrushes with bristles that taper into a wedge are fine. Make sure the bristles don't come off. Some artists' brushes are also useful, especially flat brushes, but this is a matter of personal preference. A great variety of styles is available, at widely ranging prices. Experiment to see what works best for your applications. Whatever types of brushes are selected, keep them clean and use them only for paste. (PVA and mix, used in book repair, are impossible to remove completely from brushes. These brushes are always stiffer than brushes used for paste alone.)
- Soft brushes for removing dust and eraser crumbs
- Erasers, cleaning sponges
- Good scissors; a large pair and a small one
- Mounted needle or fine awl
- Fine tweezers
- Metal rulers or straightedges
- Water brushes (e.g., Niji, size Small, made by Yasumoto) or felt-tip pens (such as Letraset no. 73215) filled with plain water
- Tacking iron or small travel iron
- Hair dryer

Equipment

The following items are optional, but very useful:

- Sieve for straining paste. Round sieves with flat tops are available from Asian grocery stores.
- Fine mist sprayer
- Light box
- Dry mount press; this is usually used cold, so it need not be in working condition

Other Supplies

Other supplies include the following:

- Several bricks, to be used as weights. Store them indoors until they are completely dry, then wrap them in heavy paper to protect countertops and materials being mended.

- Small weights, up to 2" or 3" (5 or 7.5 cm) in length or diameter. They can be purchased from suppliers, but many objects can be used as weights, for instance, small boxes or film canisters filled with sand or lead shot (or a combination of the two). Old lead type can be tied or taped together and wrapped in heavy paper, or placed in small boxes.
- Several wooden pressing boards, at least 16" × 20". Sheets of thick (at least ⅜") acrylic glazing (Plexiglas) can be used as well.
- A stack of acid-free binder's board, for flattening and drying operations
- Blotters. White, acid-free blotting paper is available from conservation suppliers. It is useful to have whole sheets as well as pieces cut to smaller sizes, e.g., 3" × 3" for small mends; 3" × 10" for drying hinged pages, and so on, are useful.
- Spun polyester web (Hollytex, Reemay). This is a nonwoven fabric that allows moisture and air to pass but prevents adhesives from sticking to blotters or other materials. Cut some to same sizes as blotter pieces.
- Polyester film (e.g., Mylar or Mellinex) for moisture barriers, and for tracing the outline of "fills"
- Waste paper (unprinted newsprint) for pasting on, covering surfaces, etc.

TECHNIQUES FOR HANDLING PAPER

People who handle documents and other paper objects all the time develop a certain ease that allows them to work quickly without damaging the materials (or getting paper cuts). If you are new to this kind of work, start by working slowly and methodically; give yourself time and the ease will come with practice.

Preparing Materials before Putting Them into Enclosures

In section 3 we discussed a number of storage containers, or preservation enclosures. Documents should be examined for harmful fasteners, surface dirt, insect evidence, and mold before being placed into enclosures. Any items with evidence of insects or mold should be treated as described in "Mold" in section 1, p. 17, or sent to a conservator.

Removing Fasteners and Rubber Bands

Staples and paper clips are the two metal fasteners that are most commonly found on archival or research materials. The fastener often rusts and the rust proceeds to eat away the paper around the fastener. Clips also cause indentations and creases in the paper.

PAPER CLIPS

Removing sound paper clips from strong paper is a quick operation. Place the document on a clean blotter, for padding, with the long part of the paper clip against the blotter. Hold the long leg of the clip down through the document and lift the short leg with fingertip or nail and pry up a bit so the document can slide out. The tip of a microspatula can be used, gently, if it is more convenient.

The leaves of the document can then be held together by placing them in an acid-free envelope or in a fold of paper. Another option (again, for strong paper only) is to fold a small piece of heavy acid-free paper over the leaves to be held together and then put a stainless steel paper clip over it.

Plastic paper clips or plastic-coated metal clips do not rust, but they do make big indentations in the paper. They are not for archival materials.

Clips that have just begun to rust can be removed if the clip has not yet become attached to the paper. Do it very carefully.

If the clip is so rusted that it has completely fused with the paper, do not try to remove it. Simply enclose the whole document in a buffered paper envelope to protect its neighbors from the rust. A conservator may be able to remove the fastener and repair the paper.

STAPLES

Regular staples rust if stored in humid areas, the same as paper clips, but they don't distort paper as much as clips do. Removing staples is a bit more complicated than removing clips. If the relative humidity in the storage space is strictly controlled, it may not be necessary to remove all staples, particularly those holding pamphlets together.

To remove a staple from a document in good condition, place it on a piece of blotter, for padding, with the legs of the staples facing up. Use a small, dull blade to pry each leg up. Then turn the document over and carefully insert the blade under the staple to lift it out. Micro-spatulas work well, but sometimes they get scratched in the process and can snag delicate papers if used for other purposes afterwards. (They can be polished with very fine sandpaper or a fine sharpening stone, or, simply dedicate a microspatula for staple removal and don't use it for anything else.)

If the paper is fragile or the rust has spread from the staple to the document, it may not be possible to remove the staple without further damage to the paper. When in doubt, enclose the document in a buffered envelope to isolate it from other materials and consult a conservator.

When staples are removed from a pamphlet, another method has to be used for holding it together. If the paper is in good condition, stainless steel or other non-rusting staples can be used. Otherwise, sew it with linen thread as described in "Pamphlets" in section 5, p. 144. It may be necessary to repair or reinforce the paper in the area where the staple was removed.

RUBBER BANDS

Cut the rubber band and then remove it from the object. If the rubber band has already begun to deteriorate, it may be stuck to the paper. Remove as much as comes off easily in pieces. A microspatula may help. Don't pull off bits that refuse to budge; be careful not to damage the paper. If the residue is still sticky, place the object into an individual enclosure to isolate it from its neighbors.

To keep the documents as a group, they can be placed into an acid-free envelope or other convenient enclosure.

When sorting through a box of documents, broken rubber bands in various stages of decomposition are often found at the bottom. Get rid of them. As rubber breaks down, it gives off gases that are noxious to paper. There are no "safe" kinds of rubber bands.

OTHER FASTENERS

Old documents sometimes have old, unusual fasteners made of metal, string, wax, and other materials. Consult the librarian or curator to find out if these fasteners should be removed. The fasteners might add to the historical or monetary value of the document. If this is the case, leave the fastener in place and simply enclose the document in an acid-free envelope.

For more information on the topic, consult NEDCC Technical Leaflet 54, "Removal of Damaging Fasteners from Historic Documents."

Surface Cleaning

Cleaning dust and debris from book pages and documents is the next step after removing harmful fasteners. It is time-consuming but must be done carefully in order not to damage the paper. One of the main benefits is that it forces the worker to look at the whole surface of the object; this often reveals conditions not noticed at first glance. These should be taken into account when determining if further treatment is necessary.

Some works may refer to the "dry cleaning" of paper; this is an older term for surface cleaning and does not imply the use of chemicals or solvents. Surface cleaning removes surface dirt; it will not remove embedded stains such as greasy fingerprints.

Various brushes, sponges, vinyl erasers, eraser crumbs, cloths, and cleaning pads have been used over the years for surface cleaning. The cleaning pads are composed of fine eraser crumbs inside a small, knit bag. The cleaning crumbs are forced out through the fabric onto the paper; then the bag is used to rub the crumbs over the paper. We do not use these because the fine crumbs cause a lot of airborne dust, and it is sometimes hard to get all the crumbs out of the gutters of books when cleaning pages. A simple arsenal of a soft brush, cleaning cloths, cleaning sponges, and vinyl erasers is generally sufficient for most work.

Start by placing the document on a large sheet of clean newsprint. This makes it easier to catch the crumbs. Clean the surface with a soft brush. Sometimes a cleaning cloth, such as a Dust Bunny, works well for the initial wiping. If more cleaning is needed, use cleaning sponges or erasers. As you work, make sure no crumbs get under the document, between it and the work surface beneath. This makes the surface of the paper uneven and can cause damage as the eraser goes over the lumps. Work from the middle out (fig. 4-9). When close to the edges, rub toward and off the edge to prevent tearing. Among brands of erasers currently recommended are the Staedtler Mars vinyl eraser and the Eberhard Faber 1954 Magic Rub. They can be purchased from conservation and art suppliers.

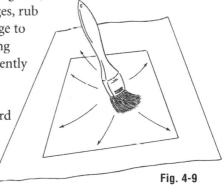

Fig. 4-9

Rubber cleaning sponges without additives, such as those made by Gonzo, are available from conservation catalogs. They should always be used dry, *not wet*. The plain, natural color sponges are very useful for cleaning book pages, documents, and maps (fig. 4-10). They are excellent for removing soot from paper and other materials.

Fig. 4-10

Cut the sponge into two or three pieces. As each erasing surface gets dirty, cut it away with large scissors or a serrated knife. The sponges can be washed but take several days to dry thoroughly; they don't work as well after washing as they do when new, and we replace sponges rather than wash them.

The sponges can be used to clean light mold, as described in "Mold" in section 1, p. 17. Be sure to discard them immediately after use, to prevent spreading the mold to other materials.

Erasers are helpful for removing spots. As with the sponges, rub in one direction only, not back and forth: this can cause wrinkles and tears. Rub toward and off the edges to prevent tears. When cleaning is completed, inspect the work and brush all eraser residue from the pages and from the gutter of the book.

BRITTLE PAPER

Clean paper that is brittle with a soft brush *only;* do not use the other methods described above.

REMOVING DEBRIS
FROM THE GUTTER OF A BOOK

A lot of extraneous matter can be found in the gutters of books. Dirt accumulates over the life of the book and, in addition, people often leave things in books. Almost every imaginable object has been discovered in the process of surface cleaning the pages of a book, from slips of paper to pressed flowers to slices of ham.

To clean the gutters, lay the book on the counter and begin at the front, or back, according to your preference. Open the pages one by one and brush the debris out with a brush (fig. 4-11). Reserve the brush for this purpose only and replace it when it gets too filthy or misshapen.

For more detailed instructions on surface cleaning, see Greenfield, *Books: Their Care and Repair;* Kyle, *Library Materials Preservation Manual;* and NEDCC Technical Leaflet 46, "Surface Cleaning of Paper," by Sherelyn Ogden.

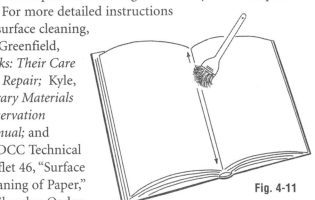

Fig. 4-11

Relaxing and Flattening Paper

In the course of a rehousing project, it is common to come upon great quantities of documents, maps, or posters that have been stored folded for many years. When the objects are opened, they usually will not lie flat because the paper has acquired a memory of the folds. The same applies to materials that have been rolled up for a long time. In order to store them in folders, sleeves, or envelopes, the paper must be flattened *gradually*. Flattening by force, such as by placing in a press, will damage fragile paper. Furthermore, as soon as the document is removed from the press, it is likely to revert to its former shape.

Note: If the paper is brittle, or if there is a lot of adhesive tape or other unusual conditions, a conservator should be consulted. Works of art on paper or materials with high monetary or historical value should also be referred to a conservator.

HUMIDIFYING FOLDED OR
ROLLED DOCUMENTS

In order to flatten a document that has been folded or rolled, it is a good idea to humidify it. This is especially important during the heating season, when indoor air is very dry, since dryness makes paper more brittle. Attempts at flattening brittle paper often result in the paper splitting.

Moisture must be introduced very gradually and evenly. Paper stretches when it gets wet, as we discussed earlier in the segment on determining grain. Spraying water or wetting the paper with a sponge are likely to result in overly wet areas as well as dry areas. This means that the document will stretch at different rates, depending on how wet each area is. Furthermore, overwetting might cause inks to run. Tide lines (water stains) are also likely. A gradual increase in humidity over the whole document can sometimes relax it enough so that it will lie flat.

In areas with humid summers, it may well be possible to relax a rolled map or folded document by simply leaving it uncovered for a week or more in a room that has no air conditioning. Check periodically to make sure there is no mold development. It might be a good idea to schedule a project that includes flattening materials for the summer months in order to take advantage of the head start afforded by the weather. Even if the materials need more humidification, they will be more pliable than during the heating season.

The safest way to further humidify rolled and folded materials is to enclose them in a chamber where the humidity can be raised significantly without the object coming into contact with water. Many types of containers can be used for this purpose; we give directions for two here.

Humidification Chamber

A simple humidification chamber can be made using a large, shallow plastic container with a tight-fitting lid, such as those sold for storing rolls of gift wrap. A container with sloping sides works well. Place a couple of blotters in the bottom and soak them with water. Cut a piece of plastic "egg crate" grid (sold in electrical supply stores) or any lightweight, rigid plastic grid to size so it sits about 3"–4" (7–10 cm) from the bottom, resting on the sloping sides. Set the container in a place where it can stay without being disturbed. Keep it out of the sun to reduce condensation. Lay a piece of dry blotter on the plastic grid and cover it with polyester web, e.g., Hollytex.

Unfold the documents or loosen the rolled materials a little without causing strain to the paper. Place them on the grid, on top of the polyester web and blotter. Put another piece of web loosely over the documents and a blotter over that, to catch condensation that might form on the inside of the lid and drip on the objects. (See fig. 4-12)

Horton Humidifier

Carolyn Horton, a noted conservator active from the 1950s to about 1990, began using a plastic humidity chamber in the 1960s.

It consists of a clean plastic trash can with a tight-fitting lid. Place a smaller plastic can inside. Arrange one or more damp blotters *between* the two cans (fig. 4-13).

Cut a piece of dry blotter so it fits snugly into the lid. This blotter will catch any condensation that might form on the underside of the lid and drip onto the documents.

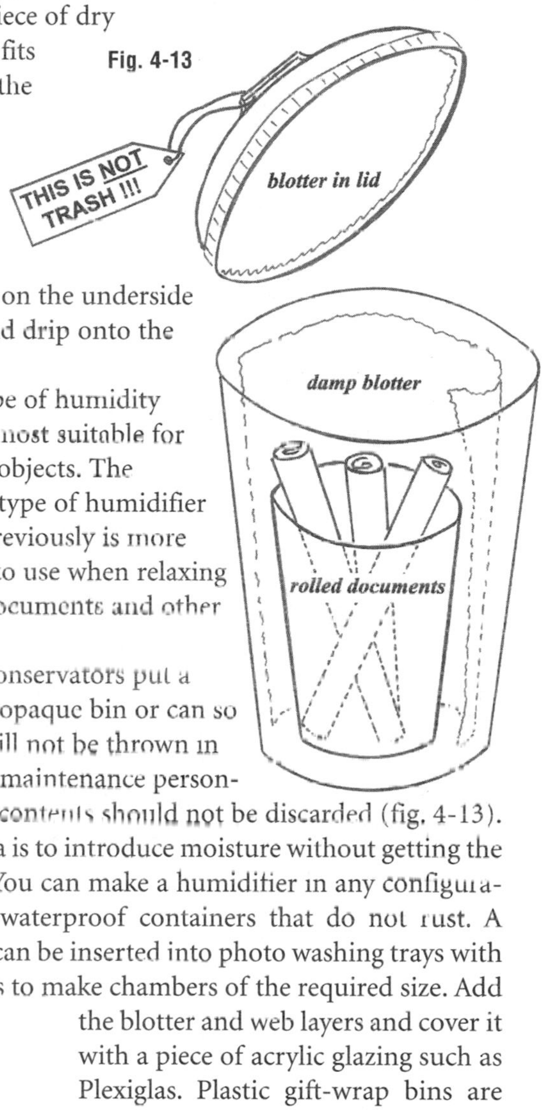

This type of humidity chamber is most suitable for large rolled objects. The storage bin-type of humidifier described previously is more convenient to use when relaxing letter-size documents and other small items.

Many conservators put a sign on any opaque bin or can so that trash will not be thrown in and to alert maintenance personnel that the contents should not be discarded (fig. 4-13).

The idea is to introduce moisture without getting the object wet. You can make a humidifier in any configuration, using waterproof containers that do not rust. A plastic grid can be inserted into photo washing trays with sloping sides to make chambers of the required size. Add the blotter and web layers and cover it with a piece of acrylic glazing such as Plexiglas. Plastic gift-wrap bins are also available in an upright design, to accommodate rolls 40"–44". Blotters and a smaller container to hold the rolls can be placed inside, as in a Horton Humidifier.

Fig. 4-13

blotter in lid

THIS IS NOT TRASH !!!

damp blotter

rolled documents

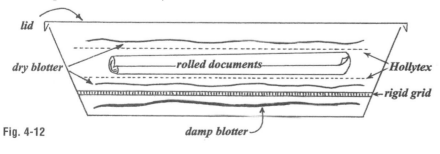

lid

dry blotter

rolled documents

Hollytex

rigid grid

damp blotter

Fig. 4-12

Look inside the humidifier after a couple of hours to make sure all is well. Don't let condensation drip on the objects; adjust the position or quantity of blotters as necessary.

Check on the documents or rolls to see if they are becoming more flexible and relaxed. This may happen in an hour or two but it may take longer, sometimes several days. If the process takes more than a day, change the damp blotters periodically and examine the materials in the humidifier carefully for any signs of mold. *Mold is always a threat* but it is more likely to develop on materials with a history of inadequate storage. Humid weather is also a contributing factor. Notice if any smell comes out of the container when you open it; this is a sign of trouble and the documents or rolls should be removed immediately and placed in a dry place to air dry. Never leave materials in a humidifier over a weekend. It is safer to remove them from the humidifier and start again on Monday than to risk the development of mold.

Pressing Humidified Paper

Once the documents or rolls have relaxed enough that they will lie flat with very little or no restraint, they should be dried under *light* pressure. Place the objects between dry blotters and put a pressing board or a piece of ½"-thick Plexiglas on the blotters. (Plate glass can be used but acrylic is safer.) Change the blotters after 15–30 minutes, and repeat this in an hour or two and once again if necessary.

Note: If there are any areas of the flattened documents that might be at all sticky, put a smooth, unwrinkled piece of polyester web between the object and the blotter. Don't use silicone release paper, glassine paper, or wax paper because the humidity from the documents often wrinkles the release paper and the wrinkles can get pressed into the document.

Dry Mount Press

A cold dry mount press can also be used for pressing the humidified documents. Simply place the document between blotters into the press and close it. Light pressure is desirable; extra boards will probably not be needed. (See "Presses" in section 2, p. 40, for suggestions on using a dry mount press.)

If there are any areas of the flattened documents that might be at all sticky, put a smooth, unwrinkled piece of polyester web between the object and the blotter. Don't use silicone release paper, glassine paper, or wax paper.

Proper Storage of Flattened Materials

Store the flattened objects in appropriate envelopes, sleeves, or folders and place them in boxes or drawers as desired. Some pressure or restraint is often needed to prevent the documents or maps from trying to revert to their folded or rolled shapes.

FLATTENING AND DRYING STATION

During a rehousing project or just in the course of day-to-day mending operations, there are many times when something needs to be flattened or dried. Blotters and pressing boards or acrylic have to be assembled and a space found where the stack can stay undisturbed.

If there is a sturdy work surface that can be dedicated to this purpose, purchase a bundle of fairly heavy acid-free binder's board, e.g., .098 or .123, from one of the suppliers listed in appendix B. The numbers refer to the thickness of the board in inches. A bundle of full-size (usually 26" × 38") sheets always weighs 50 pounds, so the number of sheets per bundle varies according to the thickness of the board. There will be about 15 sheets in a .098 bundle and 12 in a .123 bundle. Some suppliers also sell individual sheets and half sheets, which might be more useful if space is limited. (Binder's board cannot really be cut down accurately without a board shears or other heavy cutter; see "Cutters" in section 2, p. 36.)

Keep the boards in a stack and reserve them for flattening and drying operations *only,* so they will stay clean and always be available.

Binder's board has a smooth surface and is much more dimensionally stable than blotters. This means that it doesn't cockle and wrinkle very much when it gets damp, and therefore it doesn't transfer wrinkle marks to the object being pressed. Place the document in a folded blotter (using smooth, unwrinkled polyester web if needed) and place it between two pieces of binder's board. As noted above, the board is heavy, so the lower in the stack the document goes, the more pressure it will get. After the first pressing, a document that was simply humidified should be dry enough that it can be put between the binder's boards (in a different area, to continue the drying) without blotters. Fold a large piece of polyester web in half and place the document inside; the web can stick out of the pile to facilitate finding the document later.

If more pressure is desired, distribute pressing boards, Plexiglas, or other weights evenly over the top of the pile.

Note: Glassine paper, wax paper, and silicone release paper are not recommended for use as barrier sheets or other applications where moisture might be present because they wrinkle and pass the cockling on to the object being pressed.

Flattening Creases

The creases in folded documents can be minimized by humidifying the whole document and pressing it, as described above. When book pages have creases, such as bent corners, humidification has to be introduced locally.

AVOIDING TIDE LINES

One of the characteristics of most papers, but especially older ones, is that they can be stained by partial wetting. These stains are produced by sizing and impurities in the paper that begin to move as they dissolve in water. When they reach the edge of the wet area, they cannot go any further so they accumulate there. These are the familiar water stains or "tide lines" that are seen in books or prints that have been wet.

To humidify a book page with the least chance of causing tide lines, mist a piece of blotter with a fine mist sprayer. To avoid having droplets of water fall on the blotter, hold the blotter vertically while spraying. Any droplets that form will fall on the countertop or floor rather than on the blotter. The blotter should not be soaking wet, just a little bit damp. If the blotter is not moistened all the way through, place it in a plastic bag for a half hour or so. This will draw the moisture evenly throughout.

Put a scrap piece of polyester film (Mylar) under the creased page, to protect the rest of the book and to concentrate the moisture where you need it. Place a piece of dry blotter between the creased page and the film.

Unfold the crease, using clean fingers, microspatula, or other fine tool to manipulate it into the correct position. Put a scrap of paper over it and rub gently with a bone folder. A Teflon folder is ideal for this purpose. Remove the paper scrap and put the dampened blotter over the crease. Put a weight over it. The moisture should travel gradually through the page and into the bottom blotter. Allow it to dry.

This method is most appropriate for smaller creases on sound paper. Creases that go across the whole page are difficult to remove and should not be attempted in-house.

Unfolding creases in brittle paper may cause the paper to split open or break off, so it is usually better to leave them as they are. This is a common problem when the corners of brittle pages have been folded for a long period. If a crease splits open accidentally or a corner breaks off, mend the paper as described in "Paper Repair Techniques" later in this section.

Picking Up and Moving Large Flat Items

When moving a big piece of paper, such as a print or map, first make sure that the drawer or surface where it is going is large enough to accommodate it and there is a clear path to that location, since your view may be impeded by the object you are carrying. Pick it up by two opposite corners, as shown in figure 4-14. Allow the paper to sag down in the middle as you move it. Set it down gently, letting the middle rest on the surface, and then allow the corners to *drop* down. This method helps avoid denting or creasing the paper.

Fig. 4-14

If a piece is too large or too fragile to be picked up this way, carefully slide a rigid support, such as mat board, Plexiglas, or acid-free cardboard under the piece. Two people can then move the item on its "tray." Large objects are often heavy and unwieldy. Don't attempt to move a big stack of maps or several bundles of rolled drawings all at once, to avoid damaging them and possibly injuring yourself.

Be especially careful when moving fragile materials, such as old mounted photographs or prints, no matter what size. Mounts were often made from poor-quality materials. Although the print itself might be in good condition, the mount may have deteriorated and become brittle. If you pick up mounted art by one corner, a piece of the mount may break off and part of the photograph or print may come off with the corner. This is especially likely in the case of larger pieces, but to be safe, always use a rigid support to move mounted items, even if they don't look really fragile.

PAPER REPAIR TECHNIQUES

The best, most long-lasting paper repairs are made with Japanese paper and wheat or rice starch paste. This traditional Eastern method was adopted by Western conservators in the mid-twentieth century and is now the norm. The repairs are flexible, strong, and easily reversible. As with anything, practice is needed to produce inconspicuous, smooth repairs.

As discussed earlier, starch paste must be mixed with water and cooked before use. It can be made in different consistencies that are suitable for various applications. Paste does not stain or pucker paper when used correctly and it dries with a very matte finish. However, it does not keep very long. Depending on the weather, paste can spoil and mold in a day or two. Moldy paste cannot be reconstituted and should be thrown out. For a small facility that does paper repairs only occasionally, the short shelf life can be a drawback.

An acceptable substitute for most uses of paste is methylcellulose. Methylcellulose also comes as a powder and must be mixed, but then it will keep for months if not contaminated. Repairs made with methylcellulose sometimes have a slightly shinier look, especially around the edges of the mend. This can be reduced by applying it sparingly, so that not much oozes out from under the paper. This adhesive does not have as strong a hold as paste but is quite adequate for most routine mending. With a suitable adhesive always available, there is less inclination to resort to tapes for a quick mend.

See "Adhesives" earlier in this section, p. 79, for instructions on mixing adhesives. All of the repairs described below can be carried out with either paste or methylcellulose.

It's good to have a few different Japanese papers of various weights and shades. The repair paper should be thinner and somewhat lighter in color than the page. Some papers are very thin and transparent and are suitable for repairs over printed pages. Sekishu and Kizukishi are two widely used papers, of different weights, for different applications. These and many other papers can be purchased from conservation suppliers. If you are not familiar with Japanese papers, purchase a sample book from the supplier and order a few sheets at a time till you build up an assortment that works well for your needs. Very small pieces are used for mending, so a sheet will last a good while.

Preparing a Work Surface

When getting ready to do many paper repairs, line the work surface with clean, flat blotters and cover them with polyester web. That way, you can set a repair down to dry anywhere on the counter and not worry about putting a blotter under it.

Tearing Japanese Paper

Repairs will blend better into the page if you tear the strips of Japanese tissue instead of cutting them. Furthermore, the long fibers give the repair a soft edge that will not cut weak or brittle paper. The longest fibers and softest edges are obtained by "water tearing."

You will need a ruler and a felt-tip pen filled with water or a water brush, each available from art supply stores. Felt-tip pens are good for tearing a lot of strips relatively quickly. The Letraset no. 73215 is sold empty and comes with three interchangeable tips of different sizes. Water brushes are made for Japanese calligraphy, but they are sold empty and can be filled with plain water. The Niji brush, size Small, made by Yasumoto, is a good choice. The brushes are excellent for tracing the outlines of "fills" and odd-shaped tears.

A small brush or a ruling pen dipped in water can also be used to "water tear" paper.

Determine the width needed for the repair strip and place a ruler parallel to the grain of the paper. With the water pen or brush, draw a line along the length of the ruler (fig. 4-15).

Gently tear the strip away by pulling it against the ruler (fig. 4-16).

You can also "needle tear" the Japanese paper strips. Instead of using the water pen or water brush, score the paper very lightly with a needle or an awl, along the ruler, and then pull the strip away. Moreover, some papers can be torn dry, using the ruler, though the fibers will be shorter. These are faster methods than water tearing, and quite satisfactory for many applications.

Paper with Tear Lines

Some suppliers sell sheets of Japanese paper manufactured with parallel tear lines at varying intervals. The paper is thinner at the lines and can be torn without wetting.

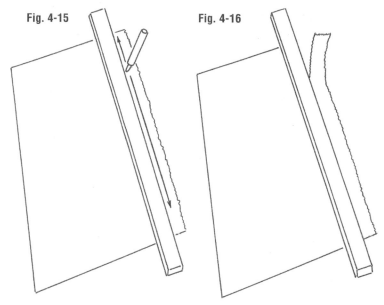

Fig. 4-15   Fig. 4-16

Once the paper has been removed, check to see if there is adhesive residue on the paper. If there is, use a clean, barely damp cotton swab to clean it.

After the mend and the adhesive have been removed, put a piece of polyester web and a blotter over the area and press. After 10–15 minutes, remove the weight and blotter and check on the work. If the paper appears damp, put a dry blotter on the area and replace the weight for a half hour or so.

Note: If the document has wrinkled where the mend or hinge was removed, it will be necessary to humidify the whole piece and then flatten it, as described in "Relaxing and Flattening Paper" on p. 84.

Undoing (Reversing) Repairs Made with Paste or Methylcellulose

This technique is also used for removing hinges from artwork. Place the repaired document or hinged artwork on a blotter, with the mend or hinge on top. When reversing repairs on book pages, place a blotter under the page and a piece of Mylar between the blotter and the rest of the pages. Dampen a cotton swab and roll the cotton tip over a scrap of blotter or a paper towel to work off excess moisture. If the swab is too wet, the extra water will cause a water stain or tide line and possibly wrinkle the paper as well.

Roll the barely damp swab over the mend or hinge to be removed. Do it a few times, till the moisture penetrates through the Japanese paper and starts softening the paste. Gradually pull the mend off the paper. Patience is important; if the mend doesn't come off right away, continue treating it with the swab.

Another method is to dampen a piece of blotter *lightly* with a mist sprayer, as in flattening creases, described above. Place the dampened blotter over the mend for a few minutes, with a small weight on top, till the moisture penetrates through the Japanese paper and starts softening the paste. Don't leave the dampened blotter in place for a long period; check to make sure the document or book page does not get very wet or it will cockle and possibly develop a tide line. Gradually remove the mend. If it resists, replace the damp blotter for another minute or two.

Mending Edge Tears

Some tears are feathered, with overlapping edges; this is because the paper has split in layers. When mending these tears, it is helpful to work on a light box to make sure the edges are aligned properly. Light boxes are available from conservation and art suppliers but they can be improvised very simply. Put a sheet of Plexiglas (acrylic glazing) over a small fluorescent fixture. Support the Plexiglas on bricks to raise it up a few inches. Or put the fluorescent fixture inside a shallow washing tray and place the acrylic on top of the tray. Make sure the acrylic is supported firmly before starting to work on it.

The paste or methylcellulose should be thick but still easy to spread in a thin layer with a brush. This will produce less cockling and water staining.

Place a piece of polyester web (Reemay or Hollytex) under the tear, and a piece of blotter under the polyester. (Or work on a large blotter covered with polyester web.)

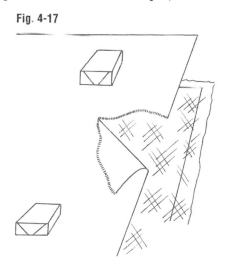

Fig. 4-17

Align the edges of the tear and *match the print or image carefully.* Put a small weight on each side of the tear, to keep it in position (fig. 4-17).

Gently separate the tear and apply a thin coat of paste to each edge of the tear. Set the edges back together, cover with polyester web and blotter, and rub down gently with a bone folder.

Change blotters if they feel damp. Put a weight over the repair and leave it for an hour or so.

Repair long, irregularly shaped tears in short segments, an inch or two at most, allowing each repaired section to dry before proceeding to the next (fig. 4-18). If the overlapping surfaces are wide, this may be sufficient; for additional strength, finish the repair with Japanese tissue as described below.

Fig. 4-18

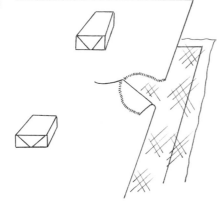

Mending a Simple Edge Tear with Japanese Paper and Paste

A strip or patch of Japanese paper is needed for reinforcement when repairing cuts and tears without overlapping edges. Choose a paper of a lighter weight than the paper to be repaired.

Tear a strip to size. Apply a light coat of paste or methylcellulose to it. (If you place the mending strips on a blotter when applying paste, some of the moisture will be absorbed by the blotter and the repair will dry faster.) Pick up the pasted strip with a microspatula and place it over the tear. Allow about ¼" (6–7 mm) to extend beyond the edge of the paper (fig. 4-19). The excess will be cut off later, after the repair dries.

Fig. 4-19

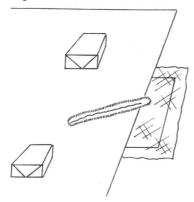

Place a piece of polyester web over the repaired tear, then a piece of blotter on top. Rub gently to absorb excess moisture and paste. Change the blotters, and place a small weight on top (fig. 4-20). Let dry under weight. When dry, cut the excess flush with the edge of the page.

Fig. 4-20

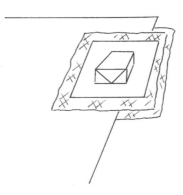

It is easier and neater to repair long tears, especially curved ones, using short strips of torn Japanese paper placed end to end (fig. 4-21). The feathered edges blend into each other. There is less pulling and buckling as the repair dries.

Fig. 4-21

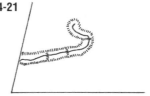

Repairing Holes and Missing Corners

When there is a hole or "loss" in a page or document, make a patch to fill it. Place the page on a light box and put a scrap of Mylar over the hole or missing corner, as a moisture barrier. Select a Japanese paper that coordinates with the color of the page and is of similar thickness, or a little thinner.

Trace the outline of the loss on the Japanese paper, using a water brush or fine water pen. Make the tracing just a little larger than the hole, so that the torn fibers will overlap the edges of the hole. Very carefully, tear the patch away from the sheet of Japanese paper.

Place the document over a blotter covered with polyester web.

Turn the patch over and apply paste to the feathered edges. Turn it over again and position it over the hole (fig. 4-22). Place a scrap of polyester web and a blotter over the repair and rub down with a bone folder.

Fig. 4-22

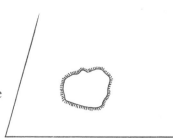

Change blotters and put a small weight on the repair (fig. 4-23). Allow to dry.

If the mend seems thin, repeat the process on the other side of the document. This produces better results than using one layer of thick paper.

Fig. 4-23

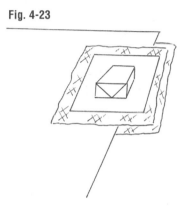

When a corner is missing, place the document on a light box and put a Mylar scrap on the document. Place a piece of Japanese paper over the loss and trace the outline of the area where the corner broke off, using a water pen or brush (fig. 4-24). Leave the other two sides oversize; they will be trimmed after the repair is dry.

Fig. 4-24

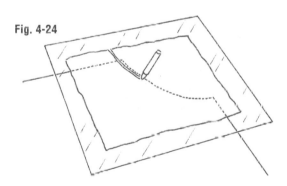

Tear the patch away and attach it to the document, overlapping the edges as described above and allow to dry (fig. 4-25).

Fig. 4-25

You may want to repeat the process one or more times to build up the thickness of the new corner to match the document. Attach each added layer at a slightly different distance from the edge of the document to lessen the thickness at the edge of the repair. (A few layers of thin paper work better than one layer of heavy paper.)

When the repair is dry, trim the edges of the corner in a line with the edges of the page, as shown in figure 4-26. (See "Cutting and Trimming" in section 2, p. 49, for directions on cutting and trimming.)

Fig. 4-26

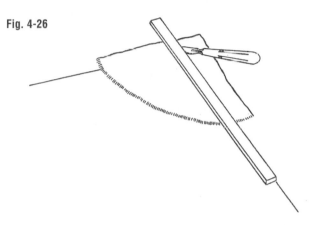

If the corners of the other pages in the book have become rounded from wear, snip off a tiny bit from the point of the new corner so it will blend in better.

Attaching Hinges to Pages

A hinge is a narrow strip of paper attached lengthwise (like a piano hinge) to the page to be inserted into a book. Choose a Japanese paper of suitable weight and color. It should be thicker than that used for repairing tears but thinner than the paper the page is printed on. Sekishu, which comes in either white or natural tones, is frequently a good choice, but thinner papers are often used. The thinner the hinge paper is, the less extra bulk will be added in the gutter. This keeps the book from becoming distorted.

Sometimes the page to be hinged needs to be trimmed a little in order to accommodate the added hinge. It is better to trim the gutter edge than the fore edge, especially if the edges of the book are gilt or marbled. Determine ahead of time how much needs to be trimmed off the gutter edge so that the hinged page will line up with the fore edge of the book. However, if the fore edge is very damaged, trim a small amount (say,

⅛", or 3 mm) off the leaf at the fore edge. When a leaf has been detached from a book for some time, all the edges are often frayed. In that case, trim all the edges, just the minimum amount needed to cut off the fraying. (Long tears should be mended rather than cut off.) The page will then fit better in the book and will be less likely to tear further. These instructions apply to books from circulating or research collections. Do not trim the pages of old or rare books.

Tear a strip of mending paper approximately ⅝" (1.6 cm) wide by a bit longer than the height of the page to be hinged. Tear the hinge so that the grain runs the length of the strip.

Place the page to be hinged on a sheet of waste paper. Place another piece of waste paper on top, about ¼" (6–7 mm) away from the edge where the hinge will be placed. Apply adhesive to the exposed area (fig. 4-27). Remove the top waste sheet and move the page onto a clean, absorbent surface, such as blotter covered with polyester web. Discard the used waste paper.

Fig. 4-27

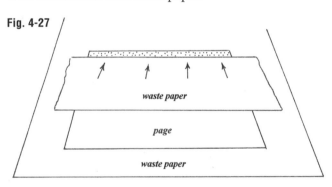

Position the strip of Japanese paper over the pasted area, as shown in figure 4-28. *Be careful not to stretch the pasted strip or the repair will buckle when it dries.* Cover with web and blotter and rub down with a bone folder. Replace the blotter with a dry one and let dry under weight.

The page is now ready to be inserted into the book. This will be described in "Hinging" in section 5, p. 109.

Fig. 4-28

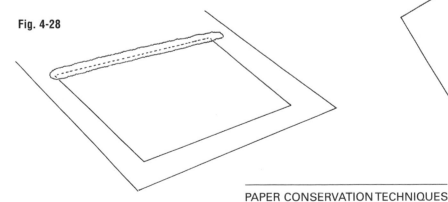

Guarding Two Leaves

The term "guarding" refers to the joining of two leaves using a narrow strip of paper (the "guard") in order to create a fold between the leaves. A guard is a type of hinge.

To make it easier to align the tops of the leaves accurately, use a straightedge to make a simple jig.

Tape the straightedge to the countertop to prevent it from moving (fig. 4-29), or put a weight on the straightedge.

Position two leaves on a sheet of waste paper. Jog the tops of the leaves against the jig and adjust the space between them. Place a weight on each leaf to hold it in place.

Tear a strip of Japanese paper approximately ⅝" (1.6 cm) wide and slightly longer than the leaves. The grain should be long. Place this guard on a piece of waste paper and apply adhesive to it. Pick it up with a microspatula and center it, adhesive side down, on the inner edges of the leaves (fig. 4-30). Rub down through polyester web and blotter using a bone folder. Place dry blotter on the repair and let dry under weight. Trim excess at each end when dry.

Fig. 4-29

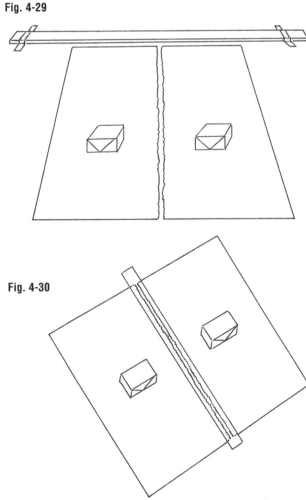

Fig. 4-30

This two-page section can be "tipped" directly into the gutter of a book, as described in "Inserting Guarded Leaves" in section 5, p. 110.

TIPPING PAGES

"Tipping" is a term used for attaching one or more pages to a book without the use of an added hinge. It will be discussed in "Tipping" in section 5, p. 108.

Mending Torn Pages in Books

When mending a torn page in a book, provide support to the book so that the pages lie flat without any strain on the binding (fig. 4-31). You may need to prop the book open with weights or place another book of suitable thickness under the open board.

Fig. 4-31

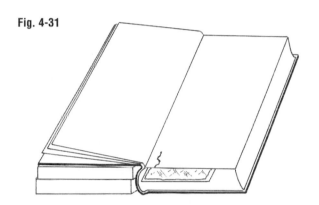

Place a small blotter covered with polyester web under the page to be mended and proceed with the mending repair as discussed earlier in "Mending Edge Tears." Put a piece of web and a blotter over the repair and allow it to dry under a weight.

If the repair is not too close to the gutter, you may be able to close the book, with the blotters in place, and put a weight on the book, over the area of the repair. Be careful not to distort the book; if the cover of the book won't stay closed with the blotters in place, leave the book open and allow the repair to dry under a weight, as described above.

Mending Tears in Foldout Maps

Before repairing a map that folds out beyond the edge of the pages of a book or atlas, build up the surface under the map to match the thickness of the book. Use boards or other books. Cover the stack of boards with a blotter and polyester web (fig. 4-32).

Fig. 4-32

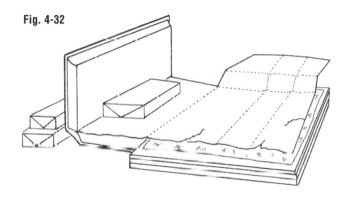

Allow the repairs to dry completely before refolding the map. If the folds are torn, it is often better to repair them on both the front and the back, using thin paper. This usually gives a more flexible repair than one layer of thicker paper, and if any print is covered by the repair strip, it is more readable. Do all the mending from one side first, then turn the map over and adjust the supports so you can mend the other side.

Book Conservation Techniques

and Terminology 95**

Parts of a Book 95

Techniques for Handling Books 100

Removing a Book from the Shelf 100

Call Number Flags 100

Opening a Book 101

Supporting Fragile Books 101

Packing and Moving Books 102

**Supplies and Equipment Needed
for Book Repairs 103**

Adhesives 103

Cloth 104

Western and Japanese Papers 105

Boards 105

Thread 105

Hand Tools 106

Equipment 107

Other Supplies 107

Book Repair Techniques 107

Simple Repairs between the Covers 107

Simple Repairs to the Case 119

Repairs to the Text Block and the Case 126

Pamphlets 144

Children's Books 147

BOOKS ARE DECEPTIVELY FAMILIAR. WE HAVE BEEN surrounded by them all our lives and it is easy to take them for granted. But as with all useful things, having some background knowledge of the nature of books makes it easier to care for and repair them.

This section is divided into four parts.

1. "Brief Review of Bookbinding Structure and Terminology" briefly describes bookbinding structure, including some historical details that explain why books are the way they are. Figures 5-1A and 5-1B depict the various parts of a modern case-bound book.

2. "Techniques for Handling Books" provides tips for cleaning, moving, packing, and opening books, since handling books correctly is an important aspect of preventive preservation.

3. "Supplies and Equipment Needed for Book Repairs" describes the tools and supplies needed in setting up a work area. We discuss adhesives, hand tools, and repair materials.

4. "Book Repair Techniques" provides directions for carrying out book repairs, beginning with very simple steps and progressing to more complicated techniques. Some steps are based on traditional bookbinding techniques, but we do not cover binding books "from scratch" because this requires much more training than we can convey in a manual. In any case, most libraries send very damaged books to library binders or else replace them.

The repair methods described in part 4 are intended for books that circulate or have research value. Consult a conservator before treating rare books or materials from special collections.

BRIEF REVIEW OF BOOKBINDING STRUCTURE AND TERMINOLOGY

Parts of a Book

Figures 5-1A and 5-1B give the terminology for various parts of a common hardcover book, such as would come to the preservation department for repair.

Text Block

The text block of a traditional book is composed of groups of leaves, commonly called "signatures" or "sections." (The terms "gathering" and "quire" may also be found occasionally.) Signatures result from the traditional way that the pages of books are printed on sheets of paper.

A whole piece of hand- or machine-made paper is called a "sheet." Paper is available in many sheet sizes, and a printer selects a size that will produce a book of the desired dimensions with the least waste. The text of a book is printed on several large sheets. Many pages are printed on the front and back of each sheet in a very specific arrangement so that the pages will be in order and right side up when the sheet is folded several times. Each folded sheet is a signature or section.

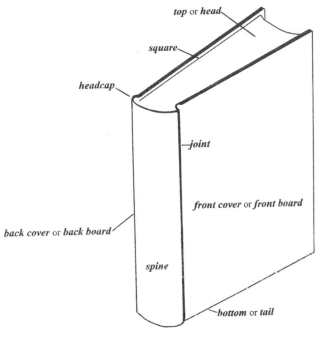

Fig. 5-1A Parts of a book

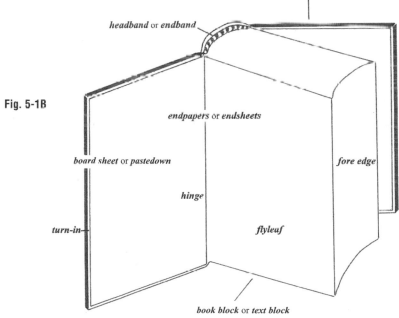

Fig. 5-1B

FOLIOS

The word "folio," from the Latin word for "fold," is commonly used in libraries to signify a large book. The term originally meant that the pages of the book had been printed on sheets that were folded just once (fig. 5-2). Figures 5-3A and 5-3B show both sides of a folio layout. These were usually large books, and the term eventually came to refer to any large volume.

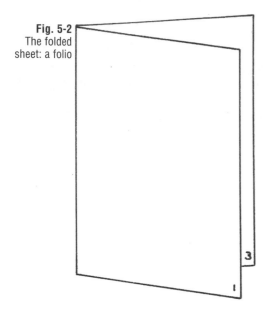

Fig. 5-2
The folded
sheet: a folio

Fig. 5-3A

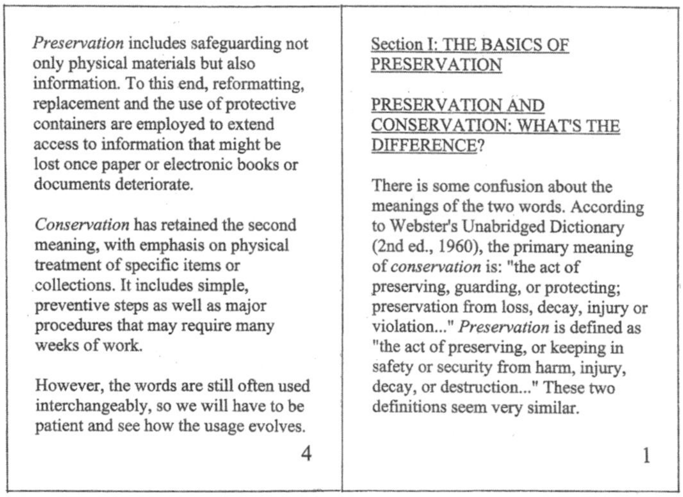

Preservation includes safeguarding not only physical materials but also information. To this end, reformatting, replacement and the use of protective containers are employed to extend access to information that might be lost once paper or electronic books or documents deteriorate.

Conservation has retained the second meaning, with emphasis on physical treatment of specific items or collections. It includes simple, preventive steps as well as major procedures that may require many weeks of work.

However, the words are still often used interchangeably, so we will have to be patient and see how the usage evolves.

4

Section I: THE BASICS OF PRESERVATION

PRESERVATION AND CONSERVATION: WHAT'S THE DIFFERENCE?

There is some confusion about the meanings of the two words. According to Webster's Unabridged Dictionary (2nd ed., 1960), the primary meaning of *conservation* is: "the act of preserving, guarding, or protecting; preservation from loss, decay, injury or violation..." *Preservation* is defined as "the act of preserving, or keeping in safety or security from harm, injury, decay, or destruction..." These two definitions seem very similar.

1

Fig. 5-3B

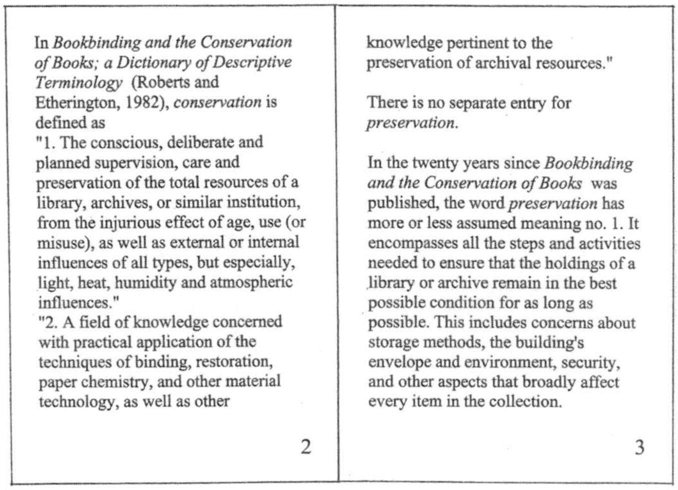

In *Bookbinding and the Conservation of Books; a Dictionary of Descriptive Terminology* (Roberts and Etherington, 1982), *conservation* is defined as
"1. The conscious, deliberate and planned supervision, care and preservation of the total resources of a library, archives, or similar institution, from the injurious effect of age, use (or misuse), as well as external or internal influences of all types, but especially, light, heat, humidity and atmospheric influences."
"2. A field of knowledge concerned with practical application of the techniques of binding, restoration, paper chemistry, and other material technology, as well as other

2

knowledge pertinent to the preservation of archival resources."

There is no separate entry for *preservation*.

In the twenty years since *Bookbinding and the Conservation of Books* was published, the word *preservation* has more or less assumed meaning no. 1. It encompasses all the steps and activities needed to ensure that the holdings of a library or archive remain in the best possible condition for as long as possible. This includes concerns about storage methods, the building's envelope and environment, security, and other aspects that broadly affect every item in the collection.

3

QUARTOS

Figures 5-4A and 5-4B show both sides of a quarto layout, in which the sheet is folded twice, with the folds at right angles, producing four leaves or eight pages (fig. 5-5). Note that some pages are printed upside down.

An *octavo* format is the result of folding the sheet three times, each fold at right angles to the preceding one, which produces eight leaves or sixteen pages. Booksellers' catalogs often use the word "octavo" to indicate a book size, about eight to ten inches (20–25 cm) high.

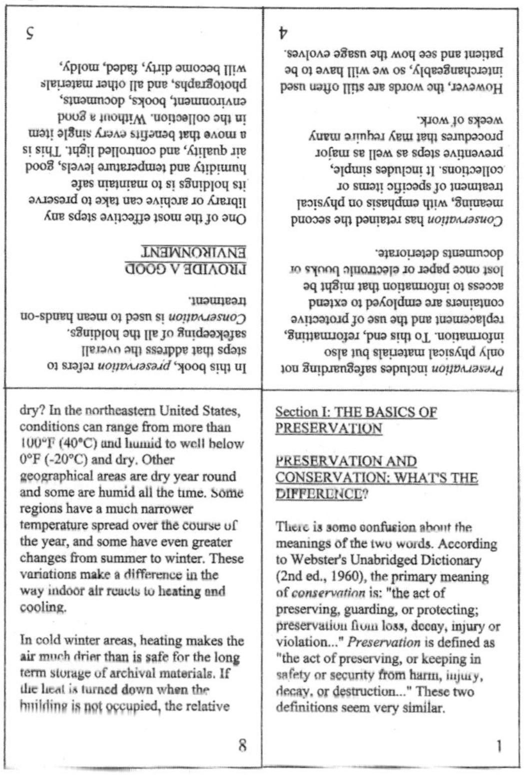

The result of the folding is pairs of *leaves,* one on either side of the fold at the spine edge or *gutter.* A pair of folded leaves are said to be "conjugates."

Each leaf consists of two *pages,* one in front (the *recto*) and one in back (the *verso*). When a book is open, the page on the right is the recto and has an odd page number, and the page on the left is the verso and has an even number.

Occasionally, you may see at the bottom of a page a small letter or number that is not the page number. The marks appear in sequential order, at regular intervals

Fig. 5-4A

Page 5 (printed upside down): In this book, *preservation* refers to steps that address the overall safekeeping of all the holdings. *Conservation* is used to mean hands-on treatment.

PROVIDE A GOOD ENVIRONMENT.

One of the most effective steps any library or archive can take to preserve its holdings is to maintain safe humidity and temperature levels, good air quality, and controlled light. This is a move that benefits every single item in the collection. Without a good environment, books, documents, photographs, and all other materials will become dirty, faded, moldy,

Page 4 (printed upside down): *Preservation* includes safeguarding not only physical materials but also information. To this end, reformatting, replacement and the use of protective containers are employed to extend access to information that might be lost once paper or electronic books or documents deteriorate.

Conservation has retained the second meaning, with emphasis on physical treatment of specific items or collections. It includes simple, preventive steps as well as major procedures that may require many weeks of work.

However, the words are still used interchangeably, so we will have to be patient and see how the usage evolves.

Page 8: dry? In the northeastern United States, conditions can range from more than 100°F (40°C) and humid to well below 0°F (-20°C) and dry. Other geographical areas are dry year round and some are humid all the time. Some regions have a much narrower temperature spread over the course of the year, and some have even greater changes from summer to winter. These variations make a difference in the way indoor air reacts to heating and cooling.

In cold winter areas, heating makes the air much drier than is safe for the long term storage of archival materials. If the heat is turned down when the building is not occupied, the relative

Page 1: Section I: THE BASICS OF PRESERVATION

PRESERVATION AND CONSERVATION: WHAT'S THE DIFFERENCE?

There is some confusion about the meanings of the two words. According to Webster's Unabridged Dictionary (2nd ed., 1960), the primary meaning of *conservation* is: "the act of preserving, guarding, or protecting; preservation from loss, decay, injury or violation..." *Preservation* is defined as "the act of preserving, or keeping in safety or security from harm, injury, decay, or destruction..." These two definitions seem very similar.

Fig. 5-4B

Page 6 (printed upside down): is to maintain the desired temperature is harmful to many materials; the key days per year. Frequent fluctuations storage areas, 24 hours per day, 365 temperature around 60°F (16°C) for recommended RH of 50% and many preservation specialists have temperatures. Since the late 1960's, relative humidity (RH) and moderate storage spaces emphasize controlled Guidelines for archival and library

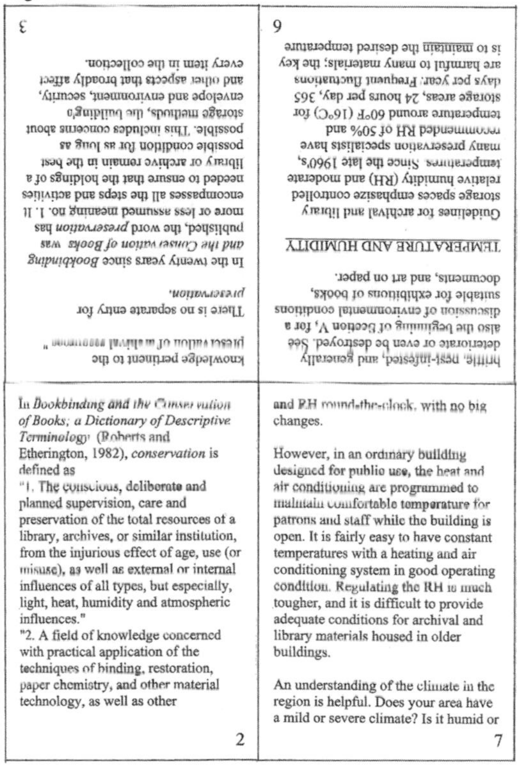

TEMPERATURE AND HUMIDITY

also the beginning of Section V, for a discussion of environmental conditions suitable for exhibition of books, documents, and art on paper.

brittle, pest-infested, and generally deteriorate or even be destroyed. See

Page 3 (printed upside down): knowledge pertinent to the preservation of archival materials."

There is no separate entry for preservation.

In the twenty years since *Bookbinding and the Conservation of Books* was published, the word *preservation* has more or less assumed meaning no. 1. It encompasses all the steps and activities needed to ensure that the holdings of a library or archive remain in the best possible condition for as long as possible. This includes concerns about storage methods, the building's envelope and environmental security, and other aspects that broadly affect every item in the collection.

Page 2: In *Bookbinding and the Conservation of Books; a Dictionary of Descriptive Terminology* (Roberts and Etherington, 1982), *conservation* is defined as
"1. The conscious, deliberate and planned supervision, care and preservation of the total resources of a library, archives, or similar institution, from the injurious effect of age, use (or misuse), as well as external or internal influences of all types, but especially, light, heat, humidity and atmospheric influences."
"2. A field of knowledge concerned with practical application of the techniques of binding, restoration, paper chemistry, and other material technology, as well as other

Page 7: and RH round-the-clock, with no big changes.

However, in an ordinary building designed for public use, the heat and air conditioning are programmed to maintain comfortable temperature for patrons and staff while the building is open. It is fairly easy to have constant temperatures with a heating and air conditioning system in good operating condition. Regulating the RH is much tougher, and it is difficult to provide adequate conditions for archival and library materials housed in older buildings.

An understanding of the climate in the region is helpful. Does your area have a mild or severe climate? Is it humid or

Fig. 5-5

every few pages. They are printed on the first page of each signature. The term "signature" originally referred to these marks, which were used to help the bookbinder assemble the book in correct order before sewing. Over the course of the twentieth century, the use of signature marks was replaced by graduated marks on the outside of the spine folds of each section. These marks are not visible when the book is bound.

CUTTING THE FOLDS

After the signatures are sewn together, the folds at the top, fore edge, and bottom are cut off, leaving only the fold at the spine edge. The leaves of the book are now free to turn.

In the past, especially in Europe, the folds were not cut off after sewing, leaving this task to the purchaser of the book. The folds were slit with long knives in order to open the pages.

In the event that a book with uncut pages comes to the preservation department, check with the librarian to make sure that the value of the book will not be affected by opening the folds. If so, the librarian should determine the best course of action. Place the book in an enclosure if it needs protection.

To open the pages of a book by hand, select a knife with a long blade with a rounded end. Place the blade in the fold and cut by pushing the blade out against the fold (figs. 5-6 and 5-7). Avoid a sawing motion, since this produces a jagged cut and might tear the pages.

Fig. 5-6

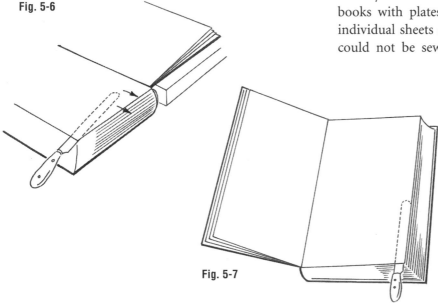

Fig. 5-7

Sewn and Adhesive Bindings

The folded sections are sewn through the inner fold and linked one to the next. This is the meaning of the term "sewn through the fold." All books were originally sewn by hand. In the 1860s, machinery for sewing book sections was invented by David Smyth, whose name has become synonymous for machine sewing through the fold. Books sewn through the fold open well.

The other common way of holding pages together is by *stab sewing* or *side sewing*. Unsewn, folded book sections or loose single pages, or a combination of the two, are sewn together with thread that goes through the whole book, from front to back, near the binding edge. It is a very quick way of assembling pages and a very strong method. Books that are stab sewn do not open very well, however. Pages often crease and break off against the line of stitching, especially at the front and back. Pamphlets and children's books are often sewn this way. Side sewing is also used in Japanese and other Asian books, but because the pages are made of very soft, flexible paper, these books open well.

In *side stitching*, wire staples are used to fasten the leaves together, in a manner similar to side sewing. This is another very strong method that results in limited openability, in other words, side-stitched books don't open very well.

"Saddle stitching" refers to holding together a pamphlet, magazine, or other single section publication by stapling through the fold with wire staples.

Oversewing came into use in the late eighteenth century. It was a very common way of assembling large books with plates because the plates were printed on individual sheets separately from the text, so the books could not be sewn through the folds without special preparation of the plates. In the early twentieth century, oversewing machines were invented and the method became the standard of library binders until the later part of the century.

Whether by hand or by machine, oversewing involves several steps. The original spine folds of the text pages are sometimes cut off for hand sewing and always for machine oversewing. This converts the sections into single leaves. Any plates or other separately printed items are put in their correct locations and then the whole book is divided into small groups of leaves. Each group is sewn together with a type of overcast stitch, producing individual sections. These sections are then connected with a complex zigzag stitch.

A good amount of inner margin is lost, between cutting off folds and oversewing. Oversewn (or overcast) books vary in openability. Some large books, with paper in good condition, open very well. But smaller books, especially if printed short grain, are very difficult to open well enough to see the inner margins. The large number of perforations needed for this method also weakens the paper and makes it more likely to break off.

After sewing a book with several sections, either through the fold or oversewn, adhesive is applied to the spine, to shape the spine.

During the last quarter of the twentieth century, new methods of holding pages together were developed to make the process faster. Among them was cleat sewing, also called Smyth-Cleat sewing, which is a combination of machine sewing and gluing. This process integrates the sewing and gluing operations.

Adhesive bindings do away with sewing altogether. This method of holding pages together was first invented in the nineteenth century, using rubber adhesives (caoutchouc). These adhesives did not age well, and it was not until the development of plastic adhesives in the middle of the twentieth century that adhesive bindings started to become common. Many kinds of adhesives have been used over the last forty years, with varying success.

"Perfect binding" is the name for a type of adhesive binding commonly used by publishers of paperbacks and magazines in the second half of the twentieth century. Today, *double fan* and other ingenious adhesive bindings are the norm for library binding and for some types of edition bindings as well. Books with good adhesive bindings open well; the leaves do not fall out even after repeated use.

HEADBANDS, ENDBANDS

Originally, headbands were part of the structure of the book, serving to help anchor the boards to the text block. Now they are a purely decorative element found at the top and bottom of the spine, usually made of a multicolored woven cloth tape. Occasionally the term "tailband"

is used to denote the bottom headband. The term "endband" is gaining in popularity; it is used to denote both the headband and tailband.

BINDING TYPES

Originally, a book's cover was built onto the text block in a continuous series of steps. The boards were fastened to the sewn pages and then the covering material was glued to the boards and to the back of the signatures, resulting in a "tight" back. (See fig. 5-8.) This is the traditional way of binding a book; it is a sturdy method, but a time-consuming one. With the great explosion of book publishing in the early nineteenth century, a quicker way to get books into the hands of readers was sought. The result was the development of *case* binding.

Fig. 5-8

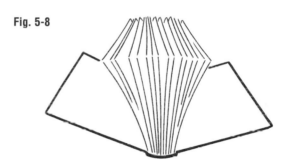

To make a typical case-bound book, the text block (sometimes referred to as the "book") is prepared as one operation while the case is being made separately. After the pages are sewn, the spine of the text block is rounded and backed. "Shoulders" are formed at the front and back of the book when a few of the outer pages bend outward in the backing process. The boards of the cover fit into the space created by the shoulders, when the text block is attached to the cover. Folded endpapers are tipped onto the shoulders of the text block (see fig. 5-43, p. 114), and fabric linings are applied over the spine and hinge area.

Meanwhile, the covers, or case, are made by gluing the covering material, normally cloth, paper, or leather, to pieces of binder's board of the correct size, with a piece of card stock in the space between the boards to accommodate the spine of the text block.

Next, the case and the book are connected by gluing the joints of the case to the shoulder area of the text block. This results in a hollow spine (see fig. 5-9), in contrast to the tight backs of earlier times when the covering material was glued directly to the back of the sewn signatures. Finally, the board sheets are pasted down to the inside of the boards.

Most books made from the mid-nineteenth century to the present have hollow spines and case bindings of some type. The repair techniques in this section are intended for use on such books. If the book seems different from the above description, it may be prudent to consult a conservator before proceeding with repairs.

Fig. 5-9

TECHNIQUES FOR HANDLING BOOKS

Removing a Book from the Shelf

A lot of damage to books can be avoided by proper handling. All staff members, volunteers, patrons, and other library users should learn this basic form of preservation.

It is not easy to remove one book out of a tightly packed shelf. Pulling on the top of the spine is the most common method; it inevitably leads to torn headcaps (fig. 5-10).

It may be possible to start moving the book toward the front of the shelf by placing one or two fingers on top of the *pages,* without touching the top of the spine (fig. 5-11).

Fig. 5-10

Fig. 5-11

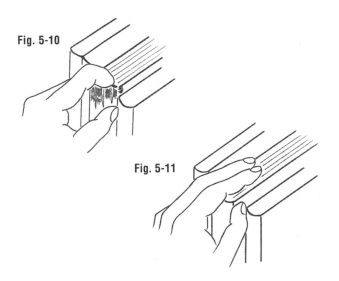

If this doesn't work, the safest way is to push in the books on either side a couple of inches so that the selected book is left protruding at the front. Then it can be grasped securely around the spine and removed without damage (fig. 5-12).

Fig. 5-12

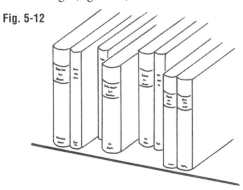

In the case of a really overpacked shelf, it may be necessary to temporarily remove several books in order to make enough room to extract the desired volume. It is easier to get two or three books out of the middle of the shelf at once than a single book at one end or the other.

Do not reshelve all the books if the fit is too tight. Notify the librarian that the area needs shifting.

Call Number Flags

Call numbers are not usually marked on books in special collections; often the number is typed on a flag of card weight stock that is inserted into the book. Plain card stock is better for this purpose than the flags sold in supply catalogs. Some flags have die-cut tabs to be hooked over a page, thus preventing them from falling into the book. However, fragile pages can be accidentally torn by the tabs. If the card is inserted into the middle of the book rather than at the title page, the book will hold the card more snugly and it will stay in place when a researcher looks at the table of contents, for instance.

Opening a Book

New Books

Brand-new books often have quite tight bindings and do not stay open well. Rather than opening a stiff book by forcing the spine to crack, take the time to open it gradually.

Rest it on its spine on the table or work counter. Allow the front and back boards to drop to the table and then begin opening pages alternately at the front and at the back. Gently smooth the pages over the boards with your hand. Keep opening pages a few at a time until you get to the middle of the book.

In the past, booksellers often gave buyers instructions for opening new books. Notices like this one can sometimes be found tucked inside early twentieth-century books (fig. 5-13). The excerpt comes from *Modern Bookbinding Practically Considered* (1889) by William Matthews.

Old Books

Old books have different problems. It is very common for the front cover of older books to have a weak joint area. When opening any book, make a habit of always cradling the front cover in your hand so that when you pick up a fragile book, the motion will be automatic. Depending on the condition of the joint, it may not be safe to open a book more than 90°. Never allow the board of an old book to flop down without supporting it, and do not open it more than 180°.

Some old books have tight spines that do not allow the pages to open well (see fig. 5-8), but they cannot usually be loosened in the same way as new books. Often these books cannot be opened more than 90° without danger of weakening the board attachment. Book supports can be helpful.

Supporting Fragile Books

When reading large, fragile, or tightly bound books, some support is needed to prevent damage to the bindings.

To keep the front board from opening more than the joint can tolerate, place a wedge-shaped support next to the spine before opening the book. Then open the front board and hold it until it comes to rest on the wedge. The angle of the wedge should vary according to how much the book can open without causing stress to the joint. You can use a combination of wedges or boards to make a temporary mount for the book, rearranging them as you progress to the middle of the book (fig. 5-14).

Fig 5-14

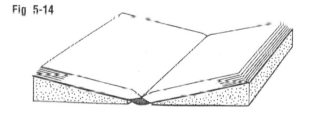

In the case of books with tight bindings, a wedge at both the front and the back of the book will make it easier to keep the book open. A variety of small weights and "snakes" (flexible weights) can be used to hold the pages open.

In "Preparing Books for Exhibition" in section 6, we discuss supports for books on display. Several kinds of wedges, stands, weights, and snakes are available from conservation catalogs. The special collections staff should keep an assortment of supports on hand and help patrons understand and accept their use.

NOTICE.

HOW TO OPEN A BOOK.

From "Modern Bookbinding."

Hold the book with its back on a smooth or covered table; let the front board down, then the other, holding the leaves in one hand while you open a few leaves at the back, then a few at the front, and so on, alternately opening back and front, gently pressing open the sections till you reach the center of the volume. Do this two or three times and you will obtain the best results. Open the volume violently or carelessly in any one place and you will likely break the back and cause a start in the leaves. Never force the back of the book.

"A connoisseur many years ago, an excellent customer of mine, who thought he knew perfectly how to handle books, came into my office when I had an expensive binding just brought from the bindery ready to be sent home; he, before my eyes, took hold of the volume and tightly holding the leaves in each hand, instead of allowing them free play, violently opened it in the center and exclaimed: 'How beautifully your bindings open!' I almost fainted. He had broken the back of the volume and it had to be rebound."

Fig. 5-13 Notice from *Modern Bookbinding Practically Considered* (1889) by William Matthews

---

Packing and Moving Books

Every library needs to pack books for moving or storage from time to time. In case of disasters, books must be packed so they can be sent to freezers. To avoid damage, a few simple rules apply.

Cleaning Books

When moving books to another section or putting them into storage, take the opportunity to remove loose surface dust from them. As the books come off the shelf, vacuum the tops of the books and other exposed surfaces. Use a vacuum cleaner with a HEPA filter or equivalent and put cheesecloth between the wand and the brush attachment, as shown in figures 1-11 and 1-12, p. 17. This quick cleaning will remove quite a bit of dirt and, possibly, mold spores as well. It also gives the person packing the books a chance to notice major problems, which should be brought to the attention of the supervisor.

Small Boxes

Books are dense, heavy objects. A large box filled with books is more likely to be dropped, causing damage to the contents. The weight can also cause injury to someone lifting or carrying it. Although the person who originally packs the books may be able to manage the box, it may well cause a problem for someone else who handles it later. Boxes or crates holding about one cubic foot are a good size.

Packing the Boxes

Books are made of "plastic" materials, i.e., materials that are pliable and adapt to new shapes. When they are not supported properly, as shown in figure 5-15, they become deformed. This is especially likely to happen if the books are stored in boxes rather than shelved immediately after a move. The severely distorted books in figure 5-16 show the results of poor packing.

Fig. 5-16

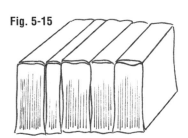

Fig. 5-15

The following are some good ways to arrange books in boxes.

1. Place the books upright on the bottom of the box, as if they were standing on a shelf. Keep them straight and don't let them sag, because this will cause them to become misshapen. Use wads of acid-free paper or other padding materials as needed to fill spaces.

2. Lay the books flat, one on top of the other, starting with the biggest books on the bottom. Don't let large books cantilever out over small ones.

3. Put books into cartons *spine side down*. If the spine faces up, the book will sag over a period of time and the pages may start to fall out of the covers.

Sometimes a combination of these methods within a box works best, e.g., put a couple of large, thin books at the bottom of the box and then some books upright or resting on their spines. Or you can have two piles of books that are lying flat. The idea is to make sure that the books are supported and do not have room to shift around, as shown in figure 5-17.

Fig. 5-17

Don't fill empty spaces with books at strange angles; use crumpled paper or spacers made from acid-free corrugated board or other conservation-quality materials.

Remember not to leave boxes of books on the floor, to avoid problems with moisture from leaks or condensation. Use judgment when stacking boxes to make sure that the contents do not get crushed. Don't stack boxes of wet books: they are particularly heavy and there is the possibility that the boxes will come apart, causing more damage to the books. Furthermore, wet books are especially likely to become distorted.

If it is necessary to stack boxes, be sure to use heavy-duty boxes that will not collapse and stack them no more than three boxes high. Consider using straight-sided, heavy-duty plastic crates designed for stacking.

Moving Books on Book Trucks

The same principles apply to placing books on book trucks. The books should be flat, or they can stand on the shelves of the truck, or they can be on their spines. They should be supported so they do not sag. Keep in mind that sometimes books stay on trucks for quite a long time.

Don't overload the trucks. If the books are going to be moved a good distance, do a trial run to make sure there is clearance for the trucks at doorways, narrow walkways, or temporary obstructions during construction. Make modifications to the route as needed before starting the move.

Sloped shelf trucks are somewhat better for moving smaller books because they hold the books a little more securely. But larger books that would protrude from this type of truck should be moved on flat shelf trucks. Consider tying a mover's woven strap around the books for added safety.

SUPPLIES AND EQUIPMENT NEEDED FOR BOOK REPAIRS

The following pages include descriptions of some of the supplies and tools of the trade. We've tried to list most items that might be used to carry out book repairs, but this doesn't mean that you must purchase everything before you can start. A modest tool kit consisting of adhesives, brushes, bone folders, microspatulas, a cutting mat, a steel straightedge, some knives, and a few weights will suffice at the beginning. Read through the techniques in "Book Repair Techniques" in this section to determine which procedures are appropriate for your collection. This will give you an idea of what equipment and supplies are necessary.

Adhesives

Repairs to the pages of books are made with starch paste or methylcellulose. Instructions for mixing and using these are given in "Adhesives" in section 4, p. 80. Straight paste and methylcellulose are used on occasion in book repair, but neither of these adhesives is strong enough for repairs to parts of the binding that must flex.

The word "glue" originally referred to protein-based adhesives derived from animals, while the term "paste" was used for adhesives made from plant starches. When synthetic adhesives were developed in the middle of the twentieth century, neither term was exactly accurate and there was some blurring of the distinction between them. Today the terms "gluing" and "pasting" are often used interchangeably. In this book, we tend to use "glue" for PVA and "paste" for paste and methylcellulose.

Hot Animal Glue, Hide Glue

Hot animal glue was used for centuries by bookbinders and restorers and can still be found in supply catalogs. It is protein-based and, when prepared and used properly, is an excellent adhesive that can be reversed with water. The glue comes in cake or granular form; it is diluted with water and then heated in an electric pot. The temperature must be regulated and water added from time to time to maintain the right consistency. The glue must be heated on a regular basis to avoid mold and decay and it must not be allowed to burn. These characteristics make it inconvenient; glue is no longer used in most institutional preservation labs.

There are a few other protein-based adhesives, such as gelatin, fish, and rabbit glues, but they are not suitable for the average in-house lab.

PVA

PVA (polyvinyl acetate) is a synthetic white glue. White glues are used by woodworkers and other craft people as well as by conservators and bookbinders. There are many formulations; those offered by conservation suppliers are pH neutral, do not give off harmful gases once dry, and do not break down over time. Polyvinyl acetate emulsion is usually white but dries clear. The bond is very strong and flexible. These qualities make it appropriate for use in certain types of conservation work.

PVAs vary in several characteristics, such as setting time and degree of reversibility. Polyvinyl alcohol, another type of white glue, is somewhat more reversible. When selecting a PVA, read the descriptions in the catalogs to see what fits your needs best and then order the smallest container to test it in use.

PVA must be applied with a light hand in order to achieve a satisfactory result. (See below for pasting tips.) However, the main drawback of this adhesive is that it is *not easily reversible*. It should not be used to repair historic bindings. A conservator should be consulted when an old, rare, or valuable book needs treatment.

When used straight out of the bottle, PVA dries too fast for most uses. While it is possible to slow the drying rate by adding water, the added liquid results in excessive wetting of the material being glued. This often causes stretching, warping, delamination, and other problems. PVA can be mixed with a slower-drying adhesive, such as methylcellulose, to provide a longer working time without the bad consequences of adding extra water. This mix is suitable for most steps in book repair.

Mix: 50-50 Mixture of PVA and Methylcellulose

To make this, combine equal parts PVA and prepared methylcellulose. (See "Adhesives" in section 4, p. 81, for methylcellulose mixing instructions.) It is much easier to apply a thin coat of this "mix" than plain PVA. Mix dries more slowly, giving the user more working time. Use mix for most work on book covers, pamphlet binders, and enclosures. Paste can also be used to make mix, but it will not keep as long.

A 50-50 mix of PVA and methylcellulose is available from a maker of fine papers and stationery, Twinrocker Handmade Paper. A PVA-paste mix is sold by Conservation Resources International. (See appendix B; more sources may be available in the future.)

Commercial Tapes

Double-coated tape is used for attaching pockets to books and for fastening polyester film jackets together. Purchase a tape that has a paper liner, such as 3-M no. 415, available from most conservation and library suppliers. The tape is sometimes called "double-stick," "double-sided," "double-faced," and probably other names as well; we use the term "double-coated" because that is what the manufacturer calls it.

Other pressure-sensitive tapes should be avoided. These tapes have two layers: the film "carrier" and the adhesive. Most of the adhesives cause staining over time or else they ooze out from under the carrier. They require solvents and technical skill for removal. It is almost impossible to remove tape and its residue from deteriorated leather or fragile cloth. Tape repairs have caused much damage to the inner hinges of books because the tape is usually so much stronger and thicker than the endpapers.

Pressure-sensitive tapes advertised as "archival" are sometimes more stable than regular tapes; they do not yellow and adhesive does not ooze out from the edges even after aging. But they are hard to remove and their aging properties are not really known yet. Do not use them for anything of lasting value. The tapes are quick and convenient fixes for circulating and other materials that are not meant to be kept, e.g., an annual directory that is discarded when the new one comes in.

Rubber Cement

Never use rubber cement! It gives off toxic gases that are harmful to the worker. As it ages, it dries up, releasing its hold and staining paper. It damages paper irreversibly.

Cloth

Several types of cloth are used in bookbinding and repair. Fabric is applied to the spine to help shape it and to reinforce the hinge area. Inner hinges are often made of cloth, as are headbands (endbands). The cloths chosen for spine linings and hinge reinforcement are usually unsized or lightly sized, to permit the adhesive to penetrate well.

The covers of many books have cloth glued to the outside. In order to use fabric this way, the adhesive must penetrate enough to attach the cloth to the boards but not so much that it goes through to the outside, or *face*, causing stains. Two methods are used to turn cloth into book cloth. The first is to put a size or coating on the cloth, which prevents the adhesive from penetrating all the way through.

Sizing can consist of a number of substances that are coated or impregnated into cloth. Vegetable starch was the traditional size used since cloth was first adapted for bookbinding in the 1830s. The term "starch-filled" refers to a cloth that is sized with vegetable starch. In the last two decades of the twentieth century, many synthetic fillings and coatings were developed and today starch-filled cloth is hard to find.

The other way to turn a cloth into book cloth is to laminate thin paper to the reverse side. Many good-quality book cloths are made this way.

In addition to preventing the adhesive from staining the face of the cloth, both of these methods make the cloth dimensionally stable. This means that it doesn't stretch or distort very much when adhesive is applied, and it handles somewhat like a piece of paper. This characteristic varies with types of cloth and the coatings or linings used. In general, very thin cloths are likely to stretch the most, and some require a practiced hand to work them onto a cover before they curl up. As with anything new, apply adhesive to a scrap of cloth to see how it reacts before starting on a project.

The grain of cloth runs parallel to the selvage, in the direction of the warp threads. (See "Grain Direction" in section 2, p. 46, for more information on determining grain.) Cloth should be cut so that the grain is parallel to the spine of the book. The joint area of the binding will work better this way.

Book cloth is available from the suppliers listed in appendix B in rolls of varying widths, from about 27" (69 cm) to about 55" (140 cm). Some suppliers also sell narrow rolls from 2" (5 cm) to 12" (30.5 cm) wide, as well as cloth cut to several sheet sizes. These last two formats are especially convenient for repairs.

Western and Japanese Papers

Practical Differences

Quite a bit of paper is used in bookbinding and repair, aside from the mending of text pages. Western and Japanese papers have very different properties, as discussed in "Overview of Western and Japanese Paper" in section 4, p. 76, and each is used for different purposes. Western papers are best for endpaper replacement, spine labels, hollow tubes, book jackets, and other applications where a strong, sized paper is preferable. Many bindings have paper-covered boards and cloth or leather spines, or they may be completely covered with paper. Japanese paper is soft and absorbent; these qualities make it less suited to these operations.

Japanese papers are preferred for repairing inner hinges and for spine lining. They are also sometimes used for repairing corners or heads and tails of spines. Japanese paper flexes and molds to desired shapes much better than Western paper, and its long, strong fibers keep it

from splitting as easily. A thin piece of Japanese paper is much stronger and more flexible than a Western paper of the same caliper (thickness). Because Japanese paper is so absorbent, it is often necessary to apply more than one coat of adhesive.

Grain

Grain direction is usually quite pronounced in Western papers. When cutting paper for book repairs, it is very important to make sure the grain runs parallel to the spine of the book. This applies also to photocopied pages used to replace missing pages. Otherwise, the stretching caused by applying adhesives or even changes in relative humidity will cause cockling and warping of the page.

Japanese paper is most often torn rather than cut. Although it flexes well in either grain direction, it tears more easily with the grain. Therefore, it is best to tear it long grain. This means hinge repairs will be made with the grain parallel to the spine, a desirable detail.

See section 4, "Overview of Western and Japanese Paper," for more general information about paper and for methods of testing grain direction.

Boards

Light board, such as bristol or card stock, is used in book repair for spine inlays and sometimes for making pockets. The grain of spine inlays must always be parallel to the spine of the book. Binder's board is used for making case bindings, but this manual does not include instruction in binding, since this is not a practical operation to perform in-house. (See the works by Diehl, Johnson, Watson, and Young in the bibliography for reference titles on bookbinding.)

Thread

Linen or cotton thread is used for sewing book pages together. There are many weights or thicknesses of thread, and several considerations affect the choice of weight when sewing a book. For a preservation department, it is adequate to have just one medium weight, for instance, 18/3. The numbers in thread sizes get smaller as the weight of the thread gets larger, e.g., 12/3 thread is heavier than 18/3. The number after the slash refers to the number of cords that are twisted together to make the thread.

Hand Tools

The following hand tools are useful in book repair.

Cutting mat. Some steps require cutting by hand; a self-healing plastic cutting mat about 9" × 12" (23 × 31 cm) is handy for trimming pages. A larger mat, at least 18" × 24" (46 × 61 cm), can be used for cutting larger items. In the past, bookbinders used thin zinc sheets to cut on. Thin, flexible plastic mats sold for cutting vegetables can be used in the same way. They do eventually get cut marks but can be replaced frequently since they are quite inexpensive.

Straightedge. For accurate cuts, a heavy straightedge, 24" or 36" (61 or 92 cm) long, is much better than a ruler, even a metal one.

Knives. Figure 5-18, at the end of the supply list, shows various kinds of knives. The second knife from the left in the photograph is a kitchen paring knife, often used dull for a variety of scraping operations. The choice of knife varies with personal preference; a heavy utility knife (third from left in fig. 5-18) gives good control when cutting heavy boards, and scalpels (fourth and fifth from left) work well for cutting paper. But many people use other types of knives with replaceable or snap-off blades, such as the sixth knife from the left. Knives and scalpels are reasonably priced and it is a good idea to have an assortment on hand.

Fig. 5-18 An assortment of knives and spatulas

Good *scissors* are needed to cut various items. As with knives, it is helpful to have a few pairs of different sizes. Keep them sharp and protect the tips from damage. Never use the blades to scrape debris or to pry things open.

Bone and Teflon folders are indispensable for most operations. They are described in "Hand Tools" in section 2, p. 45.

Microspatulas. Stainless steel spatulas of different sizes and shapes serve many purposes and can be obtained from conservation suppliers. One is shown in figure 5-18 on the extreme right. Carbon steel spatulas, sometimes called Casselli spatulas, are much thinner and are useful for lifting and splitting operations. They are more expensive than stainless steel spatulas and more delicate. They will rust if not dried after they get wet. A few suppliers carry them. A Casselli spatula is to the left of the stainless steel microspatula in figure 5-18.

Lifting knives are angled, rigid knives, often made from carbon steel. The knife on the extreme left in figure 5-18 is a lifting knife. They are useful for separating cloth or paper from boards. They come in right- and left-handed versions. A few suppliers carry them.

Needles, knitting needles. Select sewing needles about 2" (5 cm) long and not too thin. No. 3 darners are good; avoid beading or other long, thin needles because they are too flexible and hard to control. Conservation suppliers carry sewing needles; they can also be purchased in fabric or craft stores. Knitting needles are used to repair loose hinges. Select smooth metal needles, nos. 3 or 4, that are 9"–14" (23–35 cm) long. Plastic needles are usually too flexible.

Elastic bandages (e.g., Ace) are used for certain steps and may be bought in pharmacies and veterinary supply stores. Elastic bandages that cling to themselves eliminate the need for fasteners.

Brushes. An assortment of sizes, e.g., ½", 1", 1½", 2" (about 1–5 cm), is recommended. Nylon or polyester paintbrushes with bristles that taper into a wedge are fine. Make sure the bristles don't come off. A great variety of styles is available, at widely ranging prices. Wide brushes with very flat bristles are useful for various applications. You may find them in hardware stores or in stores that sell supplies for professional hair coloring. Experiment to see what works best for your applications. You can use the same *types* of brushes for both paste and for PVA or mix, but have separate sets; PVA is very difficult to remove completely from the bristles.

Spacers. These ¼" (6–7 mm) square metal or plastic rods are available from craft stores. They are optional but are useful when attaching boards to a new spine, as described in "Rebacking a Book with Detached Boards" (p. 140).

Awls are used for piercing sewing holes in pamphlet binders. Some awls have metal rings, or sharp ridges around the handle. Get awls with smooth, rounded handles.

Equipment

Some appropriate equipment in good condition will make it easier to do good work. A good cutter, a few small presses, and an assortment of wooden boards are essential. These items are described in "Equipment" in section 2, p. 36.

Other Supplies

Other supplies used in book repair include the following.

- Acid-free blotter. Pieces cut to book sizes, e.g., 9" × 12" (23 × 30 cm), are used for inserting inside the covers; some 3" × 12" (7.5 × 30 cm) pieces are used for drying hinged pages; and so on.
- Spun polyester web (e.g., Hollytex, Reemay) allows moisture and air to pass but prevents adhesives from sticking to blotters. Cut some to the same sizes as blotter pieces.

- Polyester film (e.g., Mylar or Mellinex), cut to book sizes, is used for moisture barriers.
- Waste paper (unprinted newsprint) is used for pasting on, covering surfaces, and so on.
- Wax paper is used for moisture and adhesive barriers, and for wrapping text blocks.
- Plastic wrap is an alternative for wrapping text blocks.
- Medium-fine sandpaper or sanding blocks are used for sanding spines.
- Weights are needed for many operations. They are sold by conservation suppliers, but other heavy items can be used as well. New bricks can be wrapped in several layers of wrapping paper which is then taped or glued shut. Bring the bricks indoors and allow them to dry for several days before wrapping them. Sad irons (small cast-iron implements used before the invention of the electric iron), wood-splitting wedges, and sash weights can all be cleaned and pressed into use.

  Small weights can be made by putting lead shot and sand into film canisters or small boxes that are then wrapped in paper. They should weigh at least a pound (one-half kilo) to be useful.

BOOK REPAIR TECHNIQUES

In the rest of this section we give directions for carrying out book repairs that are appropriate for research collections. The goal is to keep books on the shelf as long as possible using methods that do not cause harm. However, rare or valuable books should not be repaired in-house by these methods. A conservator should be consulted to determine a course of action that will preserve the book's value and historical integrity.

The instructions are presented starting with simpler steps and progressing to more time-consuming procedures. Because books are complex, three-dimensional objects, it is not feasible to cover every possible situation. You may have to use your ingenuity to combine various methods in order to solve a particular problem. It is often helpful to see the same technique described in a different

way. Consult other works on book repair; books on bookbinding may also help. Both types are listed in the bibliography.

If after practicing some of the steps that follow you are able to develop your own sound methods for solving problems peculiar to your institution, we will consider our work well done.

Simple Repairs between the Covers

Instructions for cleaning and repairing pages are given in "Paper Repair Techniques" in section 4. Here we deal with incorporating repaired pages into the text block and with endpaper and inner hinge repair.

Reinserting Pages into Books

When a page has come loose, examine the pages around it to see if they are still firmly attached. If the book is sewn through the folds of signatures, it is possible that the conjugate, the other half of the folded leaf, is also loose (fig. 5-19).

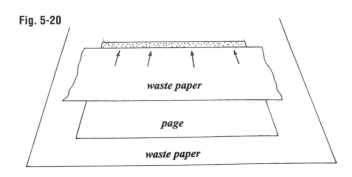

Fig. 5-20

waste paper

page

waste paper

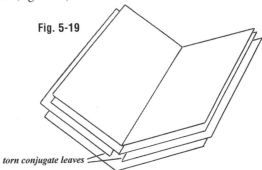

Fig. 5-19

torn conjugate leaves

There is no hard-and-fast rule about how many pages can be reinserted into a book. The important thing is not to add too much bulk at the gutter, and this will vary with the thickness of the paper and the size of the book. This also applies to replacing missing pages with photocopies from other books. If it seems that attaching all the loose pages is going to deform the spine, the book should be replaced, withdrawn, or sent to the library binder.

TIPPING

The quickest method for attaching a loose page is by tipping it in. "Tipping in" means putting a thin line of adhesive (a 50-50 mix of PVA and methylcellulose) on the edge of a piece of paper and attaching it to a page without other hinge material. A photocopied replacement page can be tipped in. A single loose page in a book and its conjugate, if necessary, can also be simply tipped in. Illustration plates in art books are often tipped on to pages; they can be reattached by this method if they become detached.

Place the leaf to be tipped in face-down on a piece of waste paper. Put another piece of waste paper on top, ⅛"–¼" (3–7 mm) away from the edge to be tipped (fig. 5-20). Apply adhesive to the exposed edge, brushing from the center out.

Remove and discard the top piece of waste paper, lift the leaf and position it in the desired location (fig. 5-21). Rub down through polyester web and blotter with a bone folder. Remove the blotter. Place wax paper on either side of the page to prevent moisture from spreading.

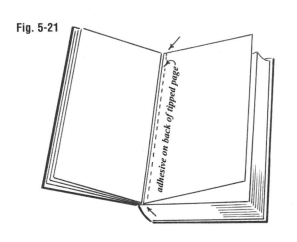

Fig. 5-21

adhesive on back of tipped page

Close the book and allow it to dry under a board and weight (fig. 5-22).

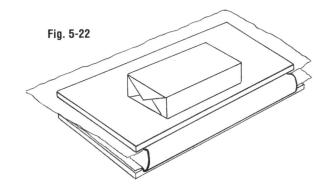

Fig. 5-22

REATTACHING LOOSE PLATES

If plates that were attached at just one edge have come loose, you can tip them back in.

Cut a piece of Mylar or card stock a little longer than the item. Apply a ¼" (6–7 mm) line of mix evenly to the card or the Mylar. Slide the card about ⅛" (3 mm) under the edge that has become detached (fig. 5-23). Rub it down gently with fingertips. This will transfer some of the adhesive from the card or the Mylar to the back of the plate. Remove the card and rub down with a bone or Teflon folder through a piece of polyester web and a blotter (or a paper towel).

Fig. 5-23

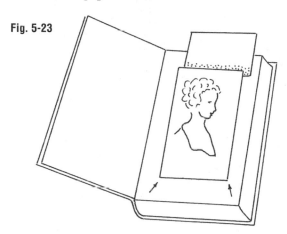

If adhesive oozes out, use less the next time.

Reapply mix to the card as needed and tack the other edges down. Or you can adhere just the corners opposite the first edge you tipped in, depending on the size of the item. Rub down through web or blotter.

Remove the blotter, leave a piece of polyester web or wax paper in place, close the book, and allow it to dry under a board and weight (see fig. 5-22).

When dry, remove polyester web or wax paper.

There are other ways of attaching loose pages or plates to books, as follows.

HINGING

If the page or the plate to be inserted is thick, it is usually better to hinge rather than tip it. This is because thick paper does not bend easily and can put undue stress on the "host" page. If the page is brittle, it can break off. In any case, a thick, tipped-in plate is more likely to become detached and fall off.

If the pages to be added are short grain, they should always be hinged.

Note: These instruction are also provided in section 4 because hinges are often attached at the same time that repairs are made to book pages. They are repeated here for convenience.

A hinge is a narrow strip of paper attached lengthwise (like a piano hinge) to the page to be inserted into the book. Choose a Japanese paper of suitable weight and color. It should be thicker than that used for repairing tears but thinner than the paper the page is printed on. Sekishu, which comes in white and natural tones, is often a good choice, but thinner papers can often be used. The thinner the hinge paper is, the less extra bulk will be added in the gutter. This keeps the book from getting distorted.

Sometimes the page to be hinged needs to be trimmed a little in order to accommodate the added hinge. It is better to trim the gutter edge than the fore edge, especially if the edges of the book are gilt, marbled, or deckled. Determine ahead of time how much needs to be trimmed off the gutter edge so that the hinged page will line up with the fore edge of the book. However, if the fore edge is very damaged, trim a small amount (say, ⅛", or 3 mm) off the leaf at the fore edge. When a leaf has been detached from a book for some time, all the edges are often frayed. In that case, trim all the edges, just the minimum amount needed to cut off the fraying. (Long tears should be mended rather than cut off.) The page will then fit better in the book and will be less likely to tear further. These instructions apply to books from circulating or research collections. Do not trim the pages of old or rare books without consulting a librarian or curator.

Attaching the Hinge

Tear a strip approximately ⅝" (1.6 cm) wide by a bit longer than the height of the page to be hinged. Tear the hinge so that the grain runs the length of the strip.

Place the page to be hinged on a sheet of waste paper. Place another piece of waste paper on top, about ¼" (6–7 mm) away from the edge where the hinge will be placed (fig. 5-24). Apply adhesive to the exposed area. Remove the top waste sheet and move the page onto a clean, absorbent surface, such as blotter covered with polyester web. Discard the used waste paper.

Fig. 5-24

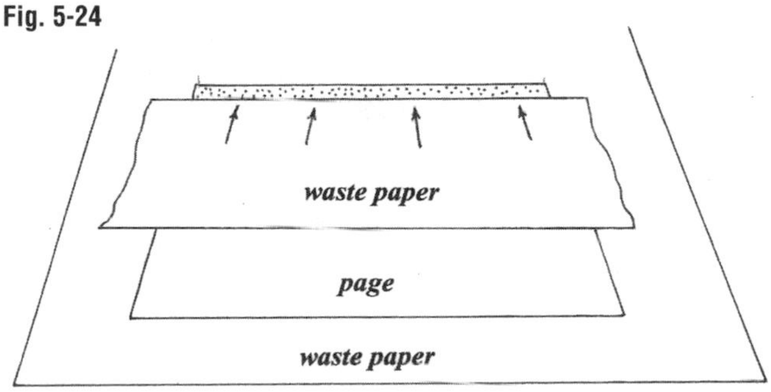

waste paper

page

waste paper

Position the strip of Japanese paper over the pasted area (fig. 5-25). *Be careful not to stretch the pasted strip or the repair will buckle when it dries.*

Fig. 5-25

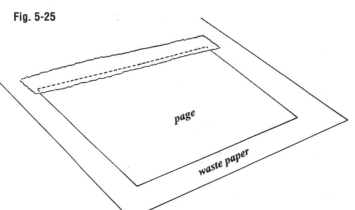

Cover with web and blotter and rub down with a bone folder. Replace the blotter with a dry one and let dry under weight.

Attaching Leaves with Hinges to the Book

Remove the weight and blotter and turn the leaf over so that the attached part of the strip is underneath.

Put a piece of wax paper or polyester film on the leaf, for a moisture barrier, and place a piece of waste paper over that. Line up the edges of the moisture barrier and the waste paper with the edge of the leaf, leaving the hinge uncovered.

Fold the hinge up over the moisture barrier (fig. 5-26) and waste paper and apply mix to the hinge.

Open the book to the place where the hinged page will go. Carefully remove the waste paper and the moisture barrier. Discard the waste paper but save the moisture barrier. Place a thin ruler within the fold of the hinge

Fig. 5-26

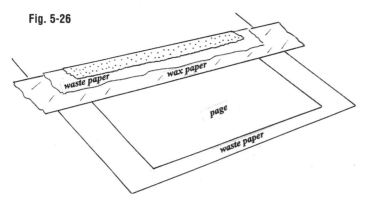

and use it to work the hinged page into position (fig. 5-27). When it is as snug into the gutter as possible, remove the ruler. Rub the hinge down gently with a bone folder, being careful not to stretch the damp Japanese paper.

Fig. 5-27

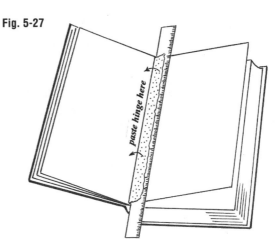

Replace the moisture barrier next to the leaf, and then put a piece of blotter and a piece of polyester web over the moisture barrier. The web will be next to the damp Japanese paper hinge. Let the blotter and web stick out of the book an inch or two at each end, to wick away the dampness. Close the book gently and place a weight over it.

If more than one page needs to be hinged, it is usually better to let the first one dry before going on to the next.

INSERTING GUARDED LEAVES

When there are two adjoining leaves to be attached, it is sometimes easier to connect them together first with a narrow strip of Japanese paper called a "guard." This is called "guarding"; directions are in "Guarding Two Leaves" in section 4, p. 92. After the guard is dry, the pair of leaves can be inserted into the book by either tipping or hinging.

TIPPING IN GUARDED LEAVES

Guarded leaves can be tipped in if the grain is long and the paper is flexible and not too thick. To tip the pages in, fold the guarded leaves neatly and place them on waste paper. Place another piece of waste paper on top, about ¼" (6–7 mm) away from the fold. Apply adhesive to the exposed area. Remove the top waste sheet and discard it.

Place a ruler between the two guarded leaves and gently push the leaves into position, making sure they go as far into the gutter as possible (fig. 5-28).

Fig. 5-28

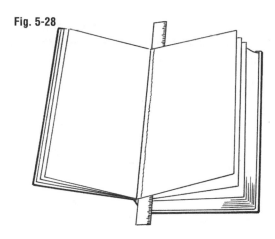

Put a piece of wax paper or Mylar between the "host" page and the pages being added, positioning it at the edge of the adhesive.

Close the book and place a board and weight on it. Allow it to dry.

HINGING IN GUARDED LEAVES

Pages that are printed on short-grain paper or are thick and stiff should not be tipped in. The action of turning would soon cause them to come loose or tear out. A hinge can be attached to the folded leaves, over the guard, in the same way as attaching a hinge to a single leaf.

When the hinge is dry, turn the leaves over so that the attached part of the strip is underneath and the rest of the hinge is spread out smoothly.

Place wax paper and waste paper over the folded leaves, lining up the edges of the moisture barrier and the waste paper with the edge of the folded, guarded leaves. Leave the hinge uncovered.

Fold the hinge up over the moisture barrier and the waste paper and apply mix to the hinge (fig. 5-29).

Fig. 5-29

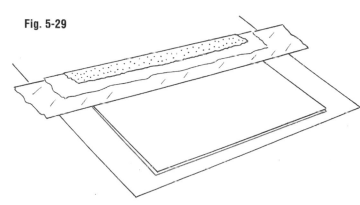

Discard the waste paper; remove the moisture barrier and set aside.

Open the book to the place where the guarded, hinged pages will go. Place a thin ruler within the fold of the guarded pages and use it to work them into position, as close to the gutter as possible (fig. 5-30). Remove the ruler. Rub the hinge down gently with a bone folder, being careful not to stretch the damp Japanese paper.

Fig. 5-30

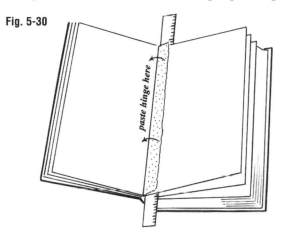

paste hinge here

Put the moisture barrier between the damp hinge paper and the guarded leaves. Close the book and put a board and weight on it. Let dry.

Reinserting a Signature

Occasionally a whole signature may come loose. To repair and reinsert it, the signature can be sewn to a strip of Japanese paper; the strip is then attached to the pages on either side. This method secures all the loose pages and permits them to turn freely.

If the conjugates are broken, they will need to be guarded together. To make sure the pages will fit into the book, trim a small amount off the gutter edge, perhaps ¹⁄₁₆" (2 mm). We prefer to apply the guarding strip on the *inside* of the inner folio (pair of folded leaves); this gives a firm base for the sewing. The other conjugates may be guarded on the outside. Leaves with intact folds should not be guarded, to save time and reduce bulk in the gutter area.

Note: Occasionally the outer folio of the signature will remain attached to the last page of the previous signature and to the first page of the following signature. If it is firmly attached, leave that folio in place and proceed with the other steps below.

Nest the folded sheets in correct order.

Tear a strip of Japanese paper, about an inch (2.5 cm) wide and the height of the pages. Fold it in half lengthwise. Fold it around the outside of the nested pages. The strip will form a hinge on each side of the signature (fig. 5-31). The two hinges help fix it in position.

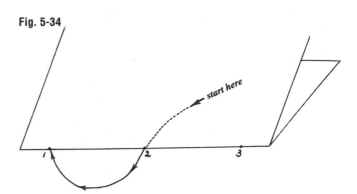

Fig. 5-31

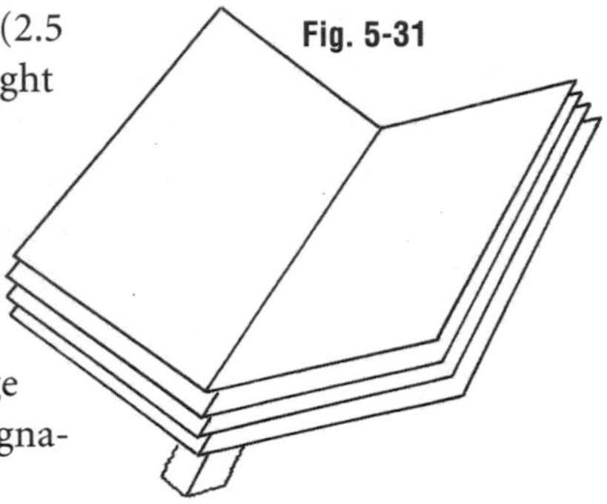

SEWING LEAVES TOGETHER

Align the nested leaves so the edges match, and wrap the folded Japanese paper strip around them. Hold the strip and pages together with paper clips (fig. 5-32).

Fig. 5-32

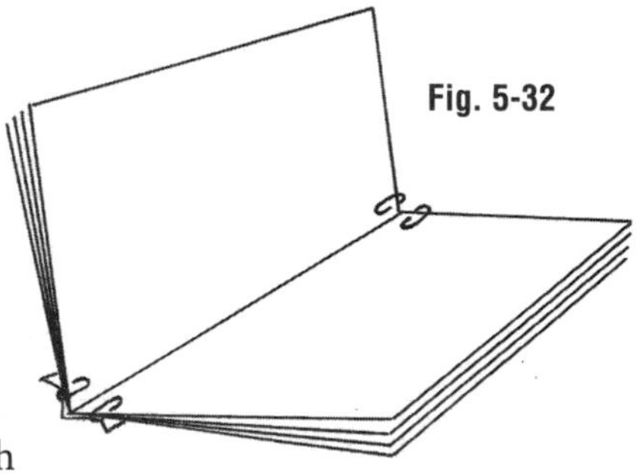

Cut a length of linen thread about 2½ times the height of the pages. Thin thread makes less bulk in the hinge area, but it is more likely to cut the paper. Use a medium thread, no. 18, or light-medium, no. 25. Thread a needle.

To mark the sewing holes, cut a strip of paper the height of the pages. Fold it in half. Make a fold about an inch (2.5 cm) from each end. When you open out the strip, there should be three folds (fig. 5-33).

Fig. 5-33

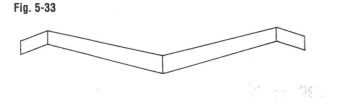

Place the opened strip inside the signature and use the needle to pierce holes through the pages and through the Japanese paper, at each fold mark.

Sew in the following pattern: begin at the center hole (2) and go from the inside of the signature to the outside (fig. 5-34). Leave about 4" (10 cm) of thread inside.

Fig. 5-34

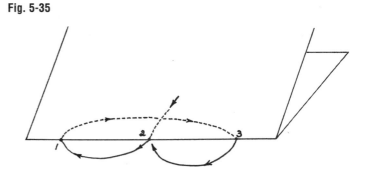

Go back from the outside to the inside through hole 1. Skip the middle hole and go out through hole 3. Gently pull the thread snug, *parallel* to the center fold (fig. 5-35). If you pull at right angles to the fold you risk tearing the pages with the thread.

Fig. 5-35

Now bring the needle back inside the signature, where the tail end of the thread is (fig. 5-36).

Fig. 5-36

Make sure that the needle goes on the other side of the long stitch between holes 1 and 3 from where the tail is. Snug the thread again and tie a square knot, *catching the long stitch* (fig. 5-37). (See "Sewing Single-Section Pamphlets into a Binder," p. 146, for a description of a square knot.)

Fig. 5-37

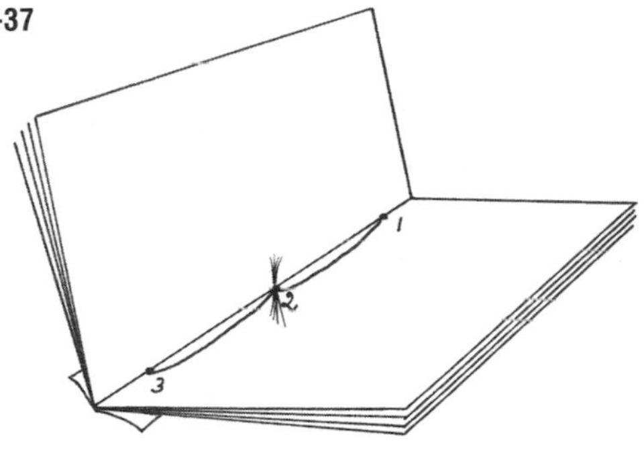

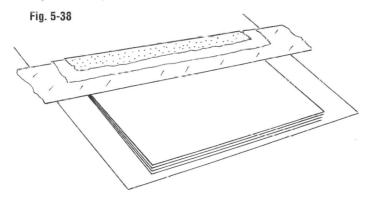

ATTACHING THE SIGNATURE TO THE BOOK

Next, the signature is attached to the book using the Japanese paper strip sewn on in the previous step. The strip forms two hinges; each hinge is attached to a "host" page as a separate step. Using two hinges helps fix the signature so that it remains aligned with the rest of the pages and does not sag or shift out of position.

Attaching the First Hinge

Place the sewn signature on a piece of waste paper and insert waste paper and wax paper or Mylar, as a moisture barrier, between the hinge and the outermost page of the signature (fig. 5-38).

Fig. 5-38

Apply mix to the hinge. Discard the waste paper; remove the moisture barrier and set it aside to use later.

Open the book to the place where the signature will go. Insert a moisture barrier behind each host page (fig. 5-39).

Fig. 5-39

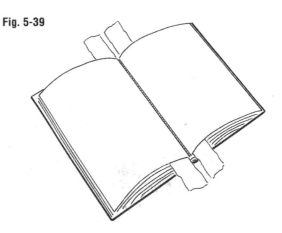

Place a ruler within the fold in the center of the signature. Use the ruler to guide the signature as far into the gutter as possible (fig. 5-40). Make sure that the top and bottom of the pages are aligned with the text block. Remove the ruler.

The pasted hinge will start attaching to the facing page as you push the signature into the gutter. Gently rub it down with a bone or Teflon folder, being careful not to stretch the damp Japanese paper.

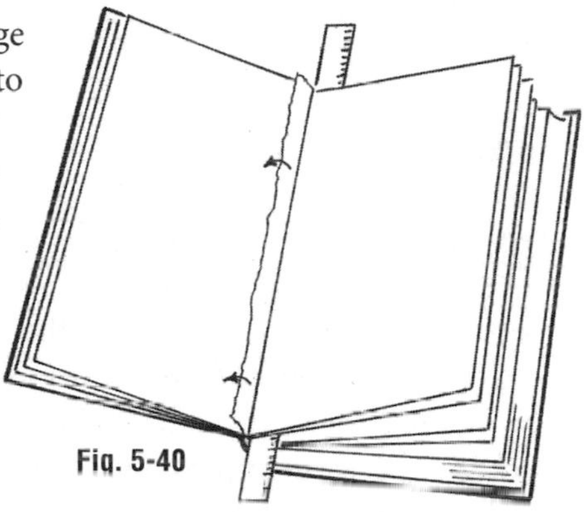

Fig. 5-40

Put a moisture barrier between the damp hinge paper and the signature and then put a piece of blotter and a piece of polyester web *over* the moisture barrier. The web will be next to the damp Japanese paper hinge. Let the blotter and web stick out of the book an inch or two at each end, to wick away the dampness.

Close the book gently, place a weight on it, and allow the hinge to dry for an hour or two.

Open the book and check that the first hinge is down correctly. If the signature is not quite straight, you may be able to realign it slightly when putting down the second hinge.

Attaching the Second Hinge

If the binding is loose enough, attach the second hinge in the same manner as the first. However, if the binding is tight and it is difficult to brush mix on the hinge neatly, use a scrap of card, as described earlier in "Reattaching Loose Plates," p. 108.

Paint mix on the card, then hold it with the adhesive facing the signature being reinserted. Carefully slip it behind the Japanese paper hinge, to transfer adhesive to it (fig. 5-41). Work the hinge into the gutter, using a Teflon folder, if available, or a bone folder without a very sharp point.

Fig. 5-41

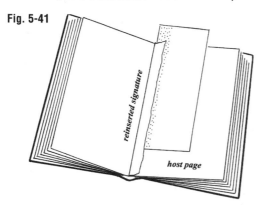

reinserted signature

host page

Put a moisture barrier next to the signature, then a blotter, and finally a piece of polyester web next to the hinge. Close the book, put a weight on it, and allow it to dry.

After the hinges are both dry, remove the blotter and barriers. See if the signature fits neatly in the book and check whether the pages turn well. If any of the pages stick out a little, trim them so they are the same size as the rest of the book. (See below for instructions.)

Some books have very tight bindings and it may be difficult to reinsert signatures into them. It might be better to send such books to the library binder.

Trimming Pages

After reattaching one or more leaves or inserting a photo-copied replacement for a missing page, a page may stick out of the book a little bit. Here is how to trim it.

Place a small cutting mat under the page to be trimmed. Put a thin steel ruler over the page and align the ruler with the pages above it.

Hold the pages closed firmly and cut along the ruler with a scalpel or small utility knife, making several light cuts (fig. 5-42).

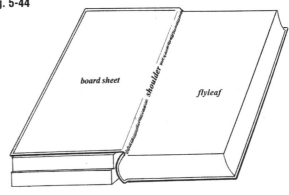

Fig. 5-42

Remember to keep pressure on the closed pages until the cut is complete to avoid a ragged cut.

Repeat the procedure at the other edges if necessary.

Endpapers

The *endpapers* or *endsheets* of a modern case-bound book consist of folded sheets of medium-weight paper that are tipped onto the *shoulders* of the text block, one in front and one in back, before the covers are attached (fig. 5-43). The shoulders are the edges of the spine that are bent over in the backing process to accommodate the thickness of the boards, as described on p. 99.

Fig. 5-43

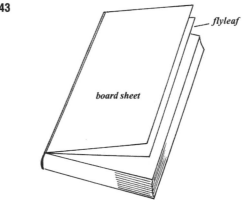

flyleaf

board sheet

The *board sheet* is the part of the endpaper that is pasted to the inside of the cover, or board, in the process of *casing in* (attaching the cover to the text block). It is sometimes called a "pastedown." The *flyleaf*, or *free end-paper*, is the half that is next to the text block (fig. 5-44). The endpapers are sometimes decorative, but their primary function is to protect the contents of the book when the cover is opened. When flyleaves are torn or missing, that first layer of protection is gone.

Fig. 5-44

board sheet　　*shoulder*　　*flyleaf*

Replacing Missing Flyleaves

If the flyleaves are torn but have no missing areas, they can be mended as described in section 4, "Mending Torn Pages in Books," p. 93. When the flyleaves are more damaged or very crumpled, it is usually better to replace them. New buffered paper flyleaves can also be made if the book has acidic boards that are staining the text block.

In the process of binding the book, the flyleaves were tipped onto the first page of the text block. Examine this area. If the remains of the flyleaf are firmly attached and the hinge area is not damaged, insert a thin cutting mat as far as possible under the flyleaf and cut it off neatly using a straightedge and knife. (If the hinge area is damaged, repair it as described below in "Repairing Hinges before Applying New Flyleaves" before proceeding with the next step.)

Select a medium-weight paper for the replacement flyleaf. Acid-free wrapping paper is available in several colors and is an economical choice. Conservation suppliers offer many other suitable papers; some are called "endpaper" in the catalog. You can use thinner acid-free papers in very small books.

Cut a piece of paper, the height of the text block and a little wider than the text. The grain must run parallel to the spine. Tip it onto the shoulder, over the remains of the old flyleaf, being careful to line up the top and bottom of the new flyleaf with the pages. It will stick out at the fore edge and will be trimmed afterwards. Put a piece of polyester web and a blotter over the tipped area, close the book, and put a weight on it. When the repair is dry, turn the book so the new flyleaf is at the bottom and trim the fore edge (fig. 5-45), as described in "Trimming Pages," p. 114.

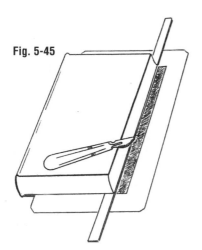

Fig. 5-45

Repairing Hinges before Applying New Flyleaves

Occasionally the paper over the inner hinge is loose or cracked. Carefully remove any loose, broken paper from the hinge. This should expose the spine lining (called the "super," "crash," or "mull"), which extends from the spine over each board, covering about 1" (2.5 cm) of the board. The super is what keeps the text block attached to the boards. *Do not disturb any paper that is firmly attached,* to avoid tearing the super. Cut the flyleaf off with a knife and straightedge, using a cutting mat.

If the flyleaf is peeling away from the text block, gently finish removing it using a microspatula or knife blade if necessary. Try not to tear the first page of the text block when doing this, but if it does tear, mend it with Japanese paper and paste, as explained in "Mending Edge Tears" in section 4, p. 89, and allow it to dry before proceeding.

Place a support under the book cover so that the board opens to 180°, i.e., flat (fig. 5-46). Place a small weight on the board to keep it in position.

Fig. 5-46

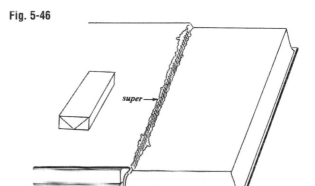

Brush a tiny amount of mix wherever the super is exposed, and work it gently into the hinge area. Use a small brush, microspatula, bone folder, down any loose pieces of paper still on the hinge.

While this dries, cut a new flyleaf, the height of the pages and a little wider than the text. The grain must be parallel to the spine. Tip it onto the shoulder of the book (fig. 5-47).

Fig. 5-47

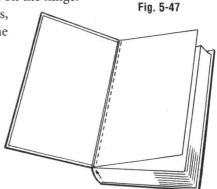

When both the hinge and the tipped-in flyleaf are dry, consolidate the repair by attaching a strip of Japanese paper over the hinge, covering the edge of the new flyleaf (fig. 5-48). Use paste or methylcellulose for a neater look; mix can also be used but may result in a shinier mend. Let it air dry for about fifteen minutes before closing the book. This allows the repair to set and minimizes wrinkling.

Fig. 5-48

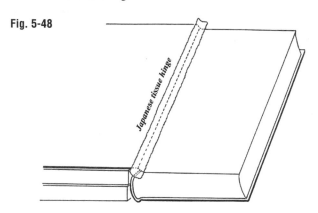

Japanese tissue hinge

Trim the repair strip with a small scissors or knife, being careful not to cut the binding.

This method tightens the hinge in addition to replacing the flyleaf.

BOARD SHEET REPLACEMENT

Replacing the board sheet part of the endpaper is more complicated because adding a layer of paper over the old board sheet is almost certain to cause the board to warp. It is better to just change the flyleaf neatly, using a paper compatible to the original, than to end up with warped boards which can let dirt accumulate inside the book. A warped book is also difficult to shelve next to other books.

If the old board sheet is badly damaged, consider whether the book should be sent to the library binder or replaced.

Tightening Book Hinges

Books become loose in the inner hinge area when the spine lining and the endpapers are partially unglued from the covers (sometimes called "shaken" in booksellers' catalogs). The contents of large, heavy volumes stored upright tend to sag away from their cases. Improper shelving can also cause loose hinges: the text blocks of oversize books stored on their fore edges start sagging and separating from the case, and books at haphazard

angles, unsupported by bookends, also get distorted. Books thrown down book-return chutes suffer similarly, and so do books that have been wet. A simple method for regluing these damaged volumes uses a knitting needle (no. 3 or 4) and PVA or mix.

Dip the knitting needle all the way into a plastic bottle containing PVA or mix (fig. 5-49). (Snip off the tip of the cap to accommodate needle size.) As you pull the needle out of the bottle, just enough glue will remain on the needle. (You can also "paint" the needle with a thin coat of adhesive if you don't have a plastic bottle handy.)

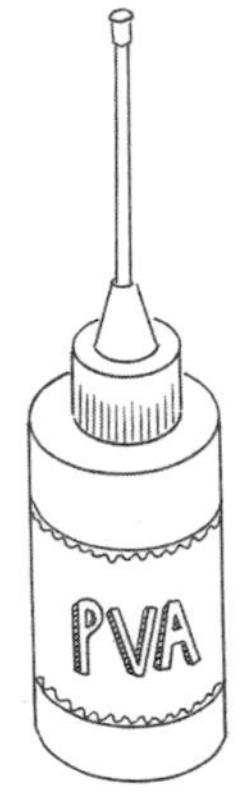

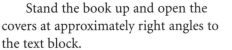

PVA

Stand the book up and open the covers at approximately right angles to the text block.

Fig. 5-49

Insert the needle into the loose area between the endpaper and the hinge (fig. 5-50). Be careful not to pierce the endpaper at the inner hinge. Move the needle gently up and down to coat the area. Turn the book upside down and repeat the process from the other end. Recoat the needle with PVA as needed.

Fig. 5-50

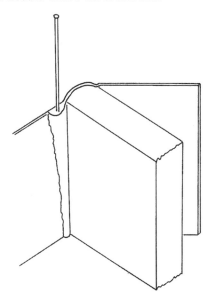

If a wide area of the hinge is loose, you may use a small brush to insert glue, very carefully, behind the paper and super. This will need to be smoothed down. Put the book down, open the cover, and support it on boards or on another book (fig. 5-51).

Put a blotter or paper towel over the freshly glued area and rub down gently with the flat part of a bone or

Fig. 5-51

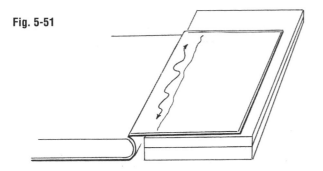

Teflon folder. Clean any adhesive that might ooze out from under the endpaper.

Insert a piece of wax paper or polyester film and close the book. If the glued area was extensive, put polyester web next to it and cover it with a blotter, then close the book.

From the outside, work the cloth into the joint using the edge (not the point) of a bone or Teflon folder. Be careful not to split the cloth or paper covering.

Repeat these steps on the other hinge if needed.

Place the book between boards (brass-edged if available) and let dry overnight under a weight. Note the position of the joints of the book at the edges of the boards (fig. 5-52). (See "Boards, Pressing Boards" in section 2, p. 43, for a description of brass-edged boards.)

After tightening the book in its case, it may be neces-

Fig. 5-52

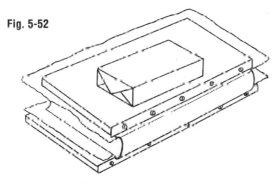

sary to consolidate weakened or cracked paper at the inner hinges with Japanese paper. The traditional adhesive for this step is starch paste, but methylcellulose also works well. Mix can be used but the result will be a shinier, more noticeable repair. See the directions at the end of "Hinge Reinforcement" below.

Hinge Reinforcement

When the paper over the hinge area is cracked, it is not practical to tighten the hinge by the knitting needle method. However, the broken paper gives access to the super and adhesive can be introduced through it.

Open the book and support the cover with boards. Examine the hinge area to see whether the super is broken (fig. 5-53). If it is, the book should be repaired using the instructions for "Repairing One Broken Hinge," p. 126, or "Reattaching the Text Block to the Case," p. 129. If the super is largely intact, continue with this process.

Fig. 5-53

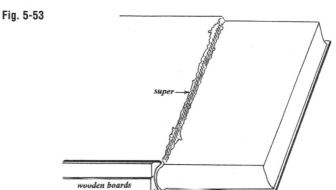

super→

wooden boards

With a small brush or a microspatula, work some mix into the super, going between the broken edges of the endpaper.

Next, tack the edges of the paper down, trying to match the original pattern, if any.

Put a piece of wax paper over the hinge area and rub the repair very gently in order to set the paper without stretching or disarranging it.

Allow this step to dry completely.

Select a medium-weight Japanese paper such as Sekishu. Cut or tear a strip the height of the text block by approximately ½" (1.3 cm) wide. The width should vary according to how damaged the hinge paper was. In general, the narrower the strip, the neater the repair will look. Thinner tissues can be used; the repair will be more transparent, allowing the original paper to be seen. Japanese papers are available in many colors that can blend well into endpapers.

Paste up the Japanese tissue strip. Pick it up, holding one end with a microspatula and the other with your fingers. Position it over the joint (fig. 5-54). Pat it down gently

Fig. 5-54

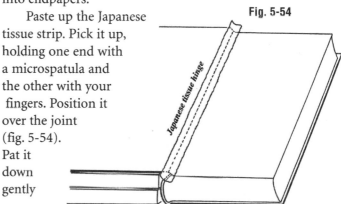

Japanese tissue hinge

with fingertips, then rub with the flat part of a bone or Teflon folder through a piece of polyester web. Let it air dry for about fifteen minutes before closing the book. This allows the repair to set and minimizes wrinkling. You can speed up the drying with a hair dryer set on "low."

Trim the paper strip to the height of the endpapers, using small scissors, or use a scalpel or small utility knife, being careful not to cut through to the binding. When dry, close the book and repeat on the other side if necessary.

If you need to close the book before the repair is dry, insert a piece of wax paper next to the hinge.

Pockets for Maps or Other Enclosures Found in Books

The simplest way to prevent loose materials in books from becoming separated is to attach a pocket to the back board of the book. This is an accepted procedure for circulating or reference books as long as the loose materials are not too thick, because excessive bulk will cause distortion to the binding. Pockets can also be added to pamphlet binders, to hold maps or other items that can't be sewn into the binder.

Pockets may not be appropriate for special collections materials; consult the librarian or curator before working on such books.

BASIC POCKET

A basic pocket can be made out of 10-point acid-free card stock or bristol. For light materials, acid-free wrapping paper or cover stock paper is also suitable. The pocket is open on two sides for easy insertion and removal of the materials, yet it still provides plenty of support for them.

Cut a piece of bristol board approximately the width of the back board and about ⅔ the height of the board.

Score and fold the bristol ½" (1.3 cm) from the bottom edge and ½" from the right edge. Cut the corners as illustrated (fig. 5-55). Fold the flaps under. Cut the top left part of the pocket at a low angle. Apply a strip of double-coated tape to each flap. Position the pocket on the inside of the back board;

Fig. 5-55

it can be aligned on the edges of the endpaper. Place a small weight on it. Remove the paper liner from the tape and smooth it down with a bone folder.

If the enclosed materials are small, the pocket need not cover the whole back board. It can be just a little bigger than the inserts.

POCKET WITH GUSSETS

For thicker inserts, a pocket with gussets on three sides is more secure. The gussets are made by scoring and folding the card stock twice.

Cut the bristol or card stock approximately the width of the back board plus 2" (5 cm) and about ⅔ the height of the board plus 1" (2.5 cm). For smaller materials, the pocket can be made narrower or shorter. Adjust the measurements accordingly. Have the grain running from top to bottom so that the vertical folds will be with the grain.

The pocket should end about ½" (1.3 cm) from the inner hinge to avoid puckering the materials and to prevent distortion of the binding. It should not stick out of the book at the bottom or fore edge.

Make two sets of marks ½" (1.3 cm) apart at the sides and bottom of the bristol. Make the marks with an awl so they will be visible from the back as well.

Score two lines on the sides and bottom of the pocket.

Cut the corners as shown in figure 5-56.

Begin by folding the inner lines.

The second fold is a reverse fold; the line may have to be scored again lightly. Use the marks made with an awl for guidance. Make the second fold.

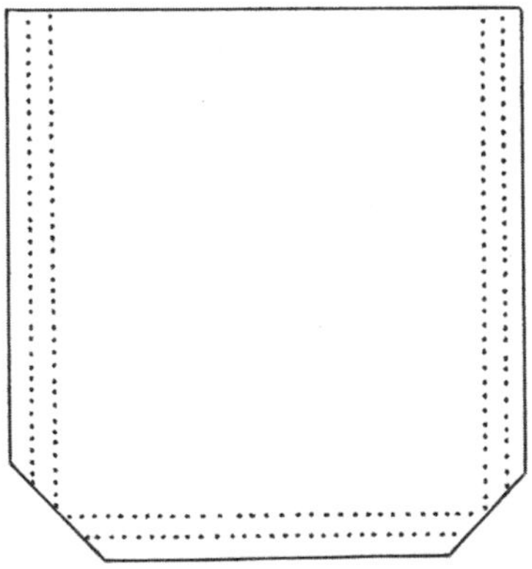

Keep the gussets folded and put double-coated tape on the three flaps made by the second fold.

Fig. 5-56

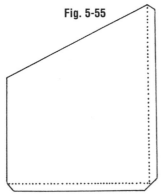

Position the pocket on the board, put a small weight on it, and carefully remove the paper liner from the tape. Rub down well.

You can also make pockets using modified acid-free envelopes. Cut them down to the appropriate size, remove flaps, slit open one side if desired, and adhere to the back board of the book using mix or double-coated tape. Alternatively, cut an L-seal polyester sleeve to the right size and attach to the board with double-coated tape. Make sure that the pocket does not stick out of the book.

Simple Repairs to the Case

The primary purpose of a book's binding is to protect the text or contents. When the case begins to deteriorate, it is time to decide whether it can be repaired. Sometimes rebinding or replacing the book is more cost-effective than repairing it. The book should not continue in use once the covers are damaged because the contents are likely to be damaged. The following pages deal with several types of repairs that can be made to the case in order to make the book sound and usable. We do not suggest making new cases (rebinding) in-house. This operation requires much more training and equipment than is usually available in smaller institutions and is always done more economically by a library binder.

Wrapping the Text Block

When repairing the case of a book, it is sometimes helpful to wrap the text block, including the flyleaves, to protect them from staining.

Wrapping paper can be used, but many conservators prefer to use wax paper or plastic wrap (polyethylene) because these materials provide a better moisture barrier.

Cut a length of the wrapping material approximately three times the height of the book and insert it between the back flyleaf and the back cover of the book (fig. 5-57).

Fig. 5-57

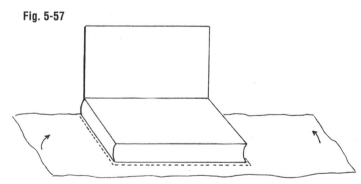

Fold the top and bottom over the text block and tape in place. Then fold the paper at the fore edge of the book and bring it up over the text. Tape in place (fig. 5-58).

Fig. 5-58

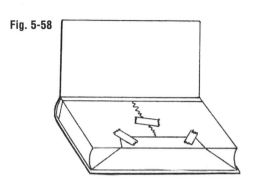

Regular masking or other adhesive tapes can be used, but remember that over time, tape can deteriorate and ooze adhesive which could stick to the board sheet of the book. Wrapping is a temporary step and should be removed as soon as the repair is completed.

Consolidating Leather Rot (Red Rot)

Many collections have large numbers of books in rotting leather bindings of no historical importance. While it would be ideal to rebind these books eventually, it is sometimes necessary to keep them in use in their deteriorated state for some time.

Unfortunately, once leather starts rotting, it cannot be restored to its original condition. The powder continues to stain the pages of the book, nearby books, shelving, and the hands and clothing of readers.

A number of coatings have been used to try to stop leather from powdering. These are not a cure, but they do consolidate the surface for a period of time. Hydroxypropylcellulose is available from conservation suppliers under the name Klucel G. It is a powder similar to methylcellulose and must be mixed with alcohol and other substances to produce a gel. In the 1990s a premixed form was developed and is available under the name Cellugel. This ready-to-use formulation is much more convenient to use. Since it is made with alcohol, be sure to have good ventilation in the work area.

Remember that this treatment is recommended for books from circulating or research collections only. Consult a conservator for advice on preserving leather books from special collections.

METHOD OF APPLICATION

Wrap the text block as described above.

If the book is fairly small, hold it by the wrapped text block as shown in figure 5-59 and apply a thin, even coat of Cellugel over the binding. Use a soft brush, 1"–2" (2.5–5 cm) wide. Paint the edges of the boards and the turn-ins (see "Parts of a Book," p. 95) if they need it, using a small brush with a chisel edge. It is okay (but not necessary) to paint over paper or cloth areas of the binding, since the gel does not stain. It dries very quickly.

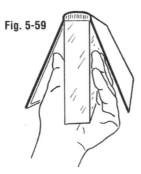

Fig. 5-59

The book can be stood up to finish drying with the covers open (fig. 5-60). If the book doesn't stand well on its cover, put it down flat on clean newsprint or some other disposable, absorbent surface.

Place larger books flat on newsprint, rather than holding them up in the air, and paint all the exposed areas. Treat a few books, then go back to the first ones done to check if they are dry. Turn them over to coat the rest of the bindings.

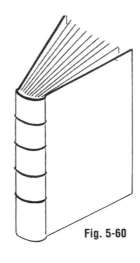

Fig. 5-60

The more rotted areas of certain leathers may darken more than the rest of the binding. But this is a treatment of last resort, and the darkening is probably preferable to the untreated red rot. As always, when in doubt, consult a librarian or curator to make sure that the treatment is appropriate for the book.

After treating the bindings, it may be advisable to put a Mylar or paper tube jacket on the book, for added protection. Directions for this are in "Polyester Dust Jackets" in section 3, p. 72.

Reattaching Spine Labels

Some bindings have labels that are printed on a separate piece of paper or leather. When these start to come loose (fig. 5-61), it is easy to tack them down again before they come off completely or get torn.

Put the book in a finishing press (fig. 5-62). In "Presses" in section 2, p. 40, we describe various types of presses that can be used for this purpose.

Fig. 5-61

Note: When putting a book in a press, it is traditional to have the head (top) of the book at the *left.* While this is not absolutely necessary, it is a very good habit to form and will save you from attaching labels or spines upside down. When a book is flat between boards, or in a nipping press, the head should likewise be on the *left* unless there is a technical reason to do otherwise.

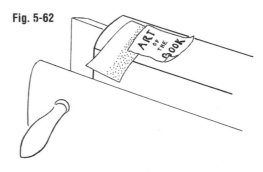

Fig. 5-62

To reattach the label, use a variation of the tipping technique. Cut a piece of Mylar or card stock 2"–3" (5–7.5 cm) wide. Apply a light coat of mix evenly to one side of the card or Mylar. Slide the card carefully under one of the corners of the label, just as far as it will go without forcing. This step can also be carried out with the book standing up (fig. 5-63). Rub it down gently. This will transfer some of the adhesive from the card or the Mylar to the back of the label.

Remove the card and rub the label down *gently* through a piece of wax paper (or a paper towel). Sometimes it helps to simply hold the label down with your hand for a minute until the adhesive starts to set.

Repeat the procedure at other corners or loose areas.

Fig. 5-63

Reattaching Flapping Spines

This is a quick fix for the spines of hollow back books that have broken at one hinge, usually the front. It is not a long-lasting repair and therefore not really suitable for reference works, but it is an appropriate treatment for circulating books that are otherwise in good condition. The board attachment must still be sound; if it is not, the book should be repaired by one of the methods described in "Repairs to the Text Block and the Case," or it can be sent to the library binder.

Put the book in a finishing press as shown, with the joints of the book at least an inch or two (2.5–5 cm) above the jaws of the press (fig. 5-64).

Fig. 5-64

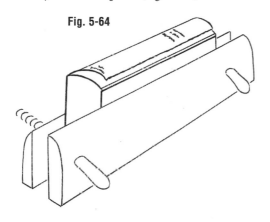

Note: In this case, the head of the book is on the right, because it is the *front* joint that is broken and this position is better for carrying out the repair.

Move the flapping spine away from the text block (fig. 5-65). Check to see if the spine linings are firm. Peel off or tack down any loose bits. (If the spine linings are very damaged, this is probably not a good way to repair the book.)

Check also to make sure the strip of card or

Fig. 5-65

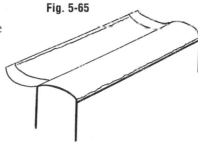

paper that stiffens the spine (the "spine strip") is in good condition. Tack it down if it has begun to come loose.

If the spine strip needs replacement, the book may need other repairs as well. Examine it carefully to decide what should be done. "Replacing a Torn Spine Strip" is described on p. 130.

Hollow Tubes

Hollow tubes may be found in some publisher's bindings, especially larger books. They are sometimes referred to as "hollows" or simply as "tubes." A tube helps attach the text block to the case and also creates a hollow spine (see fig. 5-9). New tubes are used in some types of repairs.

A hollow tube is made from a piece of medium-weight Western paper, such as wrapping paper or heavy bond, according to the size of the book. The paper is folded twice to produce three panels; the outer flaps are glued together to create a hollow tube the same width as the spine of the text block. The single side is adhered to the spine of the text block and the double side to the spine of the case.

MAKING A HOLLOW TUBE

To make a tube, cut the paper just a little shorter than the height of the text block by slightly less than three times the width of the spine. (See "Measuring" in section 2, p. 45.) The grain must be parallel to the spine so that the folds will be with the grain.

Make a mark on the paper, a little less than the width of the spine. Make a second mark, the exact width of the spine. Use a straightedge and bone folder to score two lines down the length of the paper. This will produce three sections (fig. 5-66). The middle panel will be the width of the spine and the two outer flaps slightly narrower, to make it easier to overlap them in the next step.

Apply mix to flap A and fold it over flap B (fig. 5-67). Smooth down with a bone folder. When the flaps are glued together, pop the tube open to make sure it is not stuck shut (fig. 5-68). You may slide a strip of wax paper

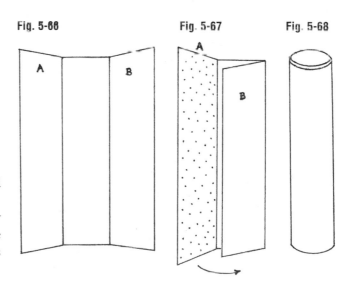

Fig. 5-66   Fig. 5-67   Fig. 5-68

in it; it should be about the same width as the tube and stick out at each end. Let the adhesive set for a few minutes so the tube doesn't come apart when you handle it.

ATTACHING THE TUBE

Apply mix to the tube on its *single* layer side. Then attach the tube to the spine of the text block (fig. 5-69). Line it up so it covers the spine from shoulder to shoulder and is straight. Be careful not to damage the joint of the flapping spine.

Rub down very well and make sure the tube sticks to the spine at the edges. Set the book aside to dry. If the edges of the tube separate from the

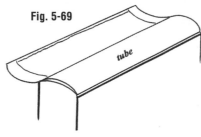

Fig. 5-69

tube

spine as it dries, insert mix or PVA under it with a micro-spatula and rub it down. You may hold it down with your fingers until it starts to dry.

If you put wax paper inside the tube, remember to remove it when the tube is dry. Occasionally, adhesive gets on the wax paper and it is difficult to slide it out. In that case, remove the book from the press and open the pages to the middle. This will pop the tube open and will make it easier to remove the wax paper. Next time, use a little less adhesive when making the tube.

PUTTING DOWN THE FLAPPING SPINE

Bring the spine down over the tube to see how it fits (fig. 5-70). Often, the edges fit together well without trimming. If the edge of the material covering the spine or board is ragged, trim neatly with scissors. In older books, the cloth over the

joints is often stretched, so that the spine might slightly overlap the area of the broken joint, or even the edge of the board. Trim the torn cloth edges a little so they don't overlap. When gluing the spine down

Fig. 5-70

in the next step, be sure it is centered well on the tube.

If the tube sticks out from under the edge of the spine, the tube is too wide. Rip the tube off the book,

removing as much paper as comes off the spine easily. Make a narrower tube.

If the fit is good, apply mix to the top of the tube.

Be careful not to get any adhesive *inside* the tube. You may stick a little piece of wax paper or Mylar inside each end of the tube to prevent the adhesive from going in, and remove it after the repair is dry.

Bring the loose spine up over the tube, centering the spine strip on the tube, and rub it down through a piece of paper. Rub the edge of the spine especially well and hold it down for a moment. Put a piece of polyester web over the spine and wrap the book with an elastic bandage to keep light pressure on the spine until it is dry (fig. 5-71).

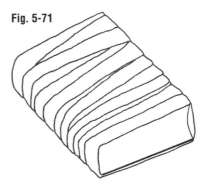

Fig. 5-71

If you used a small wooden press, leave the book in it and wrap the book *and* the press, for best support (fig. 5-72).

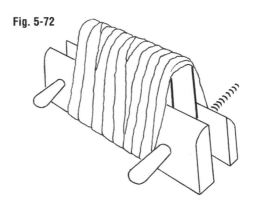

Fig. 5-72

Repairing Corners

A binding with frayed, bumped, crushed, or delaminated corners does not protect the contents as well as one with hard corners. Damaged corners can often be straightened out and reinforced by the following methods.

If the damage is limited to fraying book cloth, rub a small amount of mix or paste into the cloth and pat down the loose fibers along the edges of the corner to adhere them to the board. Mix dries faster, but paste is less likely to show on cloth.

If the cloth or paper over the corners has started to peel up, the covering can be tacked down again using a scrap of Mylar or card.

Apply adhesive to the scrap and slip it, adhesive side up, under the loose cloth or paper (fig. 5-73). Rub lightly with fingertips to transfer the adhesive to the back of the cloth or paper.

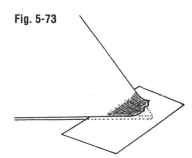

Fig. 5-73

Slide a piece of mat board (or other thin, rigid board) under the cover, for support, and place wax paper or Mylar between the support and the corner. Slide the Mylar or card out and rub the cloth or paper gently with a bone folder (fig. 5-74). (If you rub too hard, the cloth or paper may

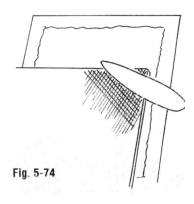

Fig. 5-74

become shiny and the adhesive may come through.) Align cloth threads as needed and shape the corner with fingers and bone folder. Air dry, without pressing.

When the corners of a binding are delaminated as well as frayed, separate the layers a bit more with a micro-spatula or with the blade of a knife (fig. 5-75). Pick up adhesive with the tip of a microspatula and insert a dab between each layer.

Press the layers together firmly and wipe off any excess adhesive that oozes out (fig. 5-76).

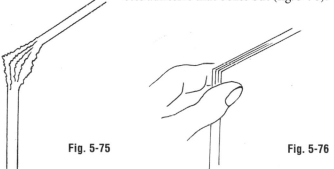

Fig. 5-75   **Fig. 5-76**

With a support and moisture barrier in place, shape the corner with a bone folder (fig. 5-77). Let air dry. It is not necessary to clamp the corner while it dries, but it must remain undisturbed until fully dry and hard.

Fig. 5-77

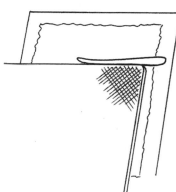

Occasionally, the cloth (or paper) covering the corner may be so worn that it is necessary to cover the exposed board. Slit the cloth or paper with a knife as illustrated (fig. 5-78) and lift it about 1"–2" (2.5–5 cm). Insert the knife flat under the cloth and keep it parallel to the board. Push it slowly with a rocking or circular motion; try to lift as little of the board as possible.

Consolidate the layers of delaminated board if necessary. Allow it to air dry, without pressing.

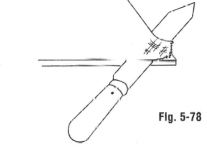

Fig. 5-78

For most books, a thin book cloth, such as one of the tissue-lined rayon cloths sold by some suppliers, will give better results than heavier cloths and will be much easier to work with. A strong paper can be used if the original covering is paper. The repair can also be made using Japanese papers, which are available in colors.

Measure by placing the corner of the board on a piece of book cloth. Measure and mark ½" (1.3 cm) margins around the corner. Cut a triangle of cloth or paper for each corner that needs repair.

Apply adhesive on the back of the repair cloth. Pick up the cloth or paper on the corner of the board and slide the repair under it. Approximately ½" (1.3 cm) should extend on each side of the corner; these flaps will be turned in over the board (fig. 5-79). (The drawing shows the three portions of the cloth that will be trimmed off in the next step as white areas.)

Fig. 5-79

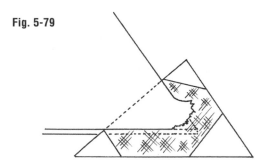

Rub down with a bone folder through a scrap of waste paper.

Repeat this step on the other corners.

Open the cover and trim the tips of the repair cloth as illustrated in figure 5-80. (The broken lines indicate the corner of the board, under the repair cloth.)

Fig. 5-80

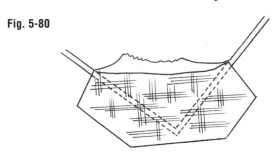

Apply adhesive to the flaps (fig. 5-81) and turn them in one after the other as illustrated. Before turning in the second flap, tuck in the corner tip with the point of the bone folder (or your fingernail) to make sure it completely encloses the tip of the board (figs. 5-82 and 5-83). Paste down the second flap.

Fig. 5-81

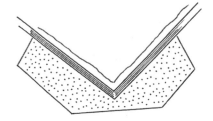

Fig. 5-82

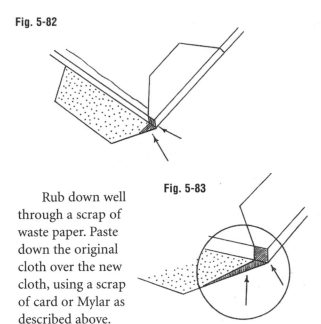

Rub down well through a scrap of waste paper. Paste down the original cloth over the new cloth, using a scrap of card or Mylar as described above.

Fig. 5-83

VARIATION: ATTACHING THE REPAIR CLOTH OVER THE OLD CLOTH

The preceding repair requires some practice and may be too time-consuming for many situations. You can also repair corners by consolidating delaminated layers of board and then pasting the new cloth or paper *on top* of the old cloth and endpaper. This is much faster and would be perfectly suitable for many reference books. In addition, trying to lift fragile book cloth or paper is not easy; applying the repair *over* such materials generally gives a neater result and is just as strong.

Repairing Tops and Bottoms of Spines

Like some forms of corner repair, this technique requires a good deal of practice. Before deciding to repair the top or bottom of the spine, examine the book critically to be sure that it is still solidly cased in (the joints should be in good condition) and that the endpapers are strong. If there are problems beyond torn headcaps, it would probably be more sensible to *reback* the book, or send it to the library binder.

Select a cloth that is compatible with the original book cloth in weight and color. Cut it about twice the height of the damaged portion of the spine and the width of the spine, plus 2" (5 cm). You may round the corners if you wish.

Slit the inner hinges of the book about ½" (1.3 cm) at top and bottom to accommodate the new cloth (figs. 5-84 and 5-85).

Fig. 5-84

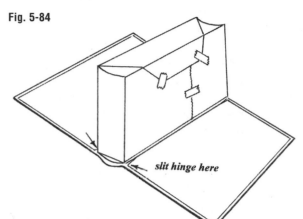

slit hinge here

Fig. 5-85

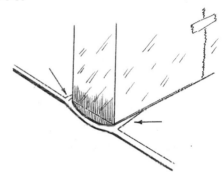

If the cloth on the original spine is crumpled and has frayed edges, smooth it out and trim off the ragged bits (fig. 5-86).

Close the book.

Apply adhesive to the new cloth and center it on the damaged area of the spine, leaving about ½" (1.3 cm) sticking out beyond the end of the spine. The repair should cover all the torn parts of the spine and extend about 1" (2.5 cm) over each joint, onto the front and back boards (fig. 5-90).

Fig. 5-86

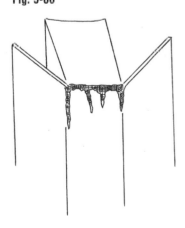

Put a piece of paper over the repair and rub it down with the flat part of a bone folder. Work the cloth into the joints with the edge of the bone folder (fig. 5-87).

Lay the book down on an absorbent surface and let the cloth dry for at least a half hour.

Stand the book up, with the pages facing you and the ½" (1.3 cm) flap sticking up at the top. Apply adhesive to the flap (fig. 5-88).

Fig. 5-87

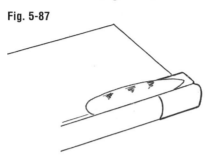

Fig. 5-88

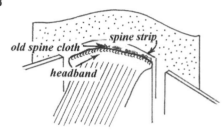

spine strip
old spine cloth
headband

Tuck the flap into the hollow of the spine with the tip of a bone folder (fig. 5-89). Slip each side of the flap through the slits made in the front and back hinges (fig. 5-90). There are two hinges, two slits.

Fig. 5-89

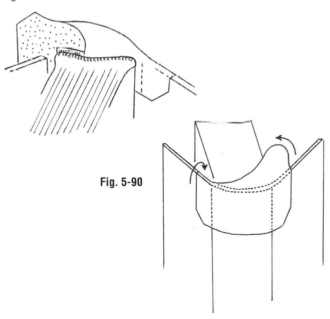

Fig. 5-90

Rub the cloth down over the board sheets with a bone folder.

Place the bone folder inside the hollow and smooth the flap so it creases at the top and adheres well to the remains of the old spine (fig. 5-91).

Fig. 5-91

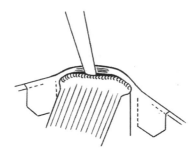

Close the book and shape the headcap with a bone folder before it dries completely (fig. 5-92).

Turn the book upside down and repeat on the tail (bottom) of the spine, if needed.

The repair cloth can also be inserted under the original cloth of the case. This technique is similar to that described in "Repairing Corners." It can leave more of the original titling and spine decoration visible. However, it does take considerably longer and requires *much* more skill in order to do this neatly. We suggest you contact a conservator or bookbinder for training or demonstrations in this and other complex steps if you are interested in going further.

Fig. 5-92

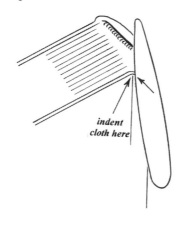

indent cloth here

Repairs to the Text Block and the Case

This segment describes ways of repairing books where the case and the text block (sometimes referred to as the "book") are no longer properly attached to each other. It builds on some skills described earlier in the section, and it may be useful to review the steps in the previous pages before proceeding.

Repairing One Broken Hinge

In situations where the cloth covering the case is undamaged and only one inner hinge is broken, the book can often be repaired in a few simple steps. (It is usually the front hinge that is broken.) One method uses a hollow tube. Another way to do it is to attach a lining over the spine, which extends to form a hinge. Sometimes a combination of the two methods is best.

Open the cover and examine the inside edge of the board, next to the broken hinge. There will usually be ragged bits of paper or super. To trim these off, place a straightedge on the board, about ⅛" (3 mm) from the edge. Hold the straightedge down firmly and cut with a utility knife or scalpel, cutting through the endpaper and the super. Peel the strip off (fig. 5-93).

Fig. 5-93

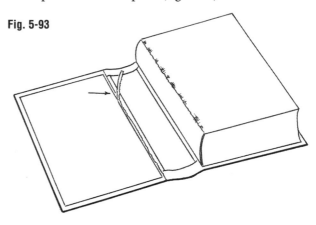

The trimmed edge of endpaper and super should be firmly attached to the board. If the edge is loose, insert some mix with a spatula or a piece of card and tack it down. Rub with a bone folder through a paper towel.

Trim off any loose bits of paper or super from the edge of the shoulder of the text block.

Place the book at the edge of the work surface, the side with the broken hinge on top. Open the cover and let it hang in front of the counter so the spine is exposed, as shown in figure 5-94 below. Place a clean blotter or board over the flyleaf and put a weight on it. (You may also wrap the text block if you prefer.) Peel off any loose spine

Fig. 5-94

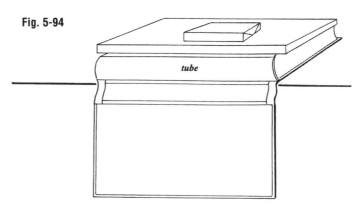

tube

linings, being careful not to damage the sound hinge at the bottom. Leave undisturbed anything that doesn't come off easily.

USING A TUBE TO REPAIR A BROKEN HINGE

If the book is small to average in size and the spine of the text block is quite sound, a tube may provide the quickest repair.

Measure the spine; you may have to stoop down to see the lower edge of the spine, next to the unbroken hinge.

Make a tube as described in "Making a Hollow Tube," p. 121. The tube should come just to the edge of the shoulders of the text block but it should not go down into the shoulder area. Attach it to the spine using mix.

Rub the tube well with a bone folder, paying special attention to the sides, until the adhesive has begun to set and the tube stays stuck. Let dry.

When the tube is dry, check to make sure that it is securely attached to the edges of the spine. You may remove the weight at this point and pick up the book to make it easier to see the edge of the spine next to the unbroken hinge. If necessary, insert mix or straight PVA under any loose areas and hold down with your fingers till set.

Close the cover over the text block and check for fit. If it is hard to get the board back into alignment with the bottom board, the tube may be too wide. Rip it off and make a narrower one.

If the top board fits well when the cover is closed, open the cover again. Insert small pieces of wax paper or Mylar into the ends of the tube (fig. 5-95). Apply a thin coat of mix to the inside of the case, just on the area of the spine and joints.

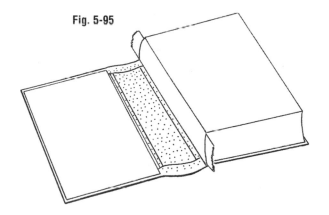

Fig. 5-95

Position the book at the edge of the work surface and open the cover, as shown in figure 5-94 above. Place a piece of wax paper or Mylar on the flyleaf as a moisture barrier. Apply a thin coat of mix to the tube and bring the case over the text block. Align the top board with the bottom board.

Work the cloth down into the joint, gently, with the *edge* of a bone folder (fig. 5-96). Rub the spine thoroughly to make sure the inside of the spine sticks to the tube.

Fig. 5-96

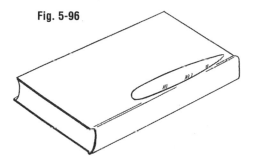

Carefully place the book between boards (with brass edges if possible), put a weight on it, and allow it to dry for a couple of hours (fig. 5-97).

Fig. 5-97

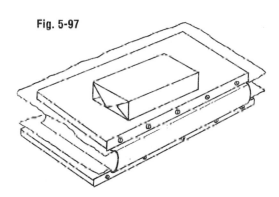

When dry, open the front cover (or the back cover, depending on which side was repaired) and support the cover with wooden boards or a book of similar thickness. Check to see if the tube, text block, and cloth joint of the cover are all firmly attached in the hinge area. Insert adhesive to tack down any loose areas and allow it to dry. If all is well, finish the repair by covering the hinge area with a strip of Japanese paper as described in "Hinge Reinforcement," p. 117.

USING A SPINE LINING
TO REPAIR A BROKEN HINGE

When the spine of the text block is not as firm as it should be, it can be reinforced by applying a spine lining.

Place the book on the edge of the work counter, with the cover hanging down over the edge (fig. 5-98). (If repairing the front hinge, the head of the book will be on the left.)

Fig. 5-98

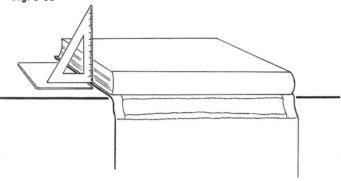

If some signatures are high or low, adjust them so a solid top edge is produced, perpendicular to the counter. To do this, make a platform next to the bottom board of the book. It should be the same thickness as the book board.

Put a triangle or square against the top of the text block, resting on the platform and the square of the book board (fig. 5-98). Adjust the pages as much as possible. Try to make the spine and fore edge gently rounded and make the first signature line up with the bottom signature (put the triangle or square against the fore edge to check on this).

When you have reshaped the text block as much as possible, put a board over the flyleaf and a heavy weight on the board, to maintain the correct shape until the next step is completed.

Note: If the book was bound after around 1970, it was probably glued up with a plastic glue. These glues are difficult to reshape and you may not be able to do much adjusting.

Apply a thin coat of mix to the spine and allow it to dry. This will set the signatures into position.

Cut a piece of lining fabric, such as super, muslin, cotton lawn, etc. It should be a little shorter than the spine by the width of the spine plus 1.5" (4 cm).

Apply a second coat of mix to the spine and attach the lining fabric, making sure it goes to the edge of the spine on the side where the hinge is sound. There should be a 1½" (4 cm) flap sticking up; this will be the new

hinge. Angle the ends for a neater appearance (fig. 5-99). Let dry.

Fig. 5-99

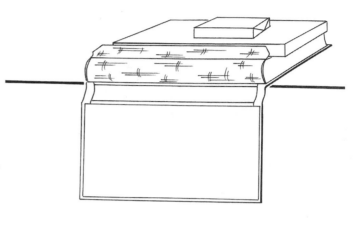

When dry, remove the pressing board and weight. Close the cover over the text block to check the fit. If all is well, put a piece of wax paper or Mylar over the flyleaf. Place waste paper over that.

Fold the new hinge down over the waste paper and brush mix on it, making sure not to get adhesive on the spine (fig. 5-100). Carefully remove the waste paper.

Fig. 5-100

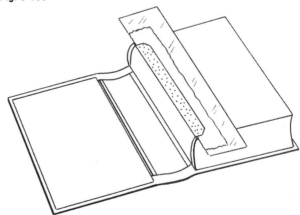

Bring the cover over the text block, aligning the front edges of the top and bottom board. (You might need to hold the book down with one hand as you start to bring the cover over, to make sure that the glued-up hinge is not disturbed in the process.)

With the edge of a bone folder, gently work the book cloth down into the joint.

Place the book between boards, brass-edged if available, and put a weight on it (fig. 5-101). Let dry. When dry, remove the moisture barrier.

Fig. 5-101

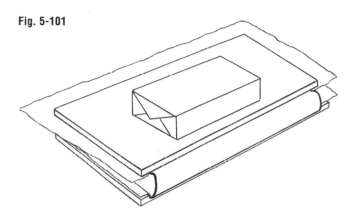

USING A SPINE LINING AND A TUBE TO REPAIR A BROKEN HINGE

If the book is very heavy or thick, it might be desirable to use a combination of the two methods. The added layers help keep the spine in shape. Since this method produces greater bulk, be sure that the cover can accommodate the extra layers.

First, apply the lining cloth to the spine, with the new hinge flap. When that is dry, measure the spine and make a tube. Attach it over the cloth spine lining. Fold the hinge flap down over the flyleaf and insert wax paper and waste paper under it.

The double layer of the tube must be glued to the spine strip. To finish the repair, apply a thin coat of mix to the inside of the spine area of the case, from the edge of the back board to the edge of the front board, including the spine strip.

Apply a thin coat of mix to the tube and to the new hinge flap, then bring the case over the text block. Align the top board with the bottom board.

With the edge of a bone folder, gently work the book cloth down into the joint.

Place the book between boards and put a weight on it. Let dry.

Reattaching the Text Block to the Case

This technique can be used to repair books with sound cases that have become separated from the text block. It is also a good way to repair a book with a broken front hinge and a weak back hinge (or vice versa), even if it isn't quite broken. When this is the case, separate the cover from the text block by cutting the back hinge using small scissors. Be careful to cut only the endpaper and the super and not the book cloth at the joint of the cover.

If the cloth is abraded or cracked at the joints, the book needs to be *rebacked* as described in "Rebacking a Book with Detached Boards," p. 140.

PREPARING THE TEXT BLOCK

Note: If the spine is sagging or the glue has deteriorated and the spine no longer keeps the signatures in correct alignment, lay the text block flat on the counter, with the shoulder over the edge, and reshape it, using a triangle, as shown in figure 5-98. The spine should be gently rounded and the shoulder at the top should be directly over the one at the bottom, at right angles to the counter. Place a weight on the book, apply a coat of mix, and allow it to dry before proceeding. It may not be possible to reshape the spines of books glued up with plastic (white) glues.

Put the text block in a finishing press and peel off any loose spine linings. Do not disturb the sewing or any linings that are firmly attached. If necessary, sand *lightly* to smooth out irregularities.

Trim off any ragged bits of paper or super from the shoulders of the book (fig. 5-102).

Fig. 5-102

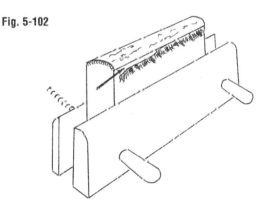

If the book has endbands (headbands), check to determine if they are in good condition. They can be glued down with mix if loose. Endbands serve no structural purpose and they can simply be removed if they are damaged. Headbanding tape is available from some suppliers, and you can attach new ones if you wish.

Check that the flyleaves are in good condition and firmly attached. New flyleaves can be attached at this point if needed. (See "Replacing Missing Flyleaves," p. 115.)

Apply a coat of mix to the spine and allow it to dry. This will help consolidate the old linings.

Cut a piece of lining fabric, such as super, muslin, cotton lawn, etc. It should be a little shorter than the spine, by the width of the spine, plus 3" (7–8 cm).

Apply a second coat of mix to the spine and attach the lining fabric; make sure it is well adhered to the whole spine, especially at the edges. Use just enough mix to make the lining stick to the spine but not so much that adhesive oozes out when you rub down.

Rub down well with a bone or Teflon folder, without stretching the lining. There should be a 1.5" (4 cm) flap on each side of the spine (fig. 5-103); these are the new hinges that will be used to attach the book to the case. Angle the corners for a neater appearance. Let dry.

Fig. 5-103

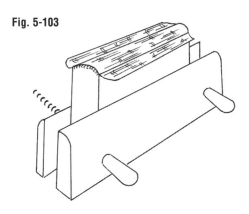

PREPARING THE CASE

Turn the case so the inside faces up. The edges of the boards may be a little ragged, with bits of endpaper sticking up as well as shreds of super. If so, trim the edges by cutting through the endpaper and the super, as described in "Repairing One Broken Hinge," p. 126, about ¼" (6–7 mm) from the edge of the board. Peel the strip off (fig. 5-104).

Fig. 5-104

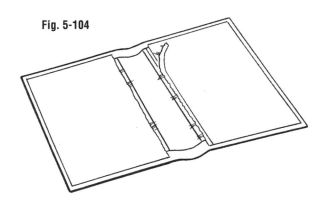

The endpaper and super should be firmly attached to the board at the trimmed edge. If not, insert some mix in the loose areas, using a spatula or a piece of card, and tack them down.

Next, check the "spine strip," the piece of bristol, paper, or card stock lining the cloth in the spine area of the case. It should be sound and firmly attached to the cloth (fig. 5-105). If the spine strip is in good condition but peeling up at the edges, tack the edges down by inserting some mix with a piece of card or with a microspatula.

Fig. 5-105

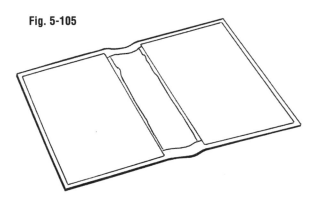

The "turn-ins" (cloth at the top and bottom of the spine) may be partly detached from the spine strip; if so, tack them down in the same way. Rub down with a bone folder. Place a weight (or series of small weights) on the spine strip, covering the edges.

REPLACING A TORN SPINE STRIP

If the spine strip is torn or creased, or doesn't seem like an adequate support for the spine, replace it with a new one. Skip the previous directions for "Preparing the Case" and start at this step

Cut a piece of bristol or card stock, the same width as the spine of the *text block* and the height of the *covers*, less a hair or two, to allow for the thickness of the cloth. Make sure the grain runs in the long direction.

Make slits in the turn-ins, about ¼" (6–7 mm) from the spine, at the top and bottom of the front and back boards (fig. 5-106). Cut neatly through the endpapers and the cloth at the turn-ins with a sharp scalpel or utility knife. (Be careful not to cut the book cloth on the joints.) Peel the cloth up. Bits of board may come up as you unfold the cloth; this is okay.

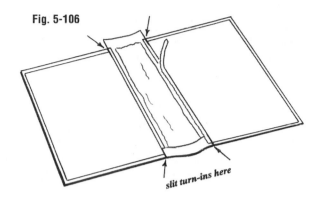

Fig. 5-106

slit turn-ins here

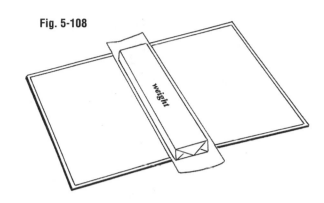

Fig. 5-108

Remove the old spine strip, peeling it off as much as possible. You may need to scrape a little with a spatula or sand gently with fine sandpaper to get a smooth surface on the cloth. It is not necessary to remove every trace of the old spine, but it is important to have a smooth, solid surface with no scraps of loose paper.

Look at the cloth in the area of the turn-in. If the cloth at the fold is weak or beginning to fray, reinforce it by pasting a piece of Japanese paper over the damaged area (fig. 5-107).

Fig. 5-107

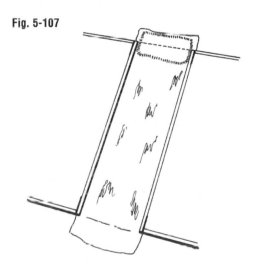

Glue the new spine strip in place using mix, centering it between the edges of the boards. Rub down well. Place a piece of polyester web or wax paper over the spine strip. Add a narrow weight that covers it from edge to edge, and allow it to dry (fig. 5-108).

When dry, apply mix to the turn-ins and fold them back in place. Rub down with a bone or Teflon folder. Work the cloth down into the joint area and align the cut edges of the slits on the boards. Allow the turn-ins to dry.

JOINING THE CASE AND TEXT BLOCK

When the spine linings are dry, remove the text block from the press.

Open the case flat on the counter, with the inside facing up, and position the text block on the back board so it covers the board sheet at the three edges. Make sure the book is right side up on the case.

Close the cover over the book. Pull the case gently as you close it and check if the joints fit well over the shoulders of the text block.

If all is well, open the front board and put a piece of wax paper or Mylar over the front flyleaf. Place waste paper over that.

Fold the new front hinge over the waste paper (fig. 5-109). Brush mix on the hinge, making sure not to get adhesive on the spine. Carefully remove the waste paper.

Fig. 5-109

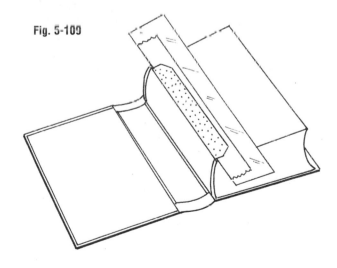

Close the cover over the book and work the cloth gently into the joint with the edge of a bone folder (fig. 5-110). Do not open the front board until the hinge is dry.

Carefully turn the book over and open the back board. Attach the back hinge in the same way.

Fig. 5-110

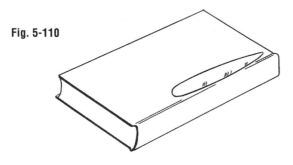

Place the book between boards and put a weight on it (fig. 5-111).

Allow it to dry for an hour or two before opening the covers.

Fig. 5-111

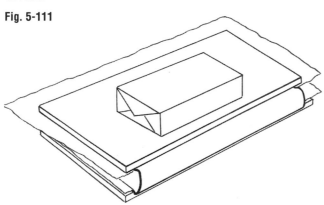

The new hinges will cover about an inch (2.5 cm) of the board sheets. You can cut the spine lining narrower as you get more practice, so the hinges will not cover as much of the board sheets.

A tube can be used in addition to the spine lining to reattach heavy books to their cases. Proceed as described in "Using a Spine Lining and a Tube to Repair a Broken Hinge," p. 129, remembering that the double-layer side of the tube must be firmly attached to the spine strip of the case. (This may be thought of as the "belt-and-suspenders" method.)

Repairing a Broken Text Block

When preparing to reattach a book to its case by some of the methods we've just discussed, you may sometimes find that the text block has split into two or three seg-

ments. The following method can be used to repair sewn or adhesive-bound books. Check the sewing or adhesive within each split part. If the sewing is broken or pages are coming loose from an adhesive binding, the book needs to be sent to the library binder. However, if the sewing or adhesive of each split section is still sound and all the pages are firmly attached, the book can be repaired as follows.

Place the text block at the edge of the work surface. If the book has just one broken inner hinge and the other one is sound, let the cover hang down (fig. 5-112).

Fig. 5-112

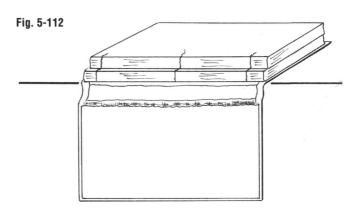

(If the text block is completely separated from the case, put the broken book sections on the counter, with the shoulder of the book hanging off the edge. Place a weight on the book and proceed to the following steps.)

Peel off as much *loose* paper from the spine lining as necessary to obtain a solid surface. You may scrape lightly with a spatula or blunt knife but be very careful not to damage the sewing.

Remove the weight, then align the broken sections so that the spine is rounded and the top edge of the book is as smooth as possible. Use a triangle, as shown in figure 5-113.

Fig. 5-113

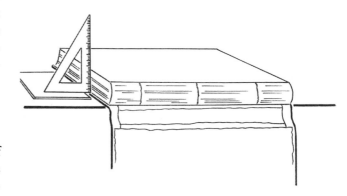

Place a board on the text block, lined up to the shoulder, and put a weight on top (fig. 5-114).

Apply a layer of mix to the spine and allow it to dry.

Fig. 5-116

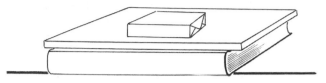

Fig. 5-114

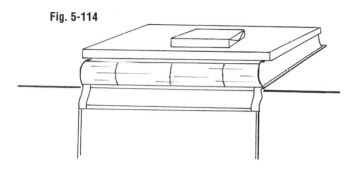

If the text block was completely detached from the case, complete the repair as described in "Reattaching the Text Block to the Case," p. 129.

CONSOLIDATING THE TEXT BLOCK USING A TUBE

Follow the steps in "Repairing a Broken Text Block," p. 132, for reshaping and gluing up the broken text block. Put a board and weight on it.

Make a tube according to the directions in "Making a Hollow Tube," p. 121. Glue it to the spine, using mix. Rub it down so it sticks securely, especially at the edges (fig. 5-115).

CONSOLIDATING THE TEXT BLOCK USING A CLOTH LINING

Another way of consolidating the text block is to use a cloth spine lining, cut wide enough to make a flap—or two flaps, in the case of a book that was completely detached from the case (fig. 5-117). The flaps serve as hinges. Follow the directions in "Using a Spine Lining to Repair a Broken Hinge," p. 128.

When dealing with a thick, heavy book, you should attach a cloth lining with flaps first and allow it to dry *thoroughly*. Apply a tube over that. Use the flaps as hinges, and finish the repair as described in "Using a Spine Lining and a Tube to Repair a Broken Hinge," p. 129.

Fig. 5-115

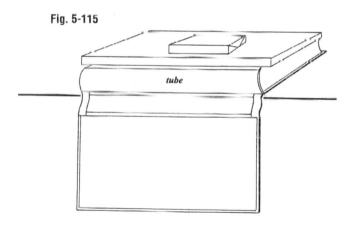

tube

Fig. 5-117

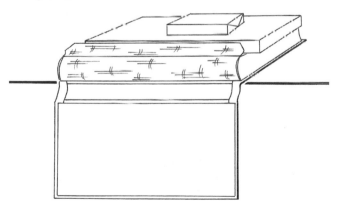

Allow the tube to dry completely.

Remove the weight and board from the book and turn the book so that the cover is resting on the work surface. Complete the repair as described in "Using a Spine Lining to Repair a Broken Hinge," p. 128.

Close the book, letting the shoulder hang over the edge of the counter. Place a board and a weight on the book (fig. 5-116).

Rebacking a Book with Boards Still Attached to the Text Block

When the boards of a book are still securely attached at the inner hinges but the spine is separated (or ready to break off) from the case along the joints, the book can be "rebacked" by the following method. Rebacking also provides a more permanent repair for books with flapping spines than the method described in "Reattaching Flapping Spines," p. 121.

If the original spine is completely detached, put it aside for later use.

Make ¼" (6–7 mm) cuts along the edges of the boards, as shown by the arrows in figure 5-119 below.

Lay the book on the counter and put a steel ruler on the front cover, about ¼" (6–7 mm) from the edge of the joint. Cut through the cloth (or paper) covering the boards, being careful not to cut into the hinge area of the book. Peel the strip away (fig. 5-118). Turn the book over and repeat on the back cover.

Fig. 5-118

If the spine is not quite detached but the cloth over the joints is damaged, proceed as follows.

Lay the book on the counter and put a steel ruler on the front cover, about ¼" (6–7 mm) from the edge of the joint. Cut through the cloth (or paper) covering the boards, being careful not to cut into the hinge area of the book. Turn the book over and repeat on the back cover.

Make ¼" (6–7 mm) cuts along the edges of the boards so that the strips can come away easily. (See arrows in fig. 5-119.)

Fig. 5-119

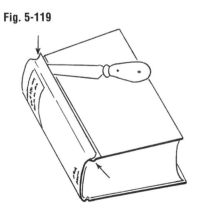

Lift the cut cloth away from the boards. The spine will usually come away with the two strips from the boards. You may have to slit the book cloth at the top and bottom

of the spine to separate the turn-ins. (If the cloth is deteriorated, the turn-ins may already be separated from the spine.)

Set aside the spine. It will be trimmed and reapplied at the end.

Open the boards and note whether the cloth turn-ins in the hinge area are ragged (see arrows in fig. 5-120). Cut away any cloth that is not firmly attached to the board, using either a small scissors or a sharp scalpel or utility knife. If the turn-ins were separated from the spine earlier, cut away any remnants still left on the board. *Be careful not to cut the super in the hinge area.*

Fig. 5-120

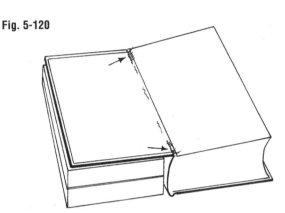

Put the book in a finishing press with about 2"–3" (5–8 cm) showing above the jaws of the press (fig. 5-121).

(If the spine of the text block is solid, well rounded, and has no loose scraps of lining, proceed to "Making a Tube" below.)

Fig. 5-121

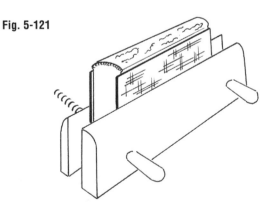

Otherwise, peel off as much *loose* paper spine lining as necessary to obtain a firm surface. You may scrape lightly with a spatula or blunt knife, or sand with medium-fine sandpaper. Be careful not to damage the sewing. If the book is adhesive-bound, do not disturb the adhesive.

If the endbands (headbands) are loose but in good condition, glue them down.

An endband should be positioned so that only the embroidered strip shows just beyond the end of the spine, sitting on top of the pages. The tube will cover the plain part of the cloth tape. Endbands in case-bound books are purely decorative and may be discarded if desired.

MAKING A TUBE

Select a piece of acid-free paper (bond weight) with the grain running parallel to the spine. Cut it about ¼" (6–7 mm) less than the height of the text block by slightly less than three times the width of the spine. Fold the paper as directed in "Making a Hollow Tube," p. 121, and glue the flaps together (fig. 5-122).

When the adhesive is dry, make ½" (1.3 cm) slits at the top and bottom of the tube, as shown in figure 5-123. Place the tube on the work surface with the two-layer side on top. Using a straightedge and a bone folder with a sharp point, score a line across the top and bottom of the tube, connecting the ends of the slits. Fold each flap up. Use a knife to cut off *just the double layer* (fig. 5-124), leaving the single layer of the tube its full length.

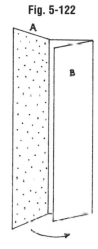

Fig. 5-122

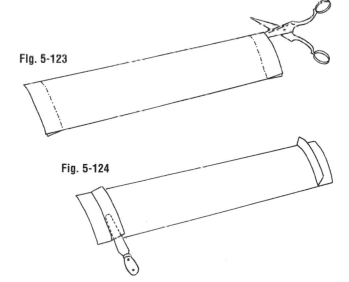

Fig. 5-123

Fig. 5-124

Attach the single layer of the tube to the spine, following the directions in "Attaching the Tube," p. 122. The two-layer side of the tube will end a little over ½" (1.3 cm) away from the top and bottom of the spine (fig. 5-125). Allow the tube to dry on the book, then check to see if it is stuck down securely all around. Using a spatula, insert a dab of mix or straight PVA under any loose spots.

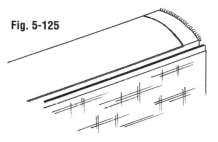

Fig. 5-125

Take the book out of the press.

Open the back board and carefully make slits in the endpaper where it covers the inner hinge, about ½" (1.3 cm), at the top and bottom (fig. 5-126). (The super usually extends to about 1", or 2.5 cm, from the top and bottom of the hinge; if it comes closer to the top and bottom of the book, it may be cut a very small amount at the same time that the endpaper is slit.)

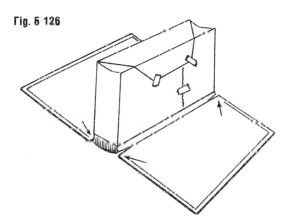

Fig. 5-126

Repeat at the front of the book.

Open the book to pop the tube open and insert pieces of wax paper at the top and bottom. This will help avoid getting mix inside the tube and will protect the endbands, if they were retained.

PREPARING A NEW CLOTH SPINE

Select a book cloth that matches or coordinates with the original cloth. The grain should run parallel to the spine. Cut it the height of the spine plus 1½" (4 cm), by the width of the spine of the text block, plus 2" (5 cm). Angle the four corners of the cloth as shown in figure 5-128.

Make a new bristol spine strip, the exact width of the spine of the text block by the height of the covers. The grain must be parallel to the spine. Mark the center of both the spine strip and the cloth by pinching lightly or making a pencil mark at top and bottom (fig. 5-127).

Fig. 5-127

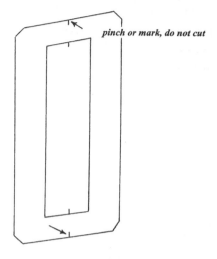

pinch or mark, do not cut

Apply adhesive to the spine strip and position it on the reverse side of the repair cloth, aligning the center marks.

Rub down well through waste paper and let dry under weight.

ATTACHING THE NEW SPINE

The new spine will be attached in two steps. First, the cloth and the spine strip will be glued to the tube and to the boards and joints. When that is dry, the cloth extending at the top and bottom of the book will be turned in.

Put the book back into a press, or prop it up between bricks, so you can have both hands free for the next steps.

Apply mix to the whole prepared cloth piece, including the new spine strip (fig. 5-128). Don't worry if the adhesive doesn't cover the top and bottom edges completely, since more mix will be applied to these areas later.

Make sure the waxed paper strips are in the tube.

Place the new spine on the tube, aligning the spine

Fig. 5-128

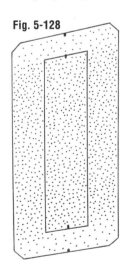

strip with the edges of the tube on both sides (fig. 5-129). The top and bottom of the spine strip should line up with the top and bottom of the boards (see broken lines in fig. 5-129). Work carefully but quickly, so that you have time to slide the new spine into the correct position, before the adhesive starts to set.

Fig. 5-129

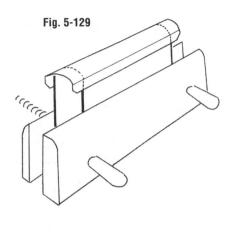

When the new spine is correctly attached to the tube, use the edge of a bone folder to work the cloth into the joints and over the boards.

Remove the book from the press or bricks and lay it flat on the counter. Put a piece of waste paper over the board and rub the new cloth with a bone folder, smoothing it over the boards and into the joints (fig. 5-130). Repeat on the other side.

Leave the wax paper inside the tube and allow the cloth to dry thoroughly.

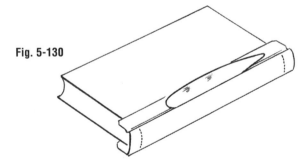

Fig. 5-130

MAKING THE TURN-INS

To turn in the cloth at the top and bottom of the spine, open the book so it is facing you. Remove the wax paper from the tube. Stand the book upside down on a board, allowing the cloth at the top of the spine to hang over the edge of the board. This will prevent the cloth from being crushed. (Wooden boards are useful for this step, but you can also use a stack of cardboard pieces or other flat objects that will raise the book up off the countertop.)

Apply mix to the flap that is sticking up (fig. 5-131) and tuck it into the hollow area of the spine, using the tip of a bone folder. (The cloth should fit well in the area where the tube was slit and cut. If not, extend the slits a little, very carefully.)

Fig. 5-131

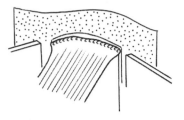

Slip each side of the flap through the slits in the hinges (fig. 5-132).

Fig. 5-132

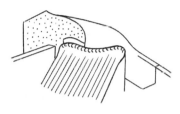

Fold the flap down over the spine strip and pull snugly over the edges of the boards so the new cloth doesn't make a big hump. The edges of the boards should be as smooth as possible where the repair cloth goes over the original cloth.

Fig. 5-133

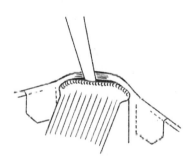

Rub the cloth with a bone folder until the adhesive sets on the board sheets.

Insert the bone folder into the hollow of the tube and rub the cloth at the tailcap smooth (fig. 5-133).

Close the book and shape the spine with a bone folder (fig. 5-134).

To make the turn-in at the top of the book, stand the book on the board with the newly made tailcap hanging off the edge of the board,

Fig. 5-134

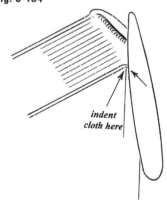

indent cloth here

to keep it from getting crushed. Repeat the previous steps to make the turn-in and shape the headcap.

Put wax paper or Mylar inside the covers as a moisture barrier. Check that the bottom of the spine did not get crushed while you were working on the top. If so, the adhesive may still be moist enough to allow you to reshape it with a bone folder.

When all is right, place the book between brass-edged boards and put a weight on it (fig. 5-135). Allow it to dry.

Fig. 5-135

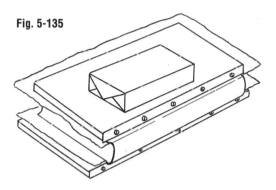

When dry, open the covers and check if the inner hinges are still in good condition. If necessary you can reinforce them with Japanese paper, as shown in figure 5-54, in "Hinge Reinforcement."

REATTACHING THE ORIGINAL SPINE

While the book dries, prepare the original cloth spine. Turn the old spine with the reverse facing up and peel or gently scrape off as much of the lining paper as possible. Sand lightly if necessary to smooth out irregularities.

Put the rebacked book into a finishing press.

Use a piece of paper to measure the new spine, just the part where you can feel the bristol spine strip under the cloth. Fold the paper to determine the midpoint of the new spine. Place the paper on the book's new spine and transfer the midpoint to the top and bottom of the new spine (fig. 5-136). Save this strip to use again later.

Fig. 5-136

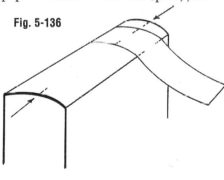

With another strip of paper, determine the midpoint of the *titling* on the original cloth. Measure the longest line, then fold the paper in half. If there are decorative lines stamped at the top and bottom of the spine, measure them instead. Make faint marks with a pencil or small holes with a fine awl at the top and bottom of the original cloth spine to note the midpoint (fig. 5-137A).

Place the strip of paper with the width of the new spine over the original spine and align the midpoints. Make a set of marks at the top and bottom of the original spine, transferring the width of the new spine from the strip of paper.

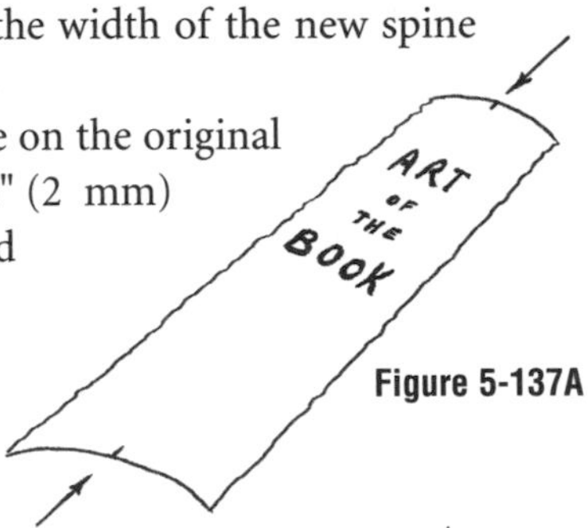

Place a straightedge on the original spine. Align it about ⅟₁₆" (2 mm) *inside* the marks, toward the center of the spine (fig. 5-137B). Hold the straightedge down firmly and cut with a sharp scalpel or utility knife.

Figure 5-137A

Figure 5-137B

Note: To cut old cloth without damaging it, use the rounded part of a scalpel blade, such as a no. 23, rather than the point of a blade. Make sure the straightedge holds the cloth securely to prevent it from shifting.

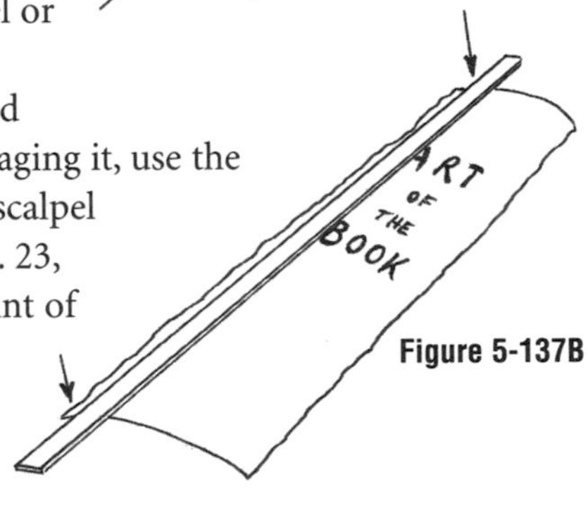

Repeat on the other side of the old spine, again setting the straightedge inside the marks. This will make the old spine slightly narrower than the new spine, to ensure that it will not extend beyond it.

Cut the top and bottom of the old spine neatly, using stamped lines (if there are any) as guides. Cut off any ragged cloth edges. The old spine should be at least ¼" (6–7 mm) shorter than the new spine.

Apply mix to the reverse of the old spine and attach it over the new spine, centering the old cloth on the midpoint marks on the new spine (fig. 5-138). Put a piece of paper over the spine and rub down gently with a bone or Teflon folder for a couple of minutes.

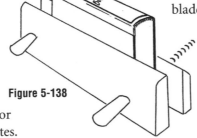

Figure 5-138

Pay particular attention to the edges and insert mix under any areas that are loose, then rub again.

Leave the book in the finishing press. Cover the spine with wax paper and wrap the book and the press with an elastic bandage, as shown in figure 5-71 in "Reattaching Flapping Spines." Do not overstretch the bandage. Allow it to dry.

If the spine is damaged but the titling is legible, cut that area out of the old spine. Trim it neatly, so that the title is centered and the piece of cloth has square corners. Attach it to the new spine as a label.

Make new labels for the title and call number if the original spine is missing or not usable. Computer-generated foil-backed labels are a good option.

VARIATION: LIFTING THE OLD CLOTH

Applying the new cloth *over* the old cloth on the boards is the fastest and easiest method. However, if you want to save titling or decoration on the covers, the original cloth can be lifted so that the repair cloth can be inserted under it. Either method is structurally sound, but lifting cloth or paper requires a lot of practice in order to achieve a neat result. Bookbinders use rigid knives with angled ends, called "lifting knives," for this operation. However, you can probably get acceptable results with a thin, wide, carbon steel spatula or possibly with a thin knife, not too narrow, with a rounded end.

The following instructions are for lifting the original cloth from the boards. If only the front cover has titling or decoration, you can lift the cloth on just the front cover.

Remove the old spine as described in "Rebacking a Book with Boards Still Attached to the Text Block," p. 134, and set it aside.

Lay the book flat on the counter. Using a scalpel or utility knife, slit the cloth at the top and bottom of the boards, cutting about 1" (2.5 cm) starting at the joint.

Insert a wide spatula or a thin knife with a rounded end under the trimmed edge of the book cloth. Begin at a spot where the knife can be inserted easily, often at one end or the other where the cloth was slit, then slide the blade up and down with a rocking motion. At the same time, angle the blade up a bit every so often to loosen the cloth from the board (fig. 5-139). Try not to cut into the board. Some cloths are much harder to lift than others, and paper covers are very likely to be damaged from lifting. Work cautiously and patiently to avoid ripping through the cloth.

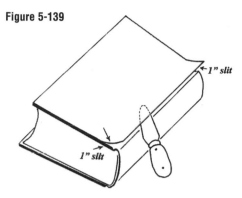

Figure 5-139

1" slit

1" slit

Lift the cloth at least 1" (2.5 cm). Don't fold it back or crease it; the crease mark will show as a line after the cloth is pasted down later.

Put the book into a finishing press with about 2"–3" (5–8 cm) showing above the jaws of the press.

Clean up the spine of the text block, construct and attach a tube, and make a new cloth spine with a bristol spine strip in the same way as in the previous version of this rebacking method.

VARIATION: ATTACHING THE NEW SPINE

The new spine will be attached in four steps. First, the cloth and the spine strip will be glued to the tube. Then the cloth will be attached to the boards, under the lifted cloth. When that is dry, the cloth extending at the top and bottom of the book will be turned in. Finally, the lifted cloth will be reattached over the new cloth.

1. Put the book into a press, or prop it up between bricks, so you have both hands free for this step. Apply mix to the bristol spine strip of the prepared cloth piece. Place the new spine on the tube, aligning the spine strip with the edges of the tube on both sides. The top and bottom of the spine strip should line up with the top and bottom of the boards. Work carefully but quickly, so that you have time to slide the new spine until it is in the right position, before the adhesive starts to set.

When the new spine is correctly positioned on the tube, rub it down with a bone folder. Allow it to dry in the press.

2. When the new spine is firmly attached to the tube, remove the book from the press or bricks. Rest it on its spine while you brush mix on one of the flaps of the new spine (fig. 5-140). Be careful not to get adhesive on the old cloth.

Lay the book flat on the counter. Gently insert the pasted flap under the lifted cloth and rub it down with a bone folder (fig. 5-141). Use the edge of the folder to work the cloth into the joints.

Fig. 5-141

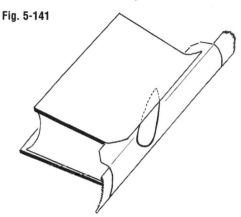

If the cloth was lifted on both boards, glue the other flap under the original cloth in the same way.

Insert strips or wax paper or Mylar between the old cloth and the new spine; otherwise, moisture from the freshly glued flaps might stain the old cloth.

Allow the repair to dry between boards with a weight on top.

3. Open the book to pop the tube open and put pieces of wax paper into each end. Make the turn-ins and shape the headcaps as described in "Repairing Tops and Bottoms of Spines," p. 124.

4. When the new spine is dry, apply a thin coat of mix to the underside of the lifted cloth of the front board, using a card or spatula, as described in "Reattaching Spine Labels," p. 120. If you use too much adhesive, it may ooze out when the cloth is rubbed down. Pat the cloth down gently with your fingertips.

Put a piece of waste paper over the board and rub the old cloth with the flat part of a bone or Teflon folder, smoothing it over the new cloth. Rub very gently; old cloth may be damaged or stained by too much pressure. Repeat on the other side. If adhesive oozes out, clean it with a paper towel or pick it up with a spatula.

Place the book on an absorbent surface and let it air dry completely, *without pressing it.* (Applying pressure on old cloth after it has been pasted can force adhesive through it. This will show as dark stains on the face of the cloth.) Prepare and reattach the old spine as described in "Reattaching the Original Spine," p. 137.

Fig. 5-140

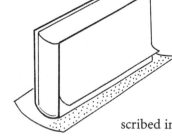

Rebacking a Book with Detached Boards

This procedure can be used to repair a book with boards that have come off completely. The spine is usually detached as well but may still be attached to one of the boards, or it may be missing altogether. It combines some of the techniques used in "Rebacking a Book with Boards Still Attached to the Text Block" with those used in "Reattaching the Text Block to the Case."

This is the most complex technique presented in the manual. Before deciding to repair a book in this way, make sure that the boards are sturdy, with sound corners and cloth in good condition. If the boards are detached and the cloth is fraying around the edges and, in addition, the corners need rebuilding, the spine is very damaged or missing, and the endpapers are ripped, the book should be sent to the library binder or replaced. The same applies if a board is cracked, even if the cloth over the break hasn't split.

PREPARING THE TEXT BLOCK

Note: If the spine is distorted or the signatures are no longer in correct alignment because the glue has deteriorated, lay the text block flat on the counter, with the shoulder over the edge, and reshape it using a triangle, as described in "Using a Spine Lining to Repair a Broken Hinge," p. 128. The spine should be gently rounded, with the shoulder at the top directly over the one at the bottom and at right angles to the counter. Place a weight on the book, apply a coat of mix, and allow it to dry before putting the book into a finishing press.

Note: It may not be possible to reshape the spine of books glued up with plastic (white) glues. Just do the best you can with such books; consider replacing very misshapen books or sending them to the library binder.

If the spine does not need to be reshaped, proceed as follows.

Put the text block into a finishing press and peel off any loose spine linings. Do not disturb the sewing or any linings that are firmly attached. If necessary, sand *lightly* to smooth out irregularities.

Trim off any ragged bits of paper or super from the shoulders of the book, using scissors (fig. 5-142).

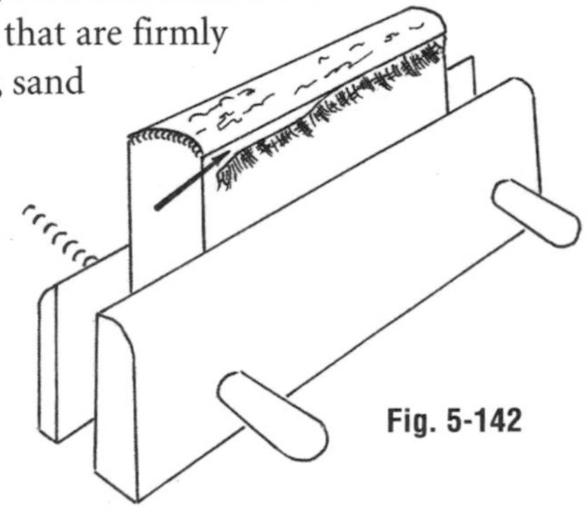

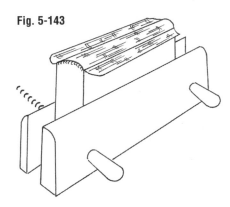

Fig. 5-142

If the book has endbands (headbands), check if they are in good condition. They can be glued down with mix if loose. Endbands serve no structural purpose and can simply be removed if they are damaged. Headbanding tape is available from some suppliers and you can attach new ones if you wish.

Check that the flyleaves are in good condition and firmly attached. New flyleaves can be attached at this point if needed. (See "Replacing Missing Flyleaves," p. 115.)

If necessary, consolidate any loose spine linings with a thin coat of mix. Otherwise, go to the next step.

Attaching a New Cloth Lining

Cut a piece of lining fabric, such as super, muslin, cotton lawn, etc. It should be a little shorter than the spine, by the width of the spine, plus 3" (7–8 cm).

Apply a coat of mix to the spine and attach the lining fabric; make sure it is well adhered to the whole spine, especially the edges. If any adhesive oozes out, wipe it up.

Rub down well with a bone or Teflon folder, without stretching the lining. There should be a 1.5" (4 cm) flap on each side of the spine; the flaps are the new hinges that will be used to attach the book to the repaired case (fig. 5-143). Angle the corners for a neater appearance. Let dry.

Fig. 5-143

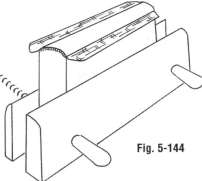

Attaching a New Paper Lining

Cut a piece of acid-free paper (bond weight) the height and width of the spine (fig. 5-144). The grain should be parallel to the spine. Heavier Japanese papers, such as some Sekishus and Okawara, are also good choices for the spine lining.

Fig. 5-144

Apply mix to the new paper lining and attach it to the spine. Rub well with a bone or Teflon folder. Use just enough mix to make the lining stick to the spine but not so much that adhesive oozes out when you rub down. Let dry.

If the spine needs more support to maintain a rounded shape, add one or two more layers of paper, allowing each layer to dry before applying the next. Several thin layers give better support than one thick layer.

Using a Tube

For heavy, thick books such as dictionaries or encyclopedias, add a tube over the paper linings. If you find that having a tube makes it easier to attach the text block to the case, you can put tubes on small books that are at least ¾" (2 cm) thick, instead of the paper linings. Narrower tubes are more difficult to work with. See "Making a Hollow Tube," p. 121, for directions on making a tube, and also consult the directions for using a tube when "Rebacking a Book with Boards Still Attached to the Text Block," p. 134.

You can leave the text block in the finishing press until the case is ready, unless the press is needed for another task.

REPAIRING THE CASE

If one or both boards are still partly attached to the text block, separate them along the joints with a scalpel or with small scissors. Be careful not to cut into the shoulder of the book.

Remove the spine; it will be trimmed and reattached at the end.

The following instructions are for rebacking the case with the repair cloth *under* the old cloth. However, the new cloth can be attached over the old cloth for a quicker repair. Also, if the cloth or paper covering the boards is fragile, it is usually better not to attempt to lift it.

Preparing the Boards

Place one of the boards, cloth side up, on the counter and put a straight-edge on it about ¼" (6–7 mm) from the spine edge. Cut through the cloth and peel the strip away (fig. 5-145).

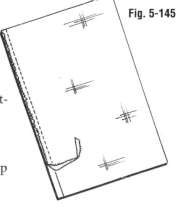

Fig. 5-145

Using a scalpel or utility knife, cut a 1" (2.5 cm) slit in the cloth at the top and bottom edges of the boards.

Insert a lifting knife, wide spatula, or a thin knife with a rounded end under the trimmed edge of the book cloth. Begin at a spot where the knife can be inserted easily, then slide the blade back and forth with a rocking motion. At the same time, angle the blade up a bit every so often to loosen the cloth from the board (fig. 5-146). Try not to cut into the board. Some cloths are much harder to lift than others; paper covers can be easily damaged from lifting. Work cautiously and patiently to avoid ripping through the cloth.

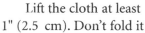
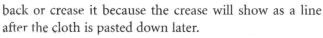

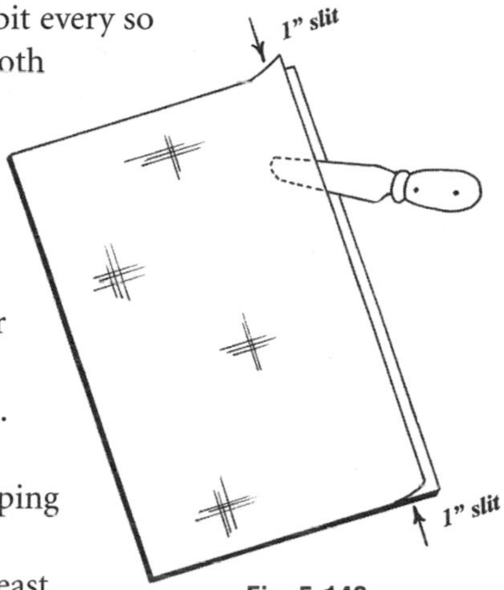

Fig. 5-146

Lift the cloth at least 1" (2.5 cm). Don't fold it back or crease it because the crease will show as a line after the cloth is pasted down later.

Turn the board over and trim the inner edge, cutting through the board sheet (endpaper), the super, and the cloth turn-in. Peel the strip away (fig. 5-147). It may be necessary to insert a spatula or knife blade under the strip, from the edge of the board, in order to get it started. There should be ¼" (6–7 mm) of board exposed. If the super or board sheet is loose, insert a little mix under it with a microspatula and smooth it down.

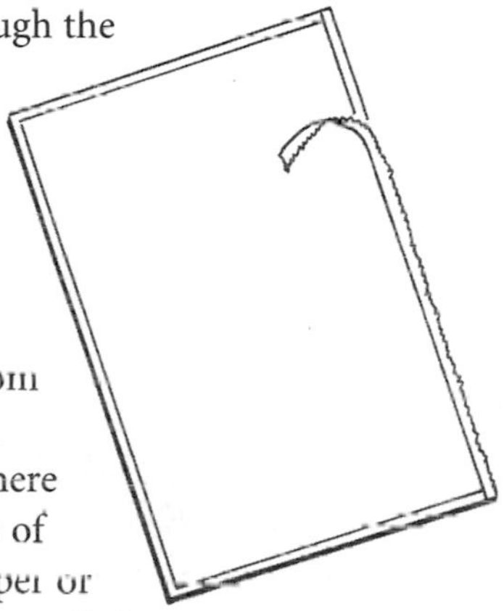

Fig. 5-147

Prepare the other board in the same way.

If the corners on either board are beginning to fray, repair them at this point and allow them to dry thoroughly. See "Repairing Corners," p. 122, for directions.

Gently pick up the lifted cloth on the outside of the board and brush a thin coat of mix on the exposed *board*. Do not put very much adhesive near the area where the lifting stopped, to avoid lumps. The adhesive will size the board and make it easier to attach the cloth spine. Let the boards air dry, cloth side up.

PREPARING A NEW CLOTH SPINE

Make a new cloth spine as directed on p. 134, in "Rebacking a Book with Boards Still Attached to the Text Block" (fig. 5-148).

Place the prepared spine on waste paper, with the bristol strip facing up. Draw a pencil line ¼" (6–7 mm) on each side of the spine strip. Use a ¼"-square metal or plastic rod as a spacer, if you have one. They are available from craft stores.

Apply mix to the cloth on one side of the spine strip, up to the line, as shown in figure 5-149.

Fig. 5-148

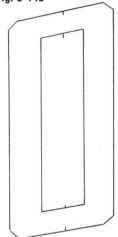

Fig. 5-149

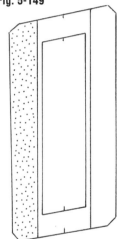

ATTACHING THE BOARDS TO THE NEW SPINE

Pick up the front board, with the board sheet facing up, and slide the new cloth under the lifted cloth, aligning the edge of the board with the line on the new cloth (fig. 5-150).

Make sure the top of the board and the top of the bristol spine strip are in a straight line.

When the cloth is correctly positioned, lay the board down again and press it with your hand for a moment, to tack the cloth down.

Fig. 5-150

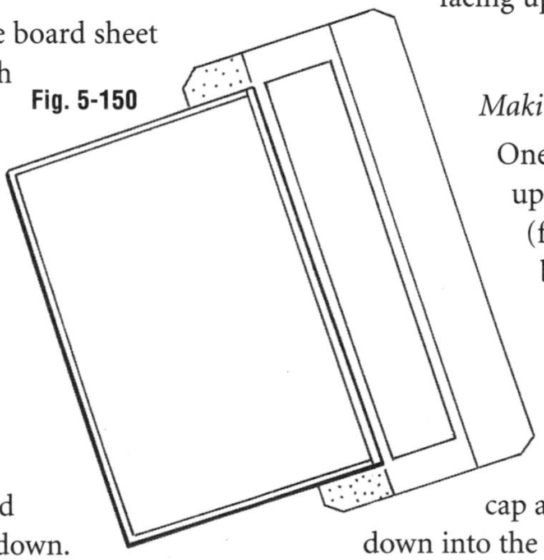

Carefully turn the board and new spine over. Hold the old cloth up gently with a spatula while rubbing the new cloth down firmly with the flat part of a bone folder, until the adhesive starts to set (fig. 5-151). Insert a strip of wax paper or Mylar between the lifted cloth and the new cloth, as a moisture barrier. (If moisture seeps into the old cloth at this stage, it may stain.) Allow it to dry a few minutes.

Fig. 5-151

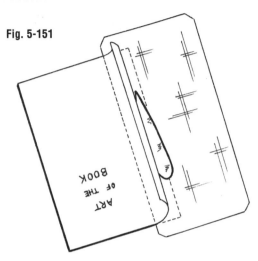

Apply mix to the other side of the new spine, up to the pencil line, and attach the back board, sliding the new cloth under the lifted cloth. Turn over and rub down, as above. Insert wax paper or Mylar between the lifted cloth and the new cloth, as a moisture barrier.

Let the repaired case dry with the cloth side up so the lifted cloth is not damaged.

When the new cloth is completely dry, remove the moisture barriers. Turn the case so the inside is facing up and lay it on a piece of waste paper.

Making the Turn-Ins

One at a time, apply mix to the flaps sticking up at the top and bottom of the new spine (fig. 5-152) and turn them down over the bristol spine strip and over the boards (fig. 5-153).

Pull tightly as you bring the cloth over the boards so that the top and bottom edges of the boards are as smooth as possible. Smooth the headcap area with a bone folder, working the cloth down into the area between the boards.

Fig. 5-152

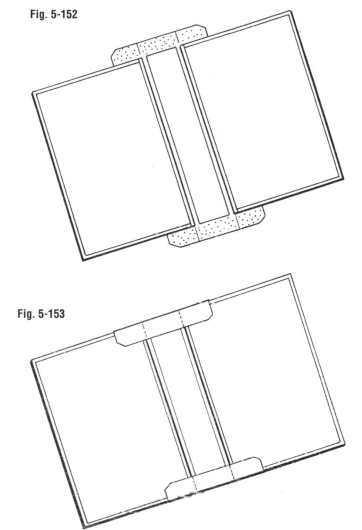

Fig. 5-153

Turn the case so the *outside* is facing up and work the cloth into the joints with the edge of a bone folder.

Pasting Down the Lifted Cloth

Apply a thin, even coat of mix to the underside of the lifted cloth of the front cover, using a card or spatula, as described in "Reattaching Spine Labels," p. 120. Pat the cloth down gently with your fingertips.

Use just enough mix so the cloth sticks down but not so much that adhesive oozes out when you rub down.

Put a piece of waste paper over the board and rub the old cloth with the flat part of a bone or Teflon folder, smoothing it over the new cloth. Rub gently; old cloth may be damaged or stained by too much pressure. Repeat on the back board. If adhesive oozes out, clean it with a paper towel or pick it up with a spatula.

Allow the repaired case to air dry without pressing before joining it to the text block.

JOINING THE REPAIRED CASE TO THE TEXT BLOCK

Remove the text block from the finishing press. When the case is thoroughly dry, open it flat on the counter, with the inside facing up.

Position the text block on the back board so it covers the board sheet at the three edges. Make sure the book is right side up on the case.

Close the cover over the book. Pull the case gently as you close it and check if the joints fit well over the shoulders of the text block.

If all is well, open the front board and put a piece of wax paper or Mylar over the front flyleaf. Place waste paper over that.

Fold the new front hinge over the waste paper. Brush mix on the hinge, making sure not to get adhesive on the spine (fig. 5-154). Carefully remove the waste paper. Leave the moisture barrier in place.

Fig. 5-154

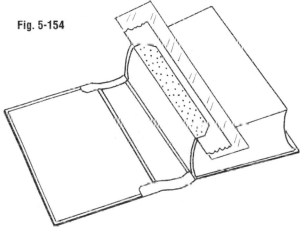

Close the cover over the book and work the cloth gently into the joint with the edge of a bone folder (fig. 5-155). Do not open the front board until the hinge is dry.

Carefully turn the book over and open the back board. Attach the back hinge in the same way.

Fig. 5-155

Note: If you put a tube on the text block, it must be attached to the new spine strip. After attaching the front hinge as described above, turn the book over, open the back cover, and place wax paper and waste paper under the back hinge. Apply a thin coat of mix to the inside of the new spine area, from the edge of the back board to the edge of the front board, *including* the spine strip. Then apply mix to the tube and the back hinge, close the cover, and work the cloth into the back joint. See "Repairing One Broken Hinge," p. 126.

Place the book between brass-edged boards and put a weight on it, as shown earlier in figure 5-97, on p. 127. You can also put the book between *regular* wooden boards, lined up to the edges of the joints, and place a weight on the top board, as shown in figure 5-101, on p. 129.

Alternatively, you can put the book between boards into a nipping press (fig. 5-156). Tighten the press very gently, and *do not crush.*

Fig. 5-156

Allow the book to dry for an hour or two before opening it.

The new hinges will cover about an inch (2.5 cm) of the board sheets. You can cut the spine lining narrower as you get more practice, so the hinges will not cover as much of the board sheets.

REATTACHING THE OLD SPINE

Prepare and reattach the old spine as described in "Re-attaching the Original Spine," p. 137. If the spine is damaged but the titling is legible, cut that area out of the old spine. Trim it neatly, so that the title is centered and the piece of cloth has square corners. Attach it to the new spine as a label.

If the spine is missing, make labels for the author, title, and call number, following the information in your catalog.

Pamphlets

Sewing Single-Section Pamphlets into a Binder

Pamphlet binders have been used in libraries for many decades. They provide a quick and inexpensive way to protect thin pamphlets or booklets so they can be stored on shelves among books on the same subject.

Various styles of binders were used in the twentieth century, with different ways of attaching the pamphlet to the binder. One style still in common use has a length of gummed cloth tape stitched to the cloth spine of the binder. The pamphlet is attached to the gummed tape. The cloth tape has sharp edges and often damages the covers of the pamphlet. Other types of binders are meant to be attached to the pamphlet by stab sewing (see "Sewn and Adhesive Bindings," p. 98), which causes the book to lose at least ½" (1.3 cm) of inner margin. Furthermore, until the 1980s most commercially made binders had acidic boards, which stained the covers of the pamphlets.

So it is not surprising that pamphlet binders acquired a bad reputation in conservation circles. Fortunately, manufacturers have met the need for good-quality, acid-free binders, and a wide variety is available from library and conservation suppliers. The binders come in many stock sizes, but they can be made to specific sizes by certain suppliers. We give directions for sewing a single-section pamphlet into a simple pamphlet binder, without the gummed cloth tape.

PREPARING THE PAMPHLET

Single-section pamphlets are normally held together by "saddle stitching," which consists of two or more staples attached through the fold.

Since wire staples can rust very quickly when stored in locations without perfect climate control, it is best to remove the staples whenever possible. See the instructions in "Removing Fasteners and Rubber Bands" in section 4, p. 82. If the paper is fragile or the staples have already begun to rust, the pamphlet is too delicate to be put into a binder and should be housed in a sleeve or envelope or in a binder with flaps, such as those described in "Making Simple Enclosures" in section 3.

Check the folds to make sure they are sound, especially the cover (sometimes called the "wrapper") and the fold in the middle of the pamphlet. Mend the folds with Japanese paper and paste or methylcellulose as needed, and mend tears in the text in the same way. See "Guarding Two Leaves" in section 4, p. 92.

BUFFERED BARRIER SHEET

Pamphlet binders that are sold by conservation suppliers are acid-free, as are many binders sold by regular library suppliers. (Test with a pH pen, as described in "PH Testing" in section 3, p. 58.) However, if you have any doubts about the quality of the binder, you can fold a piece of buffered paper around the pamphlet as a barrier. The extra paper can also be added to provide additional protection to a very thin or somewhat fragile pamphlet, even if you are using an acid-free binder.

Use buffered wrapping paper or other medium-weight paper. Cut it the height of the pamphlet by a little more than twice the width, with the grain going in the short direction. Fold the paper in half, with the grain, and put the pamphlet inside the fold.

SEWING THE PAMPHLET INTO A BINDER

Select a binder close to the size of the pamphlet. When the pamphlet is in the binder, the "squares" (the part of the board that shows around the top, fore edge, and bottom of the pamphlet) should be at least ¼" (6–7 mm).

Open the binder, then open the pamphlet to the center and place it in the binder. Carefully secure the pamphlet (and the folded barrier sheet, if one was added) to the binder with large paper clips. Use plastic-coated paper clips if available; they are somewhat less likely to damage the paper. Make sure the spine of the pamphlet is positioned accurately on the fold of the binder's cloth spine.

Using an awl, pierce holes through the center fold of the pamphlet *and* the binder.

For a small pamphlet, up to about 7"–8" (17–20 cm), three holes are adequate. Make five holes in bigger pamphlets. Try to use some of the staple holes.

It may be easier to make the holes if you partly close the binder-and-pamphlet assembly and insert the awl at a low angle, from the inside of the pamphlet to the outside of the binder. This will enable you to see the outside of the spine, to note whether the awl is coming out at the right point.

Note: Some awls have metal rings or sharp ridges around the handle. When ordering supplies, get awls with smooth, rounded handles. Be careful not to damage the pages of the pamphlet when piercing. You may wish to put a piece of waste paper over the page on the side of the pamphlet that is flat on the counter. (That's where you will be pushing the awl toward the fold.)

If the folds of the pamphlet were extensively guarded, so that none of the staple holes are visible, make a piercing jig as follows.

Three-hole piercing jig. Cut a strip of paper the height of the pamphlet and fold it in half. Make folds about ½" (1.3 cm) from the ends (fig. 5-157).

Fig. 5-157

Five-hole piercing jig. Fold the strip as above, then bring the middle fold up to meet the folds near the ends. Crease. When you open up the strip, there will be five evenly spaced marks (fig. 5-158).

Fig. 5-158

Place the piercing jig at the center fold of the pamphlet and secure it with two paper clips. Use the awl to pierce the pamphlet and binder at the crease marks on the jig (fig. 5-159).

Fig. 5-159

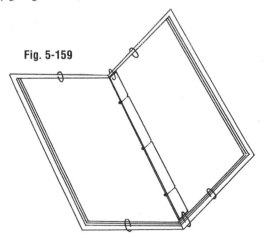

Keep the pamphlet and binder clipped together. Thread a needle with medium-weight linen thread, e.g., no. 18. Use a needle 2"–2½" (5–6.5 cm) long; darning needles are easy to thread.

Sew as shown in figure 5-160.

Fig. 5-160

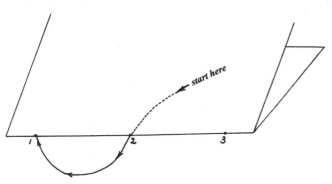

Begin inside the pamphlet, at the center hole, 2. Leave a 4½" (11.5 cm) tail of thread inside the pamphlet. Go back in from the outside, through the binder and the pamphlet, at the top hole, 1. Skip hole 2 and bring the needle out again through the bottom hole, 3. This leaves a long stitch inside the binder, from hole 1 to hole 3.

Bring the needle to the inside at hole 2, being careful not to pierce the long stitch inside the pamphlet (fig. 5-161).

Fig. 5-161

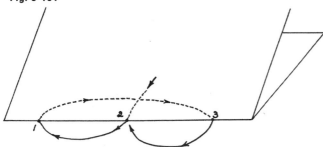

The needle must come back into the pamphlet on the *opposite* side of the long stitch from where the tail of the thread is (fig. 5-162).

Fig. 5-162

Snug the thread, so the stitching is taut but does not pucker the pamphlet (fig. 5-163). Tie a square knot, catching the long stitch in the knot. Verify that the knot is secure, then snip off both tail and needle thread, leaving about 1" (2.5 cm) inside the pamphlet.

Fig. 5-163

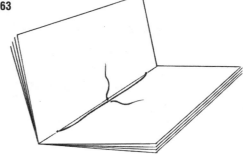

A square knot is made by putting the left end over the right and then the right over the left, as in figure 5-164.

Fig. 5-164

Sew a larger pamphlet using five holes, following the pattern in figures 5-165 and 5-166.

Fig. 5-165

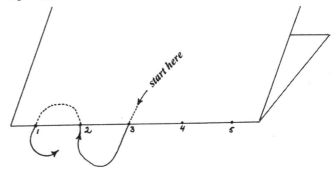

Fig. 5-166

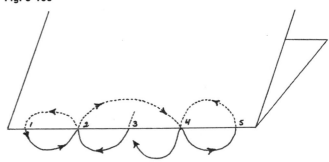

If barrier sheets were added, trim the fore edge of the barrier sheets as described in "Trimming Pages," p. 114, after the sewing is completed.

Stab-Sewn (Side-Sewn) Pamphlets

There are several types of binders available for multisection pamphlets or thin, softcover books made of single sheets with no folds. The pamphlets and binders are sewn together near the binding edge, not through the folds. It is a very quick way of assembling pages, but pamphlets that are stab sewn do not open very well. Pages often crease and break off against the line of stitching, especially at the front and back.

If the materials are of permanent value, it is usually better to send them to the library binder. However, for very limited-retention items, this type of pamphlet binding may be adequate. Conservation and library supply vendors provide instructions for attaching pamphlets to the various types of binder.

If there are pamphlets in your collection in old binders that cannot be rehoused immediately, insert loose barrier sheets of buffered paper between the boards and the pamphlet for a short-term solution. Place the pamphlet in an acid-free envelope if more protection is needed.

Children's Books

Some library edition children's books are basically like pamphlets. They can often be repaired by sewing a piece of cloth to the text block and then gluing the flaps to the inside of the cover. Make any *quick* repairs to the case first; if it is extensively damaged, it may be more economical to replace the book.

Single-Section Children's Books

1. Check to see if the inner folded sheets are solidly attached, as well as the first and last pages. Mend with Japanese paper and paste or methylcellulose if necessary.

2. Cut a piece of lightweight book cloth, just a little shorter than the height of the text block by about 3" (7–8 cm). Angle the corners. Fold it in half the long way, wrap it around the spine of the book and sew it on. Use five of the original sewing holes if possible (fig. 5-167).

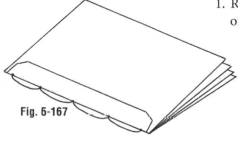

Fig. 5-167

3. Position the text block on the back cover of the case, so the back board sheet is completely covered.

Put pieces of waste paper and wax paper under the newly attached cloth hinge and apply adhesive (fig. 5-168). Discard the waste paper but leave the wax paper in place.

Fig. 5-168

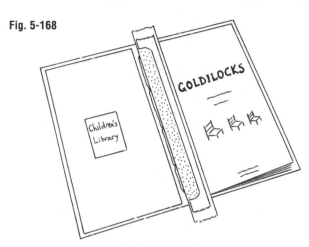

4. Carefully close the front cover, making sure everything is aligned. Place a weight on the book for a minute. Open to check.

Make corrections if needed; otherwise, turn the book over carefully and attach the other hinge in the same manner.

You may smooth down the new inner hinges with a bone or Teflon folder after pressing for a moment, but for a quicker repair, just place a board and weight on the book after attaching the second hinge. Leave the wax paper in place until dry.

Multisection Children's Books

These books are usually stab sewn. Unsewn, folded book sections or loose single pages, or a combination of the two, are sewn together with thread that goes through the whole book, from top to bottom, near the binding edge. Pages often crease and break off against the line of stitching, especially at the front and back.

1. Reattach any pages that have broken off, using Japanese paper and paste or methylcellulose.

2. Make new hinges by cutting a piece of thin book cloth, a little shorter than the height of the text block by about 3"–4" (7.5–10 cm) wide,

depending on the size of the book. Don't cover up more of the endpapers than necessary. Angle the corners of the cloth.

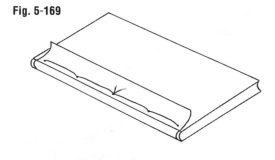

Fig. 5-169

Wrap the cloth snugly around the spine and secure it temporarily with large clips, clothespins, or other clamps. Feel through the new cloth to locate the line of sewing.

Mark five evenly spaced spots. With an awl, enlarge the sewing holes near the marks. Sew the cloth on, using the same pattern described for sewing pamphlets through the fold (fig. 5-169).

3. and 4. Same as above.

Small Exhibitions

MOST LIBRARIES AND MANY ARCHIVES PRESENT exhibitions from time to time. Library galleries are often community gathering spots where local artists exhibit their work. An institution can mount a show as part of its educational activities, to let patrons know about new acquisitions, to commemorate a particular event, or for various other reasons. Exhibitions are also a major activity for historical societies. Designing and putting up an exhibition can be a big project and may take several months. This is especially true when some of the materials are borrowed from other institutions or from private owners.

Our main goal is to make sure that documents, books, prints, and other objects on display are not damaged in the course of mounting them or as a result of environmental conditions over the duration of the show. In this section, we will address some matters relating to the preservation of book and flat paper materials on exhibit.

This section is divided into six parts.

1. "Designing the Exhibition with Conservation in Mind" gives guidelines for safe exhibit practices, including environmental controls, security, insurance, and lending and borrowing.
2. "Mounting an Exhibition" discusses exhibit cases.
3. "Exhibiting Flat Paper Items" gives techniques for displaying flat paper items.
4. "Mounting, Hinging, Matting, Framing" gives instructions for mounting, matting, and framing artworks and paper.
5. "Preparing Books for Exhibition" addresses proper methods of displaying books, with detailed instructions for making mounts and cradles.
6. "Closing the Show" covers some of the details that need attention when the show is over.

DESIGNING THE EXHIBITION WITH CONSERVATION IN MIND

When a show is first being planned, the emphasis rightly falls on content and design. However, the physical safety of the materials must also be considered from the beginning. The designer of the show should work closely with a conservator or preservation specialist. If the library or archive does not have such a person on its staff, seek advice from other institutions. It is often helpful to contract with a conservator to provide advice and services during the planning and mounting of an exhibition. The availability of a conservator, on staff or on contract, may help convince an owner to lend materials to a show. Some institutions and private owners stipulate that a conservator must be involved in the planning and mounting before they will agree to lend materials. Contact institutions in your area for references to conservators who have experience in setting up exhibitions.

Some aspects of a show, such as the size and shape of the gallery, are more or less predetermined. Some features of the space and display furniture may be less than optimal. But with a few exceptions, a gallery can be adapted to house an exhibition safely. Lenders generally want to know what sort of conditions will prevail during the time that their materials are on loan. By the same token, if another institution wishes to borrow materials from yours, it is your responsibility to determine how they will be housed and displayed.

As with any space containing collections, a main consideration is whether an acceptable environment can be maintained in the gallery for the whole length of the exhibition, 24 hours a day. If this is not possible, the space is not suitable for exhibiting original materials.

Environment in the Gallery

A gallery in which books and papers are displayed has the same temperature and humidity requirements as a special collections storage area. Consult "Monitoring Environmental Conditions" in section 1 for descriptions of the equipment used to monitor temperature and relative humidity (RH). Relative humidity should be constant and moderate for the length of the show, to avoid problems with distortion and mold. During the warm months, the air conditioning should be on 24 hours a day. In some parts of the country, additional dehumidification may be necessary to maintain an even RH around 50%. Modifications to the heating, ventilation, and air conditioning

(HVAC) system may be required to permit dehumidification when outside temperatures are too cool for air conditioning. Freestanding dehumidifiers can be used as well; make certain that the water receptacles are checked and emptied regularly. If possible, attach a hose to the receptacle and let it empty directly into a sink or drain.

If the building is not equipped to humidify air in winter, do not add moisture by using humidifiers. Instead, lower the temperature in the gallery. This will have the effect of raising the relative humidity. Keep in mind that in cold regions, indoor relative humidity can plummet to single digits during the winter when the heat is kept around 75°F (24°C).

When first selecting an exhibition area, *monitor the space a year in advance,* to see what you can realistically achieve at different times of the year. When planning a show featuring materials that are sensitive to low humidity, schedule it for a time when the gallery will be able to maintain moderate humidity levels, at least 35–40%. By the same token, if there are times of the year when the humidity cannot be kept below 55% around the clock, avoid scheduling exhibitions during those weeks or months.

Materials that are most likely to be damaged by *low* humidity include:

parchment-covered books

parchment documents

photographs of all kinds

leather-covered books

books with wooden boards

All library and archival materials are subject to damage in conditions of *high* humidity.

Air Quality

In general, in order to have the best possible air quality in the gallery, windows should be sealed. This is especially true for buildings in urban areas where air pollution can be a danger to the materials on exhibit. But even in rural areas, dust, pollen, and insects will come in even if screens are in place. Air exchange should be through the HVAC system. Of course, the system must be kept in good order. All filters should be changed on schedule, the ducts should be cleaned as needed, and other maintenance work performed regularly.

Lighting

Paper, photographs, textiles, parchment, and leather are all harmed by exposure to light. The quality and quantity of light that falls on exhibits must be controlled to prevent damage. (See also "Light" in section 1, p. 7.)

NATURAL LIGHT

Although natural light is the most pleasant type for people, it is not a good choice for a gallery that is used to show books, photographs, documents, and other paper objects. Sunlight emits a very high level of ultraviolet (UV) radiation. This is the type of light that is most damaging to paper-based materials, textiles, leather, many plastics, and all kinds of photographic processes. Fading, color changes, brittleness, cracking, and delaminating are all results of the accelerated aging that is caused by UV light.

Visible light not in the UV range causes many of the same problems, although to a lesser degree. Damage from light is irreversible, and it is cumulative. This means that the longer the material is exposed to light, even at low levels, the more serious the effect will be.

Furthermore, sunlight generates significant amounts of heat. This can play havoc with regulating the temperature and humidity in the gallery.

Skylights and windows should be covered with shades or coated with paint containing zinc white or titanium dioxide. These pigments reflect light (and heat) and absorb UV radiation. UV-filtering plastics, either in the form of roll-up shades or as acrylic sheets placed next to the glass, help reduce the amount of UV radiation but are by no means as effective as opaque coverings. The exact solution will depend on many factors, including whether the room is used for other types of functions at times when there are no materials on exhibit. In that case, opaque shades or other adjustable window covers would be a good choice.

ARTIFICIAL LIGHT

Even though indoor lighting is much less bright than sunlight, it can still cause fading and deterioration. There are several types of artificial lighting in common use. Each has different properties.

Fluorescent Tubes or Lamps

This is the kind of lighting most commonly found in institutional buildings. The light can be rather blue-green and quite cool in color. "Full spectrum" tubes and lamps are available; their light is more pleasant to the eye. Fluorescent light is economical and does not give off very much heat from the tubes themselves. The fixtures, especially the ballasts, do give off heat. If this type of lighting must be used, see if the ballasts can be installed outside the cases, and provide adequate ventilation.

Fluorescent light is a rich source of UV rays. Some tubes have a much smaller output of UV rays than others. All fluorescent tubes or lamps should be covered with filtering plastic sleeves or sheets; be aware, however, that these do not filter 100% of the UV. The ends of the tubes emit the most UV, so make sure the filter sleeves are the right length. Some manufacturers state a ten-year life expectancy for sleeves or rigid sheet filters. (See appendix B for suppliers.)

Incandescent (Tungsten) Lamps

The normal light bulbs found in homes are tungsten lamps, also called incandescent lamps. They give off very little UV and their warm-colored light is much safer for paper-based materials. They do give off a significant amount of heat. Using low-wattage lamps (20–35 watts) will help keep the light and heat at low levels. Both light and heat have to be taken into account when positioning lamps for a show.

An incandescent lamp must be at least four feet from the exhibit. Tungsten lamps should not be installed inside cases because of the possible fire hazard and because of the heat they give off. As the heat builds up, the air trapped in the display case will become much drier, leading to distortion and other damage. A spotlight aimed at an object in a display case will also heat the air in the case, in the same way that the inside of a car left in the sun becomes much hotter than the outside air.

Tungsten-Halogen (Quartz-Halogen) Lamps

These small, efficient lamps are powerful light sources and, depending on the model, give off significant levels of UV radiation. Filters are available for them. They also produce a lot of heat, sometimes more heat than light. Some fixtures have the transformer separate from the lamp; this helps to reduce heat in the gallery. Halogen lamps should not be installed inside cases. Sufficient ventilation should be provided to exhaust the heat from any enclosed space. Halogen fixtures should be shielded to prevent any contact with flammable materials and should be placed where they are inaccessible to the public.

Fiber-Optic Lighting

A fiber-optic lighting system has three main components: a projector light source (the illuminator), fiber cables that transmit the light, and focusing mechanisms that aim and control the light. The light from a halogen bulb in the projector is focused on the ends of dozens of small-diameter cables that are bundled together to connect to the projector. The cables, called "fibers" in the industry, come in different diameters, and are capable of transmitting varying amounts of light. Light travels to the ends of the fibers, where it is focused into beams of the desired intensity, size, and shape by various lenses. The lenses are sometimes called "luminaires."

There are three types of optical fibers in use for exhibition lighting, at present.

1. *Glass fiber.* Very small glass fibers bonded together with epoxy to form "tails" that transmit light to the luminaires. The epoxy can degrade in intense light and heat. Spaces between the fibers do not transmit light, limiting the output of the tail. Glass fiber transmits both UV light and heat.

2. *Solid core fiber.* Solid core fibers are made of large-diameter flexible plastic that does not transmit UV or heat. The light is slightly yellow and the fiber tends to turn more yellow and brittle as it ages.

3. *Acrylic fiber.* Acrylic PMMA (polymethyl methacrylate) fiber efficiently transmits light and, by its nature, does not transmit UV or heat. The white light has the same color balance as natural sunlight, without its harmful qualities. Acrylic fibers can remain in good condition for over ten years when used with a high-quality projector. (Plexiglas is acrylic PMMA in sheet form.)

Each projector can power dozens of fibers, and multiple light sources can be created by splicing several fibers or by running more than one fiber to the exhibit. Several luminaires can be placed inside enclosed display cases, to illuminate individual exhibits. The amount of light and shape of the beam can be adjusted to appropriate levels easily. Having the light source inside the case eliminates many reflections. Since no heat is transmitted and the fibers do not carry electricity, the system can be on (lighted) during installation. Good-quality projectors are quiet and can be installed in the light attics of cases or at some distance from the display cases. Since the halogen bulbs in projectors produce considerable heat, sufficient ventilation must be provided to exhaust the heat from any enclosed space.

This method is gaining in popularity as its merits are understood, and it is the safest way to place lights inside display cases.

For more information on lighting exhibits, consult Appelbaum, *Guide to Environmental Protection of Collections;* and NEDCC Technical Leaflets 13, "Protection from Light Damage," by Beth L. Patkus, and 14, "Protecting Paper and Book Collections during Exhibition," by Mary Todd Glaser.

Suppliers are listed in appendix B.

MEASURING LIGHT LEVELS

Ultraviolet Light Meters

Ultraviolet light, which is invisible to the human eye, can be measured with a meter. UV meters are much more expensive than visible light meters, however, and if your institution does not own one, simply assume that any natural light (even on cloudy days) as well as light from fluorescent or halogen fixtures is rich in UV rays and needs to be blocked or at least filtered.

The lower the overall light level, the less UV light. Filters on fluorescent fixtures are more effective than film or sheet filters on windows or skylights that let in the noonday sun. Opaque covers are needed in those situations. Reducing the visible light to the recommended levels will automatically greatly reduce the amount of ultraviolet light.

If borrowing materials from an owner who requires UV light measurements, you may be able to borrow a meter from a local museum or other institution.

Visible Light Meters

Fig. 6-1

A light meter (fig. 6-1) is an essential tool for an institution that mounts exhibitions. These instruments are very simple to use and the price starts at around $125. They are available in foot-candle or lux versions; some models show both. The foot-candle is the measurement commonly used in North America; lux measurements are used elsewhere. A foot-candle equals 10.76 lux. If you have a lux meter, just divide the reading by 10 for a close-enough foot-candle reading. (Suppliers are listed in appendix B.)

Take a light meter reading right next to each exhibit (figs. 6-2 and 6-3). It doesn't matter how much light is coming out of the lamp; the important thing is how much reaches each object. Hold the sensor parallel to the plane of the object, i.e., flat over a book in a display case and vertically next to a hanging framed item. The recommended limits are 5–15 foot-candles. Adjust the angle of spot- and floodlights so that the readings fall within the guidelines. If necessary, use smaller bulbs, or aim lamps at the ceiling to diffuse the light.

Fig. 6-2

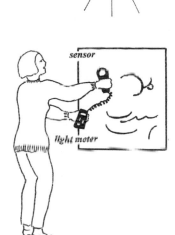

sensor

light meter

Fig. 6-3

sensor

light meter

LOW LIGHT LEVELS OVERALL

To aid viewers in adapting to the low light levels, it helps to have them enter the exhibition by way of one or more areas with lower light levels than outdoors. This allows the eyes to adjust.

There will be much less trouble with reflections from case glazing if the light level inside the case is *higher* than that in the gallery. Indirect lighting in the room (lamps aimed at the ceiling or placed behind soffits) is also helpful. When adjusting the lamps in cases, notice whether the light in one case is spilling out to nearby cases.

Turn the lights off, if it can be done safely, when the exhibition is not open to the public. If the room cannot be darkened significantly, a good solution is to cover cases or frames holding particularly light-sensitive materials with black cloth when the gallery is closed. This will reduce the total amount of light exposure. When very light-sensitive originals are shown, many institutions install blackout covers as curtains for the duration of the show. The visitor moves the curtain aside to view these delicate items.

Another possibility is to keep some or all lights off in the gallery *except* when a visitor is in the room. This solution permits the gallery to be open many more hours, without added damage to the materials. Motion-sensor switches turn lights on when someone enters the room and turn them off a certain number of minutes after they leave. Or a sign can be installed at the entrance asking visitors to turn lights on and off as needed.

If light cannot be sufficiently controlled, the space is not suitable for exhibitions of book and paper objects.

Assess Risk of Water Damage

Determine whether there are pipes running overhead. Consider also the location of restrooms on floors above the gallery. Have there been roof leaks caused by ice dams or blocked gutters? Another common cause of water damage is leakage from skylights. Don't place exhibits under skylights. If the gallery is located below grade, the possibility (or past history) of flooding should be studied. Even if the risk is small, install water alarms in logical areas, selecting models that ring at a central station, the same as fire or burglar alarms. (Alarms that sound only at the spot where they sense water are obviously much less useful.) For suppliers, see appendix B. When compiling a disaster plan, make sure to include the gallery.

Never leave materials on the floor, not even over-night. Even if a deep flood is unlikely, a small leak or spill is always a possibility, and water tends to run along the floor until it finds a drain or is stopped by some absorbent material such as a box of books or a framed piece leaning against the wall.

Length of the Exhibition

One of the factors that influences how well original materials will fare is the length of the show. Open books will eventually begin to distort; colored prints, leather, and cloth will start to fade; paper will begin to deteriorate from exposure to light. So no matter how long it takes and how much it costs to put together a show, it cannot stay up indefinitely.

Unfortunately, there is not a single ideal maximum length for an exhibition. The nature and preparation of the materials and the environment in which they will be displayed must be considered when making this decision.

When materials are borrowed from other institutions or private owners, the lender often specifies a time limit. Shows lasting one to three months are common. A fact to remember is that after a couple of months, patrons will be much less interested in the show and its message.

Security

There is no simple formula for the level of security needed for an exhibition. Much depends on the type and location of the institution, the location of the gallery within the building, the kinds of materials to be shown, and the availability of staff.

The insurance company may set certain minimum requirements for coverage; this is a good place to start. Add whatever other measures seem logical in your situation. These might include alarmed doors (especially fire-exit doors) and windows, reinforced glazing for the cases, concealed opening systems for cases, frames attached to walls with screws, vibration switches on cases and frames, and a variety of other sensors that can be connected to a central station. Water alarms should also be connected to a security system. It is a common practice in most museums and special collection libraries to require visitors to check coats and packages.

Remember also that a secluded gallery can be a hiding place for people up to no good. Electronic monitoring devices, such as closed-circuit cameras and motion sensors, can be installed in unobtrusive ways. Determine which staff members should have keys to the room. A gallery in a passageway might be easier to monitor than one in a separate room but would be more difficult to secure when the exhibit is closed.

A larger institution may have security personnel. The gallery should be included in their rounds, and they should be kept informed about the hours the gallery is open, as well as events such as deliveries, exhibition openings, and so on.

It is assumed here that the building complies with the local fire code and that the gallery has the appropriate smoke or heat sensors, sprinklers, fire extinguishers, and emergency light system. If you are not sure, the local building and fire departments may be able to give you valuable advice.

Insurance

Consult with the administration to see what kind of coverage the institution carries. Determine whether the insurer requires any special security measures, documentation, shipping arrangements, and so on. In the case of traveling exhibitions or materials borrowed or lent, coverage should be door-to-door. Insurance coverage is often provided by a rider on the owner's policy; the cost is paid by the borrower. Insurers require a dollar value for coverage; when rare books or unique documents are involved, an appraiser may have to be consulted.

Lending and Borrowing

Lending

When lending materials for an exhibition at another institution, find out what sort of conditions will prevail there. This includes environmental conditions, security arrangements, exhibition furniture and frames, and length of the show. Try to get some documentation about such things as average relative humidity (24/7) during the time of year when the show is planned and the type of exhibition mounts and matting that will be used. Inquire whether a conservator will be involved in the planning and mounting. Specify that no treatment will be performed on your object without your written permission. When lending an irreplaceable object, it is your responsibility to make sure it will be safe. If you have any doubts, it might be better to refuse the loan for the time being.

LENDING AGREEMENT

Once your institution decides to proceed with the loan, a lending agreement should be drawn up. This document stipulates exactly what pieces are being lent, special preservation requirements (including environment, mounts, etc.), and who pays for insurance, packing, and shipping. It should also indicate how conservation work will be handled if an item arrives damaged or is damaged during the exhibition.

Prepare a detailed condition report on each item going out and take pictures. (See "Condition Reports" below.) Send a copy of the report with the loan and retain another copy. Make a record of what is being lent. Packing and shipping should be done by reliable art movers. They should be able to make special crates if needed. Get referrals from other institutions and ask for the mover's references, proof of insurance, bonding, and so on. The cost of packing, shipping, and insurance is normally borne by the borrower.

When the materials come back, prepare another condition report and compare with the report and photographs from before the show.

Borrowing

If you are the borrower, be prepared to satisfy the owner about details of the planned exhibition. Many institutions draw up a description of the conditions in the gallery that can be sent to the prospective lender whenever a loan is being considered. When you receive borrowed materials, record each item and prepare your own condition report and documenting photographs. Compare it carefully to the condition report that was sent with the piece.

Be especially certain that there are no traces of mold because putting a moldy object in an enclosed case is a sure way to spread the spores to your own materials. (See "Mold" in section 1 for more information on identifying mold.) If you have any doubts about the condition of an item, contact the owner. Never undertake any repair on a borrowed object, no matter how minor, without the owner's *written* permission. Be sure to label and save all packaging, to use when it is time to return the borrowed item. In case of damage in transit, the shipper will need to examine the packing.

Condition Reports

A condition report can be written on a plain piece of paper; it notes key features of an artwork such as its accession or call number, title, author or artist, size, and present condition. Additional information can be added according to the circumstances. This system may be adequate for small institutions that have shows only infrequently. But when a museum or library presents numerous shows, involving a greater number of staff members, it is more convenient to prepare a standard form. This lets any person who is working on the show know what information must be recorded. The information can be entered into the condition report in the computer, but the form can also be printed and filled out by hand if preferred. The sample condition reports on pp. 156 and 157 can be modified to help staff record the information appropriate to each institution.

Sample Condition Report Form for Flat Items

CONDITION REPORT

Photographs, Prints, Drawings, Maps, Documents

INCOMING   (Circle one)   **OUTGOING**

Person Responsible for Report _____   Date of Report _____

Institution/Owner_____

Exhibition Dates _____   Location _____

Accession #_____   Date of Work _____

Artist (or Author) _____

Subject/Title of Work _____

    Type of Work/Medium _____   Size _____

    Markings/Signatures _____

    Inscriptions on Verso _____

    Frame Size and Type _____   Condition _____

    Mat Size _____   Condition _____

Condition   *[Sketch or Photo]*

  ___ Surface Dirt/Dust
  ___ Stains
  ___ Mold
  ___ Foxing
  ___ Fading
  ___ Flaking Surfaces
  ___ Abrasions
  ___ Mat Burn
  ___ Tape (paper, plastic, or cloth)
  ___ Losses (missing pieces)
  ___ Tears/Cracks
  ___ Holes/Punctures
  ___ Brittleness
  ___ Wrinkles, Cockling, Distortion
  ___ Insect Damage

Additional Comments

Signature _____

CONDITION REPORT
Books

INCOMING   (Circle one)   **OUTGOING**

Person Responsible for Report _____   Date of Report _____

Institution/Owner_____

Exhibition Dates _____   Location _____

Call # or ID #_____   Date of Pub., Edition # _____

Author_____

Title _____

Covering Material

Cloth _____   Paper _____   Leather _____   Parchment _____   Plastic _____   Other _____

Size (H x W x Th)_____   Number of Pages _____

Binding Condition

Surface Dirt _____   Stains _____   Mold _____   Tape _____   Tears _____

Joints Damaged or Need Tightening _____   Spine Damage _____   Insect Damage _____   Abrasions _____

Missing Pieces _____   Leather Rot _____

Text Block Condition *(Note page number of damage)*

Brittle Paper _____   Surface Dirt _____   Stains _____   Mold _____   Tape _____

Tears _____   Foxing _____   Missing Areas or Pages _____   Distortion _____

Condition of Endpapers _____   Weak Sewing _____   Endbands _____

Broken or Fragile Inner Hinges _____

Additional Comments   *[Photo]*

Signature _____

MOUNTING AN EXHIBITION

There are two main ways to exhibit library and archival materials: enclosed in a display case or hanging on a wall. Flat paper materials, such as prints, maps, and documents, are generally displayed in some sort of frame or mat, hanging vertically. Books are three-dimensional objects and are best shown in an exhibit case, supported by cradles or other props. Small flat items are often intermixed with books in display cases. And occasionally, a book will be enclosed in a shadow-box frame to create a particular effect.

Exhibit Cases

Books and other objects are placed in cases to protect them from dust and insects, to prevent visitors from handling them, and to guard against theft and vandalism. A good design also provides a favorable environment. Tightly sealed cases help even out daily fluctuations in relative humidity in galleries that do not have optimal HVAC systems. The glazing material can help reduce all light entering the case or just light in the ultraviolet range. But with airtightness come problems as well.

Light, Heat, and Relative Humidity inside Cases

One of the most common problems is heat buildup. There should be no incandescent or other heat-producing bulbs inside a case. Many cases have a compartment at the top, called a light attic, where fixtures are hidden from view. Make sure that there is a way to exhaust the heat from the attic; otherwise, the case itself will get hot. Small cases are often lit from outside, with incandescent or halogen lamps which generate heat. Sunlight from windows and skylights can also significantly raise the temperature in the room and within cases. Observe the extent of the greenhouse effect by placing a pink-to-blue temperature/humidity card, a calibrated thermohygrometer, or a data logger inside each case. (See descriptions below.)

Cover windows and skylights and adjust the size, angle, and distance of lamps. After making these changes, monitor the cases for a few days to make sure that the changes have brought the temperature and, most important, the relative humidity to acceptable ranges.

Remember that when the temperature goes up, the capacity of the enclosed air to hold moisture increases and its relative humidity goes down. This means that moisture will leave the books and be absorbed by the air.

Then, when the lights are turned off, the air in the case will gradually cool. Now the relative humidity will go up. If the RH goes up enough, there may be more water in the air than it can hold at that temperature; the excess will condense, like dew. Drops of moisture may fall from the top of the case onto the exhibits. Even when fluctuations are less dramatic, book covers and pages, photographs, and other materials can become distorted after a short period.

Sealed cases may offer enough buffering of RH variations within a 24-hour period, especially if the show is scheduled to last no more than a month or two. But make sure that there is no heat buildup inside cases from lights in the gallery or from natural light.

OTHER METHODS OF REGULATING RELATIVE HUMIDITY IN EXHIBIT CASES

Silica Gel

Silica gel is a desiccant, commonly found in sachets or little canisters used for keeping shoes, cameras, pills, etc., dry during transit and storage. For stabilizing conditions in sealed display cases, various conservation-grade varieties are available. Silica gel can be purchased as loose granules or beads, but it also comes in premeasured amounts in trays or tiles and in a mat form that can be cut to size. Water vapor is adsorbed into the internal pores of the granules or beads so they remain dry on the outside. In exhibit cases, silica gel can work in two ways: it can bring the RH in a case to a desired level, or it can act as a buffer in situations where the RH changes frequently.

When the relative humidity in the gallery cannot be kept in the safe range, silica gel can be used to modify the RH in the case. Careful conditioning is necessary, and it is best to purchase the gel from a specialized supplier that can supply it already conditioned to provide whatever RH you specify. (See appendix B.) Monitor the RH in the exhibit case; when it starts departing from the specified level, the gel needs to be reconditioned. Follow the directions of the supplier.

If the RH in the gallery is generally acceptable but sometimes spikes or drops sufficiently to cause the RH in the display case to go outside the safe limits for the object on display, silica gel can be used to buffer these changes. It will absorb excess moisture in the air and give it up when the air is dry. Gel used for this purpose can be purchased conditioned to 50% and should not need to be reconditioned during the show.

Silica gel is not a magic cure and requires a good understanding of its capabilities and limitations. It is a good idea to purchase it from a supplier who specializes in environmental controls and who can help you determine what will work best. For detailed information on the use of silica gel, see Appelbaum, *Guide to Environmental Protection of Collections;* and the Canadian Conservation Institute's Technical Bulletin 10, "Silica Gel," by Raymond H. Lafontaine.

MONITORING TEMPERATURE AND RELATIVE HUMIDITY IN EXHIBIT CASES

There is more information on monitoring equipment in "Monitoring Environmental Conditions" in section 1. Suppliers of the equipment are listed in appendix B.

Temperature/Humidity Cards

These cards give approximate but consistent readings, do not need to be calibrated, and are very inexpensive. Cards with both temperature and humidity indicators measure from 80% to 20% RH and have a lavender-colored border. The relative humidity will be in the range of the square that most closely matches the color of the border. Another type of card shows the RH only, from 10% to 100%. It does not have the colored border. They are available from conservation suppliers and also from the manufacturer, Süd-Chemie (formerly Humidial), in quantities of 100 or more. They remain accurate for a long time, but to be on the safe side, replace them once a year or immediately if they become wet.

Hygrometers

Very small instruments of this type are available, e.g., the Arten, which is only 2" (5 cm) long. It has a dial for temperature and one for RH and also a row of squares along the bottom that show RH by color change from pink to blue. Since the color change strip remains accurate indefinitely, a marked difference between the RH dial and the strip means that the instrument needs calibration. A kit is sold for this purpose.

There are various other small humidity meters on the market. All hygrometers tend to overestimate humidity over time, sometimes by more than 10%. When selecting one, ascertain whether and how it can be recalibrated. (Thermometers do not need to be recalibrated.)

Data Loggers

Another way of monitoring conditions in an exhibit case or frame is to place a data logger inside. Several models are made, some quite small, and their price continues to drop as time goes by. Some data loggers can be read from a remote location. This is a very useful feature when the exhibition is in a different building from where staff members normally work. One or more loggers can be placed in selected cases and checked frequently during the workday. An unsatisfactory reading would alert the staff to go to the gallery and investigate further. Some loggers can set off an alarm at a central station or other designated location. Many institutions place a data logger in frames when lending materials, and they sometimes enclose them in packing crates to monitor conditions during transit.

Safe Designs and Materials for Exhibit Cases

When designing a case with it own lighting system, make sure that it will be possible to change light bulbs or make other adjustments without having to remove all the exhibits from a case. The same applies to cases that have compartments for silica gel. If the budget will not allow the installation of fiber-optic lighting at the time that the cases are built, leave space to put it in later. (If working with an existing case that does not provide separate access to the fixtures, have a curator or conservator oversee any maintenance and move exhibits as necessary for safety.)

Many materials used in the construction of exhibit cases and mounts give off volatile organic compounds for varying lengths of time. These gases can cause damage to the materials on exhibit. Since a well-sealed case permits very little air exchange, it is important to keep the atmosphere inside as pure as possible.

Wood and wood products, adhesives, paints, varnishes, and gasketing are commonly used in the construction of display cases because they are easy to obtain and work with. Fabrics are often used to line cases and cover supports. All of these materials give off gases, especially when they are new.

MATERIALS TO AVOID FOR CASE INTERIORS

Some woods never stop off-gassing; these include oak, a traditional and attractive construction material. All plywoods and composition boards should be avoided because the adhesives and other additives in them may be harmful. Manufacturers may change the composition of these boards, so that a product that was safe last year may cause damage when it is reformulated. Try to avoid having any exposed wood on the inside of the case.

Oil-based or alkyd resin paints are unsuitable for case interiors, as are contact cements and rubber cement. Plastics that should be avoided include polyurethane foams and polyvinyl chloride (PVC). Rubber-based adhesives or gaskets can give off sulfur as they degrade and cause damage. All these materials continue to give off gases indefinitely.

BETTER CHOICES IN CONSTRUCTION MATERIALS

Acrylic glazing (Plexiglas) and glass are very safe choices, and they can make up a very large part of the case. Select glass shelves whenever possible; they don't need to be lined.

Anodized aluminum, stainless steel, and powder-coated metals are good, as are high-pressure plastic laminates (e.g., Formica).

Acrylic, Teflon, and silicone adhesives and caulks are suitable, as are hot-melt adhesives. Acrylic or latex paints and water-based polyurethane finishes can also be used. Any material that has to dry gives off gases until it has cured. Therefore, be sure to allow at least four weeks before the exhibits need to be mounted.

CASE LININGS

Linings are used as part of the overall design, to cover unattractive parts of cases, and to serve as barriers. Light-weight exhibits can be attached to linings in various ways. All materials used should be acid-free or inert in order to maintain good air quality in an enclosed space.

Remember that light-colored case linings reflect light. This helps illuminate the exhibits with less added light. Conversely, dark linings absorb light and may make exhibits harder to see.

Fabrics

The best choices for lining cases and covering mounts are undyed, unbleached cotton, linen, or polyester fabrics. Cotton-polyester fabrics can also be used. They should be washed in hot water without detergent to remove any surface coatings. Avoid wool, silk and any fabric that has a discernible smell after washing it in hot water.

Paper Products

Acid-free paper is perfectly safe for library and archival materials on exhibit. Many types are available in roll form, which is economical and permits installation with fewer seams. It is often used to cover the floors of cases or to wrap mounts and supports.

Barrier Products

When a less than ideal case must be used, stable barriers can be used to minimize off-gassing into the case and avoid direct contact with the exhibits. All the unsuitable interior parts of the case must be covered. Good barrier materials include polyester film (e.g., Mylar or Mellinex), four- or eight-ply acid-free mat board ("museum board"), and polyethylene foam sheeting (Ethafoam, Volara). All can be attached to vertical surfaces with double-coated tape such as 3-M no. 415.

Aluminum laminate vapor-barrier sheeting (e.g., Marvelseal) is a useful material that is impermeable to gases and moisture and can be bent or wrapped as needed. It has a heat-sensitive adhesive on the back and can be ironed onto many woods. It can also be attached using double-coated tape.

Suitable fabric or paper can be used to cover the barriers and integrate them into the overall design of the show. This is especially important if polyester film is used as a barrier because it can cause numerous reflections and make it more difficult to modulate the light. When there are vertical panels, such as on the back of a case, a neater effect can be achieved by wrapping the decorative paper or fabric around the edges of the barrier sheet and taping it down to the back of the barrier. Then the whole panel can be attached to the side or back of the case.

Scavenger products that react with pollution in air-tight cases and neutralize it are a fairly new development in barrier materials. Activated carbon and zeolites are among the active ingredients. In general, it is better to rely on good air quality in the gallery and to use safe materials in the cases and frames.

Exhibiting Other Objects Together with Library or Archival Materials

Occasionally objects made of materials that are likely to give off harmful gases, such as rubber, are included in a show. If possible, do not put them in the same cases as paper-based materials, especially original photographs. When they must be together, perhaps the questionable object can be in a small acrylic case within the larger case.

EXHIBITING FLAT PAPER ITEMS

Use Facsimiles Whenever Possible

It is often not necessary, or possible, to exhibit original prints, documents, and photographs. Good-quality copies can be made of deteriorating photographs or documents with fading ink. Sometimes the copies are easier to read than the originals. Photographs and documents frequently have inscriptions or other information on the back. Showing facsimiles makes it possible to show the back of a piece, side by side with the front. This is also a good way of including an image that belongs to another institution without having to borrow the original. And it is a very safe way to keep an image on exhibit for a long time in less than ideal conditions. The brief exposure to light during the copying process is far less damaging to the original than being on exhibit for several weeks or months. After the show, if there is a plan to use the facsimiles again soon, store them separately from the originals. But it is probably best to discard them if there is no immediate likelihood that they will be needed again. The longevity of color photocopies and inkjet prints is not proven, and the facsimiles can easily become a preservation problem.

Color Photocopying

The simplest way to make a facsimile is by color photocopying. A color copier gives more detail than a black and white machine because it scans the original four times. At present, full-size copies up to 11" × 17" can be made at most copy and office supply stores. Larger originals can be scanned and printed at professional studios (see below).

Digital Copying

Copies of almost any size can be made from digitally scanned originals. The images can be printed on regular paper or on a variety of photographic papers. Damaged originals can be manipulated in the computer; however, the skill of the technician makes a very big difference in the quality of the print. Professional equipment is expensive and needs to be updated or replaced frequently, so it is not usually practical to set up an in-house digitizing studio. This is a very fast-changing field and there are new developments every few months.

Photographic Copying

Excellent-quality facsimiles can be produced at a professional photo studio by photographing the original to produce a copy negative. The negative can be in a larger format than the normal 35-mm one, according to the size of the original, for greater detail. A print can be made on various photographic papers, full-size, larger, or smaller, as needed. This method is much more costly than color copying but it produces the best quality, and it also provides the institution with a copy negative for future use.

Copying Photographs

Extremely faithful copies can be made of fading or unstable photographs. A professional photographer can make a copy negative and photographic prints. The original photograph can also be scanned and printed on photographic paper by a professional studio. And lay people with a scanner, inkjet printer, and some skill with the right software can print very fine pictures on special paper made by each printer manufacturer. The technology of digital photography is advancing practically by the hour.

Copying Parchment Documents

Archives and historical societies often have parchment documents. (Parchment is also called vellum; see the glossary for more information.) Because this animal skin product is so likely to cockle and shrink from changes in humidity, it is a real challenge to exhibit deeds, diplomas, proclamations, and so on that are printed or written on parchment. This is most dramatic during the winter when heating makes indoor conditions very dry and parchment shrinks, distorts, and hardens. Gold and paint on manuscript illustrations is likely to flake and lift off. Parchment needs relative humidity in the 50–60% range around the clock. And framing parchment documents correctly is not easy. Add to this the fact that the inks are frequently light-sensitive or actually fading, and the benefits of making a facsimile are plain.

Call photo studios in your area and discuss the project. Not all will be interested in this type of work. To keep the parchment flat while in transit, place it in a rigid folder, put it in a plastic bag, and tape the bag shut. (If the document is cockled, it should first be flattened by a conservator. Do not attempt to do this in-house. *Never* put parchment into a dry mount press.) At the photo studio, explain the need to keep the document restrained and in its plastic bag until the moment the photographer is ready. (This will also reduce its exposure to light.) It is always easier to work with parchment during the warmer months when the heat is not on. The studio will probably take several shots and make proof sheets. The cost of the prints will depend on their size. If there is a small inscription on the back of a large document, the photographer can shoot just that area. When you go to look at the proofs, take the parchment back and return it to its storage place.

The surface of parchment is quite hard and sometimes a little shiny. A skillful photographer can produce a very satisfactory full-size (or other specified size) color facsimile, which can be exhibited as long as desired. The facsimile can be dry-mounted on foam or mat board, framed, or treated in other ways to coordinate with the rest of the exhibits. The copy negative and proof sheets should be stored in photograph storage sleeves or envelopes separately from the original. They can be used in the future for publications or to make other prints.

Compromise and accommodation are always necessary in the real world. If your administration or board really wants to show a very light-sensitive original, perhaps it can be exhibited during the opening or other important function. Make sure the light that falls on the object is under 15 foot-candles (use the light meter), and mat or support the object appropriately. For extra protection, a sheet of UV-filtering polyester film can be laid over a print or photograph if it is flat on a shelf, or placed behind a window mat if the print is displayed vertically. Acrylic glazing keeps UV light from reaching framed items. Keep the case or frame covered until just before the function. Afterward, substitute a high-quality facsimile for the duration of the exhibition.

Rotating Exhibits

If a print that is selected for exhibition is one of several similar pieces in a suite, it may be possible to exhibit each print in the suite for a portion of the show. This strategy will lessen each print's exposure to light.

Relaxing Rolled Materials

When planning an exhibition, note if the exhibits include materials that have been tightly rolled for a long period. In "Maps, Posters, Architectural Photoreproductions" in section 3, we give directions for gradually unrolling maps and architectural drawings so that they can be stored flat in folders. Keep in mind that it may take a while to relax and flatten rolled items, especially in winter. It may be

impossible to keep them flat unless they are restrained by mounting and matting. Adequate relative humidity in the case or frame is essential. It might be a good idea to enlist a conservator's help when preparing large pieces.

Handling Large Materials

In order to get large materials ready for exhibition, it is necessary to have several large, sturdy surfaces available for the whole of the preparation period so that materials in process can be left undisturbed. Folding conference tables can be brought in to add working space. Cover them with acid-free kraft paper, polyester film, or some other barrier material if the tops are rough or if the tables need protection.

When moving a large piece of paper, such as a print, pick it up by two opposite corners (fig. 6-4). Allow the print to sag down in the middle as you move it. Put it down gently, letting the middle rest on the work surface, and let the corners drop down. This method helps avoid denting or creasing the paper.

Fig. 6-4

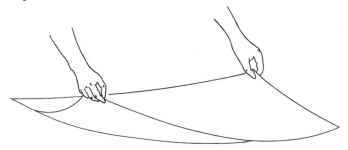

If a piece is too large or too fragile to be picked up this way, carefully slide a rigid support, such as mat board, Plexiglas, or acid-free cardboard under the piece. Two people can then move the item on its "tray." Don't attempt to move several large objects at once, such as stacks of maps or bundles of rolled drawings.

Be especially careful when moving old mounted photographs or prints, no matter what size. Mounts were often made from poor-quality materials. Although the print itself might be in good condition, the mount may have deteriorated and become brittle. If you pick up mounted art by one corner, a piece of the mount may break off and part of the photograph or print may come off with the corner. This is especially likely in the case of larger pieces, but to be safe, always use a rigid support to move mounted items, even if they don't look really fragile.

Folded Documents

Folded letters, telegrams, and other documents may be opened and relaxed in a humidity chamber as described in "Relaxing and Flattening Paper" in section 4, p. 85.

They may be matted, and framed if desired, but they can also be simply arranged on shelves or stands inside display cases. (The shelves or stands should be covered with safe linings, as described above.) A piece of acid-free paper or museum board under the document can help tie it into the design color scheme. If additional protection is needed, a piece of UV-filtering film can be placed over the document.

MOUNTING, HINGING, MATTING, FRAMING

Prints, documents, photographs, and other original works on paper are generally mounted on a support (back board) and window-matted, using acid-free materials. Then the matted object is put into a frame with appropriate glazing. If the item is going to be inside a case, e.g., hanging on the back wall of the case, it need not be framed. Framers often refer to the object being matted and framed as "the art." In this context, "art" means the whole piece of paper, not just the image area. For the sake of simplicity, we will use that term in the instructions that follow, with the understanding that it includes documents, photographs, maps, and other flat, paper-based materials.

Matting and Mounting Photographs

There are many types of photographs, and some types are more likely to react chemically with mounting materials than others. Learning to identify different photographic processes takes much time and practice, and the practical approach is to treat all paper-based photographs in the same way. Select a board that passes the PAT test. (See "PAT Test" in section 3, p. 59.) If the supplier's catalog does not state this, it may still be a safe board. Ask the supplier for specifications. Contact the customer service department of the board's manufacturer if the supplier cannot answer your questions.

Window Mats

A window mat consists of two parts, both cut from acid-free board: a backboard and a window. Four-ply board (made from four layers laminated together) is normally used; larger objects may require double or triple mats or thicker board, such as eight-ply. The backboard need not match the window; a less expensive board can be used as

long as it is of archival quality. They should be the same size and they should fit in the frame snugly. Cut both the backboard and the mat blank (window board) to size at the same time. If you have a mat cutter, the cutting head can be set to cut at 90°, and the boards for all the art can be cut at one time.

Many institutions use modular or other reusable frames in a few standard sizes (for instance, 14" × 18", 20" × 24", 22" × 28", 28" × 40") rather than having frames made to the size of each object. The borders of window mats have to be calculated so they cover the edges of the art and extend to the edges of the frame. This is different from the way matting is done at a framing studio, where the size of the mat and frame are usually determined by the shape and size of each piece.

To produce window mats with beveled edges, most people will have better results using a mat cutter with the cutting mechanism on a track. There are many models, starting at about $100. Handheld cutters require a great deal of skill and often result in a lot of wasted board. If a mat cutter is not available, the windows can be cut using a sharp mat (utility) knife and a heavy straightedge. Make the cut at 90°. A clean square cut is better than a sloppy 45° bevel. (You will also need a large self-healing cutting mat.) With practice, four-ply boards can be cut neatly by hand or with a mat cutter.

Thicker boards, double and triple mats, mats with multiple openings, and other configurations are generally too hard to cut in-house. Take several sheets of the mat board you are using to a framer and have those mats cut professionally. If your institution does not have a good mat cutter, you may wish to get a price for having all the mats cut; a framer can often do this for a small charge above the price of the board. Archival board is widely available; if in doubt, ask for a scrap and test the front, back, and *edge* with a pH pen.

Some conservation suppliers offer a mat-cutting service. This is another very good option if a mat cutter is not available. The catalogs give measuring and ordering information.

Mat board is made of layers; the grain of the layers alternates and the boards do not have very pronounced grain, but there is usually some difference in the two directions. When mounting and matting large items, try to determine the grain and have the longer side of the mat go with the grain. This will reduce the chance that the mat will cockle during the course of the exhibition. Some mat boards have a top (or front) layer of paper. The surface of this kind of board may look different depending on how it is held. Solid-core "museum"-type boards usually look much the same no matter how they are oriented.

Examine the art to be matted and determine how large the opening (the "window") should be. If a print has a large white border, leave as much of it exposed as seems balanced. A tiny print can be matted very close to the image; a big print might look better with a half inch to an inch or more of border showing. The window can be centered on the board or the mat can be "weighted," that is, the bottom border can be somewhat wider than the other three. Some artworks look better centered; others are more balanced to the eye if the mat is weighted. This is a matter of taste. There is no formula for how much wider the bottom border should be; it depends on the size and shape of the art and the mat.

Marking the Mat Blank

It is easier to cut mats from the *back* whether using a mat cutter or by hand with a utility knife. All the marks are made in pencil on the back of the mat blank. Never use pens to mark the back of window mats. The marks should be erased after cutting to avoid transferring pencil marks to the art.

Find the midpoint of the top edge of the board by measuring it with a strip of paper. Fold the paper in half and make a dot on the back of the board, as shown in figure 6-5. Mark both the top and bottom. Mark the midpoints of the sides in the the same way (fig. 6-8).

MEASURING TO DETERMINE THE WINDOW OPENING

One way to determine the size of the window is to cover the borders of the art with long pieces of mat board (figs. 6-6 and 6-7).

Fig. 6-5

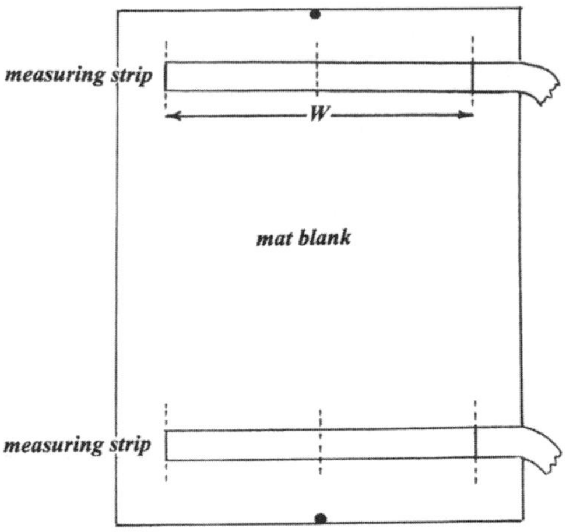

measuring strip

W

mat blank

measuring strip

Fig. 6-6

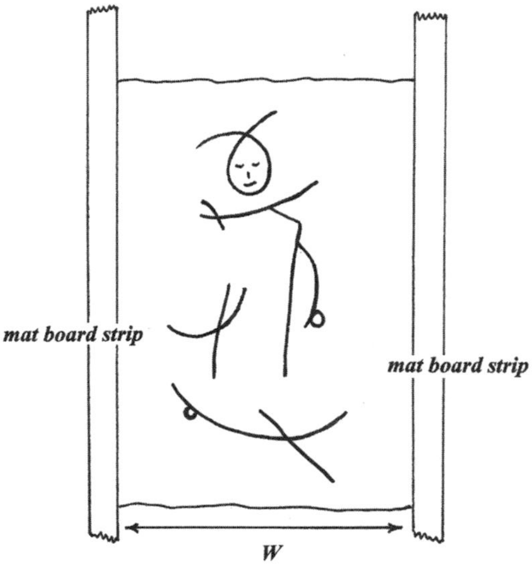

mat board strip

mat board strip

W

Fig. 6-7

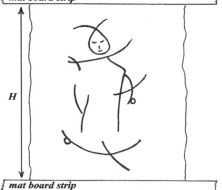

mat board strip

H

mat board strip

To find the width (W) of the opening, position the pieces of mat board on the edges of the art (fig. 6-6) and move them until you get the desired effect. (Make sure they are parallel.)

Place a weight on each piece of mat board and measure the space between them with a strip of paper. This is the width (W) of the opening. Fold the strip in half to find the midpoint.

Place the strip near the top edge of the mat blank, aligning its midpoint with the dot on the back of the board. Mark the width of the window on each side of the mat blank, both at the top and the bottom (fig. 6-5).

Determine the height (H) of the opening by placing the mat board strips at the top and bottom of the art (fig. 6-7). Measure with a strip of paper and transfer the (H) to the mat blank (fig. 6-8).

Fig. 6-8

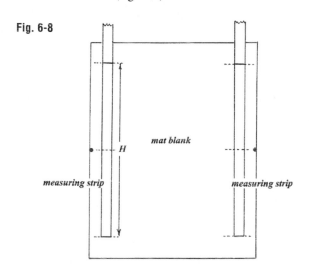

If the bottom of the window mat is going to be weighted, raise the midpoint mark a half inch or more, according to what seems pleasing. Mark both sides of the mat blank in the same way.

Draw lines connecting the marks, as shown in figure 6-9.

Fig. 6-9

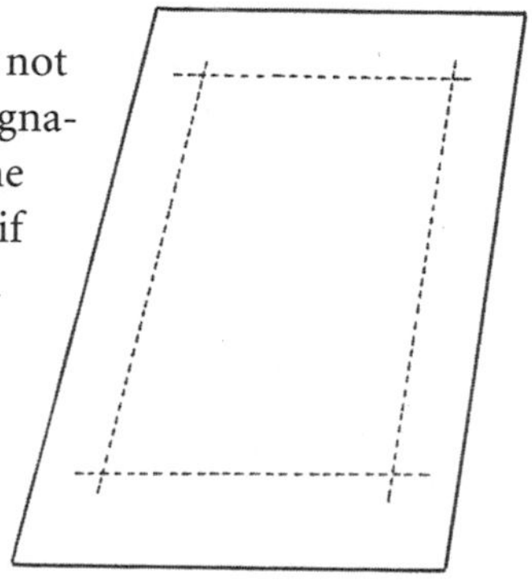

Normally, the mat should not cover any part of the image, signature, plate marks, seals, etc. The mat can be used to hide flaws if necessary, such as mat burn (a discoloration caused by acid migration from previous framing materials), and it needs to cover enough of the art to hold it down firmly.

Cutting the Window with a Mat or Utility Knife

If cutting mats with a mat knife, follow the directions for marking the back of the board. Put the mat blank on a cutting surface. Place a heavy metal straightedge on the line to be cut. For good control (and to avoid injury), hold the straightedge *very* firmly or, preferably, clamp it to the edge of the counter. Cut with a heavy utility knife with a fresh blade, at a 90° angle. Make the cuts intersect about ⅛" (3 mm) so the corners will be neat. Turn the mat right side up and use a bone folder to smooth the edge as necessary.

Cutting Mats with Beveled Edges, Using a Mat Cutter

Place a long piece of waste mat board on the bed of the mat cutter, for the blade to cut into, and shift it as it gets worn so there is always a fresh surface. This preserves the point of the blade. Once the point is dull or damaged, the neatness of the cuts will deteriorate rapidly. Always use blades made for your brand of cutter and keep a good supply on hand. Change blades as needed; the cuts will be neater and less effort will be needed to make them. Figure 6-10 shows a basic mat cutter. The operator would stand at top right in this illustration.

Logan Graphic Products, Inc.

Fig. 6-10

Practice cutting scraps until you become familiar with the cutter and the process. The cutting is done on the pull stroke, that is, from top to bottom as you stand in front of the cutter. Since the blade is at a 45° angle with the point aimed to the left, most of the mat should be to the *right* of the cutting head so that the bevel goes in the correct direction. (Trial and error will make this clear.) Mark the scraps with intersecting lines to simulate a real mat and practice beginning and ending ³⁄₁₆" (4–5 mm) beyond the intersections, as described below, in *one* motion. Stopping the cut midway usually results in a kink. Make sure the blade is cutting all the way through the board and into the waste piece below. Control will come with practice.

Place a mat blank in the cutter following the directions for your cutter. Move the cutting head along the track to the top of the mat. Press the point of the blade all the way through the board, about ³⁄₁₆" (4–5 mm) above an intersection, and right on a line. Pull the cutting head toward you in one motion, ending about 3/16" below the intersection of the lines at the bottom. Continue with the other cuts in the same way. The cuts must intersect at the corners so the bevels are cut all the way through and the middle falls out cleanly after the fourth cut.

Hinge the window mat to the backboard with pregummed cloth tape (fig. 6-11). One-inch tape is adequate for most mats. While the adhesive is still moist, close the mat and make sure the two boards are well aligned. Place a piece of polyester web in the fold and allow the mat to dry under a weight. A number of mats can be stacked to dry.

Fig. 6-11

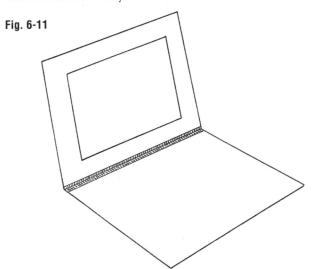

Pregummed tape is preferable to pressure-sensitive tape, which in time can ooze adhesive from the edges. The water-activated tape also permits easier alignment of the two boards.

Mounting Artwork or Documents

Art should be attached to the backboard, *not* to the back of the window mat. This reduces the danger of tearing the art if it clings to the backboard when the window is opened (fig. 6-12).

Fig. 6-12

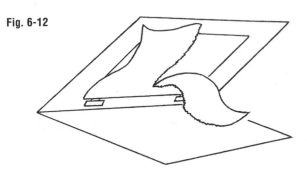

The method selected should give good support to the art, cause no chemical or mechanical damage, and be easily reversible with no trace left on the artwork. There are two techniques that meet these demands. One is hinging, which involves using a small amount of adhesive and Japanese paper. The other is using perimeter mounts or corners. At the present moment, there are no commercially available pressure-sensitive tapes that meet all the requirements for mounting items of permanent value.

Japanese Paper Hinges

There are many different ways to make hinges; we will illustrate one, the T-hinge, which is suitable for a large number of situations. For variations, see Phibbs and Volent, "Preservation Hinging"; Smith, *Matting and Hinging of Works of Art on Paper;* and NEDCC Technical Leaflets 37, "Matting and Framing for Art and Artifacts on Paper," and 50, "How to Do Your Own Matting and Hinging," both by Mary Todd Glaser.

The supplies needed are described in section 4. Instructions for tearing Japanese paper will be found there as well.

You will need the following:

Cooked paste. Methylcellulose can also be used, especially for smaller works. The adhesive should be smooth and fairly thick in consistency, just thin enough to spread easily with a brush.

Paste brush, ½ inch or 1 inch, according to preference

A piece of blotter or absorbent paper to paste the hinges on

Blotter and polyester web squares, about 3" × 3" (7 × 7 mm)

Bone folder

One- to two-pound weights

For convenience, place a large blotter covered with polyester web on the work surface, especially if putting hinges on a number of objects.

Select a Japanese paper. The hinge paper should be lighter in weight than the document or artwork. Each hinge is composed of two parts. A minimum of two hinges is needed; larger, heavier works require a hinge every 10"–15" (25–38 cm). Tear one rectangular piece for each hinge, about 1" × 1½" (2.5 × 4 cm). The second part of the hinge can be cut instead of torn to save time, since it will not come in contact with the work.

ATTACHING THE HINGES
TO THE ARTWORK OR DOCUMENT

Turn the art image side down. Determine where the hinges will be attached. They should be a little in from the corners, one to two inches, depending on the size of the art. Two hinges are enough for a piece up to about 12"–15" (30–38 cm) wide. A print up to 24" (60 cm) wide can have three hinges. If you are not working on a blotter/polyester web surface, place a blotter square covered by a web square under each spot.

Put the hinge on the pasting blotter or paper and apply a thin layer of paste to the end of the hinge. Paste about ¼"–½" (7–14 mm), according to the size of the work. Allow some of the moisture to be absorbed, then put the hinge on as shown in figure 6-13. Cover it with a blotter square and smooth gently with a bone folder. Take the damp blotter off, and cover with a polyester web square and a dry blotter square. Put a weight on top and leave for at least a half hour. Repeat the process for each hinge.

Fig. 6-13

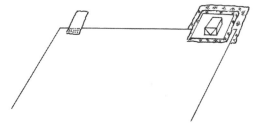

Be careful not to apply too much paste to the hinge. Excess moisture may cause water stains or wrinkles in the art. If in doubt, take the blotters off after a couple of minutes, check that all is well, and replace with dry blotters. Repeat ten minutes later.

ATTACHING THE ARTWORK
OR DOCUMENT TO THE BACKBOARD

Open the hinged mat package and place the artwork so it shows through the window, adjusting it till it is just right. Put a small blotter on the artwork and a weight on the blotter. Carefully open the window mat and make sure that the hinges on the artwork are straight and smooth.

Apply paste to the second piece of Japanese paper, over the entire surface. Place it across the part of the hinge that extends from the artwork, attaching it to the backboard (fig 6-14). The crosspiece should be at least ¼" (6–7 mm) from the art so that the art can be lifted on its hinges easily. Put web and blotter over the hinge and place a weight on top. Repeat with the other hinges. Let dry for at least an hour.

Fig. 6-14

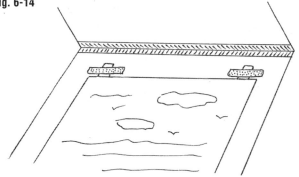

Since the crosspiece of the hinge is well removed from the art, you may use a good-quality pressure-sensitive tape for this step, such as Filmoplast P90, or gummed cloth tape.

Other Mounting Methods

It is also possible to mount objects on the backboard without attaching hinges to the artwork, which is often desirable in the case of valuable or fragile works.

PERIMETER MOUNTS

These mounts support the object on all four sides and are ideal for irregularly shaped pieces. They are made from four strips of acid-free paper, about 1½" (4 cm) wide, two for the sides and one each for the top and bottom of the artwork. They are all cut long grain and an inch or two longer than each dimension. The strips are folded lengthwise, with the fold line not in the middle but about a third of the way to one side.

Fit the top and bottom strips on the object as shown in figure 6-15. The narrower flap goes in front.

Fig. 6-15

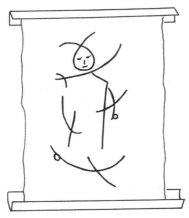

Place the folded side strips over the top and bottom strips, at the edge of the print, and make pencil marks on the folded areas of the vertical strips where they cross over the horizontal strips. See arrows in figure 6-16.

Fig. 6-16

Open the vertical strips, place them on a cutting mat, and slit the folds at the marks with a scalpel or utility knife (fig. 6-17).

Fig. 6-17

Insert the ends of the horizontal strips into the slits of the vertical strips (fig. 6-18).

Fig. 6-18

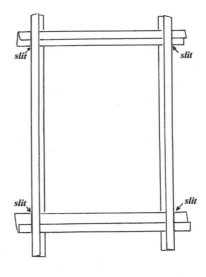

Snug the supports around the art (fig. 6-19).

Fig. 6-19

To attach the perimeter mounts to the backboard, open the hinged mat package and place the artwork so it shows through the window, adjusting it as necessary. Put a small blotter on the artwork and a weight on the blotter.

Carefully open the window mat and make sure that the mount is still snug around the artwork. Use a good-quality tape, such as Filmoplast P90 or gummed cloth tape, to attach the crossed ends of the mount to the backboard (fig. 6-20).

Fig. 6-20

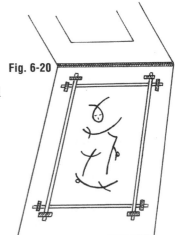

MOUNTING STRIPS

These clear supports consist of a piece of one-ply mat board (a little thicker than an index card) with a larger piece of 7-mil Mylar attached to it. A strip of double-coated tape on the back is used to attach the mount to the backboard (fig. 6-21). The strips are available from conservation suppliers.

They come in 4" (10 cm) and 12" (30 cm) lengths and can be used in many situations where a perimeter support is indicated.

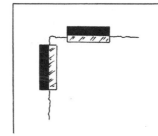

Fig. 6-21

CORNERS

Paper or polyester film corners can be purchased from most conservation suppliers. They are suitable for many small items that are both sturdy and flexible. The borders of the window mat should be wide enough to cover them. Don't use corners on brittle items, or on any object that doesn't flex well. Corners are not a good choice for valuable materials because of the danger of damage to the corners of the object.

Attaching Photographs to a Mount

Depending on the size, thickness, and condition of the photograph, use perimeter mounts, corners, or commercial mounting strips or plastic channel mounts to provide good support and avoid risk of distortion. Don't attempt to remove photographs from mounts; they are part of the artifact. Instead, accommodate the thickness of the cardboard by using perimeter mounts or commercially available mounting strips or channel mounts.

Thin photographs that do not stay flat should be prepared by a conservator. Do *not* dry mount original photographs in-house.

Always use a mat that is deep enough to keep the emulsion well away from the glazing of the frame. A double or triple mat might be needed, or a sink mat. For information on making sink mats, see NEDCC Technical Leaflets 37, "Matting and Framing for Art and Artifacts on Paper," and 50, "How to Do Your Own Matting and Hinging," both by Mary Todd Glaser; Phibbs, "Preservation Matting for Works of Art on Paper"; and Smith, *Matting and Hinging of Works of Art on Paper.*

Framing

After the art is in the mat, it can be put into a variety of frames. Modular metal frames can be reused many times. Other types of frames have a removable side to use for loading the mat package and glazing. Make certain that the type selected is sturdy and that the wire or other hanging system is securely attached. Very inexpensive wood frames sometimes fall off the wall when the eyehooks come out of soft, cheap wood.

Frames usually come with a backing board, which goes behind the mat package and makes it fit snugly in the frame. Check the pH of the board to make sure it is acid-free. If not, replace with acid-free mat board, corrugated board, or archival foam board. All are available cut to standard sizes from conservation suppliers. More than one board, or boards of different thicknesses, may be needed, according to the depth of the frame. The glazing and mat package should not be able to shift once in the frame.

To prevent damage to the frame and glazing, always work on a clean, padded surface.

Glazing

Acrylic glazing is generally preferable for exhibitions. Acrylic glazing (e.g., Plexiglas) is lighter than glass, shatterproof, and it reduces ultraviolet light transmission. It is more likely to scratch, so careful handling is needed. After a few shows, some panes may have to be replaced.

Acrylic can develop and hold a static charge, especially when the relative humidity is low. This poses a problem for works with loose media such as pastel or charcoal, or flaking paint, because the static can pull some of the color off the paper. Glass is a safer solution for such works.

UV-filtering coatings are available for both glass and acrylic. The coatings sometimes have a slight tint. Check with conservation suppliers and acrylic distributors for various options. This might be a good solution for works with very light-sensitive media.

For situations where reflections are a problem, there are various types of nonglare glass. Some also feature UV-filtering. A good framer can show you what is available and supply the glass cut to size.

Framing Alternatives

If the budget does not permit good-quality frames, it is better to use other methods than to buy cheap frames.

The mat package, a thin backing board, and acrylic glazing can be taped together at the edges using ½" polyester slide tape, available from some conservation suppliers. Other narrow, good-quality tapes may also be used.

Small, lightweight items can be held by "L" pins pushed into the wall. (The pins are shaped like the letter "L"; the longer leg goes into the wall and the shorter one holds the art.) They are not suitable for brick or plaster walls. "L" pins are good for attaching small matted pieces to the back walls of cases. The exhibit case lining material should be able to hold the pins securely. The pins are available from most conservation suppliers.

Corner clips of various types can be used to attach the package to the wall. They are sold as a set of four clips to be laced together at the back of the matted art. Follow the lacing pattern shown in figure 6-22, starting at lower left (point 1). Tension the string as you go, making sure it pulls the hooks snugly around the perimeter of the package. Hang the frame on the picture hook at point 5, where there is a double layer of string. This lacing pattern helps keep the string tight. Figure 6-23 shows the front of the picture after the lacing is completed.

For more information on framing and hanging frames, see Phibbs, "The Frame: A Complete Preservation Package"; and Phibbs, "Building a Preservation Frame."

Fig. 6-22

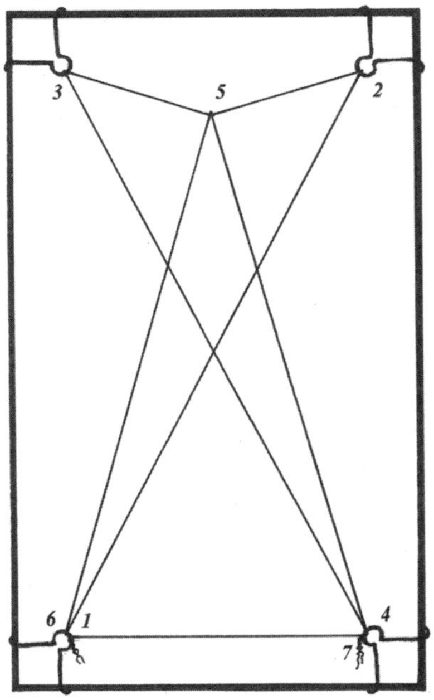

Fig. 6-23

back   *front*

PREPARING BOOKS FOR EXHIBITION

Books are three-dimensional, movable objects. These characteristics make them different from flat paper objects, and they require different preparation. The typical way to exhibit a book is to open it to a chosen page and prop it up in some way to maintain that page in good viewing position for the duration of the show. This is an unnatural thing to do to a book.

To prevent the damage that often results, conservators and curators have developed a variety of cradles and supports. These are derived from museum mount con-

struction and rightly so, because books that are chosen for exhibition usually are important as objects and not just for the information they contain.

The first step is to assess the condition of the book. You may open a scruffy old book with very loose sewing to the desired page and find that page in fine condition to exhibit. The loose or broken sewing may allow it to open perfectly flat with no further damage to the structure. Such a book can often be supported and propped up to make it look presentable during the show. If the covers are a little ragged, a simple book cover can be made following the instructions for the "Tube Book Jacket" in section 3, p. 73. After the show, a box should be made for the book until it can be evaluated for conservation. (Unless making a point, don't exhibit books that are obviously very damaged. Not only are they not attractive, but they also give viewers the impression that the library doesn't care.)

On the other hand, a book with a beautiful, intact binding might be difficult to open more than 45° and will require much more preparation before it can be exhibited without damage. Small leather-bound books with tight spines and short-grain paper are often a problem. (See fig. 5-8.) Very large books are also challenging because of their weight.

It is important to remember that the front cover of a book flexes on its hinge every time the book is opened. This is one of the areas of the binding that is most likely to be weakened from use, and care is often needed to prevent the front cover from coming off during preparation. Make a habit of always cradling the front cover in your hand when opening a book. Never allow the board to flop down or open more than 180°.

Adjustable book cradles are available from companies that specialize in museum mounts and from conservation suppliers. They work very well but are rather expensive for shows in which many books will be exhibited. A variety of wedges and supports can be made in house, with simple tools and materials.

Simplest Supports

A Stack of Paper or Board

Open the book to the page to be exhibited and determine just how much the book can open without stress. Don't force it. If the book opens very well and the page is more or less in the center of the book, it is only necessary to allow space for the spine by raising the two covers a little off the floor of the case. Place a stack of waste mat board or other archival-quality material under each cover. Acid-free copier paper will also work. Adjust the thickness of each support to keep the open book parallel to the floor of the case. The supports can be slightly smaller than the book cover, to show less, and you can cover them with paper or fabric that matches the case linings if desired.

If the selected page is toward the front of the book, e.g., the title page, only the front cover needs support, so that the board opens no more than 180°, i.e., flat.

Cushions

When the covers of a book need to be supported at an angle, an easy way to do this is with padding or rolled fabric.

Polyester batting, available from some conservation suppliers and from sewing stores, is a good material for this purpose. It is inert (does not cause damage) and can be cut to size, folded, and rolled as needed. Simply arrange the batting so it supports the book open at the desired angle (fig. 6-24). Make sure to leave space so there is no pressure on the spine. You can cover the batting with a soft, washed, undyed fabric.

Book Wedges

Foam Wedges

Fig. 6-24

In the 1980s some curators began using wedges made of foam rubber to support books. The wedges were very versatile and easy to use. They provided excellent support to heavy books with irregular surfaces and did not damage fragile bindings. However, problems were noticed with off-gassing and other signs of deterioration, so these early wedges should *not* be used in exhibit cases.

A book-support system consisting of various wedges, pads, and strips made of a stable synthetic foam is available from some conservation suppliers. The components can be arranged to suit books of all sizes and shapes and can be used to prop a book to desired page openings (fig. 6-25).

Fig. 6-25

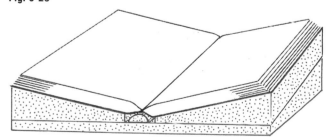

Making Book Wedges

Supports of various shapes can be made from four-ply mat board, from CFC-free polystyrene foam board (e.g., Artcare), from acid-free corrugated board, and from corrugated plastic board (e.g., Coroplast). The supports are made from one long piece of material, cut short grain, and scored, folded, and taped together. (The "grain" of corrugated boards is in the direction of the ribs.) The material must be cut with the long edges perfectly parallel and with square corners. It will be much easier and quicker to do this with a good cutter that has a clamp. A mat cutter set to cut at 90° is adequate.

SCORING THE BOARD FOR FOLDING

Scoring the boards is necessary to make neat folds. Foam board and acid-free corrugated board should be scored with a straightedge and bone folder, on the inside of the fold. Crease the board by holding the straightedge very firmly over the fold line and folding the board back over it, with the help of a bone folder (fig. 6-26). Mat board can be scored and folded this way as well, although the outside of the fold may be a little ragged.

Fig. 6-26

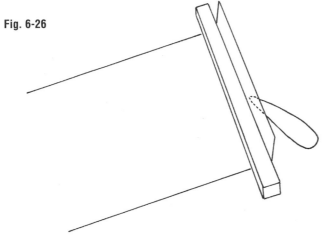

Corrugated plastic board must be scored with a knife in order to make neat folds. The scores are made on the outside of the board and cut just the outer layer of the Coroplast. After scoring, slide the board so the scored line is at the edge of the counter and push down on the board. Mat board can be scored with a knife as well; cut *very* lightly. The folds are neater this way. The instructions that follow are for scoring on the outside of the fold lines with a knife. Marking with an awl makes it easier to see the marks on the reverse. If you prefer to score mat board with a bone folder on the inside, just reverse the directions.

BASIC WEDGE SUPPORT

Measure the height (H) and width (W) of the book (fig. 6-27) and cut a piece of board about ½" (1.3 cm) narrower than the H by about 3 times the W (fig. 6-28).

Fig. 6-27

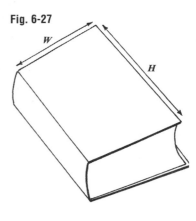

Open the book to determine how much the book can open without straining the binding. If the page to be shown is toward the front of the book, a wedge will be needed under the front cover.

Fig. 6-28

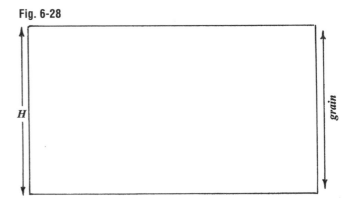

For an opening around the middle of the book, it might be better to use a wedge on each side, to keep the book at a good angle for viewing (fig. 6-29). The two wedges can be different depending on the desired opening of the book. Place the book on the counter and hold it in the desired position. Measure the distance between the top of the counter and the fore edge of the front cover.

Transfer the measurement to the end of the board.

Fig. 6-29 To leave both hands free for measuring, place temporary supports under the book covers

Draw a line in pencil; make sure it is at a true 90° angle with the edge of the board because all the other lines will be measured from there (fig. 6-30). This is panel A; it equals the distance between the fore edge of the book cover and the floor of the case.

Fig. 6-30

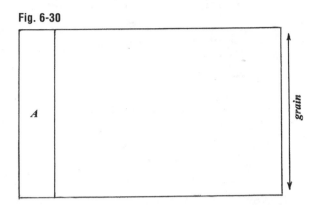

Measure the width (W) of the book board up to the joint. Transfer this measurement to the support, starting from the line at panel A. Draw another line. This is panel B, the longest side of the triangle. The book will rest on panel B.

Score the two lines very lightly with a knife.

Slide the board to the edge of the counter and fold down along the scored lines to make the creases (fig. 6-31).

Fig. 6-31

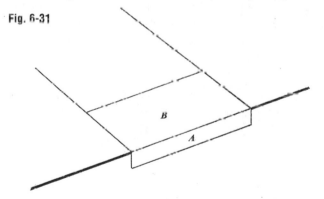

Fold panel A as shown, so that it is at 90° with the rest of the board. Mark the edge of the board where panel A rests on it with an awl (fig. 6-32). Draw a line. Make sure it is parallel to the other two lines. Score and fold. This is panel C, which will rest on the floor of the case.

Fig. 6-32

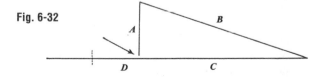

The remaining board must be cut down to create panel D, which should be about ⅛" (3 mm) narrower than panel A (fig. 6-33). Panel D fits inside panel A; the two are held together with double-coated tape (fig. 6-34).

Fig. 6-33

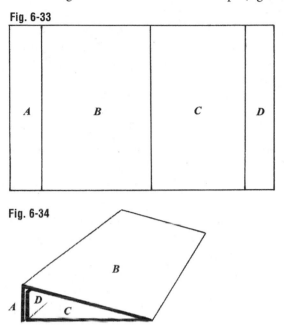

Fig. 6-34

BOX SUPPORT

When showing a page toward the front of a book that opens easily and has strong hinges, the front cover of the book can be opened flat but it must be supported. Raise it from the floor of the case so that the book does not open more than 180°. This can be done by putting a stack of acid-free board or paper under the board, as described earlier, or by making a box-shaped support (fig. 6-35). It is made in the same way as a basic wedge support (see above), with an extra panel added next to the spine of the book.

Fig. 6-35

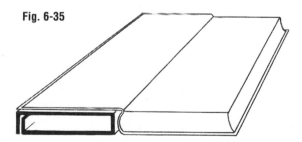

Measure the height (H) and width (W) of the book and cut a piece of board about ½" (1.3 cm) narrower than the H by about 3 times the W.

Measure the thickness (T) of the book (fig. 6-36).

Make marks about ⅛" (3 mm) less than this measurement at one end of the cut board. Draw a line in pencil; make sure it is at a true 90° angle with the edge of the board because all the other lines will be measured from there. This is panel A. (Subtracting ⅛" allows for the thickness of the front cover and should produce a support of the right height.)

Fig. 6-36

Measure the width of the book's front board and subtract ½" (1.3 cm). (This will make the support slightly smaller than the open book's board.) Transfer this measurement to the support, starting from the line at panel A. Draw another line. This is panel B.

An extra panel (X) is added now, to make the support four-sided. Make marks for panel X the same size as panel A and draw a line (fig. 6-37).

Fig. 6-37

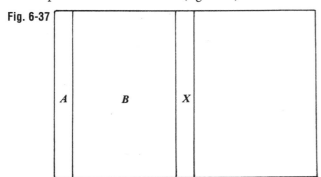

Make marks for panel C the same size as panel B and draw a line. Score the new lines and fold, on the same side of the board as before.

Make marks for panel D, about ⅛" (3 mm) narrower than panels A and X (fig. 6-38). Cut off excess board.

Fig. 6-38

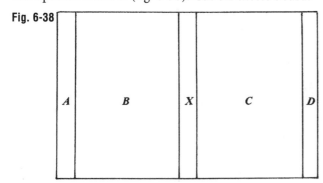

Panel D fits inside panel A; the two are held together with double-coated tape (fig. 6-39).

CROSS BRACING

If the box support sags after it is assembled, insert a cross brace inside to keep it square. The reinforcement is made from two pieces of board.

Fig. 6-39

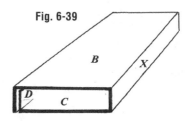

Measure the height inside the support; this will be the width (W) of both pieces. Cut a strip of board this width and long enough to make both pieces, or cut both pieces from separate scraps, from the same measurement.

Measure the width inside the box support; this will be the length of piece 1.

Cut piece 2 about two inches shorter than the length of the support, so the brace will not show (fig. 6-40).

Fig. 6-40

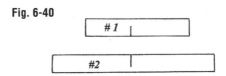

Cut a slit halfway into each of the pieces and slide each segment onto the other (fig. 6-41).

Push the cross brace into the center of the box support.

Fig. 6-41

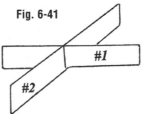

FOUR-SIDED WEDGE

When showing a page toward the front of a book that does not open well, the front board of the book should be supported at an angle *and* raised up from the floor of the case. This will support the book's cover all the way to the joint area and keep the spine from getting crowded or compressed.

A four-sided wedge is useful in these situations. It combines elements of the basic wedge support and the box support (see above). The back cover of the book can rest on another four-sided wedge, on a basic three-sided wedge, or it can lie on the floor of the case, depending on what provides the best support (fig. 6-42).

Fig. 6-42

Open the book to determine how much the book can open. If the page to be shown is toward the front of the book, a wedge will be needed under the front cover. For an opening around the middle of the book, it might be better to make a wedge for each side, to keep the book at a good angle for viewing (fig. 6-43). This also gives better support for the spine.

Fig. 6-43

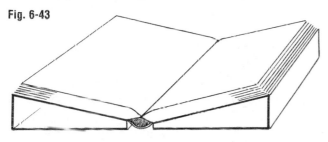

To make a four-sided wedge, measure the height (H) and width (W) of the book and cut a piece of board about ½" (1.3 cm) narrower than the H by about 3½ times the W.

Place the book on the counter and hold it in the desired position. Measure the distance between the top of the counter and the fore edge of the front cover (fig. 6-44). Transfer this measurement to the end of the board. (Repeat for back cover if there are going to be two wedges. The two wedges can be different, to accommodate the position of the book.)

Draw a line in pencil; make sure it is at a true 90° angle with the edge of the board because all the other

Fig. 6-44

lines will be measured from there. This is panel A (fig. 6-45); it equals the distance between the fore edge of the book cover and the floor of the case.

Fig. 6-45

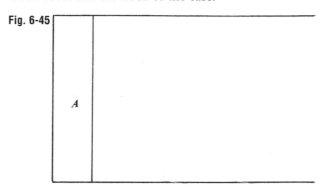

Measure the width (W) of the book board up to the joint. Transfer this measurement to the support, starting from the line at panel A. Draw another line. This is panel B, the widest side of the wedge. The book will rest on panel B.

An extra panel (X) is added here, to make the wedge four-sided.

Open the book and place it on the counter in the position it will be displayed. Measure the distance between the counter and the joint of the book. This is the width of panel X.

Make marks for panel X and draw a line (fig. 6-46).

Fig 6-46

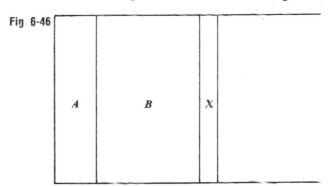

Score the lines very lightly with a knife. Slide the board to the edge of the counter and fold down along the scored lines to make the creases (fig. 6-47).

Fig. 6-47

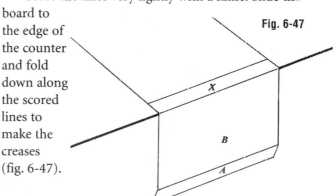

Fold panel A and panel X so they are parallel to each other, then fold the rest of the board under panel B (90° with panels A and X). Mark the board where panel A rests on it. Draw a faint pencil line. Make sure it is parallel to the other lines. Score and fold. This is panel C, which will rest on the floor of the exhibit case.

Cut down the remaining board to create panel D, which should be about ⅛" (3 mm) narrower than panel A. Panel D fits *inside* the wedge; it is attached to panel A with double-coated tape (fig. 6-48).

CROSS BRACING

The four-sided wedge may tend to collapse or sag when a heavy book is placed on it; if so, insert a cross brace inside. The reinforcement is made from two pieces of board and is similar to the one described earlier for the box support.

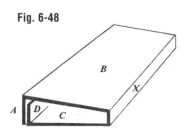

Fig. 6-48

Cut a strip of board for piece 1 (fig. 6-49) about one or two inches shorter than the length of the wedge, so the brace will not show. (The width of piece 1 will be determined later.)

Fig. 6-49

Measure the width inside the wedge (fig. 6-50); cut piece 2 this length (fig. 6-51).

Piece 2 must have the same profile as the wedge. Measure the height inside the narrow side of the wedge (panel X) and mark the board. Repeat at the high side (panels A–D). Cut piece 2.

Fig. 6-50

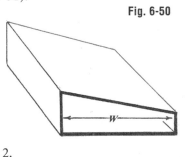

Cut a slit halfway through piece 2 (fig. 6-51).

Cut piece 1 so it is the same width as piece 2 at the slit. (Piece 1 is a rectangle; piece 2 is wider at one end.) Cut a slit halfway through piece 1.

Fig. 6-51

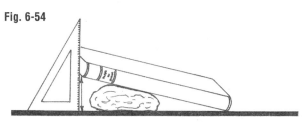

Slide each segment onto the other (fig. 6-52).

Push the cross brace into the center of the box support.

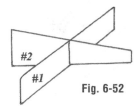

Fig. 6-52

LECTERN-STYLE SUPPORT

To display the cover of a closed book, it is often desirable to tilt the top of the book up a little. A basic wedge support (p. 172) can be used to support the book. The support works best if it is not very steep; otherwise the book may slide down and may even distort. The heavier the book, the lower the angle should be. An angle of 25° is generally considered the maximum (fig. 6-53).

Fig. 6-53

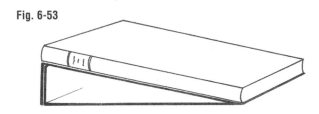

Measure the height (H) and width (W) of the book. Cut a piece of board about an inch narrower than the W of the book and about 2½ to 3 times the H.

Place the book on the counter and support it in the desired position. Measure the distance between the back cover of the book, at the top, and the top of the counter (fig. 6-54). This is the width of panel A. Mark panel A on the board, making sure that the line is at 90° with the edge.

Fig. 6-54

To mark panel B, use the H of the book minus one inch. This will make the support a little smaller than the book, so it doesn't show. Transfer the measurement to the board, and draw a line. Panel B is the longest side of the triangle. The book will rest on panel B.

Score the two lines very lightly with a knife, slide the board to the edge of the counter, and fold along the scored lines to make the first two creases. Rub down the fold between panel B and the rest of the board, so it stays creased at a sharp angle.

Fold panel A as shown, at 90° with the board on the work surface. Mark the board where panel A rests on it and draw a faint pencil line. Make sure it is parallel to the other two lines. Score and fold. This is panel C, which will rest on the floor of the case (fig. 6-55).

Fig. 6-55

Cut down the remaining board to create panel D, which should be about ⅛" (3 mm) narrower than panel A (fig. 6-56). Panel D fits *inside* the wedge and is attached to panel A with double-coated tape.

Fig. 6-56

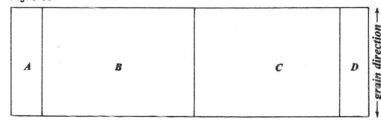

If the lectern support sags, insert a brace in it. Make it in the same way as the brace for the four-sided wedge (see above). Piece 2 does not need to come all the way to the narrow end of the lectern. A heavy book might require a brace with two or more sets of each piece.

STOP FOR LECTERN

If the angle of the lectern is low enough, a book in good condition should not slide down. But in case it does, make a stop for it.

Cut several pieces of scrap board, about an inch wide and slightly shorter than the width of the book. Stick them together with double-coated tape (or use PVA-methylcellulose mix and place the stop under a weight until dry). Make the stack high enough to keep the bottom board of the book cover in place. Cover the stack neatly with fabric or paper used to line the case, if desired.

Place the book on the lectern where it will be located in the case. Position the stop so it keeps the book in place. Attach the stop to the bottom of the exhibition case using double-coated tape. If tape won't stick to the case lining, small pins or brads can be pushed into the bottom of the

case to hold the stop in place (fig. 6-57). It might be helpful to stick the bottom of the lectern to the bottom of the case in some situations.

Fig. 6-57

A segment of acrylic rod cut slightly shorter than the width of the book can be used in the same way. It is available from stores that sell acrylic sheeting.

A low-angle lectern can be used to display art or documents. Lightweight items will generally stay on the support without having to be fastened. The bottom of mounted and matted art can rest on the floor of the case; this should keep it from sliding. Use a stop if necessary.

COMBINATIONS OF WEDGES

It is possible to use a combination of lectern and basic and four-sided wedges in order to support a book propped up *and* open to a certain angle (fig. 6-58).

Fig. 6-58

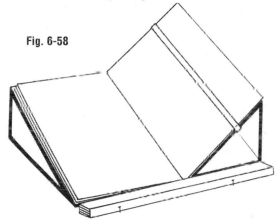

Vivak Copolyester Sheet Supports

Olga Marder, head of the conservation lab at the New York Botanical Garden, introduced us to a transparent plastic that is easy to form into cradles and other supports for lightweight materials. It is polyethylene terephthalate glycol (PETG), a member of the polyester family, and is sold under the name Vivak in the United States.

Unlike acrylic sheet (e.g., Plexiglas), it can be cut using any of the cutters described in section 2, and it can be bent and shaped without the need for heat or chemicals. Vivak comes with a protective plastic film on either side, to prevent scratches. It comes in various thicknesses or gauges; .06 is suitable for most cradles and supports. (Thicker sheets may be too difficult to cut or bend using equipment normally found in a conservation lab.) It is sold by most plastic distributors and is also available in a UV filtering version.

To cut Vivak, follow the directions for cutting in "Cutting and Trimming" in section 2, p. 49. If the edges are rough after cutting, they can be smoothed with fine sandpaper. It is also possible to round the corners with a corner-rounder. (These small machines are sometimes used to round the corners of polyester film after encapsulating documents.)

To bend the plastic, place it in a cutter with a clamp and depress the clamp. Use a bone folder to bend the plastic against the cutting edge of the cutter, as described in "Scoring and Folding" in section 2, on p. 50. Or clamp the plastic to the edge of the counter and fold the plastic over the edge with a bone folder (or the flat part of your hand), as shown in figure 6-31.

A piece of Vivak can be made into a simple wedge for an open book by bending it to the desired angle. Cut the plastic so that the wing under the book will be slightly smaller than the cover. If the angle is not satisfactory, modify it by bending the wedge more or less. The plastic will hold the new angle.

Another wedge can be placed under the back cover if needed, as shown in figure 6-59.

Fig. 6-59

You can also make lectern stands with a lip at the bottom to hold the book in place (fig. 6-60). If you have a corner rounder, round the corners of the lip. Otherwise, smooth the edges with fine sandpaper.

Experiment with the material to solve other mounting problems. The plastic can be drilled easily and the

mount can be suspended if desired. Furthermore, the supports can be bent again to new angles, as needed, and the mounts may be reused. Because Vivak bends easily, heavy books may cause the supports to sag after a time.

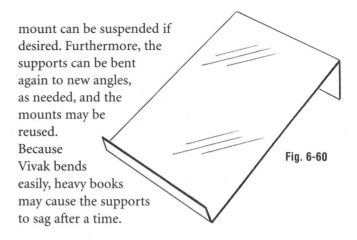

Fig. 6-60

Polyester-Film Book Supports

Faced with the need to fabricate book supports on short notice for an exhibit at the New York Academy of Medicine Library, conservator Susan B. Martin devised a cradle made of one piece of 5-mil polyester film. The design can be adjusted so that each book in a show can be opened to an appropriate angle and be evenly supported across the boards and spine. Each cradle can be made in about 15 minutes.

The polyester film structure is a flexible support that can conform to irregularities in the shape of the book's boards, and it distributes the weight of the book evenly. If desired, front and back boards can be supported at very different angles from each other. The film's smoothness will not cause any abrasion on the binding. Polyester is archivally sound, relatively inexpensive, and readily available. After installation, the support is nearly invisible.

When the show is over, the adhesive tape should be removed from the supports and they can then be stored flat for future use.

Construction of Polyester-Film Book Supports

The following instructions were kindly furnished by Susan B. Martin, and are reprinted in their entirety with her permission.

1. As a rough measurement, cut a rectangle of 5-mil polyester film approximately three times the girth of the book by slightly less than three times the height of the book (the point being to have a support slightly smaller than the book). Fold the film into thirds lengthwise to form a long strip three times the girth of the book by slightly less than the height of the book. Make all creases sharp and straight with your bone folder. Place the book

on a firm surface and hold it open to the display pages, creating the exact configuration you desire. Continue to check this position as you proceed with each step of the construction. Do not force a book to open wider than is comfortable and safe for it.

2. With the seam side down, crease the polyester film ("valley" fold AA' in fig. 6-61) with a bone folder to the left of the center of the folded strip to create the left side of the spine area. Next, crease the polyester film one spine's width to the right ("valley" fold BB') for the right side of the spine; now there is an exact place for the spine of the book to rest. *Note:* Some books will not need a spine's width area; they may require only one valley fold to create a "V" shape, and this will be apparent when you first observe the book open to its display position as mentioned above.

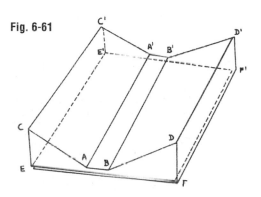

Fig. 6-61

3. To form the wedge shapes: make a "mountain" fold (CC') just slightly less than the width of the front board from the spine fold and make a corresponding "mountain" fold (DD') for the back board. It is important at this point to place the book in the exact position desired for display in order to determine the height of the boards above the base. Front and back boards may not need to be at the same height; they can be displayed at whatever angle is most appropriate. Measure the height of the front board's fore edge from the table and make a corresponding "mountain" fold in the polyester film (EE'). This forms the left turn-in for the support's base, a right angle (CEA). The same process is repeated to form the other right angle (DFB). This completes the folding of the polyester film. Place the open book in its exhibit position on the nearly completed support and adjust the base sections to maintain the right angles and to establish the finished shape of the support. If the two base pieces are longer than necessary, trim off the excess. Because the

cradle is made of *folded* polyester film, it is helpful to tuck one side of the base into the other side of the base for added stability; a small piece of double-sided tape will further hold the configuration you desire (fig. 6-62).

Fig. 6-62

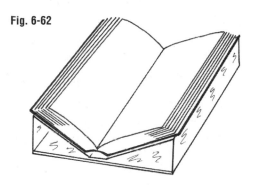

If necessary, the displayed pages can be secured with polyester film "ribbon" wrapped around the supporting surface of the cradle and the opened book, and fastened with double-sided tape underneath.

4. For especially heavy or large books, one can cut four-ply mat board "legs" the height of the sides (CE and DF) and simply insert these into the pockets formed by the folded polyester film. This greatly adds to the strength and stability of the cradle and is not visually intrusive. This method has been used successfully to support books up to 10" × 14", 4" thick, and weighing over 10 lbs (25 × 35 × 10 cm thick, weighing over 4.5 kg).

Preventing Distortion

Polyester Film Ribbon

No matter what type of support is used, it is sometimes necessary to hold the book open securely. A common way to do this is with thin ribbon or tape made of polyester, polypropylene, or polyethylene film (fig. 6-63). The ribbon is shown in figure 6-58, for example. The thin, flexible, transparent material is sold in rolls in various widths. The polyester is more transparent, but the polyethylene and polypropylene tapes can be softer. Thick polyester tape may cut pages; select a thin tape, .5 mil or less. Thread the ribbon through the cradles and stick the ends together with double-coated tape. Slide the taped ends inside the cradles carefully.

If there is a possibility that the ribbon could damage the paper, place a piece of thin acid-free card stock or two-ply mat board (according to the size of the book) under the ribbon to act as a cushion next to the page. It is usually possible to put the ribbon around the page *under* the one to be exhibited and still have the book sufficiently held in place, so the cushioning and the tape will not show. There's no need to slide the ends under the cradles, but be very certain that the double-coated tape is nowhere near the edges of the ribbon.

Fig. 6-63

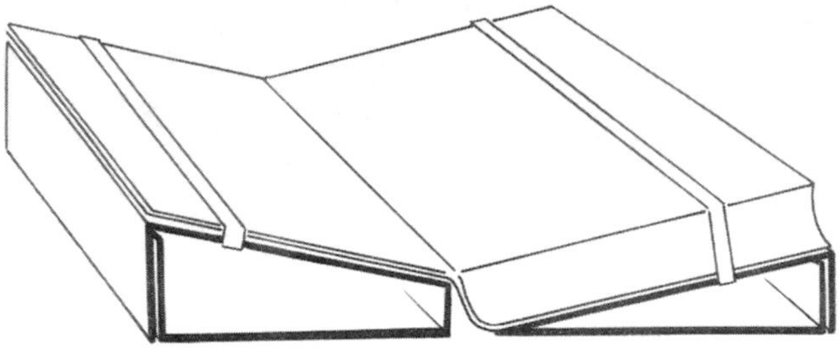

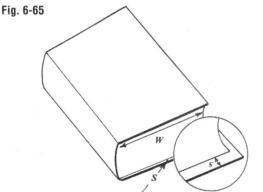

Pillow for Text

In some cases, the pages of a book may sag when it is propped up. A "pillow" can be made to support the pages.

Measure the thickness of the text (pages) of the book, and the width (fig. 6-64). Cut a piece of mat board the same width as the thickness of the text and about a half inch shorter than the width of the pages.

Fig. 6-64

Measure the part of the book cover that extends beyond the pages at the bottom. This is called the "square" (S), as shown in figure 6-65.

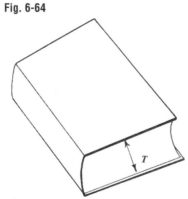

Fig. 6-65

Cut additional pieces of mat board, or thinner acid-free board, as needed to make the pillow the same thickness as the square (fig. 6-66). Attach them together with double-coated tape (or use PVA-methylcellulose mix) and place the pillow under a weight for a couple of hours to make sure it is flat.

Fig. 6-66

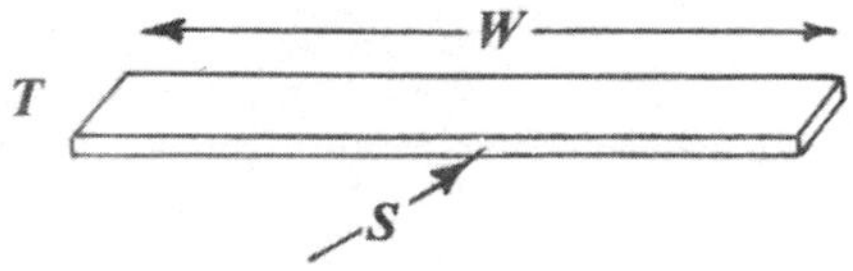

Fit the pillow in the space below the text block, between the covers. The pillow and the bottom edge of the book cover should be flush. It can be held in place with polyester or polypropylene ribbon around the pages, for convenience.

Exhibiting Books as Museum Objects

Books that are permanent exhibits in museum settings such as historic houses should be treated as objects. They have quite different requirements from books that are part of a research collection in a library or archive. Since they are not used, you need not worry about the condition of the pages and can concentrate on making the covers look good, especially the spines.

As with all permanent exhibits, there are dangers. If possible, remove any books with research or historical value and substitute similar items of less importance.

The most obvious effect of permanent display is fading of the exposed surfaces from light damage. It is a common experience to remove a book with a tan spine from a shelf and discover that the book has brilliant green sides. The cloth, paper, or leather covering the boards was protected from light and retained the original color while the spine gradually faded.

To prevent further damage, lights should be turned off and windows covered whenever the room is empty. (This will benefit all the other exhibits as well.)

Insects and vermin can set up housekeeping on shelves behind the books. Mold may also start growing in these dark, undisturbed air pockets. Periodically remove books from the shelves and inspect and clean them as described in "Cleanup Procedure" in section 1, p. 17, and in "Cleaning Books" in section 5, p. 102. Reshelve the cleaned books.

Arrange books in an attractive and neat manner. Line them up evenly at the front of the shelf. They should not look as if they have been left abandoned for fifty years or a century.

Books are sometimes displayed leaning at angles, for a more casual effect. This will certainly cause severe distortion in a short time and should be avoided unless the books are considered completely disposable.

Other hazards include desiccation in dry conditions, as well as distortion and possible mold growth in damp conditions. In winter, keep the heat at moderate levels (below 70°F, or 21°C) in rooms with book collections; in summer, keep the relative humidity below 50%.

Vandalism and theft are always possible with open shelves or tables.

When books are displayed in casual arrangements on tables, make sure they are supported properly. Make unobtrusive cradles or other small mounts and pillows. They should be as hidden as possible but if they show a little, they will give visitors the message that the museum cares about the objects.

Books with detached or very fragile boards may still be displayed on shelves. Place the boards in position and tie the book up with cotton twill tape. Cross the tape over one board and tie it at the top, as shown in figure 6-67.

If the spine is flapping, tie the book up in the other direction. Position the tape as inconspicuously as possible, e.g., under the raised bands in a leather book. Make the knot at the fore edge (fig. 6-68).

White twill tape is available from conservation suppliers. You can tone it with acrylics to blend in with the book; let it dry completely before tying it on. Colored twill tape can be purchased from fabric stores and is appropriate for use with display books.

If after these measures the books still look sad, a book conservator may be able to furbish the visible parts, often on-site, using various cosmetic techniques.

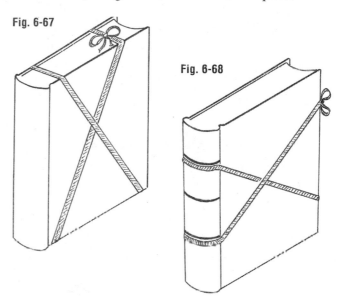

Fig. 6-67

Fig. 6-68

CLOSING THE SHOW

Removing Materials from the Exhibit

After the show is over, close books gently and gradually. The materials that make up books, especially paper, leather, parchment, and adhesives, retain a "memory" of the shape or position they have been in for an extended period of time. If a cover doesn't close fully, leave the book flat overnight on a surface where it will not be disturbed. The next day, turn it over so it is resting on the other cover. Repeat this a few times until the book closes on its own. It may take a week or two for a book to close fully after being in a cradle for several weeks. A book in good condition will eventually return to its pre-exhibition shape.

Examine all the items in the show and fill out a condition report form for each one. (See "Condition Reports," p. 155.) Compare it with the condition report from before the show and notify the librarian, curator, or other person in charge if there are any changes. *Do not make any repairs to books, art, or documents that are on loan.* Advise the lender that the item is being returned damaged; it is up to the owner to evaluate the situation and determine a course of action. The borrower is normally responsible for conservation costs, which may be covered by insurance.

Package and return all borrowed items, in the original shipping containers if possible. The lending agreement may specify that art movers do all the packing, or state which commercial carrier should be used. In some cases, a lending institution may send its own staff to pack and transport the materials.

Matted art or documents can be left in their mats for storage. You may place a piece of acid-free paper inside the window, over the art. Mats of the same size can be stacked and placed in a labeled, acid-free flat storage box; larger pieces can be put in flat file drawers.

If desired, the art may be removed from the backing board by simply cutting the hinges (carefully!) with a scalpel or sharp utility knife, as far as possible from the edge of the art. The small bit of Japanese paper may be left attached to the back of the item. It can be removed at a later time if necessary. (See "Undoing [Reversing] Repairs Made with Paste or Methylcellulose" in section 4, p. 89, for directions.) The documents or prints should be returned to their storage boxes.

In the case of books with damaged bindings or pages, the condition report form should state whether minor repairs or full treatment are needed. In either case, the book should be stored in a box until it can be repaired.

Storage of Exhibit Materials

Take a hard look at the cradles, frames, mats, Plexiglas, case linings, and all other items used in the show. Discard anything that is damaged or will obviously never be used again for any reason. Dedicate a storage space for materials that can be reused. Pack or stack everything so it will remain in good condition until needed again. Label boxes and packages.

Frames are a major expense in exhibitions. Always work on a padded surface when framing or unframing art. For storage, leave the glazing material and a backboard in the frame and wrap it in corrugated cardboard, bubble wrap, or other padding material. In order to preserve the frame in the best possible condition, store it *upright* in a rack. (See "Framed Art Storage" in section 1, p. 25.) Larger frames should be separated with corrugated cardboard or with foam board.

A *single, small* frame with glazing can be stored flat in a box, if well padded. Label the box clearly to prevent heavy objects from being placed on top. Larger framed items stored flat in drawers frequently suffer damage from sliding around as the drawer is opened and closed, as well as from other items being stacked on top of them over time.

Take special care when handling and storing acrylic glazing (e.g., Plexiglas) because it scratches very easily. Larger pieces are likely to sag if not well supported. If the glazing does not belong in a frame, interleave Plexiglas with scrap mat board or with corrugated or foam board. Place upright in a storage rack.

Commercial book wedges and cradles are meant to be used repeatedly; keep them in good condition by packing them in boxes with plenty of padding. Wedges made in-house can very often be used again if stored carefully.

Think Ahead to the Next Show

After all the exhibits and props are put away, consider what went well about the show, as a production, and what gave you trouble. Make notes so you will have this information for the next show.

And now, take a well-earned break!

———◆———◆———◆———

Care of Photographs

Ana B. Hofmann is a conservator of photographs and works on paper. In her teaching and consulting work, she found that certain questions kept coming up frequently. She compiled the following information to help curators and private owners care for their collections.

Many of the guidelines that apply to the proper storage and display of photographs are also valid for other paper-based materials and are similar to information found elsewhere in this book. However, if your collection consists largely of photographs, it may be convenient to have this information together in one place. We thank Ana Hofmann for permitting us to print her work here.

HOW TO HANDLE PHOTOGRAPHS

- *Never* smoke, eat, or drink near the artwork.
- Have a flat, clean, dry surface to work on:
  - cover the work surface with clean, white blotter or lint-free cloth
  - when handling fragile items, pad the work surface with a folded towel
- Wash and dry your hands thoroughly before handling photographs:
  - dirt, sweat, and oils can leave permanent marks on photographic emulsions
- Use clean, white cotton gloves or latex gloves when handling objects prone to finger marks such as color prints, high-gloss prints, and glass plate negatives. Gloves should be snug-fitting and should not have raised grips on the fingertips.
- Avoid touching the image area of the photograph.
- Use a flat, rigid support such as a piece of mat board or Plexiglas to transport fragile objects.

- Use two hands to pick up large and fragile objects. Never pick anything up by one corner or one edge.
- To turn over large, soft (floppy), or brittle photographs, place the photograph in a sandwich of blotters or board and turn the whole package over.
- *Never* try to pry apart photographs which are stuck together.
- *Never* try to remove a photograph which is stuck to glass.
- *Never* try to unroll a tightly rolled photograph which appears brittle.

Unframing

- Before removing a photograph from a frame:
  - look carefully to make sure no area of emulsion is stuck to the glass
  - if the emulsion is stuck to the glass, do not attempt to unframe the photograph, as this can cause the stuck area to separate from the rest of the photograph
  - if the stuck area has already separated from the photograph, save the glass with the fragment on it. A conservator may be able to remove the fragment from the glass and reattach it to the photograph
  - handle photographs that are hinged to their mounts or overmats carefully: they can flop around and be damaged
  - lift photographs off their mounts carefully, making sure they are completely detached before lifting
- *Do not disassemble historical cased images* such as daguerreotypes and ambrotypes.

183

STORAGE OF PHOTOGRAPHIC MATERIALS: REHOUSING

Why Rehouse?

To Preserve Your Materials

Proper housing protects materials from acids and pollutants in the environment and surrounding materials.

To Protect Your Materials

In a disaster situation, photographs that are housed properly stand a much better chance of surviving in good condition.

Easier Access and Safer Handling of Materials

Most modern photograph enclosures are designed for easy access. Good-quality storage materials increase respect for the collection. People are more likely to be careless with photographs when they are stored carelessly.

Opportunity to Catalog and Survey Your Materials

Cataloging should really be the first step in rehousing. Rehousing provides an excellent opportunity to do an item-by-item survey of your collection. Photocopies can be made of each object before rehousing to make a visual catalog of the collection. This reduces future handling of the collection.

Considerations When Making Storage Decisions

Type of Photograph

Different types of photographs can have different housing needs. Photographs of unusual shape or size will need special enclosures, some of which you may have to devise yourself.

Condition of Photograph

Damaged or fragile photographs require special housing materials. Fragile photographs need sturdy enclosures.

Use of Collection

A collection that is heavily used will usually require more protection than one that is seldom used. Choosing an appropriate style of envelope can help protect a photograph from careless handling.

Budget

Money and time are needed for any rehousing project. Space must also be budgeted. Rehousing a collection almost always increases the need for shelf space.

Prioritize

Don't expect to rehouse a large collection all at once. Assess condition, use, and value and create a long-term rehousing plan which can be implemented in stages, as money becomes available. Future rehousing projects should build on, not supersede, current ones.

STORAGE MATERIALS FOR PHOTOGRAPHS

Paper vs. Plastic Enclosures: Pros and Cons

Paper Enclosures: What Kind of Paper?

Acid-free
PH neutral (unbuffered) or
Alkaline (buffered)
100% rag paper content or
Lignin-free wood pulp
Should pass Photographic Activity Test (PAT test)
White, or not highly colored

Advantages of Paper

Paper "breathes": prevents buildup of moisture and gases
Paper is opaque: provides protection from UV radiation
Paper is usually cheaper than plastic
Paper is easy to write on with pencil

Disadvantages of Paper

Paper is opaque: photograph must be removed for viewing

Plastic Enclosures: What Kinds of Plastic?

Polyester Marketed under brand names Mylar (DuPont) and Mellinex (formerly ICI, now DuPont). "Polyester" is common name for polyethylene terephthalate. The most stable and inert of the plastics. In its film form, polyester is used for storage enclosures. Usually the most expensive of the plastics. Polyester is manufactured with different coatings or uncoated. Enclosures should be made from uncoated polyester such as Mylar D or Mellinex no. 516.

Polyethylene	A chemically stable, soft highly flexible plastic used for sleeves, bags, and plastic sheeting. Can be transparent or translucent. Good for wrapping large objects. Very flexible, provides no rigid support
Polypropylene	A chemically stable plastic. Can be rigid or flexible. Similar to polyester in film form but not quite as rigid. Can be almost as soft and flexible as polyethylene, but scratches less easily; good for binder sleeves. Can also be very stiff; used for film storage canisters.
Polyvinyl Chloride (PVC)	Sometimes called "vinyl." Chemically unstable, emits hydrochloric acid as it deteriorates. Has a "plastic" smell. Never use PVC as a storage material.

Advantages of Plastic

• Plastic is clear. Photograph can be viewed without removing it from the enclosure. Good for heavily used collections.

• Plastic provides protection from pollutants in atmosphere.

Disadvantages of Plastic

• Plastic does not breathe. Does not allow gases and moisture to escape. Plastic enclosures should not be used for nitrate and acetate negatives.

• Plastic, especially polyester, creates a static charge. Plastic is not recommended for photographs with loose emulsion flakes or coloring media such as pastels.

• Plastic is usually more expensive than paper.

• It is best to purchase enclosure materials from conservation material suppliers to ensure quality.

ENCLOSURES AND BOXES

Enclosures

Enclosures can be made of paper, plastic, board, or a combination of materials. Choose an enclosure of appropriate size for the object: loose enough to allow easy insertion and removal, but not so loose that the object slides around a lot.

Envelope	Sealed on three sides. Seams should be down the sides of the envelope, not the center. Secure, but sometimes difficult to insert and remove object.
Folder	Open on three sides. Folders are often used in combination with other enclosures. Easy to insert and remove object, but not very secure; object easily slips out.
L-Velope	Sealed on two adjacent sides. Slightly more secure than a plain folder, but still easy to insert and remove object.
Four-Flap Folder	Has four flaps which fold in to seal all four sides of the package. Useful for fragile glass plate negatives and cased objects.
Sleeve	Sealed on two opposite sides and open at both ends. Sometimes a sleeve is actually a folder with a flap on the open side that can be folded over to lock closed.
Ring Binder Page	To be used in three-ring binders. Made of polyester, polyethylene, or polypropylene.

Boxes and Albums

Boxes and albums should be made of good-quality, acid- and lignin-free board, archival-quality corrugated cardboard, or corrugated polypropylene. Metal reinforcement at corners allows for stacking of boxes. Leather-covered boxes and albums should be avoided, as leather is an inherently acidic material. Choose a box of an appropriate size for the photographs. Try to store similar sizes together to avoid creating uneven pressure. If you must store different sizes together, stack them so that the heaviest and largest objects are at the bottom. If photographs are to be stored vertically (on edge) in boxes, they should be supported by inserting a piece of archival corrugated cardboard every few photographs. Do not allow photographs to sag unsupported. Do not overfill boxes.

Clamshell Box	Top is attached along one side. Top has a substantial lip which comes down over bottom portion of box. Objects are stored vertically.
Shoebox	Shallow lid is not attached to bottom. Objects are stored vertically or flat.
Drop-Front Box	Shallow box that has one side which folds down. Has a deep lid which is not attached. Objects are stored flat.
Album	Usually has a three-ring binder mechanism in the spine to accommodate storage pages.

SUGGESTED ENCLOSURE STYLES FOR DIFFERENT TYPES OF PHOTOGRAPHS

(*Note:* If you have a large collection of photographs, consider having a conservator or curator identify the different types of photographs. This will enable you to follow the suggestions below. —Nelly Balloffet)

These are only suggestions, not hard-and-fast rules.

Daguerreotype	Unbuffered, bristol four-flap envelope or box. For loose daguerreotypes: plastic sleeve with museum board insert for support (if needed). Sink mat.
Ambrotype	Same as above.
Tintype	Same as above.
Albumen Print	Unbuffered, acid-free paper or plastic sleeve, envelope, or folder. Use museum board insert for very fragile and brittle photographs, or a combination plastic-and-board folder. Protect albumen photographs from light when not being viewed.
Gelatin Print	Same as above.
Collodion Positive	Same as above.

Carbon Print/ Woodburytype	Same as above.
Salted Print	Same as above. Protect from light.
Platinum Print	Same as above.
Cyanotype	Same as above. Paper enclosures must be unbuffered. Protect from light.
Collodion Wet Plate Negative	Unbuffered paper four-flap envelope, or regular envelope or sleeve. Sandwich broken negatives between museum board or place in a sink mat.
Gelatin Dry Plate Negative	Same as above.
Cellulose Nitrate Negative	Buffered paper envelope. Store separately from other types of photographs.
Cellulose Acetate Negative	Same as above.
Panorama	Store flat (if possible) in plastic sleeve or unbuffered paper or board folder. If already rolled, store in protective box of appropriate size.
Oversized Photograph	Store in museum board folder or in flat file drawer. Store flat.
Album, Domed or Odd-Shaped Photograph	Clamshell or drop-front box of appropriate size. Pad with acid-free tissue to prevent shifting. Interleave album pages with acid-free paper.

STORAGE ENVIRONMENT FOR PHOTOGRAPHIC MATERIALS

"Perhaps the most important thing to remember about photographs is that they often consist of several dissimilar materials, each of which will react somewhat differently—and perhaps in opposition to one another—in response to changes in the environmental conditions. This can result in stress and dimensional instability, and perhaps in the loss of the image" (Ritzenthaler, Munoff, and Long, "Preservation of Photographic Materials," in *Archives and Manuscripts: Administration of Photographic Collections*).

A lot of damage and deterioration can be avoided or slowed down through proper environmental control.

Environmental Factors to Consider

Temperature

Heat is an energy source for deterioration reactions. The rate of deterioration of photographic materials is doubled for every 18°F (10°C) increase in temperature. Therefore, all else being equal, photographs stored at 60°F (16°C) will last twice as long as ones stored at 78°F (26°C). Lowering the temperature to 42°F (6°C) from 78°F will decrease the deterioration rate by a factor of four, and so on.

The maximum temperature for the storage of most photographic materials is 70°F (21°C). This is a compromise between what is best for photographs and what is comfortable for humans. However, the cooler the better, as long as relative humidity can be controlled at the same time. The maximum temperature for the storage of nitrate and acetate films is 55°F (13°C).

Relative Humidity

Relative humidity is the amount of water vapor in the air, expressed as a percentage of the maximum amount of water that the air could hold at a given temperature. Temperature and relative humidity are interdependent: the warmer the air, the more water it can hold.

The optimum relative humidity for the storage of photographic materials is 30–50%. Higher relative humidities encourage mold growth and insect activity and can accelerate certain chemical reactions. Very low relative humidity will cause photographs to become desiccated and embrittled.

Cellulose nitrate and acetate films require a relative humidity of no more than 20–30%. These films emit gases as they deteriorate. The gases combine with water in the atmosphere to form acids which will attack the film images themselves as well as surrounding materials.

Cycling

"Cycling" denotes large, rapid, and frequent changes in temperature and relative humidity. This causes materials to repeatedly expand and contract, resulting in a great deal of stress and leading to more rapid deterioration. In an ideal world, both temperature and relative humidity in collection storage areas should be kept constant 24 hours a day, 365 days a year. In real life, this is often impossible, so changes in temperature and relative humidity should be kept as small and gradual as possible, as the seasons progress. If regulation of temperature and relative humidity of the whole building is not possible,

locate the collection storage area in a room which can be closed off and regulated separately. Monitor temperature and relative humidity daily or weekly and create a log to record readings. Inexpensive monitoring devices include digital psychrometers, Arten mechanical hygrothermometers, and temperature/humidity indicator cards.

Light

Light, and particularly ultraviolet light, is a catalyst or energy source for deterioration reactions. It will cause fading of unstable silver images, as well as embrittlement and discoloration of paper. Excessive exposure to ultraviolet (UV) radiation will cause fading or color changes in inks and the color dyes in color photographs. UV radiation is more concentrated in sunlight and fluorescent light. Photographic processes which are particularly susceptible to fading from exposure to UV radiation include cyanotypes, salted and albumen prints, color photographs, and the color media of hand-colored photographs. Damage caused by light is cumulative: it depends on the intensity and length of exposure. Ideally, storage areas should be kept dark when not in use, which will also help to keep temperatures down. Light levels are measured in lux or foot-candles; ten lux equal one foot-candle (approximately). Light meters calibrated in lux are available to measure light levels.

Ventilation

Good ventilation of storage areas is very important. Certain photographic materials, nitrate and acetate negatives in particular, emit harmful gases as they deteriorate. A well-ventilated storage area will allow these gases to dissipate as they are formed. Good ventilation will also discourage mold growth and insect activity.

Cold Storage

A cold-storage area must be frost-free. Cold storage is especially recommended for deteriorating nitrate and acetate negatives, as well as some color materials. Deterioration rates are greatly reduced at low temperatures. Photographs which are to be placed in cold storage must be packed in airtight containers or in polyethylene bags which have had their openings taped shut. This will keep moisture levels within the package fairly constant and will help in acclimatizing the photographs when they are removed from the refrigerator. When removing items from cold storage, do not unseal the package until it has come to room temperature. This will prevent moisture in the room-temperature air from condensing on the surface of the photographs; it will, instead, condense on the outside of the plastic bag. It is important to remember that cold storage is a long-term storage option. If the materials are going to be removed from cold storage every other day, this amounts to repeated cycling of temperature, which can be detrimental.

Housekeeping

Housekeeping is essential for any collection. Soot and dust can abrade and stain photographic materials. Dirty and untidy conditions will also encourage insect and rodent activity. Smoking, eating, and drinking should be prohibited in the storage area and especially when photographs are being handled. Regular dusting and sweeping will also discourage mold growth.

Location of Storage Area

- Do not locate storage areas in basements or attics. Extremes in temperature and relative humidity are most likely in these two areas.
- Do not place shelving underneath overhead water pipes. Be aware of any pipes that may be located in walls and ceilings and try to stay away from them. A burst pipe is truly a disaster which can cause a huge amount of damage to your collection.
- Never store anything on a shelf lower than six inches from the ground.
- Do not locate shelving near heaters or air ducts.
- Do not place shelving against a damp outside wall.
- Make sure that the floor can support the weight of a fully loaded shelving system or other storage furniture. This is especially important in historic houses.

TYPES OF DAMAGE

(*Note:* The following information will be helpful when filling out condition reports. —Nelly Balloffet)

Major Causes of Damage to Photographs

- Environment
    high temperature

extremes in relative humidity
cycling of temperature and relative humidity
pollution
poor-quality storage and framing materials
light
biological agents
- Handling
    carelessness and accidents; vandalism
- Inherent Vice
    when the materials that make up an object possess properties that will cause the deterioration of the whole
- Poor Processing Techniques

TWO MAJOR CATEGORIES OF DAMAGE

Mechanical Damage

Mechanical damage occurs as a result of a physical event, such as careless handling. Can be a break, tear, etc.

Chemical Damage

Chemical damage occurs as a result of chemical interaction between the photograph or the components which make up the photograph and another substance, such as residual processing chemicals or acidity from adjacent materials. Chemical damage is usually manifested in the form of stains, discoloration, fading, and embrittlement. Chemical and mechanical damage are not mutually exclusive.

Specific Types of Damage

Tear/Break/ Crease/ Abrasion	Almost always caused by poor handling, framing, or storage practices.
Loss	A missing area of the photograph's image or base layer.
Dimensional Distortion	The photograph (or mount) is out of plane (cockled, wavy, bulged, etc.). Often occurs when the photograph expands and contracts in fluctuating humidity.

Embrittlement	Fragile brittleness. Caused by acidity, dehydration, and excessive exposure to UV radiation.
Cleavage	Separation of image and support layers or a photograph from its mount. Evident as flaking, bubbles, lifted areas, etc.
Stain/ Discoloration	Stains and discolorations of the photographic emulsion or support can be caused by acidity, food, adhesives, mold, residual processing chemicals, water, and more. Stains can be localized or overall.
Fading	Fading of the photographic image can be localized or overall and is caused by many of the same things that cause stains.
Mirroring	A silvery, reflective coating on the surface of silver gelatin prints. More prevalent in darker shadow areas of print. Very common in silver prints.
Mold	Evident as a stain, a furry growth, or a dull area on the surface of the photograph. Mold weakens gelatin emulsions, making them extremely water-soluble and fragile. Also weakens paper supports. Mold is always a serious problem which must be dealt with immediately.
Foxing	Small, reddish-brown spots in paper and board mounts and also in paper-based photographs, especially albumen, salted, and platinum photographs. Thought to be caused by the presence of iron particles or mold in paper. Foxing is common in papers which have been exposed to high humidity.
Insect Damage	Common signs are the insects themselves, larvae, frass (feces), losses, holes, or chewed-up areas. Insects will attack both the image layer and paper support of a photograph.
Ferrotyping	A type of surface damage which occurs when a gelatin emulsion has stuck to glass or some other smooth surface during a period of high humidity and has subsequently come off, leaving a shiny spot in that area. The gelatin essentially conforms to and takes on the surface quality of the glass.
Dirt	Dirt will cause a photograph to look dull and dingy. It can deteriorate, stain, and abrade the image layer.
Accretion	Stuff that sits on the surface of the photograph. Can be anything: adhesives, food, mud—you name it. Accretions can cause stains, fading, and weakening of the image layer.
Weeping Glass	A form of glass deterioration which occurs when potassium salts in the glass migrate to the surface. Looks like droplets or crystals on the surface of the glass.

How to Look for Damage

- Employ safe handling practices—damaged objects are usually fragile ones.
- Look at both the front and back of the photograph.
- Look carefully at both the photograph and its mount (if present).
- Look at the photograph from different angles.
- Look at the photograph in different types of light: artificial, daylight, head-on, raking angle. Some types of damage are more evident in certain kinds of light.

Documentation of Condition

- Photographic Documentation
    - visual record of condition
    - write date and accession number or other ID on a small piece of paper and place it alongside the object so it is included in the picture
    - include a color chart in the picture
- Photocopy Photograph
    - "quick and dirty" visual documentation

useful for documenting inscriptions

do not force photograph flat on copy machine. Make copy with copy machine lid open.

• Condition Report

can be brief or in-depth

documents present condition of photograph

jogs memory during inspection

DISPLAYING PHOTOGRAPHS AND WORKS ON PAPER

Temperature

Heat is an energy source for deterioration reactions. The maximum temperature in your display area should be 70°F (21°C). This is a compromise between what is best for the art and what is comfortable for humans. Cooler is always better, as long as the relative humidity can also be kept down as the temperature is lowered.

Relative Humidity

This is the amount of water vapor in the air, expressed as a percentage of the maximum amount of water that the air is capable of holding at a given temperature. Temperature and relative humidity are interdependent: the warmer the air, the more water it can hold. The optimum relative humidity for paper and photographs is 30–50%. Higher relative humidity encourages mold growth and insect activity. Very low relative humidity causes desiccation and embrittlement. Control relative humidity with the use of air conditioners, dehumidifiers, and humidifiers.

Cycling

"Cycling" refers to large, rapid, and frequent changes in temperature and relative humidity. This causes materials to expand and contract, resulting in stress and leading to more rapid deterioration. Try to keep changes in temperature and relative humidity as small and gradual as possible as the seasons progress.

Light

Light radiation, and particularly ultraviolet (UV) radiation, is an energy source for deterioration reactions. It can cause fading, discoloration, and embrittlement of photographs and paper. Damage caused by light is cumulative: it depends on the intensity and length of exposure. Sunlight and fluorescent light contain the most UV radiation. Avoid hanging art next to windows or under fluorescent lights. Use incandescent light sources to illuminate art, but be aware that this type of light source generates heat. Keep light levels to a minimum and turn off lights when they are not needed. If art is fragile and deteriorated or if it is displayed in areas with fluorescent or sunlight, use UV-inhibitor glazing in the frame.

DISPLAY CONDITIONS FOR PHOTOGRAPHS

Temperature	70°F (21°C) maximum.
Relative Humidity	30–50%.
Light	Measured in lux or foot-candles; 1 foot-candle equals 10 lux.
Light Levels	For exhibition of sensitive photographs: 3–5 foot-candles or 30–50 lux.
	For other types of photographs: 10 foot-candles or 100 lux.

Light Source

Sunlight	Contains the most UV radiation. Not recommended as a source of illumination for photographs on display. Sunlight in a display area should be filtered with UV-inhibitor shades or window films, as well as curtains and venetian blinds. Difficult to regulate intensity and to direct.
Fluorescent	Contains a lot of UV radiation. Not recommended as a source of illumination for photographs on display. Fluorescent lamps in display area should have UV-inhibitor filters in the form of tube sleeves or sheets which sit in diffusing panel of light fixture. Fluorescent light is difficult to direct and can have an unpleasing color.

Tungsten	Produces little UV radiation, but produces quite a lot of infrared radiation. Infrared radiation does not produce photochemical damage like UV, but it does raise the temperature of objects that absorb it.
	Regular incandescent bulbs are a tungsten light source. Tungsten light sources convert most electrical energy they use to heat, so the main problem they can create is overheating and drying.
	Warm, pleasing color; easy to direct.
Halogen	Produces a lot of UV radiation, which is easily transmitted through the quartz-halogen bulb housing. Use UV-protective glazing when using halogen spotlights.

Very sensitive photographs and those in very bright display areas should be protected with UV-inhibitor glazing in their frames. However, ultraviolet radiation is not the only type of light which damages photographs, so filtering out UV rays does not mean that the danger of light damage is eliminated.

Length of Display Time

Prolonged exposure to light will cause fading and color changes. No photograph should be put on permanent display, and certain sensitive materials such as hand-colored albumen photographs or cyanotypes can fade within a matter of weeks. Concrete light levels and time limits for the display of photographs do not exist.

As a general rule: light levels should be 3–10 footcandles and duration should be 3–6 months. Monitor photographs regularly during exhibit for signs of fading and color change. Fading and color changes are most easily detected at the edge of the overmat.

Displaying Facsimiles

This should be considered when a permanent display is necessary, or for very sensitive and fragile images. Good facsimiles can be made through photographic copying techniques, digital (computer) imaging, or good-quality color photocopies. Be careful that fragile images do not get damaged by careless handling during copying.

GENERAL GUIDELINES FOR DISPLAY

The following are general guidelines for display, to which there are many exceptions.

- Any photograph that is in bad shape (discolored, faded, embrittled, etc.) should be exhibited at very low light levels for very short periods of time—or not at all. Consider using facsimiles.
- Duration of exhibition: 3–6 months of 10-hour days with rest periods of 1–3 years between exhibition cycles. Light damage is cumulative, so if possible, turn lights off or down when gallery is not in use.
- To make viewing easier under low light conditions, provide a transition area with medium-intensity illumination just before the exhibit area. This will allow viewers coming in from the bright light of the outdoors to become accustomed to lower light levels.

Suppliers,
Conservation
Binders, and
Salvage
Companies

SUPPLIERS

The suppliers listed below are known to us; there may well be other suppliers of similar products, and we do not imply that the ones listed are the only good sources.

Alpina Manufacturing
2532 N. Elston Ave., Chicago, IL 60647
(800) 915-2828; fax: (800) 217-9431
http://www.quickchangeframes.com

> Framing supplies. Quick-change display frames.

American Frame Corporation
400 Tomahawk Drive, Maumee, OH 43537-1695
(888) 628-3833; fax: (800) 893-3898
http://www.americanframe.com

> Framing supplies. Frames and mats made to order, customer installs art in frame.

Archival Matters, Inc.
16 Long Hill Road, Leverett, MA 01247
(413) 549-1060; fax: (413) 549-1052
http://www.archivalmatters.com

> Framed art storage systems, crating and assembly of traveling exhibitions.

Archivart
7 Caesar Place, Moonachie, NJ 07074
(800) 804-8428
http://www.archivart.com

> Paper, boards, storage containers, polyester film, blotting paper, adhesives, etc.

Art Preservation Services
315 East 89th, New York, NY 10128
(212) 722-6300; fax: (212) 427-6726
http://www.apsnyc.com

> Products for environmental control and monitoring.

Atlantic Protective Pouches
P.O. Box 1191, Toms River, NJ 08754
(732) 240-3871; fax: (732) 240-4306
http://www.atlanticprotectivepouches.com

> Custom-made polyester enclosures: folders, sleeves, "L" seals, etc. They also ship polyester film in roll form, or in sheets cut to size.

Benchmark
P.O. Box 214, Rosemont, NJ 08556
(609) 397-1131; fax: (609) 397-1159
http://www.benchmarkcatalog.com

> Exhibit supplies: mount-making materials, rare book stands and supports, including adjustable brass and acrylic book cradles.

Bookmakers
8260 Patuxent Range Rd., Suite C, Jessup, MD 20794
(301) 604-7787; fax: (301) 604-7176
http://www.bookmakerscatalog.com

> Book and paper conservation supplies, bookbinding equipment and supplies. (Bookmakers ships many Metal Edge products to East Coast customers.)

CMI Archival Boxes
10034 East Lake Road, Hammondsport, NY 14840
(607) 569-2738; fax: (646) 349-1058
http://www.archivalboxes.com

Custom-made protective boxes.

Cole-Parmer Instrument Co.
625 East Bunker Court, Vernon Hills, IL 60061
(800) 323-4340; fax: (847) 247-2929
http://www.coleparmer.com

Environmental monitoring instruments.

Conservation Resources International, LLC
5532 Port Royal Rd., Springfield, VA 22151
(800) 634 6932; fax: (703) 321-0629
http://www.conservationresources.com

Conservation supplies for museums, libraries, and archives.

Dickson
930 South Westwood Ave., Addison, IL 60101-4917
(800) 323-2448; fax: (800) 676-0498
http://www.dicksonweb.com

Data loggers and other monitoring instruments.

Direct Safety
2005 West 14th St., #132, P.O. Box 27648, Tempe, AZ 85285-7648
(800) 528-7405; fax: (800) 760-2975
http://www.directsafety.com

Supplies for emergency response, personal protection, and industrial safety.

Dorlen Products
6615 West Layton Ave., Milwaukee, WI 53220
(800) 533-6392; fax: (414) 282-5670
http://www.wateralert.com

Water alarms.

Gaylord Bros.
P.O. Box 4901, Syracuse, NY 13221
(800) 448-6160; fax: (800) 272-3412
http://www.gaylord.com

Library supplier; also carries wide line of book and paper conservation items.

Harcourt Bindery
51 Melcher St., Boston, MA 02210
(617) 542-5858; fax: (617) 451-9058
http://www.harcourtbindery.com

Bookbinding equipment and supplies, including fine book cloths. Custom-made protective boxes; hand binding and limited edition binding.

Hiromi Paper International
2525 Michigan Ave. #G9, Santa Monica, CA 90404
(866) 479-2744; fax: (310) 998-0028
http://www.hiromipaper.com

Large assortment of Japanese papers, including paper in rolls. Conservation and bookbinding supplies.

Humidial: *see* **Poly Lam Products Corp.**

Lab Safety Supply, Inc.
P.O. Box 1368, Janesville, WI 53547-1368
(800) 356-0783; fax: (800) 543-9910
http://www.labsafety.com

Supplies for emergency response, personal protection, and industrial safety.

Light Impressions
P.O. Box 787, Brea, CA 92822-0787
(800) 828-6216; fax: (800) 828-5539
http://www.lightimpressionsdirect.com

Book and paper conservation supplies; specializing in photograph conservation and framing.

Metal Edge, Inc.
6340 Bandini Blvd., Commerce, CA 90040
(800) 862 2228; fax: (888) 822-6937
http://www.metaledgeinc.com

Book and paper conservation supplies; storage products. (Many of its products are shipped to East Coast locations from Bookmakers in Maryland.)

New York Central Art Supply Co.
62 Third Ave., New York, NY 10003
(800) 950-6111; (212) 477-0400; fax: (212) 475-2513
http://www.nycentralart.com

Papers, boards, adhesives, art supplies.

NoUVIR Research
20915 Sussex Highway 13, Seaford, DE 19973
(302) 628-9933; fax: (302) 628-9932
http://www.nouvir.com
> Fiber-optic lighting for exhibits and galleries.

Poly Lam Products Corp.
(distributor for Süd-Chemie Performance Packaging)
80 Earhart Drive, Williamsville, NY 14221
(716) 633-1977; (800) 836-9648;
fax: (716) 633-2007
http://www.polylam.com
> Humidity-indicating cards and temperature/humidity-indicating cards, cat. no. 6203-LCC. Sells in quantities of 100 or more.

PRG, Inc.
Box 1768, Rockville, MD 20849-1768
(800) 774-7891; fax: (301) 279-7885
http://www.prginc.com
> Environmental monitoring instruments; water alarms.

Shat-r-Shield Inc.
116 Ryan Patrick Drive, Salisbury, NC 28147-5624
(800) 223-0853; fax: (704) 633-3420
http://www.shat-r-shield.com
> Plastic-coated, shatterproof lamps can be supplied with UV-filtering coatings upon customer request.

Sonin, Inc.
2345 Route 52, Hopewell Junction, NY 12533
(800) 223-7511; fax: (845) 226-8701
http://www.sonin.com
> Inexpensive moisture meters and water alarms.

Spacesaver Corporation
1450 Janesville Ave., Fort Atkinson, WI 53538-2798
(800) 492-3434; fax: (920) 563-2702
http://www.spacesaver.com
> Mobile storage systems, compact shelving, framed art storage.

Süd-Chemie Performance Packaging: see **Poly Lam Products Corp.**

TALAS
20 West 20th St., 5th Floor, New York, NY 10011
(212) 219-0770; fax: (212) 219-0735
http://www.talasonline.com
> Conservation supplies for museums, libraries, and archives. Bookbinding supplies and equipment.

Twinrocker Handmade Paper
P.O. Box 413, Brookston, IN 47923
(800) 757-8946; fax: (765) 563-8946
http://www.twinrocker.com
> Handmade papers, adhesives, including PVA-methylcellulose mix.

United Mfrs. Supplies, Inc.
80 Gordon Drive, Syosset, NY 11791
(800) 645-7260; fax: (516) 496-7968
http://www.unitedmfrs.com
> Framing supplies.

University Products
P.O. Box 101, Holyoke, MA 01041-0101
(800) 628-1912; fax: (800) 532-9281
http://www.universityproducts.com
> Conservation supplies for museums, libraries, and archives.

Utrecht Art Supplies
6 Corporate Drive, Cranbury, NJ 08512-3616
(800) 223-9132; fax: (800) 382-1979
http://www.utrecht.com
> Art supplies, mat cutters, self-healing mats, straightedges, mat board, brushes.

COMMERCIAL CONSERVATION BINDERS

In cases where books are somewhat fragile or have value as objects, using the services of a library binder that has a separate conservation department may be a better choice than a regular library binder.

The establishments listed below are able to provide many special services, such as hand sewing, conservation of original bindings, box making, deacidification, and encapsulation, and they can be relied upon to use archival materials. They can also make photocopies of brittle books in the form of bound books with acid-free pages. This may be a more desirable reformatting choice than microfilm in certain cases.

We list the following vendors because we have worked with them in the past; other library binders may have conservation departments now or in the future, and we do not mean to imply that the ones listed are the only acceptable choices.

Bridgeport National Bindery, Inc.
P.O. Box 289, Agawam, MA 01001-0289
(800) 223-5083; (413) 789-1981; fax: (413) 789-4007
http://www.bnbindery.com

Etherington Conservation Center, Inc.
7609 Business Park Drive, Greensboro, NC 27409
(877) 391-1317; (336) 665-1317; fax: (336) 665-1319
http://www.donetherington.com

Ocker and Trapp, Inc.
P.O. Box 314, Emerson, NJ 07630-0314
(800) 253-0262; (201) 265-0262; fax: (201) 265-0588
http://www.ockerandtrapp.com

SALVAGE AND FREEZE-DRYING COMPANIES

Except as noted, these companies can provide comprehensive recovery services and a great deal of advice in the event of a disaster. They can be reached by phone at any time. Several have offices throughout the United States.

American Freeze Dry Operations, Inc.
39 Lindsey Ave., P.O. Box 264, Runnemede, NJ 08078
(800) 817-1007; (856) 546-0777
http://www.americanfreezedry.com

Belfor USA (formerly Disaster Recovery Services)
2425 Blue Smoke Court South, Fort Worth, TX 76105
(800) 856-3333; fax: (817) 536-1167
http://www.belforusa.com

BMS Catastrophe, Inc.
303 Arthur St., Fort Worth, TX 76107
(800) 433-2940; fax: (817) 332-6728
http://www.bmscat.com

Disaster Recovery Services: *see* **Belfor USA**

Document Reprocessors
East Coast:
5611 Water St., Middlesex, NY 14507
(716) 554-4500; (800) 437-9464; fax: (716) 554-4114

West Coast:
1384 Rollins Road, Burlingame, CA 94010
(650) 401-7711; (800) 437-9464; fax: (650) 401-8711
http://www.documentreprocessors.com

Munters Moisture Control Services
79 Monroe St., P.O. Box 640, Amesbury, MA 01913
(800) 686-8377
(call center, will direct to nearest regional office)
http://www.muntersmcs.com

National Library Relocation
70 Bridge Road, Central Islip, NY 11722
(631) 232-2233; (800) 486-6837; fax: (631) 232-2236
http://www.nlrbookmovers.com

Solex Environmental Systems
P.O. Box 460242, Houston, TX 77056
(800) 848-0484; fax: (713) 461-5877
http://solexrobotics.com

This list includes some organizations that can help with advice and referrals. It is not exhaustive; we regret if we have omitted anyone who should be mentioned. Many of the web addresses provide links to other useful sites.

Abbey Publications

7105 Geneva Dr., Austin, TX 78723

http://palimpsest.stanford.edu/byorg/abbey

> Nonprofit organization dedicated to the preservation of library and archive materials. Newsletters cover research, techniques, health issues, etc.; available online.

American Institute for Conservation of Historic and Artistic Works (AIC)

1717 K Street, NW, Suite 200, Washington, DC 20006

(202) 452-9545; fax (202) 452-9328

http://aic.stanford.edu

> National membership organization of conservation professionals. Can supply referrals to conservators in private practice.

American Red Cross

2025 E Street, NW, Washington, DC 20006

(202) 303-4498

http://www.redcross.org

> Services and disaster planning information.

American Society of Heating, Refrigerating and Air-Conditioning Engineers (ASHRAE)

1791 Tullie Circle, NE, Atlanta, GA 30329

(800) 527-4723

http://www.ashrae.org

> This organization engages in research, sets standards, publishes a journal, and provides referrals.

Amigos Library Services

14400 Midway Road, Dallas, TX 75244-3509

(800) 843-8482; (972) 851-8000; fax: (972) 991-6061

http://www.amigos.org

> Services include cataloging, reference, resource sharing, preservation, digital imaging, consulting, and training.

Canadian Conservation Institute (CCI)

1030 Innes Rd., Ottawa ON K1A 0M5, Canada

(613) 998-3721; fax: (613) 998-4721

http://www.cci-icc.gc.ca

> Devoted to the conservation of cultural heritage; focuses on helping clients and on achieving results. Engages in research and produces many publications, including a newsletter. All publications and other information available in English and French; most of the CCI Notes are also available in Spanish.

Conservation Center for Art and Historic Artifacts (CCAHA)

264 South 23rd St., Philadelphia, PA 19103

(215) 545-0613; fax: (215) 735-9313

http://www.ccaha.org

> Regional conservation center serves institutional and private clients; research, disaster assistance, preservation assessments, and other consulting available. Publishes newsletters and other technical leaflets.

Conservation On Line (COOL)

http://palimpsest.stanford.edu

> Links to conservation and cultural organizations.

The Exhibition Alliance
1370 Route 12B, P.O. Box 345, Hamilton, NY 13346
(315) 824-2510; fax: (315) 824-1683
http://www.exhibitionalliance.org/

> Professional exhibition support for museums, galleries, and other exhibiting organizations. Provides an art transit service, assistance with the design of exhibitions, crating of works of art, and a fine-art insurance service. Website has technical briefs, resource links.

Federal Emergency Management Agency (FEMA)
http://www.fema.gov/library

> FEMA's online library is divided into four sections: information about FEMA operations; preparation and prevention; response and recovery; and what to do when a disaster or emergency strikes in your local area. Some information available in Spanish.

Guild of Book Workers, Inc.
521 Fifth Ave., New York, NY 10175-0083
http://palimpsest.stanford.edu/byorg/gbw

> Organization devoted to increasing public awareness of the hand book arts. Produces an annual Standards of Excellence Seminar with demonstrations by experts. Publishes a study opportunities list and a list of suppliers. Provides referrals to bookbinders, conservators, and other specialists.

Image Permanence Institute (IPI)
Rochester Institute of Technology
70 Lomb Memorial Dr., Rochester, NY 14623-5604
(585) 475-5199; fax: (585) 475-7230
http://www.rit.edu/~661www1/

> Nonprofit photographic research laboratory. Testing, surveys, workshops, publications. Library and study collection.

Library of Congress Preservation Directorate
Washington, DC 20540-4500
(202) 707-5213; fax: (202) 707-3434
http://lcweb.loc.gov/preserv

> The website gives access to Library of Congress publications, provides preservation information for librarians and archivists, and has links to other organizations. Many useful publications are available under the heading "Caring for Your Collections."

Lower Hudson Conference
2199 Saw Mill River Rd., Elmsford, NY 10523
(914) 592-6726; fax: (914) 592-6946
http://lowerhudsonconference.org

> Provides workshops and technical assistance to museums, historical societies, archives, libraries, and related cultural institutions.

National Film Preservation Foundation (NFPF)
870 Market St., Suite 1113, San Francisco, CA 94102
(415) 392-7291; fax: (415) 392-7293
http://www.filmpreservation.org

> A public charity, affiliated with the Library of Congress's National Film Preservation Board. Grants to libraries, museums, and archives to help preserve films and make them available for study and research. Information on film preservation issues.

National Fire Protection Association (NFPA)
1 Batterymarch Park, Quincy, MA 02169-7471
(617) 770-3000; fax: (617) 770-0700
http://www.nfpa.org

> Fire, electrical, building, and other safety products and services, including seminars and publications.

New York State Library
Program for the Conservation and Preservation of Library Research Materials Discretionary Grant Program
10-B-41 Cultural Education Center, Albany, NY 12230
(518) 474-6971
http://www.nysl.nysed.gov/libdev/cp

> Information on state grants for preservation of library and archival materials. Workshops. Publications on preservation topics. Support for local and cooperative activities that increase access to research materials.

Northeast Document Conservation Center (NEDCC)
100 Brickstone Square, Andover, MA 01810-1494
(978) 470-1010; fax: (978) 475-6021
http://nedcc.org

> Regional conservation center serves institutional and private clients; research, disaster assistance, preservation assessments and other consulting services are available. Publishes newsletters, and the NEDCC's technical leaflets are available on its website. Some publications available in Spanish.

Southeastern Library Network (SOLINET)
1438 West Peachtree St. NW, Suite 200, Atlanta, GA 30309-2955
(800) 999-8558; fax (404) 892-7879
http://www.solinet.net

Field services program provides education, training, information, and consulting. Publications, videos, bibliographies. Some publications available in Spanish. Disaster assistance.

Western Association for Art Conservation
http://palimpsest.stanford.edu/waac

Nonprofit membership organization for professional conservators. Most members in western United States, but membership open to all. Produces a newsletter and other technical publications, including some in Spanish.

accelerated aging tests   Trials used to determine the expected lifetime of materials. Some tests involve heating the materials in a chamber under controlled humidity and other conditions. The results are only approximate, since the actual permanence of paper, ink, leather, and other components of books and documents varies greatly depending on the conditions found in the storage area and on interactions between components.

acid-free   Describes materials that are pH neutral (about 7) or alkaline (above 7) on a scale of 1 (very acidic) to 14 (very alkaline). *See also* **buffered.**

acid migration   Acid transfer from an acidic item to another (less acidic) item by physical contact.

adhesive binding   A process for holding single sheets or signatures together by an adhesive, such as PVA or a hot melt, instead of by sewing.

alkaline   Describes materials that have a pH above 7 on a scale of 1 (very acidic) to 14 (very alkaline).

alkaline buffer, alkaline reserve   An extra quantity of alkaline substance added to paper during the manufacturing process to counteract (buffer) gradual deterioration caused by acid migration.

ANSI (American National Standards Institute)   A private, nonprofit organization that administers and coordinates the U.S. voluntary standardization and conformity assessment system. Website: www.ansi.org.

archival   In book conservation, this term often refers to materials such as paper, board, or other items that are acid-free or inert and therefore not harmful when used with archived objects such as documents, photographs, etc., that are being stored for preservation. "Archival" adhesives may be reversible, but this is not always the case. Materials that are labeled "archival," such as file folders, are expected to last longer and protect objects better than ordinary ones sold as office supplies. However, it is a good idea to check what the basis for the "archival" designation is before buying materials.

artifactual value   The value that an item may have as a "collectible" object, a museum piece, a bit of memorabilia, a piece of art, etc., i.e., not its informational value.

awl   A small pointed metal tool with a plastic or wooden handle that is used for making holes in paper and board.

bands   The raised strips across the spine of a leather-covered book.

binder's board   Stiff gray cardboard used for the covers of books. Binder's board comes in various weights and densities. Acid-free board is available from several suppliers. Sometimes spelled "binders board."

blotter   Thick, absorbent paper that is used in many drying operations. It is made without any sizing and is not very strong, especially when wet. White, acid-free blotters are used for conservation work. Also called "blotting paper."

board shears   Heavy-duty cutter.

board sheet   That portion of an endpaper pasted to the inside of a book board. Also called "pastedown."

boards   1. Wooden pressing boards used in bookbinding operations. 2. Binder's board, mat board, press board, and other paper boards of various thicknesses. 3. Hard covers on a book (front board, back board).

bone folder   A small, flat tool, usually between 4" and 8" (10 and 20 cm) long, that is used to score and fold, rub down pasted areas, mark distances, burnish materials, and for other tasks as well. Most folders are made from animal bone, but some are now made from Teflon. Also called "folder."

book block: *see* **text block.**

book cloth   A cloth glued to the outside of the covers of a book. The cloth has been treated to prevent adhesive from penetrating all the way through, and is dimensionally stable so it doesn't stretch or distort when handled. Book cloth can be coated with a size or it can be laminated to a thin paper backing.

bristol   Paper board such as is used for file folders. It is available in 10- and 20-point thicknesses. Also called "folder stock," "card stock," "cover weight."

buckram   Heavy, strong book cloth. The starch-filled type is usually preferable.

buffered   Describes materials that have been made with or provided with some alkalinity to counteract acidity in the environment or in the manufacturing process.

caliper   The thickness of paper or paperboard.

card stock: *see* **bristol.**

case   The protective hard cover around a book, made separately and then joined to the text block.

casing in   Attaching a case to the text block.

clamshell box   A protective container with two trays; the book fits into the smaller tray and the second tray closes over it. Also called "drop-spine box," "tray case," "portfolio box," "book box," or other names, depending on the supplier.

coating: *see* **sizing.**

cockling   A wrinkled condition in paper, board, leather, or vellum caused by humidity, nonuniform drying, shrinkage, incorrect grain direction, or incorrect use of adhesive.

collating   In book conservation, this term refers to checking the proper order of all numbered and unnumbered pages before taking a book apart. The conservator may number the pages in pencil, beginning with the first leaf of the text block and continuing to the last. When the pagination is straightforward, often only the first few and last few leaves are marked. The page order may also be noted on a separate worksheet.

conjugate leaves   Two leaves consisting of a single piece of paper folded at the spine; because of the structure of the signature, conjugate leaves are not necessarily adjacent to one another. Also called "folios."

crash: *see* **super.**

daylight   Space between the base and platen of a press.

deckles, deckled edges   The feathered edge(s) of paper as it emerges from the mold in the papermaking process. Deckled edges are usually trimmed straight but are sometimes kept for artistic effect.

dry cleaning   An older term for **surface cleaning**.

encapsulation   In conservation, the protection of a document between two sheets of polyester film sealed on all sides.

enclosure   1. An item included with a letter in the same envelope. 2. An item found in a book, such as a letter or newspaper clipping. 3. An envelope, folder, box, or other container used to protect books or documents.

endband: *see* **headband.**

endpapers, end sheets   Blank leaves at the beginning and end of a book or pamphlet. In publishers' bindings such endpapers consist of a board sheet, attached to the inside of the cover, and a flyleaf next to the text block. They can be plain or decorated. Endpapers serve an important function by providing an additional layer of protection for the book.

envelope   An enclosure made from paper or Tyvek and sealed on three sides. The fourth side may have a flap or be open.

ferrule   Iron band surrounding a wooden or plastic shaft to strengthen the shaft or to hold a joint between the shaft and some other part, e.g., the bristles of a brush.

fill   A paper mend used to repair or fill a hole.

flyleaf   The free-swinging, usually blank leaf next to the text block that is structurally part of an endpaper.

folder   1. A simple enclosure, made from various light boards, that is folded once. Folders range in size from letter size to quite large ones that are suitable for the storage of maps or prints. Smaller folders can be stored upright or flat; larger ones should always be stored flat. Hanging folders have metal rods with hooked ends that ride on rails in file cabinets. 2. A small tool; *see* **bone folder.**

folder stock: *see* **bristol.**

folio   1. A sheet of paper folded once, which forms two leaves or four pages. 2. Conservators often use the word to mean two conjugate leaves. 3. Librarians and booksellers use the term to refer to a large book.

fore edge   The edge opposite the spine of a book.

foxing   Rust-colored spots that develop in paper, often due to high humidity and impurities present in the paper.

fume hood   A hood equipped with an exhaust fan to draw noxious fumes away from a work area or process.

gouge   A type of chisel.

grain direction   A characteristic of paper, board, and cloth resulting from the alignment of their fibers during the manufacturing process. It determines the ease of bending, folding, and tearing, i.e., the material bends more easily in one direction (grain direction) than in the perpendicular direction. Also called "machine direction."

guard   1. A strip of paper (usually Japanese) used to mend or join two leaves together. 2. A strip of paper or cloth attached to plates so that they can be sewn with the signatures through the fold. 3. The act of reinforcing the fold of a signature.

guillotine   A single-bladed, heavy-duty cutter used for cutting thick bundles of paper or thick board, e.g., in trimming whole text blocks. Both ends of a guillotine blade are connected to upright supports, whereas the blade of a board shears is hinged at one end only.

gutter   The inner margins of the pages, close to the spine.

head   Top of the book or top of the spine.

headband   A decorative embroidered strip of cloth glued at the head and tail of the spine of the book. In early bindings and in hand binding they are often embroidered by hand around a core of leather or string. Also called "endband."

headcap   The top and bottom of the spine of a binding.

hinge   1. A strip of paper to which a leaf or tip-in is attached. 2. The flexible area inside the binding where the spine of the text block is connected to the boards. The hinge is between the board sheet and the text block when looking at an open book.

hollow tube: *see* **tube.**

Hollytex: *see* **polyester web.**

host page   The page onto which another page is attached, either by hinging or by tipping-in.

hot melt   The adhesive used in perfect-bound books. It is applied hot and sets as the paper absorbs the adhesive and the liquid medium evaporates.

hygroscopic   Describes materials that readily absorb, retain, and give up moisture. Materials that are hygroscopic expand and contract quickly in response to changes in relative humidity

inert   Describes materials that are chemically stable, not reactive.

interleaving   The insertion of a blank page (interleaved page) between two printed pages, sometimes for the protection of an illustration, sometimes to allow for handwritten notes.

joints   The flexible areas on the outside of the binding, where the spine of the binding and the boards of the book connect. The corresponding areas on the inside of the binding are the "hinges."

kettle stitch   A knot in the sewing process that connects each signature to the preceding one, at the head and tail of the book. The kettle stitch is usually between ½" and 1¼" (1.3 and 3.2 cm) from the top and bottom of the book.

leaf   A piece of paper consisting of two pages, one on each side (the recto and the verso).

loss   A missing area in a document, page, or book covering.

map folder stock: *see* **bristol.**

mat   A board with a center cutout that shows the artwork behind it and keeps the art away from the glass in a frame. Also called "window mat."

mat, mat package   A piece of art sandwiched between a window mat and one or more backing boards.

mat burn   Discoloration caused by acid migration from poor-quality window mats.

Mellinex: *see* **polyester film.**

methylcellulose   A slow-drying adhesive made from cotton fibers treated with an alkali. It is sold as a white powder and is mixed with water before use. Also spelled "methyl cellulose."

mix   Adhesive made of PVA and methylcellulose in a 50-50 mixture, or of PVA and paste in the same proportions.

moisture barrier   A material that prevents moisture from moving from one area to another, such as waxed paper, polyethylene, polyester film, etc.

monograph   1. A scholarly work on a particular restricted topic. 2. In libraries, the term refers to a work, collection, or other writing that is not a serial.

Mylar: *see* **polyester film.**

nipping press   A press, usually made of cast iron, used to set the joints of a book as well as for other operations.

oversewing   A method of assembling pages in which the folds of the signatures are cut off, resulting in single leaves. The leaves are divided into small groups. Each group is sewn together with an over-cast stitch and all the sections are held together using a zigzag stitch. The process can be carried out by hand or machine.

page   One side of a leaf.

parchment   An animal skin that has been treated with lime and stretched and scraped rather than tanned; used for writing on and in the pages and bindings of books. Also called "vellum."

paste   A slow-drying adhesive made from wheat, rice, and other starchy plants. The starch powder is mixed with water and cooked while stirring.

PAT (Photographic Activity Test)   A worldwide standard for archival quality in photographic enclosures that predicts possible interactions between photographic images and the enclosures in which they are stored. The PAT test is also used to test the components of enclosures, such as adhesives, inks, paints, labels, and tapes.

pH   A scale from 1 to 14 that describes the degree of acidity and alkalinity, where 1 is extremely acidic, 7 is neutral, and 14 is extremely alkaline.

phase box   A temporary storage box constructed of various light boards.

polyester encapsulation: *see* **encapsulation.**

polyester film   A clear, chemically inert, and stable polyester material used for encapsulation. Mylar or Mellinex are brand names.

polyester web   A strong, nonwoven material used to support wet paper or to prevent pasted paper from sticking to neighboring pages while drying. Hollytex and Reemay are brand names.

pressboard   A strong, lightweight cardboard with a hard, shiny, and sometimes mottled surface. Sometimes used to make pamphlet binders.

pressing boards: *see* **boards.**

PVA   Polyvinyl acetate or other plastic glues.

rebacking   The replacement of a worn or missing spine with new material, either cloth or leather, while retaining the original boards. Parts of the old spine may be reapplied over the new cloth or leather.

recto   The front of a leaf or document, or the right-hand page of an open book.

Reemay: *see* **polyester web.**

reformatting   Preserving information in a different format, e.g., microfilming, photocopying, digitization, etc.

rehousing   In preservation, this term refers to putting materials into envelopes or other protective containers.

relative humidity   The amount of water vapor in the air, expressed as a percentage of the maximum amount of water that the air could hold at a given temperature.

reversible   Describes processes that can be undone without damaging or altering the original materials.

saddle stitching   Stitching together a single-signature pamphlet by stapling through the fold.

scoring   Indenting a line on a sheet of paper or light board by pressing with a bone folder drawn against a straightedge.

section: *see* **signature.**

selvage   The edges of cloth as it is manufactured; the weave on the edges is specially designed to prevent unraveling, and the edges are usually removed before use.

serial   A publication issued in successive parts. Serials include newspapers, magazines, yearbooks, and other works published in a numbered or dated series.

sewing stations   The holes along the folds of a signature through which thread passes during the sewing process.

shaken   A term sometimes used in booksellers' catalogs to indicate a book that is loose in its case or
has other damage.

sheet   A single piece of hand- or machine-made paper;
paper is available in many sheet sizes.

shoulder   The shaped edges of the spine of the text
block against which the boards sit.

side sewing, stab sewing   In this method of assembling
the text block, unsewn folded book sections or loose
single pages, or a combination of the two, are sewn
together with thread that goes through the whole
book, from front to back near the binding edge.

signature   The leaves formed by the folding of a single
large piece of paper. The number of leaves in a signature depends on the number of times the sheet is
folded. Also called "section."

sizing   The treatment of paper and cloth to give some
resistance to the penetration of liquids.

sleeve   A flat, see-through enclosure. A sleeve may be
closed on one, two, or three sides. Sleeves made of
polyester, polyethylene, and polypropylene are suitable for use with documents and photographs;
acetate and vinyl sleeves are harmful.

spine   1. The bound edge of a text block, opposite the
fore edge. 2. The area of a book cover between the
boards, covering the spine of the text block.

spine lining   The cloth that is glued to the spine of the
text block to reinforce it and, in some cases, to
provide hinges. It is usually super, lawn, muslin, or
linen. One or more layers of paper are added over
the cloth.

squares   The edges of the inside of a book cover that
are visible beyond the edges of the pages.

stab sewing: *see* **side sewing.**

starch-filled cloth   A book cloth that is coated or filled
with starch.

starch paste: *see* **paste.**

stub   A lengthwise tab on the inner edge of a leaf which
is folded for sewing or used for attaching an insert.

super   A heavily sized cloth with the appearance of
coarse cheesecloth, used to line the spine in commercial bindings.

surface cleaning   Cleaning the surface of paper or
cloth with brushes and various types of erasers.

tail   The bottom edge of the book, in particular, the
bottom of the spine.

tape   In some types of bindings, the linen or cotton
tape used to anchor the sewing thread.

text block   The text pages or "insides" of a book. Also
called "book block."

tide lines   Stains caused by water soaking into paper
unevenly, wetting some areas and leaving other
parts dry. The stains tend to be darkest at the edges
of the wet areas, where the dissolved impurities in
the paper cannot flow into the dry paper.

tip, tip in   To attach an item, such as a letter or an
illustration, into a bound book by applying a
narrow line of adhesive to one of its edges.

tube, hollow tube   A piece of paper folded in three and
glued to create a hollow tube the same width as the
spine. The single side is adhered to the spine of the
book and the double side to the spine of the case.

turn-in   The covering material that is turned inside
around the edges of the boards.

Tyvek   A thin, strong material made from spun-
bonded olefin (high-density polyethylene), manufactured by DuPont. It allows vapor to escape but
resists penetration by liquids, and it also resists
punctures and tears.

vellum: *see* **parchment.**

verso   The back of a document or page, or the left-
hand page of an open book.

window mat: *see* **mat.**

wrapper   A protective enclosure for books that is
made of lightweight board.

wrappers   Soft covers on pamphlets or temporary
paper covers on books intended to be bound later.

Other glossaries may be found in the following sources.

John Carter, *ABC for Book Collectors* (New Castle, DE:
Oak Knoll, 2002).

Jane Greenfield, *Books: Their Care and Repair* (New
York: H. W. Wilson, 1983).

Hedi Kyle, *Library Materials Preservation Manual* (New
York: New York Botanical Garden, 1983).

Matt T. Roberts and Don Etherington, *Bookbinding and
the Conservation of Books* (Washington, DC: Library
of Congress, 1982).

Most of the titles listed here clearly indicate the subject matter; a few entries have been annotated.

American Association of Museums. "Revised Standard Facility Report." American Association of Museums, Technical Information Service, 1575 Eye Street, NW, Suite 400, Washington, DC 20005.
    Provides a standard form for recording information often required by institutions as a prerequisite for lending property for exhibition in other institutions. Also a useful self-assessment tool for the building and its protection systems. Disk included.

American Society of Heating, Refrigerating and Air-Conditioning Engineers. *Heating, Ventilating and Air-Conditioning Applications.* Atlanta, GA: American Society of Heating, Refrigerating and Air-Conditioning Engineers, 2003. See chapter 21, "Museums, Libraries, and Archives."

Appelbaum, Barbara. *Guide to Environmental Protection of Collections.* Madison, CT: Soundview, 1992. (Available from conservation suppliers.)

Bachmann, Konstanze, ed. *Conservation Concerns.* Washington, DC: Smithsonian Institution, 1992.
    A collection of articles about the preservation of photographs, paintings, textiles, and metal, wooden, and stone objects. Includes storage and exhibition guidelines.

Banks, Paul, and Roberta Pilette, eds. *Preservation: Issues and Planning.* Chicago: American Library Association, 2000.
    Chapters on preservation planning for libraries and archives, including building design, emergency preparedness, exhibitions, library binding, microfilming, digitization, and more.

Barclay, Robert, André Bergeron, and Carole Dignard. *Mount-Making for Museum Objects.* Ottawa, ON: Canadian Conservation Institute, 2002. (Published in English and French.)

Barrett, Timothy. *Japanese Papermaking: Traditions, Tools, and Techniques.* New York: Weatherill, 1983.

BonaDea, Artemis. *Conservation Book Repair.* Juneau, AK: Alaska State Library, 1995.

Burke, Robert B., and Sam Adeloye. *A Manual of Basic Museum Security.* Paris: ICOM, 1986. Available from Museum Consultants, Inc., 1716 17th Sreet, NW, Washington, DC 20009.

Canadian Conservation Institute. Technical Bulletin 10, "Silica Gel," by Raymond H. Lafontaine. 1984. Code 8401.

——. Technical Bulletin 22, "The Stability of Photocopied and Laser-Printed Documents and Images: General Guidelines," by David Grattan. 2000. Code 0003.

——. Technical Bulletin 25, "Disaster Recovery of Modern Information Carriers," by Joe Traci. 2002. Code 0203.
    Procedures for dealing with CDs, magnetic diskettes, and magnetic tapes that have been damaged by water, mud, heat, dust, mold, etc.

——. Technical Bulletin 26, "Mould Prevention and Collection Recovery: Guidelines for Heritage Collections," by Sherry Guild and Maureen MacDonald. 2004. Code 0301.
    Information on mold morphology, prevention of mold growth, health effects.

Carter, John, and Nicolas Barker. *ABC for Book Collectors.* 8th ed. New Castle, DE: Oak Knoll, 2002. Technical terms used in book collecting.

Clapp, Anne F. *Curatorial Care of Works of Art on Paper: Basic Procedures for Paper Conservation*. New York: Nick Lyons Books, 1987.

Collection Conservation Treatment: A Resource Manual for Program Development and Conservation Technician Training. Compiled by Maralyn Jones. Berkeley: University of California Library, 1993.
> A compilation of in-house treatment manuals contributed by the conservation departments of several academic libraries.

Diehl, Edith. *Bookbinding: Its Background and Technique*. New York: Dover, 1985.

Dorge, Valerie, and Sharon L. Jones. *Building an Emergency Plan: A Guide for Museums and Other Cultural Institutions*. Los Angeles: Getty Conservation Institute, 1999.

Ellis, Margaret Holbein. *The Care of Prints and Drawings*. Nashville, TN: American Association for State and Local History, 1987.
> Practical advice on the care of works of art on paper, including storage, environment, matting, and hinging.

Freeman, Elizabeth P. *The Exhibition of Library Materials*. 1999–2000 Kress Internship in Paper Conservation, Report. New York: New York Botanical Garden, 2000.
> Research conducted prior to designing an exhibit gallery for art on paper as well as rare books.

Getty Conservation Institute Newsletter 19, no. 1 (2004). This issue contains four articles of interest: Robert Waller and Stefan Michalski, "Effective Preservation: From Reaction to Prediction," discusses a risk management approach to curatorial practice; Sarah Stanisforth, Richard Kerschner, and Jonathan Ashley-Smith, "Sustainable Access: A Discussion about Implementing Preventive Conservation," discusses the importance of improving conditions before dedicating resources to the conservation of specific items; James Druzik, "Illuminating Alternatives: Research in Museum Lighting," examines continuing research into safer lighting methods; and Shin Maekawa and Vincent Beltran, "Climate Control for Historic Buildings: A New Strategy," presents a method for dehumidifying buildings in humid locations without the use of air conditioning.

Greenfield, Jane. *ABC of Bookbinding: A Unique Glossary with Over 700 Illustrations for Collectors and Librarians*. New Castle, DE, and Nottingham, Eng.: Oak Knoll Press and Plough Press, 2002

———. *Books: Their Care and Repair*. New York: H. W. Wilson, 1983.

Hatchfield, Pamela. *Pollutants in the Museum Environment: Practical Strategies for Problem Solving in Design, Exhibition and Storage*. London: Archetype, 2002.

Hendriks, Klaus B., and Brian Lesser. "Disaster Preparedness and Recovery: Photographic Materials." *American Archivist* 46, no. 1 (winter 1983): 52–68.

Hofmann, Ana B. "The Dog Ate It! and Other Common Types of Damage to Photographs." *Picture Framing Magazine*, October 1993.

———. "Identifying Nineteenth Century Photographic Processes." *Picture Framing Magazine*, October 1994.

Horton, Carolyn. *Cleaning and Preserving Bindings and Related Materials*. Chicago: American Library Association, 1969.
> Instructions for reconditioning a library of permanent value.

Hunter, Dard. *Papermaking: The History and Technique of an Ancient Craft*. New York: Dover, 1978.

Johnson, Arthur. *Manual of Bookbinding*. London and New York: Thames and Hudson, 1978

———. *The Practical Guide to Book Repair and Conservation*. London and New York: Thames and Hudson, 1988.

Kahn, Miriam. *Disaster Response and Planning for Libraries*. 2nd ed. Chicago: American Library Association, 2002.

Kissel, Elconore, and Erin Vigneau. *Architectural Photo Reproductions: A Manual for Identification and Care*. New Castle, DE, and New York: Oak Knoll Press and New York Botanical Garden, 1999.

Kyle, Hedi. *Library Materials Preservation Manual: Practical Methods for Preserving Books, Pamphlets and Other Printed Materials*. New York: New York Botanical Garden, 1983.

Library of Congress Preservation Directorate. *Care, Handling and Storage of Books*.

———. *Care, Handling and Storage of Motion Picture Film*.

——. *Caring for Your Photographic Collections.*

——. *Cylinder, Disc and Tape Care in a Nutshell.*

——. *Emergency Drying Procedures for Water-Damaged Collections.*

——. *Guide to Preservation Matting and Framing.*

——. *Preservation Photocopying.*

——. *Preserving Newspapers.*

> These and other useful publications are available at http://www.loc.gov/prserv under the heading "Caring for Your Collections."

Lull, William P., with Paul N. Banks. *Conservation Environment Guidelines for Libraries and Archives.* Ottawa, ON: Canadian Council of Archives, 1995.

McCrady, Ellen, ed. *North American Permanent Papers.* 3rd ed. Austin, TX: Abbey, 1998.

McMurtrie, Douglas. *The Book: The Story of Printing and Bookmaking.* New York: Dorset, 1989.

Morrow, Carolyn Clark. *Conservation Treatment Procedures.* Littleton, CO: Libraries Unlimited, 1982.

> A manual of step-by-step procedures for the maintenance and repair of library materials.

Museums and Galleries Commission Conservation Unit, Great Britain. *Science for Conservators.* Vol. 1, *Introduction to Materials.* Vol. 2, *Cleaning.* Vol. 3, *Adhesives and Coatings.* Conservation Science Teaching Series. New York: Routledge, 1992.

National Park Service, Curatorial Services Division. "Conserv-o-Grams." National Park Service, Museum Management Program, 1849 C Street, NW, Room NC230, Washington, DC 20240.

> Short, focused leaflets about caring for museum objects as well as book and archival collections. Published in loose-leaf format and available online at http://www.cr.nps.gov/museum/publications.

——. *Museum Handbook.* Available online at http://www.cr.nps.gov/museum/publications.

> Preservation topics, conservation treatment, emergency planning, security, packing and shipping, museum record keeping.

New York University. *Disaster Plan Workbook.* An updated version, including all the worksheets, may be found at http://library.nyu.edu/preservation/.

Northeast Document Conservation Center (NEDCC). *Preservation of Library and Archival Materials: A Manual,* edited by Sherelyn Ogden. 3rd ed. Andover, MA: Northeast Document Conservation Center, 1999.

> A collection of frequently updated leaflets on many conservation subjects, including preservation planning and disaster recovery. The leaflets are also available at the NEDCC website, www.nedcc.org.

——. Technical Leaflet 26. "Integrated Pest Management," by Beth Lindblom Patkus.

——. Technical Leaflet 37. "Matting and Framing for Art and Artifacts on Paper," by Mary Todd Glaser.

——. Technical Leaflet 50. "How to Do Your Own Matting and Hinging," by Mary Todd Glaser.

Nyberg, Sandra. "The Invasion of the Giant Spore." Preservation Leaflet 5, November 1987. 1994 update available. SOLINET, Plaza Level, 400 Colony Square, 1201 Peachtree St., NE, Atlanta, GA 30361.

> Guide to mold control.

Phibbs, Hugh. "Building a Preservation Frame." A Supplement to *Picture Framing Magazine,* April 2003.

——. "The Frame: A Complete Preservation Package." A Supplement to *Picture Framing Magazine,* February 1996.

——. "Preservation Matting for Works of Art on Paper." A Supplement to *Picture Framing Magazine,* February 1997.

Phibbs, Hugh, and Paula Volent. "Preservation Hinging." A Supplement to *Picture Framing Magazine,* January 1998.

Pocket Pal: A Graphic Arts Production Handbook. Memphis, TN: International Paper Company, 1998.

> A reference book that includes information on papermaking, printing, book production, and more.

Price, Lois Olcott. "Managing a Mold Invasion: Guidelines for Disaster Response: Mold, Health Concerns, First Response, Fungicides, Cleaning, Prevention." Technical Series 1. Philadelphia: Conservation Center for Art and Historic Artifacts, 1996.

Raphael, Toby, and Nancy Davis. *Exhibit Conservation Guidelines.* Harpers Ferry Historical Association, 2000. CD-ROM. Available from http://www.nps.gov/hfc/products/cons/ex-con-guidelines.htm#, and from Harpers Ferry Historical Association, P.O. Box 197, Harpers Ferry, WV 25425.

Reilly, James. *Care and Identification of 19th-Century Photographic Prints.* Publication G2S. Rochester, NY: Eastman Kodak Co., 1986.

Rempel, Siegfried. *The Care of Photographs.* New York: Nick Lyons Books, 1987.

Rhodes, Barbara, and William W. Streeter. *Before Photocopying: The Art and History of Mechanical Copying, 1780–1938.* New Castle, DE: Oak Knoll, 1999.

Ritzenthaler, Mary Lynn, Gerald Munoff, and Margery Long. *Archives and Manuscripts: Administration of Photographic Collections.* Chicago: Society of American Archivists, 1984.

Roberts, Matt T., and Don Etherington. *Bookbinding and the Conservation of Books: A Dictionary of Descriptive Terminology.* Washington, DC: Library of Congress, 1982.

Shuman, Bruce A. *Library Security and Safety Handbook: Prevention, Policies, and Procedures.* Chicago: American Library Association, 1999.

Smith, Merrily A. *Matting and Hinging of Works of Art on Paper.* Washington, DC: Library of Congress, 1981.

Story, Keith O. *Approaches to Pest Management in Museums.* Washington, DC: Smithsonian Institution, 1985.

The Story of Humidity. Madison, WI: Research Products Corp., 2001.

Swartzburg, Susan G., ed. *Conservation in the Library: A Handbook of Use and Care of Traditional and Non-Traditional Materials.* Westport, CT: Greenwood, 1983.
> Includes sections on photographs, slides, microforms, motion picture film, videotape, and sound recordings.

Tétreault, Jean. *Airborne Pollutants in Museums, Galleries, and Archives: Risk Assessment, Control Strategies and Preservation Management.* Ottawa, ON: Canadian Conservation Institute, 2003.

Trinkley, Michael. *Hurricane! Surviving the Big One: A Primer for Libraries, Museums and Archives.* 2nd ed. 1998. SOLINET and Chicora Foundation. P.O. Box 8664, Columbia, SC 29202.

Walsh, Betty. "Salvage Operations for Water Damaged Archival Collections: A Second Glance." *Western Association for Art Conservation Newsletter* 19, no. 2 (March 1997).

Watson, Aldren. *Hand Bookbinding: A Manual of Instruction.* New York: Macmillan, 1986.

Wilhelm, Henry, and Carol Brower. *The Permanence and Care of Color Photographs.* Grinnell, IA: Preservation Publishing, 1993.

Young, Laura S. *Bookbinding and Conservation by Hand: A Working Guide.* Revised by Jerilyn Glenn Davis. New Castle, DE: Oak Knoll, 1996

Zycherman, Lynda A., and J. Richard Schrock. *A Guide to Museum Pest Control.* Washington, DC: Foundation of the American Institute for Conservation of Historic and Artistic Works, Association of Systematic Collections, 1988.

Nelly Balloffet has worked in libraries and in her own book and paper conservation studio for thirty years. She received an M.L.S. degree from Columbia University and began her library career as a cataloger. She became interested in the preservation aspects of the field and began training in book and paper conservation at the Metropolitan Museum of Art, eventually establishing her own studio. Balloffet has taught classes in book and paper repair techniques for more than twenty-five years. Many of the courses were given jointly with Jenny Hille. In addition, Balloffet has engaged in a wide variety of consulting projects to help libraries and archives plan preservation activities. She is the author of *Emergency Planning and Recovery Techniques: A Handbook for Libraries, Historical Societies and Archives in the Hudson Valley* (1999). In 2001 she and Hille wrote an appendix to *Emergency Planning* entitled *Materials and Techniques for Book and Paper Repair.*

Jenny Hille is a book and paper conservator and library consultant in private practice in Riverside, Connecticut. She trained and worked at the Yale University Library's Conservation Studio and studied book conservation as well as fine binding in Europe. She holds an M.L.S. degree from Southern Connecticut State University. Hille conserves books and documents for private and large institutional clients and has taught numerous library conservation workshops. She coauthored with Jane Greenfield a technical bookbinding manual, *Headbands: How to Work Them,* in 1986, and with Nelly Balloffet in 2001 she wrote *Materials and Techniques for Book and Paper Repair.*